MW01122469

Regional China

Regional China

A Business and Economic Handbook

Rongxing Guo
Regional Science Association of China, China

With the assistance of
Luc (Changlei) Guo, iMBA

First published 2013 by
PALGRAVE MACMILLAN

Palgrave Macmillan in the UK is an imprint of Macmillan Publishers Limited, registered in England, company number 785998, of Houndmills, Basingstoke, Hampshire RG21 6XS.

Palgrave Macmillan in the US is a division of St Martin's Press LLC, 175 Fifth Avenue, New York, NY 10010.

Palgrave Macmillan is the global academic imprint of the above companies and has companies and representatives throughout the world.

Palgrave® and Macmillan® are registered trademarks in the United States, the United Kingdom, Europe and other countries.

ISBN 978–1–137–28766–3

This book is printed on paper suitable for recycling and made from fully managed and sustained forest sources. Logging, pulping and manufacturing processes are expected to conform to the environmental regulations of the country of origin.

A catalogue record for this book is available from the British Library.

A catalog record for this book is available from the Library of Congress.

10   9   8   7   6   5   4   3   2   1
22 21 20 19 18 17 16 15 14 13

Printed and bound in the United States of America

To the memory of my father-in-law Liu Genghe (刘庚和, 1927–2011), who taught me to be honest in everything I do

Contents

Acknowledgments

The final appearance of this book has benefited from helpful discussions with Luc (Changlei) Guo. Luc also generously helped me to collect and edit the data and materials for this book.

Among the Palgrave staff contributing to the publication of this book, Taiba Batool (Senior Commissioning Editor of Economics), and Anna Jenkins and Ellie Shillito (both editorial assistants at Palgrave Macmillan) kept in regular communication with me when the draft was being prepared. Taiba also gave me many useful suggestions on the final title and organization of this book.

I am also grateful to Sumitha Nithyanandan and Kate Boothby (both at Integra Software Services Pvt. Ltd, Pondicherry, India) for editing this book. All views and remaining errors, however, are my sole responsibility.

Rognxing Guo, Qiaozi, Huairou, Beijing, 2012

Notes on the Text

In this book, the geographical scope of China covers only mainland China, although Hong Kong, Macau and Taiwan are mentioned in a few cases for comparison purposes. In addition, unless stated otherwise, the data cited in this book are based on the sources described below.

The maps of the administrative divisions of Beijing, Chongqing, Shanghai and Tianjin were drawn by Luc Guo. Those of the remaining provinces were revised by Luc Guo based on files from Wikimedia Commons, which is a freely licensed media file repository. The copyright holders have released these maps into the public domain. This applies worldwide. In some countries this may not be legally possible; if so, the copyright holders also agree to grant anyone the right to use these maps for any purpose, without any conditions, unless such conditions are required by law (see http://commons.wikimedia.org/wiki/Main_Page for more information).

The data on the human development index (HDI) of the 31 provinces are from the *China Human Development Report 2009/2010* of the United Nations Development Program (2010, Beijing: UNDP and Renmin University of China).

The data on the geographical features of each province are based on the province's government website (given in the "Quick facts" section for each area's entry in Part I).

The data on the description of natural resources of each area are based on information from China's national online news service (www.china.org.cn).

The data on the economic and technological development zones of each province are based on the official websites of the relevant provincial governments.

The data on the top five companies of each area, except for those that have been collected by the author, are based on http://www.thechinaperspective.com.

The data for the "Indicators for the ease of doing business" sections are from *Doing Business in China 2008* from the World Bank (2008, Washington, DC: The World Bank Group; Beijing: Social Science Academic Press [China]).

Abbreviations

APEC	Asia-Pacific Economic Cooperation
ASEAN	Association of Southeast Asian Nations
BAIC	Beijing Automotive Industry Holding
CCP	Chinese Communist Party
CCPCC	Chinese Communist Party Central Committee
EU	European Union
FAI	fixed asset investment
FDI	foreign direct investment
GDP	gross domestic product
GRP	gross regional product
HDI	human development index
HKG	Hong Kong Stock Exchange
ISO	International Standard Organization
MNC	multi-national company
NYSE	New York Stock Exchange
PPP	purchasing power parity
PRC	People's Republic of China
R&D	research and development
SAR	special administrative region
SEHK	Stock Exchange of Hong Kong Limited
SHA	Shanghai Stock Exchange
SHE	Shenzhen Stock Exchange
SPC	sub-prefectural level county
UNESCO	United Nations Educational, Scientific and Cultural Organization
¥	yuan (Chinese unit of currency)

Units of Measurement

°C = centigrade
cm = centimeter
ha = hectare
km = kilometer
km^2 = square kilometer
kw = kilowatt
kw h = kilowatt hour
m = meter
mm = millimeter
m^2 = square meter
m^3 = cubic meter
TEU = twenty equivalent unit

Glossary

Disposable income of urban households refers to the actual income at the disposal of members of households which can be used for final consumption, other non-compulsory expenditure and savings. This equals the total income minus income tax, personal contribution to social security and subsidy for keeping diaries in a sample household. The following formula is used:

$$\text{disposable income} = \text{total household income} - \text{incometax}$$
$$- \text{personal contribution to social security}$$
$$- \text{subsidy for keeping diaries for a sample household.}$$

Ease of doing business provides a quantitative measure of regulations for such indicators as starting a business, registering property, getting credit and enforcing contracts – as they apply to domestic small and medium-size enterprises within China.

Starting a business records all procedures that are officially required for an entrepreneur to start up and formally operate an industrial or commercial business. These include obtaining all necessary licenses and permits and completing any required notifications, verifications or inscriptions for the company and employees with the relevant authorities.

Registering property records the full sequence of procedures necessary for a business (buyer) to purchase a property from another business (seller) and to transfer the property title to the buyer's name so that the buyer can use the property for expanding its business, use the property as collateral in taking new loans or, if necessary, sell the property to another business. The process starts with obtaining the necessary documents, such as a copy of the seller's title, if necessary, and conducting due diligence, if required. The transaction is considered complete when it is opposable to third parties and when the buyer can use the property, use it as collateral for a bank loan or resell it. The ranking of the ease of registering property is the simple average of the percentile rankings of its component indicators.

Getting credit measures the legal rights of borrowers and lenders with respect to secured transactions through one set of indicators and the sharing of credit information through another. The first set of indicators describes how well collateral and bankruptcy laws facilitate lending. The second set measures the coverage, scope and accessibility of credit information available through public credit registries and private credit bureaus.

Enforcing contract measures the efficiency of the judicial system in resolving a commercial dispute. The data are built by following the step-by-step evolution of a commercial sale dispute before local courts. The data are collected through study of the codes of civil procedure and other court regulations as well as surveys completed by local litigation lawyers and judges.

Engel's coefficient refers to the percentage of expenditure on food in the total living consumption expenditure, using the following formula:

$$\text{Engel's coefficient} = \frac{\text{expenditure on food}}{\text{total living consumption expenditure}} \times 100\%$$

Exports refer to commodities that are sent out from their place of origin to a consumer abroad.

Imports refer to commodities that are brought in to their place of consumption from a producer abroad.

Fixed asset investment (FAI) refers to the volume of activities in construction and purchases of fixed assets of the whole country and related fees, expressed in monetary terms during the reference period. It is a comprehensive indicator which shows the size, structure and growth of the investment in fixed assets, providing a basis for observing the progress of construction projects and evaluating the results of investment. Total investment in fixed assets in the whole country includes, by type of ownership, the investment by state-owned units, collective-owned units, joint ownership units, share-holding units and private unit individuals, as well as investments by entrepreneurs from Hong Kong, Macau and Taiwan, foreign investors and others.

Foreign direct investment (FDI) refers to the investments inside China by foreign enterprises and economic organizations or individuals (including overseas Chinese, compatriots from Hong Kong, Macau and

Taiwan, and Chinese enterprises registered abroad), following the relevant policies and laws of China, for the establishment of ventures exclusively with foreign-owned investment, Sino-foreign joint ventures and cooperative enterprises, or for the cooperative exploration of resources with enterprises or economic organizations in China. It includes the re-investment by the foreign entrepreneurs of the profits gained from the investment and the funds that enterprises borrow from abroad in the total investment of projects which are approved by the relevant government department.

Gross regional product (GRP) is also called regional gross domestic product (GDP) and refers to the final products at market prices produced by all resident units in a region during a certain period of time. It is expressed from three different perspectives – namely, value, income and products. GRP from its value perspective refers to the total value of all goods and services produced by all resident units during a certain period of time, minus the total value of input of goods and services of the nature of non-fixed assets – in other words, it is the sum of the value-added of all resident units. GRP from the perspective of income includes the primary income created by all resident units and distributed to resident and non-resident units during a given period of time. GRP from the perspective of products refers to the value of all goods and services for final demand by all resident units plus the net export of goods and services during a given period of time. In the practice of national accounting, GRP is calculated from three approaches, namely the production approach, the income approach and the expenditure approach, which reflect GDP and its composition from different angles.

Human development index (HDI) is a composite statistic used to rank countries by level of "human development". It is a comparative measure of life expectancy, literacy, education and standard of living. It is used to determine whether the country is a developed, developing or underdeveloped country, and also to measure the impact of economic policies on quality of life.

Net income of rural household refers to the total income of rural households from all sources minus all corresponding expenses. Net income is mainly used as input for reinvestment in production and as consumption expenditure for the year, and also for savings and noncompulsory expenses of various forms.

"Per capita net income of farmers" is the level of net income averaged by population, reflecting the average income level of the rural population in a given area. The formula for calculation is as follows:

$$\text{net income} = \text{total income} - \text{household operation expenses}$$
$$- \text{taxes and fees} - \text{depreciation of fixed assets for}$$
$$\text{production} - \text{gifts to rural relatives}$$

Patent is an abbreviation for the patent right and refers to the exclusive right of ownership of the inventors or designers for the creation of inventions, given by the patent offices after due process of assessment and approval in accordance with patent law. Patents are granted for inventions, utility models and designs.

Inventions refer to new technical proposals for products, methods or their modification. This is a universal core indicator reflecting the technologies with independent intellectual property.

Utility models refer to practical and new technical proposals regarding the shape and structure of a product or a combination of both. This indicator reflects the condition of technological results with certain technical content.

Designs refer to the aesthetics and industrially applicable new designs regarding the shape, pattern and color of a product, or their combinations. This indicator reflects the appearance design achievements with independent intellectual property.

The latter three indicators reflect the achievements of science, technology and design with independent intellectual property.

Primary, secondary and tertiary industries. In China, economic activities in industry are categorized into three strata:

(1) Primary industry refers to agriculture, forestry, animal husbandry and fishery, and services in support of these industries.
(2) Secondary industry refers to mining and quarrying, manufacturing, production, supply of electricity, water and gas, and construction.
(3) Tertiary industry refers to all other economic activities not included in the primary or secondary industries.

Research and development (R&D) refers to systematic and creative activities in the fields of science and technology aiming to increase knowledge and to use that knowledge for new applications. It includes three categories of activities: basic research, applied research and experimentation for development. The scale and intensity of R&D are widely used internationally to reflect the strength of science and technology and the core competitiveness of a country.

Sales of consumer goods refers to the amount obtained by enterprises (units, self-employed individuals) through direct sales of non-production and non-business physical commodities to individuals and social institutions, and revenue from providing catering services. Individuals include rural and urban households and populations from abroad; social institutions include government agencies, social organizations, military units, schools and neighborhood (village) committees.

Maps and Tables

Map 1 The province-level administrative divisions of China
Source: Courtesy of the University of Texas Libraries, University of Texas at Austin.

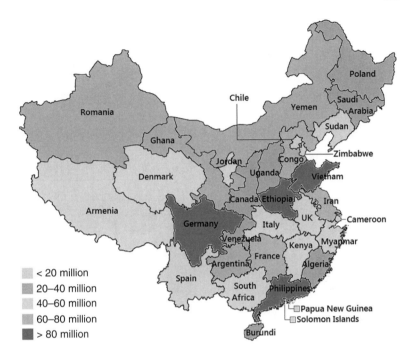

Map 2   Which countries match the population of Chinese provinces?

Notes: The equivalents are as follows: Algeria = Fujian, Argentina = Guizhou, Armenia = Tibet, Burundi = Hainan, Cameroon = Shanghai, Canada = Shaanxi, Chile = Beijing, Congo (Dem. Rep. of) = Hebei, Denmark = Qinghai, Ethiopia = Henan, France = Hunan, Germany = Sichuan, Ghana = Gansu, Iran = Jiangsu, Italy = Hubei, Jordan = Ningxia, Kenya = Jiangxi, Myanmar = Zhejiang, Papua New Guinea = Hong Kong, Philippines = Guangdong, Poland = Heilongjiang, Romania = Xinjiang, Saudi Arabia = Jilin, Solomon Islands = Macau, South Africa = Guangxi, Spain = Yunnan, Sudan = Liaoning, Uganda = Shanxi, UK = Anhui, Venezuela = Chongqing, Vietnam = Shandong, Yemen = Inner Mongolia and Zimbabwe = Tianjin. (2) Hong Kong and Macau are treated as two provincial economies, and Taiwan is an independent economy. (3) Data are as of 2010.

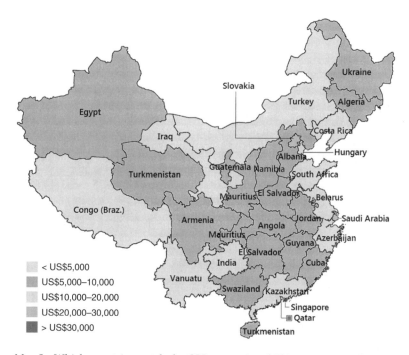

Map 3 Which countries match the GRP per capita of Chinese provinces?

Notes: (1) The equivalents include as follows: Albania = Hebei, Algeria = Jilin, Angola = Hubei, Armenia = Sichuan, Azerbaijan = Zhejiang, Belarus = Jiangsu, Belarus = Jiangsu, Congo (Brazzaville) = Tibet, Costa Rica = Liaoning, Cuba = Fujian, Egypt = Xinjiang, El Salvador = Henan, El Salvador = Hunan, Guatemala = Ningxia, Guyana = Jiangxi, Hungary = Tianjin, India = Guizhou, Iraq = Gansu, Jordan = Anhui, Kazakhstan = Guangdong, Mauritius = Chongqing, Mauritius = Shaanxi, Namibia = Shanxi, Qatar = Macau, Saudi Arabia = Shanghai, Singapore = Hong Kong, Slovakia = Beijing, South Africa = Shandong, Swaziland = Guangxi, Turkmenistan = Hainan, Turkmenistan = Qinghai, Ukraine = Heilongjiang and Vanuatu = Yunnan. (2) Hong Kong and Macau are treated as two provincial economies, and Taiwan is an independent economy. (3) Figures are in purchasing power parity (PPP) dollars and as of 2010.

< US$5 billion

US$5–10 billion

US$10–50 billion

US$50–200 billion

> US$200 billion

Map 4   Which countries match the exports of Chinese provinces?

Note: (1) The equivalents include as follows: Austria = Shanghai, Bahrain = Sichuan, Belize = Tibet, Benin = Ningxia, Bosnia and Herzegovina = Shaanxi, Botswana = Jilin, Colombia = Tianjin, Congo = Hunan, Costa Rica = Henan, El Salvador = Inner Mongolia, Gabon = Guangxi, Greece = Hebei, Hungary = Shandong, Jordan = Heilongjiang, Latvia = Jiangxi, Lebanon = Chongqing, Libya = Liaoning, Mongolia = Hainan, Namibia = Yunnan, Nepal = Gansu, Nigeria = Fujian, North Korea = Guizhou, Oman = Beijing, Panama = Macau, Rwanda = Qinghai, Serbia = Anhui, Iceland = Shanxi, South Korea = Guangdong, Sri Lanka = Hong Kong, Taiwan = Jiangsu, Thailand = Zhejiang, Trinidad and Tobago = Hubei and Uzbekistan = Xinjiang. (2) Hong Kong and Macau are treated as two provincial economies, and Taiwan is an independent economy. (3) Figures are in US dollars and as of 2010. (4) The data of Hong Kong and Macau exclude re-exports.

xxii

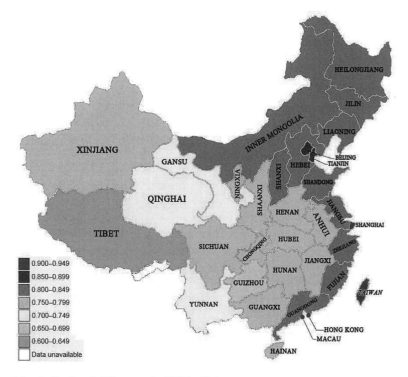

Map 5   Regional differences in HDI in China
Note: The HDI values of Hong Kong, Macau and Taiwan are included for comparison purposes.
Source: Author based on UNDP, *China Human Development Report 2009/2010*. Beijing: United Nations Development Program (UNDP) and Renmin University of China, 2010.

Table 1 Geopolitical and social status of China's provincial administrations

Provincial administration	Political form	Population (millions)	Land area (000 km²)	Capital city
Anhui	S	59.5	130.0	Hefei
Beijing	ZXS	19.6	16.8	Beijing
Chongqing	ZXS	28.8	82.4	Chongqing
Fujian	S	36.9	120.0	Fuzhou
Gansu	S	25.6	390.0	Lanzhou
Guangdong	S	104.3	180.0	Guangzhou
Guangxi	ZZQ	46.0	230.0	Nanning
Guizhou	S	34.7	170.0	Guiyang
Hainan	S	8.7	34.0	Haikou
Hebei	S	71.9	190.0	Shijiazhuang
Heilongjiang	S	38.3	460.0	Harbin
Henan	S	94.0	160.0	Zhengzhou
Hubei	S	57.2	180.0	Wuhan
Hunan	S	65.7	210.0	Changsha
Inner Mongolia	ZZQ	24.7	1100.0	Huhehaot
Jiangsu	S	78.7	100.0	Nanjing
Jiangxi	S	44.6	160.0	Nanchang
Jilin	S	27.5	180.0	Changchun
Liaoning	S	43.7	150.0	Shenyang
Ningxia	ZZQ	6.3	66.0	Yinchuan
Qinghai	S	5.6	720.0	Xi'ning
Shaanxi	S	37.3	190.0	Xi'an
Shandong	S	95.8	150.0	Ji'nan
Shanghai	ZXS	23.0	5.8	Shanghai
Shanxi	S	35.7	150.0	Taiyuan
Sichuan	S	80.4	477.6	Chengdu
Tianjin	ZXS	12.9	11.0	Tianjin
Tibet (xizhang)	ZZQ	3.0	1200.0	Lasha
Xinjiang	ZZQ	21.8	1600.0	Wurumuqi
Yunnan	S	46.0	380.0	Kunming
Zhejiang	S	54.4	100.0	Hanzhou

Notes: (1) S (sheng) = province; ZZQ (zizhiqu) = autonomous region; ZXS (zhixi-ashi) = municipality directly under the central government. (2) Hong Kong and Macau special administrative regions are not included. (3) All data are as of 2010.

Table 2 Time needed to start a business, selected nations and Chinese provinces

Nations	Days in 2010	Chinese provinces	Days in 2006
Austria, Palau	28	Guangdong	28
Tanzania	29		
India, Russia	30	Zhejiang	30
Bahamas, Benin, Nepal, Nigeria	31	Jiangsu	31
Burundi, Poland, Thailand	32		
		Jilin	33
Guyana (CR), Israel, Kenya	34		
Cameroon, Kuwait, Paraguay	35	Shanghai, Sichuan	35
Sudan	36	Hubei	36
Djibouti, Guatemala	37	Beijing, Jilin	37
China, Sri Lanka, Tajikistan	38	Hainan	38
Malawi, Nicaragua, Seychelles, Vanuatu	39	Chongqing	39
Côte d'Ivoire, Lesotho	40	Fujian	40
Guinea, Peru	41	Liaoning, Tianjin, Henan	41
Trinidad and Tobago	43	Anhui, Heilongjiang, Hebei, Hunan, Shaanxi, Yunnan	42–43
Bangladesh, Belize	44	Xinjiang	44
Bhutan, Fiji	46	Jiangxi, Guangxi	46
Spain	47	Gansu	47
West Bank and Gaza	49	Inner Mongolia	48
Bolivia, Vietnam	50	Guizhou	50
Papua New Guinea	51	Qinghai	51
Philippines	53	Shanxi, Ningxia	55

Notes: (1) "Time needed to start a business" records all procedures that are officially required for an entrepreneur to start up and formally operate an industrial or commercial business. These include obtaining all necessary licenses and permits, and completing any required notifications, verifications or inscriptions for the company and employees with the relevant authorities. (2) The figure for each Chinese province is represented by that of its capital city.
Sources: (1) *Doing Business in China 2008* from the World Bank (2008, Washington, DC: The World Bank Group; Beijing: Social Science Academic Press [China], 2008, p. 38); and (2) *Doing Business in China 2011* from the World Bank (2011, Washington, DC: The World Bank Group; Beijing: Social Science Academic Press [China], pp. 145–205).

Table 3 Time needed to register property, selected nations and Chinese provinces

Nations	Days in 2010	Chinese provinces	Days in 2006
Italy	27	Chongqing	28
China, Luxembourg, Mali	29	Shanghai	29
Bahrain, Chile, El Salvador, Zimbabwe	31	Jiangsu	31
Austria, Panama, Kosovo, Philippines	32–34		
Niger, Hong Kong, Iran	35–36	Guangdong	35
Tajikistan	37	Fujian	37
Ireland, St. Vincent and the Grenadines	38		
Gabon, Tunisia, Zambia	39	Jilin, Sichuan	39
Djibouti, Germany, Kazakhstan, Ethiopia	40–41		
Albania, Brazil, Denmark, Mozambique	42	Tianjin	42
Russia, Chad, India, Swaziland	43–44		
Latvia	45	Xinjiang	45
Paraguay	46	Anhui	46
Algeria, Morocco, Venezuela	47	Inner Mongolia	47
Liberia, Pakistan	50	Jiangxi, Shaanxi, Zhejiang	50
Iraq	51	Liaoning	51
Argentina	52	Hunan	53
Democratic Republic of Congo	54	Jillin	55
Republic of Congo, Jamaica, Kuwait	55	Heilongjiang	55
Cambodia, Vietnam, Macedonia	56–58	Hebei	58
Burkina Faso	59	Beijing, Ningxia	59
Belize, Dominican Republic, Rwanda	60	Hubei, Henan	60
Côte d'Ivoire, São Tomé and Principe	62	Shanxi	62
Gambia, Uruguay	66	Yunnan, Guangxi	66

Table 3   (Continued)

Nations	Days in 2010	Chinese provinces	Days in 2006
Fiji	68	Qinghai	69
Central African Republic	75	Hainan	76
Grenada, Uganda	77	Guizhou	77
Czech Republic, Eritrea, Uzbekistan	78	Gansu	78

Notes: (1) "Time needed to register property" records the full sequence of procedures necessary for a business (buyer) to purchase a property from another business (seller) and to transfer the property title to the buyer's name so that the buyer can use the property to expand its business, use the property as collateral in taking new loans or, if necessary, sell the property to another business. (2) The figure for each Chinese province is represented by that of its capital city.

Sources: (1) *Doing Business in China 2008* from the World Bank (2008, Washington, DC: The World Bank Group; Beijing: Social Science Academic Press [China], 2008, p. 38); and (2) *Doing Business in China 2011* from the World Bank (2011, Washington, DC: The World Bank Group; Beijing: Social Science Academic Press [China], pp. 145–205).

Table 4   Time needed to enforce contracts, selected nations and Chinese provinces

Nations	Days in 2010	Chinese provinces	Days in 2006
		Jiangsu	112
		Guangdong	120
Singapore	150		
Uzbekistan, New Zealand	195–216	Shandong	210
Belarus, South Korea, Azerbaijan	225–237	Shaanxi	235
Kyrgyz Republic, Rwanda	260	Liaoning	260
Namibia	270	Ningxia	270
Lithuania, Guinea	275–276	Hubei	277
Hong Kong, Norway, Russia	280–281		
Armenia, Georgia	285	Henan, Zhejiang, Chongqing	285–286
		Heilongjiang, Shanghai	290–292
Vietnam	295	Sichuan	295
US	300	Anhui, Shanxi, Tianjin	300
Latvia, Mongolia, Luxembourg	309–321	Hainan	310
France	331	Inner Mongolia	330

Ukraine	345	Beijing, Fujian	340–342
Japan, Moldova	360–365	Yunnan, Jiangxi	365
Macedonia, Mauritania, Finland	370–375		
Denmark	380	Hunan	382
Albania, Kazakhstan, Germany	390–394	Xinjiang	392
Australia, Hungary, Austria, Fiji	395–397	Guizhou, Guangxi, Hebei	397
China, Cambodia, Eritrea, UK	399–406		
Mexico, Iceland, Switzerland Turkey, Peru	415–428		
Tajikistan, Lao PDR	430–443	Gansu	440
Nigeria	457	Qinghai	458
United Arab Emirates	537		
Brunei, Nicaragua	540	Jilin	540
Montenegro, Niger, Portugal	545–547		

Notes: (1) "Time needed to enforce contracts" measures the efficiency of the judicial system in resolving a commercial dispute. The data are built by following the step-by-step evolution of a commercial sale dispute before local courts. The data are collected through study of the codes of civil procedure and other court regulations as well as surveys completed by local litigation lawyers and by judges. (2) The figure for each Chinese province is represented by that of its capital city.

Sources: (1) *Doing Business in China 2008* from the World Bank (2008, Washington, DC: The World Bank Group; Beijing: Social Science Academic Press [China], 2008, p. 39); and (2) *Doing Business in China 2011* from the World Bank (2011, Washington, DC: The World Bank Group; Beijing: Social Science Academic Press [China], pp. 145–205).

Introduction

During ancient times, the Chinese nation was generally regarded as being divided into nine states (or prefectures). More often than not, China, now called *zhongguo* (center under heaven or central state) in pinyin form, had an alternative name, *jiuzhou* (nine states). However, there have been a number of different viewpoints as to the states' precise classification.

For example, according to *Yugong* (the geographical records of the tribute to Yu), a book which was probably written in the Xia Dynasty (c. 1988–1766 BC), the nine states are Jizhou (on the northern side of the Yellow River), Yanzhou (on the eastern side of the Yellow River), Qingzhou (on the Shandong Peninsula), Yangzhou (in the southeast), Jingzhou (in the south), Yuzhou (on the southern side of the Yellow River), Yongzhou (in the near west), Liangzhou (in the far west) and Xuzhou (in the east, comprising the northern Jiangsu and southeast Shandong provinces).[1]

Since founding the feudal system, China's provincial administrations have been named as, *inter alia*,

- *jun* in the Qin Dynasty (221–206 BC);
- *junguo* in the Western Han Dynasty (206 BC–AD 25);
- *zhou* in the Eastern Han (AD 25–220), the Wei (AD 220–265), the Jin (AD 266–420) and the North and South (AD 420–589) dynasties;
- *dao*[2] in the Tang Dynasty (AD 618–907);
- *lu* in the North and South Song (AD 960–1279) and Jin (AD 1115–1235) dynasties;
- *zhongshu-xingsheng* in the Yuan Dynasty (AD 1279–1368);
- *xingsheng* in the Ming (AD 1368–1644) and Qing (AD 1644–1911) dynasties.

Note that the Chinese character *sheng* originally refers to the term 'ministry' (it is still used in Japan and Korea). *Zhongshu-xingsheng* and *xingsheng* (the latter has evolved into the term *sheng* in contemporary Chinese) refer to the "ministerial representative agencies of central government to provinces".

At present, China's territorial-administrative hierarchy has three different types of provincial-level units: *sheng* (provinces), *zizhiqu* (autonomous regions) and *zhixiashi* (municipalities directly under central government). In Chinese state administration "autonomous" refers to self-government by a large and single (but not necessarily majority) ethnic minority in any given unit within the territorial hierarchy. Autonomous regions are provincial-level units of state administration where the presence of an ethnic minority is officially recognized. They have the name of the specific ethnic minority incorporated into their title, as, for example, in the Guangxi Zhuang autonomous region, where Guangxi is the geographic name of the region and Zhuang is the name of a nationality. Municipalities are large cities, directly subordinate to the Chinese Communist Party Central Committee (CCPCC) and the State Council.

It should be noted that the three kinds of provincial administrations (*sheng, zizhiqu* and *zhixiashi*) have different functions. More often than not, top *zhixiashi* leaders are appointed as members of the Politburo of the CCPCC, something which has only happened to a small number of *sheng* and *zizhiqu* leaders. The autonomous regions (*zizhiqu*) are only established in areas where the ethnic minorities consist of the major portion of the population. Compared with other forms of provincial administrations, the *zizhiqu* is, at least in form, the most politically and culturally autonomous of the three kinds of provincial administration. In addition, Hong Kong and Macau – which returned to China in 1997 and 1999, respectively – are now China's two special administrative regions (SARs). It was agreed on handover that the existing political and economic systems that prevailed prior to these dates would be maintained for 50 years.[3]

While the formation of most provinces had taken place well before the foundation of the People's Republic of China (PRC), in recent decades a few of the others were either incorporated with their neighboring provinces or divided into new ones. For example, in 1954, Pingyuan Province, which was composed of the marginal administrative areas of present-day Hebei, Shanxi, Shandong and Henan provinces, was abolished; in 1988, Hainan Island, Guangdong Province, was established as a new province; and, in 1997, Chongqing City and its surrounding areas, all of which had belonged to Sichuan Province, became a province-level municipality under the direct control of central government. In addition, during the history of the PRC, some provincially marginal areas have been administratively transposed between the neighboring provinces. For example, in 1953, Xuzhou administrative region Shandong Province was placed under the administration of Jiangsu Province; and, in 1955, Yutai County was transferred from Anhui to Jiangsu Province.

There are five hierarchies of administrative divisions in China – that is, provincial, prefectural, county, township and village. The first-class administrative divisions include provinces, autonomous regions and municipalities directly under central government. The second-class administrative divisions refer to prefectures, autonomous prefectures, municipalities and other prefecture-level administrative divisions. And the third-class administrative divisions relate to counties, autonomous counties and other county-level administrative divisions. An organizational pattern involving more classes of administrative division has been generally known to have a lower level of administrative efficiency.

Recently, some provinces have been granted permission by central government to practise the reform of administrative divisions (i.e. to eliminate the second-class administrative divisions) in order to increase spatial economic efficiency. However, this administrative reform has encountered difficulties in dealing with large provinces. For example, in Henan and Shandong provinces there are more than 100 counties and county-level administrative divisions. Without the participation of the prefecture-level administrations, it would be very difficult, if not impossible, for a provincial governor to exert any direct effective influence on all of these county magistrates concurrently.

Most of China's provinces, autonomous regions and municipalities that are under the direct control of central government,[4] which are the average size and scale of a European country in population and land area, are considerable political and economic systems in their own right. These large provincial administrations, although they have some comparative advantages over the small ones in some circumstances, have been known to lack spatial administrative efficiency. Generally, the sources of benefits for large administrations may be grouped into two categories:

(1) The large administrations can make relatively efficient use of their fixed cost and hence gain considerable advantages over small administrations.

(2) Marketing in a larger economy has many benefits, but the main economies of scale from marketing include the bulk purchases and distribution potentialities.

A number of advantages can lead to larger administrations experiencing risk-bearing economies. The underlying factor is that large administrations frequently engage in a range of diverse activities, so that a fall in the return from any one unit of economy does not threaten the stability of the whole economy. While increases in size frequently confer advantages on an administration, there is a limit to the gains from growth in many cases. In other words, there is an optimal level of capacity, and increases in size beyond this level will lead to a loss of economies of scale and manifest themselves in rising average costs (see Figure 0.1). Without doubt, the increasing complexity of managing a large administration is the major source of administrative inefficiencies when its size grows beyond a certain level, and management of diverse socioeconomic affairs and risks becomes increasingly difficult.

Given China's huge size and enormous population, establishing new provincial administrations (including provinces or other provincial-level units) in the border areas of some adjacent, large provinces seems to serve two positive functions. The first concerns the increase in the efficiency of spatial administration over the marginal, adjacent areas by transferring the multitude of administrative systems into a unitary administrative structure; and the second relates to the realization of

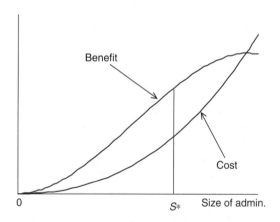

Figure 0.1   The optimum size ($S*$) of administrative divisions

increased economies of scale for provincial administration by separating the marginal areas out of the over-sized provinces.

Over recent decades, the total number of China's provincial administrations has increased from 29 in the mid-1950s to 30 in 1988 and 31 in 1997. But economic geographers and regional scientists still believe that the introduction of more (and smaller) provinces may help to improve the spatial efficiency of the Chinese economy. However, it seems unlikely that, under current political and economic systems, central government will be willing to create, and, of course, able to deal with, any more provincial administrations.

This book provides, in an easy-to-use format, a broad collection of data on China's 31 provinces. It is a resource that profiles the geography, demography, economy, political environment and business climate of each of these provinces. The chapter on each province contains:

- a brief introduction setting the geo-political and institutional background to each province's economy;
- a clear map indicating each province's geo-political relations with its neighbors, as well as its administrative divisions;
- a set of key demographic and socioeconomic indicators;
- an economic survey, divided into sections addressing the various sectors, including agriculture, industry, services, external trade, government finance and international economic cooperation;
- comparative (dis)advantage indexes of major industrial sectors in each province;
- provincial ranking of selected socioeconomic indicators from 2000 to 2010;
- a dedicated list of references for each province.

We hope that this book, which can be regularly updated with new editions to make sure that the provincial data are as up-to-date as possible, will become a useful source for researchers, businesses, government agencies and news media with an interest in either the rapidly changing provincial economies or the Chinese economy as a whole.

Notes

1. In the book titled *Lvshi Chunqiu* (historical records compiled by Lv Buwei), these states include Jizhou, Yanzhou, Qingzhou, Yangzhou, Jingzhou, Yuzhou, Yongzhou, Youzhou (in the northeast) and Bingzhou (in the north).

2. Notice that the Chinese character *dao* is still being used for "province" in both North and South Korea.
3. Note that Hong Kong and Macau SARs will not be discussed in this book.
4. In what follows, unless stated otherwise, we will use the term "province" to denote all three kinds of administrative division.

Part I
Provinces A–Z

Anhui

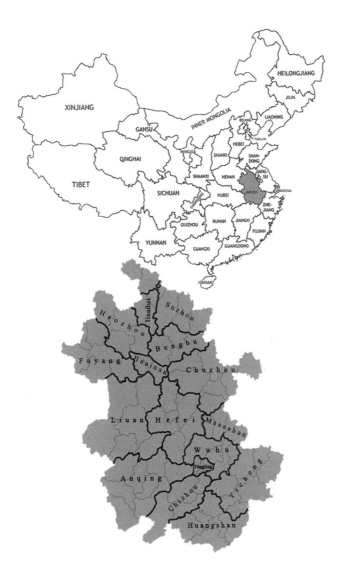

Source: The author, based on a file from the Wikimedia Commons.

Table A   The administrative divisions of Anhui

Name	Administrative seat	Population
Anqing PM	Yingjiang District	5,311,000
Bengbu PM	Longzihu District	3,164,000
Bozhou PM	Qiaocheng District	4,851,000
Chizhou PM	Guichi District	1,403,000
Chuzhou PM	Langya District	3,938,000
Fuyang PM	Yingzhou District	7,600,000
Hefei PM	Luyang District	7,457,000
Huaibei PM	Lieshan District	2,114,000
Huainan PM	Tianjia'an District	2,334,000
Huangshan PM	Tunxi District	1,359,000
Lu'an PM	Jin'an District	5,612,000
Ma'anshan PM	Yushan District	2,304,000
Suzhou PM	Yongqiao District	5,353,000
Tongling PM	Tongguanshan District	724,000
Wuhu PM	Jinghu District	3,443,000
Xuancheng PM	Xuanzhou District	2,533,000

Notes: PM = prefectural level municipality. All data are as of 2010.

Quick facts

Official name: Anhui Province
Abbreviated name: Wan
Land area: 139,400 km^2
Population (as of 2010): 59,567,000
Population density: 440/km^2
GRP per capita of 2010: ¥20,888
HDI of 2008: 0.750
Capital: Hefei
Address of government office: 221 Changjiang Road, Hefei City
Tel: 0551–260–1113/260–1114
Postcode: 230001
Website: www.ah.gov.cn

Anhui is a province of the PRC. Its name derives from the names of two cities – Anqing and Huizhou (now Huangshan City) – both of which are located in south Anhui. The abbreviation for the province is "Wan", because in ancient times there was a state called Wan in areas around the mountain called Wan in the province.

Situated in the southeast of China, and across the basins of the Yangtze and the Huai rivers, Anhui Province shares borders with

Jiangsu Province to the east, Zhejiang Province to the southeast, Jiangxi Province to the south, Hubei Province to the southwest, Henan Province to the northwest and Shandong Province to the north. It extends about 570 km from north to south, and 450 km from west to east, with an area accounting for 1.45% of the country.

There are 17 prefecture-level administrative divisions in Anhui, which are subdivided into 105 county-level divisions (44 districts, 5 county-level cities and 56 counties). Those are in turn divided into 1,845 township-level divisions (972 towns, 634 townships, 9 ethnic townships and 230 sub-districts).

Topographically, Anhui Province is quite diverse. The north is part of the North China Plain, while the north-central areas are part of the Huai River watershed. Both of these regions are very flat and densely populated. The land becomes more uneven further south, with the Dabie Mountains occupying much of southwestern Anhui and a series of hills and ranges cutting through the southeast. The Yangtze River finds its way through south Anhui between these two mountainous regions. Major rivers include the Huai in the north and the Yangtze in the south. Lake Chaohu, with an area of about 800 km^2, is the largest lake and is located in the center of the province. The southeastern part of Anhui near the Yangtze River has many lakes as well.

With the Yangtze and Huai rivers running through the province from the west to the east, Anhui is divided into three geographical regions, including Huaibei (north of the Huai), Jianghuai (between the Yangtze and the Huai) and Jiangnan (south of the Yangtze). The north of the Huai, part of the North China Plain, is a vast expanse of flatland. The middle area between the Yangtze and the Huai is a chain of undulating hills. The lands by the two sides of the Yangtze and around Lake Chaohu are low and flat, belonging to the well-known Middle-Lower Yangtze River Plain. The south mainly comprises hills.

Generally, the province can be divided into five topographical zones: the plain north of the Huai River, the hilly land between the Huai and Yangtze rivers, the Dabieshan mountain area of West Anhui, the plains along the Yangtze River and the hilly area in southern Anhui. Located in the transition region of the warm-temperate zone and sub-tropical zone, the climate is warm and humid with distinct seasons. The province's annual rainfall and weather in general varies greatly, with frequent spring droughts and summer floods.

Anhui differs in climate from north to south. The north is more temperate and has more clear-cut seasons. The average annual temperature of the province is 14–17 °C. January temperatures average −1 to 2 °C north of the Huai, and 0–3 °C south of the Huai. In July, temperatures average 27 °C or above. The average frost-free period lasts 200–250 days. Plum rains (a term used in some Chinese provinces to denote the rainy season) occur in June and July and may cause flooding. The annual average rainfalls are 800–1,800 mm. Plum rains occur in June and July and may cause flooding.

Anhui has a variety of natural resources. It has rich mineral reserves and the deposits of iron, copper, pyrite, limestone and alunite are among the top five in the nation. In addition, these resources are concentrated in distribution. Among the 138 discovered minerals, 104 have had their reserves proved. Major production sites of minerals in the province include iron in Ma'anshan, coal in Huainan and copper in Tongling, and there are industries related to these natural resources.

Covering an area of 4.33 million ha/40,907 km^2 of fertile farmland and benefiting from the mild climate, Anhui Province is rich in agricultural resources. Its major crops include rice, wheat and sweet potato. Many of its agricultural products are also famous. These include grapes, pears, pomegranates, tea and crabs. Agriculture varies according to the climate zones that the province crosses. Wheat and sweet potatoes are grown on the northern side of the Huai River, while rice and wheat are on the southern side. The total water reserve of Anhui is about 68 billion m^3. The Bishihang Irrigation Project and the Simashan Diversion and Irrigation Project are two key irrigation projects of the province. Forested areas amounted to 3.6 million ha as of the end of 2005.

Anhui is rich in plants and animals. It has 1,300 woody plants and 2,100 herbaceous plants. Among its more than 500 species of animals, 54 are listed as rare and under state protection, including the Yangtze alligator and the white-fin dolphin.

As of 2005, the province had established 31 nature reserves, including 5 at the national level, 25 at the provincial level and 1 at the county level. Its principal tourism sites include ancient villages in southern Anhui (e.g. Xidi and Hongcun [World Heritage Site]); Mount Huangshan (World Heritage Site); Mount Jiuhua; Mount Qiyun; Mount Tianzhu; the old town of Tunxi; Mount Langya; Zuiweng Pavilion, named after the poet Ouyang Xiu (AD 1007–1072); Lake Chao; Taiji Cave (the longest karst cave in East China); and the Zhenfeng Pagoda (a Ming Dynasty pagoda in Anqing City).

In 2010, Anhui's nominal GRP was ¥1.23 trillion (about US$181.1 billion) and per capita was ¥20,888 (about US$2,400). It is considered to be a mid-size province in terms of economic output. Compared with its more successful neighbors to the east, Zhejiang and Jiangsu, Anhui has lagged markedly behind in economic development, with a GRP per capita around one-third of those two provinces. There is great regional disparity as well. Regions such as Hefei, Wuhu and Ma'anshan have benefited from their closeness to the Yangtze River and so are significantly wealthier than the rest of the province due to their industrial and manufacturing industries.

Table B   Demographic and socioeconomic profile: Anhui

Indicator	2000	2010
Population (thousands)	59,860	59,567
Illiteracy rate of population aged 15 or over (%)	10.06	8.34
GRP (¥ billions)	303.82	1,235.93
Composition of GRP (%)		
Primary sector	24.1	14.0
Secondary sector	42.7	52.1
Tertiary sector	33.2	33.9
Fixed asset investment (¥ billions)	80.40	1,154.29
Status of foreign-funded enterprises		
Number of registered enterprises	2,216	5,633
Total investment (US$ millions)	9,144	30,324
Registered capital (US$ millions)	5,868	17,349
Foreign trade (US$ millions)		
Export	2,119	10,927
Import	1,570	12,453
Sales of consumer goods (¥ billions)	105	420
Per capita annual disposable income of urban residents (¥)	5,293.55	15,788.17
Engle's coefficient (%)	45.71	37.96
Per capita annual net income of rural residents (¥)	1,934.57	5,285.17
Engle's coefficient (%)	37.94	40.69
Number of patent applications granted	1,482	16,012
Inventions	104	1,111
Utility models	894	8,839
Designs	484	6,062

Note: All monetary values are measured at current prices.
Source: *Anhui Statistical Yearbook*, 2001 and 2011.

Anhui's GRP is largely driven by fixed asset investment (FAI). This, coupled with the province's pool of cheap labor and the establishment of an export processing zone in Hefei, which will offer numerous incentives (e.g. tax rebates and exemptions for manufacturers to set up shop) will likely further increase the growth of Anhui's more industrialized regions.

Anhui has several pillar industries – equipment manufacturing, metallurgy, coal exploration and chemicals. Its equipment manufacturing industry focuses on the fabrication of engineering machinery, electrical appliances and automobiles, with Wuhu City being one of the major air-conditioner production bases in China. It is highly concentrated in terms of the industrial group of products and has strongly competitive brands. However, there is a low level of creativity and high energy consumption in the industry. Examples of famous manufacturing firms in the region are Anhui HELI Corp (the nation's top company for forklift manufacturing), Meiling Corp (the leading enterprise in the China's refrigeration industry) and Chery Auto (a major enterprise in the country's automobile industry). The metallurgy industry in Anhui focuses on steel and copper. The output of refined copper products from Ma'anshan, Wuhu and Tongling accounts for one-third of the nation's total. Key enterprises in this industry are Masteel Group Corp and Tongling Nonferrous Metals Group Corp, the country's seventh largest steel producer and the world's eighth copper refiner.

Anhui's major exports include mechanical and electrical products, spinning- and fabric and related products, and land vehicles. The major imports are metal ore, metal waste material and special industrial machinery. Chile, Japan, Australia, Germany and Brazil are among the major import sources, while the US, Japan, South Korea, Hong Kong and Russia are the key export destinations.

The province receives large amounts of foreign direct investment (FDI) (more than half of the total) from Hong Kong. Other major sources are the US, Taiwan, Singapore and Japan. Manufacturing is the key recipient of FDI in Anhui. Energy supply, real estate, mining and accommodation are other noteworthy recipients.

As of 2010, compared with those of other provinces, "mining", "education" and "health, social security and social welfare" were relatively strong, while "services to households and other services", "leasing and business services" and "agriculture, forestry, animal husbandry and fishery" were relatively weak sectors (see Table C).

Since reform and an open-door policy were implemented in the early 1980s, Anhui has established four major economic and technological development zones, as described below.

Table C Anhui's comparative (dis)advantage indexes by sector, 2010

Sector	Index
Agriculture, forestry, animal husbandry and fishery	0.57
Mining	2.00
Manufacturing	0.73
Production and distribution of electricity, gas and water	1.08
Construction	1.16
Transport, storage and post	0.84
Information transmission, computer service and software	0.72
Wholesale and retail trades	0.91
Hotels and catering services	0.62
Financial intermediation	1.09
Real estate	0.81
Leasing and business services	0.52
Scientific research, technical services and geological prospecting	0.80
Management of water conservancy, environment and public facilities	1.02
Services to households and other services	0.31
Education	1.34
Health, social security and social welfare	1.22
Culture, sports and entertainment	0.91
Public management and social organization	1.14

Notes: All the sectors included in this table are determined according to China's official definitions and for urban areas only. Numerals greater than, equal to and less than 1 indicate that the province's sectors have advantages, no apparent (dis)advantages and disadvantages, respectively.

Sources: Calculated by the author based on *China Statistical Yearbook*, 2011. See Appendix for a detailed methodological description.

- **Hefei Economic and Technological Development Zone** Founded in 1993, this zone is located close to Hefei Luogang International Airport in the southwest of Hefei. It is the second largest of the development zones in Anhui in terms of land area (53 km²). It is divided into two functional areas. The east part is allocated to manufacturing and has two parks; the west part contains the business center, Hefei university town and the international community center. The pillar industries of this zone are the automobile, engineering equipment, electric appliance, daily chemical and food processing industries. In 2006 its industrial output accounted for 40% of Hefei's total industrial output. As well as this healthy output the zone upholds its quality standards and passed the ISO9001 and ISO14001 certifications in 2005.
- **Hefei Hi-Tech Industrial Development Zone** Founded in 1990, this was approved by the State Council as a state-level development

zone in 1991. With a land area of $11 km^2$, it ranks 16th in size among all the national high-tech development zones. It has more than 200 high-tech enterprises, accounting for 35% of the province's total. In 1997 the zone was ratified as an Asia-Pacific Economic Cooperation (APEC) Science and Technology Industrial Park, with special open policies to APEC and European Union (EU) members. The zone was also approved as a National High Tech Export Base in 2000 and recognized as an Advanced High Tech Zone under the Torch Program (sponsored by the Chinese Ministry of Science and Technology) in 2003. As of 2010, more than 100 hi-tech enterprises had entered the zone. Industries encouraged there include chemicals production and processing, electronics assembly and manufacturing, heavy industry, instruments and industrial equipment production, medical equipment and supplies, research and development (R&D) and telecommunications equipment.

- **Wuhu Economic and Technological Development Zone** Founded in 1993, this is the first state-level development zone approved by central government in Anhui. Located in Wuhu City, it has the largest land area ($56 km^2$) among all the major development zones in the province, and in 2006 its GRP, total industrial output value, fixed asset investment and total imports and exports reached ¥13.4 billion, ¥51.0 million, ¥4.2 million and US$704.6 million, respectively. As the hub in the west of the Yangtze Delta, the zone is an ideal place for business in Central and Eastern China (e.g. for manufacturing or as a logistics center) due to its great transportation advantage. Wuhu Port is the last ideal deepwater port in the province going through the Yangtze River. It is the main foreign trade base and overseas transportation center. It takes one hour from Wuhu to Nanjing Lukou International Airport and to Hefei Luogang Airport. The pillar industries of this zone are new construction materials, automobiles and parts, electronic and electronic appliances, biological engineering and IT.
- **Wuhu Export Processing Zone** Approved by the State Council as a national-level export processing zone, this zone has an area of about $3 km^2$. It is located close to Wuhu Airport and Wuhu Port. Industries encouraged in the zone include electronics assembly and manufacturing, heavy industry, instruments and industrial equipment production, shipping/warehousing/logistics, trading and distribution.

As of 2010 the top five companies were as follows:

1. Anhui Conch Cement Co (SHA: 600585) is a leading cement producer and distributor. It posted ¥34.51 billion revenue and ¥6.17 billion net profit for 2010.
2. Ma'anshan Iron and Steel Co (SHA: 600808) is an iron and steel producer and distributor based in the city of Ma'anshan. It posted ¥64.98 billion revenue and ¥1.1 billion net profit for 2010.
3. Guoyang Securities Co (SHE: 000728) specializes in debt service, dividend distribution, custody and authentication of securities, proprietary trading of securities, underwriting securities and asset management. It posted R¥2.24 billion revenue and ¥924.98 million net profit for 2010.
4. SDIC Xinji Energy Co (SHA: 601918) is engaged in exploration, washing, processing and distribution of coal. It posted ¥7.01 billion revenue and ¥1.25 billion net profit for 2010.
5. Tongling Nonferrous Metals Group Co (SHE: 000630) is a manufacturer and processor of non-ferrous metals and chemical products based in the city of Tongling. It posted ¥51.3 billion revenue and ¥899.21 million net profit for 2010.

Indicators for the ease of doing business

A. Starting a business

Procedures: 14
Time (days): 42
Cost (% of provincial GRP per capita): 19.4

B. Registering property

Procedures: 10
Time (days): 46
Cost (% of property value): 5.6

C. Getting credit – creating and registering collateral

Time (days): 20
Cost (% of loan value): 2.8

D. Enforcing contracts

Time (days): 300
Cost (% of claim): 41.8

Further reading

Chen, Axing, Wu yunliang, Zhao Bo (2008). *The Cooperative Economic Organization in the Circulation Area of Anhui Province* (anhui sheng liutong hezuo jingji zuzhi fazhan yanjiu). Hefei: Hefei University of Technology Publishing House.

Ding, Zhongming (2007). *The Economic Development Report of Anhui Province, 2006* (anhui sheng jingji fazhan yanjiu baogao, 2006). Hefei: Hefei University of Technology Publishing House.

Ding, Zhongming, Chen Zhongwei (2011). *Anhui Economic Development Report* (anhui jingji fazhan yanjiu baogao). Beijing: China Statistics Publishing House.

Economic Development Research Center of Anhui University of Economics and Finance (2008). *The Economic Development Report of Anhui Province, 2007* (anhui sheng jingji fazhan yanjiu baogao, 2007). Hefei: Anhui People Publishing House.

Gong, Qianwen, Zhang Junbiao (2007). "Relations between agricultural natural disasters and rural poverty based on analysis of panel data in Anhui Province, China," *China Population, Resources and Environment*, vol. 17, issue 4, July, pp. 92–95.

Ji, Kunsen (2008). *The Development of the Circulatory Economic in Anhui: Collected Papers* (fazhan xunhuan jingji, jiasu anhui jueqi luntan weiji). Hefei: Anhui University Publishing House.

Liu, Can, Runsheng Yin (2004). "Poverty dynamics revealed in production performance and forestry in improving livelihoods: The case of West Anhui, China," *Forest Policy and Economics*, vol. 6, issues 3–4, June, pp. 391–401.

Lu, Yilong (2007). *Embed Polity and Economic Transition: The Case in Xiaogang Village, Anhui Province* (qianruxing zhengzhi yu cunluo jingji bianqian: anhui xiaogang). Shanghai: Shanghai People Publishing House.

Luo, Fei (2010). *Several issues on Anhui: An Empirical Analysis* (anhui ruogan wenti shizheng fenxi yu yanjiu). Beijing: China Science and Technology University Publishing House.

Rong, Zhaozi, Li Guanglong (2008). *Economics and Anhui's Economic Development, 2008* (jingjixue yu anhui jingji fazhan, 2008). Hefei: Anhui University Publishing House.

Sun, Wanning (2002). "Discourses of poverty: Weakness, potential and provincial identity in Anhui," in Fitzgerald, John (ed.), *Rethinking China's Provinces*. London and New York: Routledge, pp. 153–178.

Sun, Ziduo (2006). *From Imbalance to Coordination: Important Economic Questions Concerning the Rise of Anhui* (cong shiheng zouxiang xietiao: anhui queqi zhongda jingji wenti yanjiu). Hefei: Anhui People Publishing House.

Sun, Ziduo, Lu Qinyi (2011). *Anhui's Economy* (anhui jingji). Hefei: Anhui Fine Arts Publishing House, Times Publishing Ltd.

Tao, Fangbiao, Kun Huang, Xiang Long, Rachel Tolhurst, Joanna Raven (2011). "Low postnatal care rates in two rural counties in Anhui Province, China: Perceptions of key stakeholders," *Midwifery*, vol. 27, issue 5, October, pp. 707–715.

Wang, Yanmin (2009). *The Coordinated Development of Resource, Environment and Economy in Anhui Province* (Anhuisheng ziyuan, huanjing, jingji xitong xietiao fazhan yanjiu). Beijing: China University Science and Technology Publishing House.

Zhang, Zongliang (2006). *Anhui, Mount Huangshan and the Hui Culture* (Panoramic China). Beijing: Foreign Languages Press.

Beijing

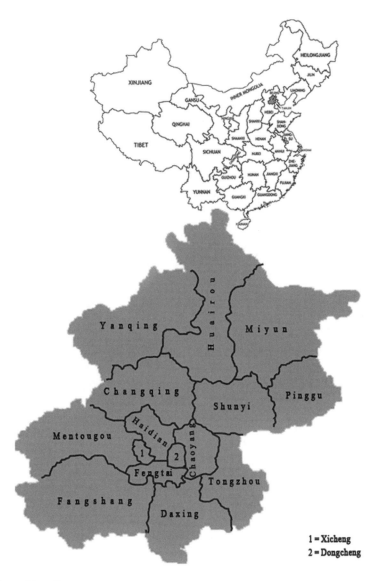

Source: The author.

Table A   The administrative divisions of Beijing

Name	Administrative seat	Population
Changping PD	Changping Town	1,661,000
Chaoyang PD	Chaoyangmenwai Ave	3,545,000
Daxing PD	Daxing Town	1,365,000
Dongcheng PD	Dongsi North Ave	919,000
Fangshan PD	Fangshan Town	945,000
Fengtai PD	Fengtai Town	2,112,000
Haidian PD	Changcunqiao Rd	3,281,000
Huairou PD	Huairou Town	373,000
Mentougou PD	Mentougou Town	290,000
Miyun SPC	Miyun Town	468,000
Pinggu PD	Pinggu Town	416,000
Shijingshan PD	Shijingshan Rd	616,000
Shunyi PD	Shunyi Town	877,000
Tongzhou PD	Tongzhou Town	1,184,000
Xicheng PD	Taipingqiao Ave	1,243,000
Yanqing SPC	Yanqing Town	317,000

Notes: SPC = sub-prefectural-level country; PD = prefectural level district. All data are as of 2010.

Quick facts

Official name: Beijing Municipality
Abbreviated name: Jing
Land area: 16,807 km^2
Population (as of 2010): 19,612,000
Population density: 1,167/km^2
GRP per capita of 2010: ¥50,467
HDI of 2008: 0.891
Capital: Beijing
Address of government office: 2 Zhengyi Road, Dongcheng District, Beijing
Postcode: 100001
Website: www.beijing.gov.cn

Beijing is a province-level municipality of the PRC and is also the capital of China. It is the country's second largest city by urban population (after Shanghai) and is the country's political and cultural center. It is home to the headquarters of most of China's largest state-owned companies. Beijing is a major transportation hub in the national highway, expressway, railway and high-speed rail network. Its Capital International Airport is the second busiest in the world by passenger traffic.

Over the past 3,000 years, Beijing has adopted numerous other names, including Ji, Yanjing, Youzhou, Nanjing, Zhongdu, Dadu, Cambaluc and Beiping. In 1421, when Emperor Yongle moved the capital of the Ming Dynasty north from Nanjing in Jiangsu Province, he renamed the city Beijing. From the Chinese characters, Beijing means, literally, the "northern capital". This official English spelling is based on the pinyin romanization of the two characters. In 1928, when the capital of the Republic of China was moved to Nanjing, the city was renamed Beiping, meaning "north peace". In 1949, it became the capital of the PRC. An older English spelling, Peking, was applied worldwide before the 1970s and is still occasionally used today.

Located at 39°56′N and 116°20′E, on the northwest edge of the North China Plain, Beijing adjoins Tianjin Municipality to the east and Hebei Province to the north, west and south. The Bohai Sea lies about 150 km to the southeast. The urban area of Beijing is in the south-central part of the municipality and occupies a small but expanding area. It spreads out in bands of concentric ring roads, of which the fifth and outermost, the Sixth Ring Road, passes through several satellite towns. Tian'anmen Square is at the center of Beijing, directly to the south of the Forbidden City, the former residence of the emperors of China. To the west of Tian'anmen is Zhongnanhai, home to the paramount leaders of the PRC. Running through central Beijing from east to west is Chang'an Avenue, one of the city's main thoroughfares.

The municipality currently comprises 16 administrative subdivisions, including 14 prefectural level urban and suburban districts and two rural sub-prefectural level counties. On July 1, 2010, Chongwen and Xuanwu districts were merged into Dongcheng and Xicheng districts, respectively. The districts and counties are further subdivided into 273 lower third-level administrative units at the township level: 119 towns, 24 townships, 5 ethnic townships and 125 sub-districts. Towns within the municipality but outside the urban area include (but are not limited to) Changping, Huairou, Miyun, Liangxiang, Liulimiao, Tongzhou, Yizhuang, Tiantongyuan, Huilongguan, Beiyuan and Xiaotangshan. Several placenames in Beijing end with *mén*, meaning "gate", as they were the locations of gates along the former Beijing city wall. Other placenames end in *cūn*, meaning "village", as they were originally villages outside the city wall.

Beijing Municipality is situated at the northern tip of the roughly triangular North China Plain, which opens to the south and east of the city. Mountains stand in the west, north and northeast, with an average elevation of 1,000–1,500 m, accounting for the 10,417.5 km² of mountain areas (or 62% of its territory). In the southeast lies the vast North China Plain of 6,390.3 km, with an average altitude of 20–60 m above sea level. The 2,303 m high Mount Lingshan on the border between the municipality and Hebei Province is the highest peak of the city. The Great Wall of China stretches across the northern part of Beijing.

Five major rivers flow across the city, including the Chaobai River in the east and the Yongding River in the west. Most of Beijing's rivers originate from the city's northern mountain areas and, after winding southeastwards across the plain area, they flow into the Bohai Sea. The 174 km long Yongding River, running through southwest Beijing, is the city's biggest river. It also has several dozen lakes (e.g. the Kunming, the Yuyuantan, the Beihai, the Zhonghai, the Nanhai, the Qianhai, the Houhai, the Xihai, the Longtan, the Taoranting and the Zizhuyuan). Miyun Reservoir, built on the upper reaches of the Chaobai River, is Beijing's largest reservoir and is crucial to its water supply. In addition, the city is also the northern terminus of the Grand Canal, which was built across the North China Plain to Hangzhou.

The municipality has four clear-cut seasons: short spring and autumn and long winter and summer. It has a rather dry, monsoon-influenced humid continental climate characterized by hot, humid summers and cold, windy, dry winters. The average annual temperature is 13 °C (averaging 25.2 °C in July, the hottest month, and −3.7 °C in January, the coldest month). The average annual rainfall is 507.7 mm (with the great majority of it falling in the summer) and the frost-free period lasts 180–200 days.

Beijing's mountain areas produce various minerals (e.g. coal and iron ores) and building materials (e.g. granite and marble). The forest coverage had reached 50.5% by the end of 2005. There are now 20 nature reserves covering an area of 1,342 km^2 and 7 ecological demonstration zones covering an area of 9,246 km^2. Human activities began in the Beijing area about 0.5 million years ago. The recorded history of Beijing as a city dates back more than 3,000 years, of which Beijing has served as a national capital for more than 700 years, being one of China's seven great ancient capitals. In this famed historical city, cultural heritage sites and scenic spots are found everywhere. Ancient palace groups, temples, parks, ancient pagodas with rock carvings, imperial gardens and tombs, and former residences of historical individuals throng the city side by side with the modern buildings of museums and memorial halls.

Beijing Municipality is not only the cultural and political center of China but also home to over 100 of China's largest companies. Its economy is based on the high-end manufacturing and service sectors, particularly the tourism, media and IT industries. Although it does not have any exchanges for securities or other financial derivatives, the capital is where the country's market watchdogs and regulators are based. Alongside Shanghai, Beijing attracts the Chinese or Asia-Pacific headquarters of many multi-national companies (MNCs).

As Chinese enterprises continue to springboard their businesses onto the global platform, Beijing's economic environment has projected an optimistic outlook over the past decade. In 2010, its GRP reached ¥787.0 billion (about US$100.3 billion). Meanwhile, its per capita GRP amounted to ¥50,467 (about US$6,428) in 2010. The service sector contributed the most to the municipal's GRP, accounting for 70% of the overall GRP in 2010. Meanwhile, the agricultural and industry sector made up 0.9% and 24.0% of the GRP, respectively (see Table B).

Table B   Demographic and socioeconomic profile: Beijing

Indicator	2000	2010
Population (thousands)	13,820	19,619
Illiteracy rate of population aged 15 or over (%)	4.23	1.70
GRP (¥ billions)	247.88	1,411.36
Composition of GRP (%)		
Primary sector	3.6	0.9
Secondary sector	38.1	24.0
Tertiary sector	58.3	75.1
Fixed asset investment (¥ billions)	128.05	540.30
Status of foreign-funded enterprises		
Number of registered enterprises	8,495	24,853
Total investment (US$ millions)	40,246	119,206
Registered capital (US$ millions)	21,738	71,477
Foreign trade (US$ millions)		
Export	7,667	30,717
Import	16,577	79,977
Sales of consumer goods (¥ billions)	144	623
Per capita annual disposable income of urban residents (¥)	10,349.69	29,072.93
Engle's coefficient (%)	36.30	32.07
Per capita annual net income of rural residents (¥)	4,604.55	13,262.29
Engle's coefficient (%)	36.47	32.36
Number of patent applications granted	5,905	33,511
Inventions	1,074	11,209
Utility models	3,463	16,579
Designs	1,368	5,723

Note: All monetary values are measured at current prices.
Source: *Beijing Statistical Yearbook*, 2001 and 2011.

As manpower, land costs and environmental pressure have been relatively higher than those of other Chinese cities, Beijing has placed
its focus on higher-value-added manufacturing. Electronics manufacturing, such as that of mobile phones and computers, is the biggest
industry in Beijing. Semiconductor Manufacturing International Corporation, the largest semiconductor foundry in China and one of the
leading foundries in the world, invested in a 12-inch wafer plant in
the Beijing Economic and Technological Development Zone. Beijing
Oriental Electronics has also established the largest thin-film transis-
tor liquid-crystal display manufacturer in China within the zone. Other
leading electronics manufacturers in the area include Nokia and Lenovo.

Beijing is also one of China's biggest automobile producers. Driven by
rising sales of automobiles, its automobile industry has grown rapidly in
the past decade. Beijing Hyundai (a joint venture between Beijing Automotive Industry Holding [BAIC] and Hyundai Motor of South Korea)
and Beijing Benz-DaimlerChrysler Automotive (a joint venture between
BAIC and DaimlerChrysler AG) are two of the major passenger car
makers in the municipality.

Within the manufacturing sector, Beijing Shougang Group had a leading role in the iron and steel industry in China. However, in an effort to
reduce the pollution levels in the capital for the 2008 Olympic Games,
the government imposed sanctions on coal-burning heavy industries,
resulting in the relocation of their facilities. All of Shougang's steel production was thus closed in 2010. In the meantime, Beijing's service
sector has achieved rapid growth. Within its retail industry, many new
shopping and commercial districts have emerged in various districts,
including Chaoyang, Haidian, Wangfujing, Xidan and Qianmen.

Beijing has placed more effort into R&D than the other municipalities.
The city's investment in this area has contributed to more than 5% of
its GRP. Meanwhile, gross added value from the high-tech industry has
accounted for a substantial portion of its overall gross industrial added
value.

As part of Beijing's 11th five-year plan, the government also pri-
oritized the development of a cultural and creative industry. This is
to function as a pillar of the region's growing economy and reinvent
its long-standing industries, which have been facing stronger domestic and overseas competition. Apart from a Beijing Creative Center in
the Dongcheng District, five other districts have plans to develop the
Shijingshan Digital Amusement Base, Zhongguncun Pioneering Base,
the National New Media Base, Deshengyuan Creative Base of Industrial
Design and the Dashanzi Arts Center. As the capital of China, Beijing

also attracts overseas and local tourists, bringing in substantial revenues for its municipal government.

During recent decades, Beijing's foreign trade has experienced rapid growth. Its largest export market was Hong Kong, followed by the US and Japan, while imports were mainly from (in order of import volume) Japan, Germany and the US.

Nearly half of the world's 500 largest enterprises had placed investments in Beijing. Its foreign investments were mainly channeled into the service industry, where the amount of utilized FDI in the service sector accounted for more than 50% of its utilized FDI. Within the sector, utilized FDI in leasing and commercial services took the largest share, followed by the real-estate sector. Hong Kong contributed the most to Beijing's overseas investment market. It invested heavily in the area's property sector, with an influx of Hong Kong developers, such as New World Development, Sun Hung Kai, Kerry Group and Cheung Kong, developing shopping centers, commercial complexes and residential buildings.

Furthermore, about 200 MNCs, such as SUN, NEC and Motorola, have developed R&D centers in the city. With the growing affluence of its residents and the development of new shopping and commercial districts in various areas of the capital (e.g. Chaoyang, Haidian, Wangfujing, Xidan and Qianmen), many foreign chain supermarkets have also set foot in its retail market. These include Carrefour, Makro and Ito Yokado.

As of 2010, compared with those of other provinces, "leasing and business services", "information transmission, computer service and software", "scientific research, technical services and geological prospecting", "real estate", "hotels and catering services", "services to households and other services", "culture, sports and entertainment" and "wholesale and retail trades" were relatively strong, while "mining", "agriculture, forestry, animal husbandry and fishery" and "production and distribution of electricity, gas and water" were relatively weak sectors (see Table C).

Table C Beijing's comparative (dis)advantage index by sector, 2010

Sector	Index
Agriculture, forestry, animal husbandry and fishery	0.17
Mining	0.16
Manufacturing	0.56
Production and distribution of electricity, gas and water	0.44

Table C   (Continued)

Sector	Index
Construction	0.63
Transport, storage and post	1.63
Information transmission, computer service and software	4.53
Wholesale and retail trades	2.09
Hotels and catering services	2.70
Financial intermediation	1.17
Real estate	3.01
Leasing and business services	5.06
Scientific research, technical services and geological prospecting	3.16
Management of water conservancy, environment and public facilities	0.81
Services to households and other services	2.50
Education	0.52
Health, social security and social welfare	0.66
Culture, sports and entertainment	2.34
Public management and social organization	0.58

Notes: All the sectors included in this table are determined according to China's official definitions and for urban areas only. Numerals greater than, equal to and less than 1 indicate that the province's sectors have advantages, no apparent (dis)advantages and disadvantages, respectively.
Sources: Calculated by the author based on *China Statistical Yearbook*, 2011. See Appendix for a detailed methodological description.

Since reform and an open-door policy were implemented in the early 1980s, Beijing Municipality has established many economic and technological development zones. Its 11th five-year plan (2006–2010) included the further development of six functional areas for high-end industries. This involved developing areas such as the Zhongguancun Science Park (ZSP), the Beijing Economic and Technological Development Zone, the Central Business District, the Olympic Central Area, the Financial Street and the Aviation Economic Area. In 2006 the six zones were attributed with approximately 50% of industrial growth, more than 50% of information industrial growth and more than 70% of financial growth within the city. Two development zones are described below.

- **Zhongguancun Science Park (ZSP)** Located in the northwestern part of Beijing in Haidian District, ZSP is China's first state-level hi-tech industrial park. Known as the Silicon Valley of China, it plays a significant role within the economy. ZSP comprises the Haidian Development Area, Fengtai Development Area, Changping Development Area, Electronics Town Science and Technology Development

Area and the Yizhuang Science and Technology Development Area. It has a high concentration of scientific and technological institutions and research resources. Featuring many renowned universities, including the Chinese Academy of Sciences, Beijing University and Qinghua University, ZSP is a development zone that focuses on the knowledge and IT industries. Over the decades, it has emerged as the largest software development center in the country. By 2006 the industrial park had attracted about 23,869 cutting-edge enterprises. In the same year the zone experienced 31.7% growth in revenue, amounting to ¥644.8 billion, while a profit of ¥37.69 billion was posted. Meanwhile, exports reached ¥12.48 billion – an increase of 32.2%.

- **Beijing Economic and Technological Development Zone** Located near the south Fourth Ring Road, this zone is one of China's state-level development areas focusing on overseas investments from high-tech enterprises and MNCs. By the end of 2006 it had registered 2,170 investors, representing an investment of US$14 billion. Within the year its revenue grew by 58.7% to ¥200 billion, while profits increased by 48.8%, reaching ¥12.5 billion. The sales value of the one's high-tech products amounted to ¥144 billion, growing by 45.4% year on year. It also reported that energy consumption per ¥10,000 of GRP in 2006 was equivalent to 0.159 tons of coal, declining by 10% from a year earlier. In 2006 it posted a 46.59% increment in export and import value, totaling US$17.5 billion. The export value from the zone reached US$9 billion, increasing by 59.77%. Meanwhile, foreign investments in the zone amounted to US$3.7 billion, representing growth of 73.41%.

As of 2010 the top five companies were as follows:

1. Aviation Industry Corporation of China (AVIC) is a Chinese state-owned company in the aviation industry, both military and civilian. It was founded in 1951 as the Aviation Industry Administration Commission. Since being established on April 17, 1951, during the Korean War as the Aviation Industry Administration Commission, the aviation industry of the PRC has been through 12 systemic reforms.
2. Bank of China Limited (SHA: 601988 SEHK: 3988) is one of the big four state-owned commercial banks of the PRC. It was founded in 1912 by the government of the Republic of China to replace the Government Bank of Imperial China. It is the country's oldest bank.

3. Central Huijin Investment Ltd, established on December 26, 2003, is an investment company owned by the government of the PRC. It is a wholly owned subsidiary of China Investment Corporation with its own board of directors and board of supervisors. Central Huijin's principal shareholder rights are exercised by the State Council.
4. Aluminum Corporation of China Limited also known as Chalco (SEHK: 2600, NYSE: ACH, SHA: 601600) is a multinational aluminum company headquartered in Beijing. It is the world's second-largest alumina producer (and the only one in China) and the third-largest primary aluminum producer (and the largest in China).
5. China Construction Bank (SHA: 601939, SEHK: 0939) is one of the "big four" banks in the PRC. Currently it is ranked as the nation's second largest, the second largest bank in the world by market capitalization and the 12th largest company in the world.

Indicators for the ease of doing business

A. Starting a business

Procedures: 14
Time (days): 37
Cost (% of provincial GRP per capita): 3.2

B. Registering property

Procedures: 10
Time (days): 59
Cost (% of property value): 3.1

C. Getting credit – creating and registering collateral

Time (days): 15
Cost (% of loan value): 2.7

D. Enforcing contracts

Time (days): 340
Cost (% of claim): 9.6

Further reading

Biao, Zhang, Li Wenhua, Xie Gaodi, Xiao Yu (2010). "Water conservation of forest ecosystem in Beijing and its value," *Ecological Economics*, vol. 69, issue 7, 15 May, pp. 1416–1426.
Chang, Sen-dou (1998). "Beijing: Perspectives on preservation, environment, and development," *Cities*, vol. 15, issue 1, February, pp. 13–25.

Cotterell, Arthur (2007). *The Imperial Capitals of China – An Inside View of the Celestial Empire*. London: Pimlico.

deLisle, Jacques (2009). "After the gold rush: The Beijing Olympics and China's evolving international roles," *Orbis*, vol. 53, issue 2, pp. 179–204.

Gu, Chaolin, Jianafa Shen (2003). "Transformation of urban socio-spatial structure in socialist market economies: The case of Beijing," *Habitat International*, vol. 27, issue 1, March, pp. 107–122.

Harper, Damian (2007). *Beijing: City Guide*, 7th Edition. Oakland, CA: Lonely Planet Publications.

He, Chunyang, Jie Tian, Peijun Shi, Dan Hu (2011). "Simulation of the spatial stress due to urban expansion on the wetlands in Beijing, China using a GIS-based assessment model," *Landscape and Urban Planning*, vol. 101, issue 3, 15 June, pp. 269–277.

Hook, Brian (1998). *Beijing and Tianjin: Towards a Millennial Megalopolis* (Regional Development in China). Oxford: Oxford University Press.

Hu, Albert Guangzhou, Gary H. Jefferson (2004). "Returns to research and development in Chinese industry: Evidence from state-owned enterprises in Beijing," *China Economic Review*, vol. 15, issue 1, pp. 86–107.

Leaf, Michael (1995). "Inner city redevelopment in China: Implications for the city of Beijing," *Cities*, vol. 12, issue 3, June, pp. 149–162.

Li, Lillian, Alison Dray-Novey, Haili Kong (2007). *Beijing: From Imperial Capital to Olympic City*. New York: Palgrave Macmillan.

Lin, Q.G., G.H. Huang (2009). "Planning of energy system management and GHG-emission control in the Municipality of Beijing – An inexact-dynamic stochastic programming model," *Energy Policy*, vol. 37, issue 11, November, pp. 4463–4473.

Simon, Denis Fred (1989). "China's hi-tech thrust: Beijing's evolving approaches to the process of innovation," *China Economic Review*, vol. 1, issue 1, Spring, pp. 73–92.

Tian, Guangjin, Jianguo Wu, Zhifeng Yang (2010). "Spatial pattern of urban functions in the Beijing metropolitan region," *Habitat International*, vol. 34, issue 2, April, pp. 249–255.

Wang, Lei, Linyu Xu, Huimin Song (2011). "Environmental performance evaluation of Beijing's energy use planning," *Energy Policy*, vol. 39, issue 6, June, pp. 3483–3495.

Wang, Zhaohua, Bin Zhang, Jianhua Yin, Yixiang Zhang (2011). "Determinants and policy implications for household electricity-saving behaviour: Evidence from Beijing, China," *Energy Policy*, vol. 39, issue 6, June, pp. 3550–3557.

Wei, Yehua Dennis, Danlin Yu (2006). "State policy and the globalization of Beijing: Emerging themes," *Habitat International*, vol. 30, issue 3, September, pp. 377–395.

Wu, Fulong, Klaire Webber (2004). "The rise of 'foreign gated communities' in Beijing: Between economic globalization and local institutions," *Cities*, vol. 21, issue 3, June, pp. 203–213.

Zhang, Jingchao, Koji Kotani (2012). "The determinants of household energy demand in rural Beijing: Can environmentally friendly technologies be effective?" *Energy Economics*, vol. 34, issue 2, March, pp. 381–388.

Zhang, Renqi (1991). "Beijing architecture since 1979," *Habitat International*, vol. 15, issue 3, pp. 99–116.

Zheng, Siqi, Matthew E. Kahn (2008). "Land and residential property markets in a booming economy: New evidence from Beijing," *Journal of Urban Economics*, vol. 63, issue 2, March, pp. 743–757.

Zheng, Siqi, Richard B. Peiser, Wenzhong Zhang (2009). "The rise of external economies in Beijing: Evidence from intra-urban wage variation," *Regional Science and Urban Economics*, vol. 39, issue 4, July, pp. 449–459.

Chongqing

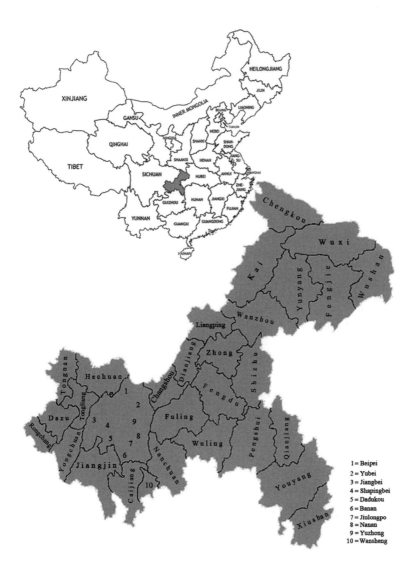

1 = Beipei
2 = Yubei
3 = Jiangbei
4 = Shapingbei
5 = Dadukou
6 = Banan
7 = Jiulongpo
8 = Nanan
9 = Yuzhong
10 = Wansheng

Source: The author.

32

Table A   The administrative divisions of Chongqing

Name	Administrative seat	Population
Ba'nan PD	Longhai Ave	918,700
Beipei PD	Shuangyuan Ave	680,400
Bishan C	Jiefang Rd	586,000
Changshou PD	Taoyuan East Rd	770,000
Chengkou C	Tucheng Rd	193,000
Dadukou PD	Shuangshan East Rd	301,000
Dazu PD	Jinhang Middle Rd	721,300
Dianjiang C	Nanyang Middle Rd	704,500
Fengdu PD	Pingdu Ave	649,200
Fengjie C	Shaoling Rd	834,300
Fuling PD	Xinghua Middle Rd	1,066,700
Hechuan PD	Xieran Ave	1,293,000
Jiangbei PD	Qufu Rd	738,000
Jiangjin PD	Binjiang Ave	1,233,100
Jiulongpo PD	Xijiao Rd	1,084,400
Kai C	Kaizhou Ave	1,160,300
Liangping C	Renmin East Rd	687,500
Nan'an PD	Jinzi St	759,600
Nanchuan D	Xinhua Rd	534,300
Pengshui Miao and Tujia AC	Shizi St	545,100
Qianjiang PD	Xingshu St	445,000
Qijiang PD	Zhongshan Rd	1,026,800
Rongchang C	Renmin Rd	661,300
Shapingba PD	Fengtian Ave	1,000,000
Shizhu Tujia AC	Xinkai Rd	415,100
Tongliang C	Longdu Rd	600,100
Tongnan C	Xingtong Ave	640,000
Wanzhou PD	Jiangnan New Area	1,563,100
Wulong C	Wulong Town	351,000
Wushan C	Wushan Town	495,100
Wuxi C	Wuxi Town	414,100
Xiushan Tujia and Miao AC	Xiushan Town	501,600
Yongchuan PD	Renmin Ave	1,024,700
Youyang Tujia and Miao AC	Youyang Tujia and Miao	578,100
Yubei PD	Yixue Rd	1,345,400
Yunyang C	Yunyang Town	912,900
Yuzhong PD	Heping Rd	630,100
Zhong C	Zhong Town	751,400

Notes: AC = autonomous county; C = county; PD = prefectural level district. All data are as of 2010.

Quick facts

Official name: Chongqing Municipality
Abbreviated name: Yu
Land area: 82,300 km^2
Population: 28,846,200
Population density: 350/km^2
GRP per capita of 2010: ¥27,596
HDI of 2008: 0.783
Capital: Chongqing
Government office address: Renmin Road, Yuzhong District, Chongqing
Tel: 023-638-5444
Website: www.cq.gov.cn

Chongqing is a province-level municipality of the PRC. A major city in Southwest China, its provincial status was approved at the Fifth Session of the Eighth National People's Congress on March 14, 1997, succeeding its status as a sub-provincial administration of Sichuan Province. Administratively, it is one of the PRC's four provincial-level municipalities (the other three are Beijing, Shanghai and Tianjin).

Chongqing (which means "double celebration") received its current name in the Song Dynasty (AD 960–1279) when Emperor Guangzong renamed the city Chongqing Fu. "Yu" is the official abbreviation of the name of Chongqing. The shortened version derives from the old name of part of the Jialing River that runs through Chongqing and feeds the Yangtze River.

Chongqing lies in the transitional area between the Qinghai–Tibet Plateau and the plain on the middle and lower reaches of the Yangtze River. Jialing River passes through the city into the Yangtze River, lending Chongqing the name of "a city on rivers". Located at the northern end of the Yunnan-Guizhou Plateau and the eastern limits of the Sichuan Basin, it is intersected by the Jialing River and the upper reaches of the Yangtze. Chongqing is also known as "a city of mountains" as it is surrounded by the Daba Mountains to the north, the Wushan Mountains to the east, the Wuling Mountains to the Southeast and the Dalou Mountains to the south. Geographically, it shares provincial borders with Hubei (in the east), Hunan (in the southeast), Guizhou (in the south), Sichuan (in the west) and Shaanxi (in the north).

The boundaries of Chongqing Municipality reach much farther into the city's hinterland than the boundaries of the other provincial-level municipalities of China, and much of its administrative area is still rural. It is divided into 38 subdivisions consisting of 19 districts, 15 counties and 4 autonomous counties.

The municipality has a monsoon-influenced humid sub-tropical climate and experiences very humid conditions for most of the year. Its average annual temperature is around 18 °C. Known as one of the "Three Furnaces" of China, along with Wuhan and Nanjing, its summers are long and among the hottest and most humid in China, with highs of 33–34 °C in July and August. However, conditions are cooler in the southeast part of the municipality due to the higher elevations there. Winters are short and somewhat mild, but damp and overcast. Chongqing is also known as the "Fog City", and a thick layer of fog shrouds it during the spring and autumn. The city's location in the Sichuan Basin causes it to have one of the lowest sunshine totals annually in China.

Chongqing is rich in mineral resources. Some 75 types of minerals have been discovered and 40 have yielded reserves. These include coal, natural gas, manganese, mercury, aluminum, marble, limestone and strontium. The region leads China and ranks second in the world in deposits of strontium. It is one of the nine largest iron and steel centers in China and one of the three major aluminum producers. Important manufacturers include Chongqing Iron and Steel Company and South West Aluminum, which is Asia's largest aluminum plant. The municipality has been selected as the site of a refinery operated by CNPC (parent company of PetroChina) to process imported crude oil from the Sino-Burma pipeline. The pipeline, after it is finished, will eventually run from Sittwe (in Myanmar's western coast) through Kunming in Yunnan Province before reaching Chongqing, and it will provide China with fuels sourced from Myanmar, the Middle East and Africa.

Agriculture remains significant in area. Rice and fruit (especially oranges) are the area's main produce. Biological resources are also plentiful. Specifically, Chongqing has more than 2,000 species of vascular plants, 380 animal species and 120 river fish. It has crisscrossing rivers and the water resources can generate 7.5 million kw of power. It has one of the three largest resources of mineral water in China.

With mountains, rivers, forests, springs, waterfalls, gorges and caves, all displaying the majesty, the fantasy, the danger and the seclusion of nature, Chongqing is proud of its popularity among tourists. Its famous tourist attractions include the Three Gorges on the Yangtze River; the night view of the City of Mountains; the rock carvings at Dazu, a World Cultural Heritage Site; the Lotus Cave near the Four-Sided Mountains; and Tiankeng (Heavenly Pit) and Difeng (Earthly Rift Valley), two rare geological spectacles at Fengjie.

Chongqing is one of the most notable cities for history and culture in China, and it serves as the economic center of the upstream

Yangtze area. The city enjoys a great cultural and natural heritage. The Three Gorges, the Dazu Stone Sculptures, the Ghost City in Fengdu, the Hot Spring Park, the Red Crag Memorial Museum, Baidicheng City in Fengjie and the Ba people's hanging coffins have attracted many tourists. Chongqing has been selected as one of the Historical and Cultural Cities of China by the State Council.

Chongqing has witnessed an average two-digit growth rate since 1997, when it was approved as the fourth municipality directly under China's central government. However, its overall economic performance is still lagging behind eastern coastal cities such as Shanghai. For instance, its per capita GRP is still below the national average. Nevertheless, there is massive government support to transform Chongqing into the region's economic, trade and financial center and to use it as a platform to open up the country's western interior to further development.

Table B Demographic and socioeconomic profile: Chongqing

Indicator	2000	2010
Population (thousands)	30,900	28,846
Illiteracy rate of population aged 15 or over (%)	6.95	4.30
GRP (¥ billions)	158.93	792.56
Composition of GRP (%)		
Primary sector	17.8	8.6
Secondary sector	41.4	55.0
Tertiary sector	40.8	36.4
Fixed asset investment (¥ billions)	57.26	668.89
Status of foreign-funded enterprises		
Number of registered enterprises	1,708	4,827
Total investment (US$ millions)	6,602	34,885
Registered capital (US$ millions)	4,419	20,350
Foreign trade (US$ millions)		
Export	1,060	6,994
Import	791	4,835
Sales of consumer goods (¥ billions)	64	294
Per capita annual disposable income of urban residents (¥)	6,275.98	17,532.43
Engle's coefficient (%)	41.45	37.59
Per capita annual net income of rural residents (¥)	1,892.44	5,276.66
Engle's coefficient (%)	32.34	48.28
Number of patent applications granted	1,158	12,080
Inventions	56	1,143
Utility models	677	6,704
Designs	425	4,233

Note: All monetary values are measured at current prices.
Source: *Chongqing Statistical Yearbook*, 2001 and 2011.

Chongqing aims to become a financial center; a manufacturing base with a focus on notebooks and IT products; a free trade zone, leveraging its railway access to Europe; and a transport hub leveraging the Yangtze River's waterway capacity and air, rail and road connections. The incorporation of Chongqing as a province-level municipality shows how serious the government is about its development.

Chongqing has increased investments in fixed assets in a bid to accelerate the economic development and living standard of its people. Areas that have attracted the largest share of fixed asset investment include real estate, manufacturing, administration of water conservancy, environment and public facilities, logistics, and electricity, water and gas production and supply. As a traditional industrial base of China, it has made an effort to restrict the high pollution and high energy-consumption industries. As a result, the fixed asset investment in the service sector has increased, accounting for over two-thirds of the total.

Chongqing is China's third largest center for motor vehicle production and the largest for motorcycles. It is the biggest auto and motorcycle production base in western China. By the end of 2006 there were 24 car-makers in the city, including 10 auto assembly firms and 14 special-purpose vehicle manufacturing enterprises. The backbone of its automobile industry is the Chang'an Group, China's fourth largest car-maker. Its joint ventures in Chongqing include Chang'an Suzuki Auto Corp and Chang'an Ford Mazda. Chongqing Lifan is China's second largest motorcycle maker. Other leading motorcycle makers include Loncin Group, Chongqing Jianshe Motorcycles, Jialing Industrial Co. Ltd and Zhongshen Industrial Group. In addition, the growth of the auto and motorcycle industry has accelerated the development of auto parts and accessories.

Recently there has been a drive to move up the value chain by shifting toward high-technology and knowledge-intensive industries resulting in new development zones, such as the Chongqing New North Zone (CNNZ). Chongqing's local government hopes to apply favorable economic policies for the electronics and IT sectors.

The city has also invested heavily in infrastructure to attract investment. The network of roads and railways connecting it to the rest of China has been expanded and upgraded, thus reducing logistical costs. Furthermore, the nearby Three Gorges Dam, which is the world's largest, not only supplies Chongqing with power but also allows ocean-going ships to reach Chongqing's Yangtze River port. These infrastructure improvements have led to the arrival of numerous foreign investors in industries ranging from auto to finance and retailing, such as Ford, Mazda, HSBC, Standard Chartered Bank, Citibank, Deutsche Bank, ANZ Bank, Scotiabank, Wal-Mart, Metro AG and Carrefour among other MNCs.

Chongqing is diversifying its industries and developing its high-tech sectors. With the government's support, the electronics industry has been developing steadily. To speed up the development of the electronics industry, local government has established the Xiyong Micro-Electronic Park, which focusses on chip production, electronic material production, and solar cell and software development, in a bid to turn the park into the "Silicon Valley" of the city. Hewlett-Packard has agreed to launch China's fourth software base in the park. The founding groups, Kingdee and Huayang, are among the first to have a seat in the park.

There are 207 enterprises producing petrochemicals, raw chemical materials and chemical products. Sinopec Fuling Chongqing Chemical Industry Co and Chongqing Chuandong Chemical Co. Ltd are two large chemical producers in the city.

Chongqing is the wholesale and retail center of southwestern China. With a large population, it is an important consumer market in the region. The retail industry is fairly competitive. Chaotianmen market is a leading wholesale center in the area. Its products include garments, plastic products and textiles. Carrefour from France, Wal-Mart from the US, Metro from Germany, B&Q from Britain and Gome from Beijing have tapped into the market. In addition, Chongqing General Trade Group and Chongqing Department Store Co. Ltd are the two largest local retailers.

Chongqing is the logistics center of western China due to its convenient transportation infrastructure. The Yangtze River and the Jialing River weave through it, making it a large inland port along the upper reaches of the Yangtze. It is also the intersection point for three railways (the Chengdu–Chongqing Railway, the Chengdu–Guiyang Railway and the Xiangfan–Chongqing Railway) and two expressways (the Chongqing–Behai Expressway and the Chongqing–Zhanjiang Expressway). Chongqing Airport Development Zone aims to set up a 48-hour logistics center through which goods are able to reach major cities around the world within 48 hours.

Chongqing has maintained steady growth in foreign trade. A breakdown of the top imported goods includes mechanical and electrical equipment, vehicles, aircraft, ships and related transportation equipment, minerals, optical and medical instruments, clocks and musical instruments, and base metals and related products. As it is one of the main manufacturing bases in western China, machinery and electrical appliances are important exports. The value of exported machinery and electrical appliances represents more than two-thirds of the total value of exports. Other major exported goods include base metals, chemicals, construction materials and textiles.

Chongqing has attracted a large number of MNCs to set up business, including ABB, Sony Ericsson, Honda and Coca-Cola. The manufacturing, real estate and finance sectors received the largest share of FDI. Hong Kong continues to be the top overseas investment source for area. Other major overseas investors are from the US, Japan and Singapore. The Chongqing government currently encourages foreign investment in infrastructure, traditional Chinese medicine, hi-tech industries and modern services.

As of 2010, compared with those of other provinces, "construction" and "real estate" were relatively strong, while "Agriculture, forestry, animal husbandry and fishery", "services to households and other services" and "Information transmission, computer service and software" were relatively weak sectors (see Table C).

There are several economic and technological development zones in Chongqing, including Chongqing Chemical Industrial Park, Chongqing Economic and Technological Development Zone, Chongqing Hi-Tech Industry Development Zone, CNNZ, Chongqing Export Processing Zone and Jianqiao Industrial Park (located in Dadukou District). Two of them are described in the following page.

Table C Chongqing's comparative (dis)advantage index by sector, 2010

Sector	Index
Agriculture, forestry, animal husbandry and fishery	0.24
Mining	0.82
Manufacturing	0.84
Production and distribution of electricity, gas and water	1.04
Construction	1.85
Transport, storage and post	1.11
Information transmission, computer service and software	0.75
Wholesale and retail trades	1.02
Hotels and catering services	1.00
Financial intermediation	1.11
Real estate	1.29
Leasing and business services	0.84
Scientific research, technical services and geological prospecting	0.92
Management of water conservancy, environment and public facilities	0.83
Services to households and other services	0.74

Education	1.08
Health, social security and social welfare	0.90
Culture, sports and entertainment	0.97
Public management and social organization	0.84

Notes: All the sectors included in this table are determined according to China's official definitions and for urban areas only. Numerals greater than, equal to and less than 1 indicate that the province's sectors have advantages, no apparent (dis)advantages and disadvantages, respectively.
Sources: Calculated by author based on *China Statistical Yearbook*, 2011. See Appendix for a detailed methodological description.

- **Chongqing Economic and Technological Development Zone (CETZ)** Established in 1993, this was the first state-level development zone in west China. By the end of 2006 it had attracted 447 investors from 22 countries. The investment amounted to US$3.53 billion and the actualized foreign investment exceeded US$1.13 billion. Ford from the US, Metro from Germany, Ericsson from Sweden, Honda from Japan and Fiat from Italy have set up operations there. The zone's GRP has maintained a two-digit growth rate for years, hitting ¥11.04 billion in 2006, up 51.93% year on year. It consists of two parks – South Park and North Park – covering an area of 9.6 km² and 83.7 km², respectively. IT, biotech and pharmaceuticals, autos and motorcycles, chemicals and new materials, food processing and textiles have formed the six pillar industries in this zone. It is targeted to have an industrial output of ¥80 billion by 2010.
- **Chongqing Hi-Tech Industry Development Zone** One of five pilot reform development zones in China, this was approved as a state-level development zone in 1993 by the State Council. It occupies an area of 73 km². More than 4,000 enterprises have been established there, including 300 from Japan, the US, Germany, France, Hong Kong and Taiwan. Major industries in the zone include IT, biotech and new medicines, new materials and mechatronics. In 2006 its gross output stood at ¥52 billion, with a value-added output of ¥11 billion. Chongqing Export Processing Zone, with a designed area of 2.8 km, was set up in the North Park of CETZ in 2001. Its total export and import value has surpassed US$300 million, while total investments amounted to nearly US$500,000 by the end of 2006. Central government has designated it as one of the seven export processing zones that will launch pilot projects to establish themselves as bonded logistics centers. It has also received regulatory approval to operate technological development and maintenance services.

As of 2010 the top five companies were as follows:

1. Chongqing Department Store Co (SHA: 600729) is engaged in the operation of department stores and supermarkets, as well as the wholesale and retail of electrical appliances. It posted ¥21.21 billion in revenues and ¥527.25 million in net profits for 2010.
2. Chongqing Iron & Steel Co (SHA: 601005) is engaged in the manufacture and distribution of iron and steel products. It posted ¥16.62 billion in revenues and ¥10.01 million in net profits for 2010.
3. Chongqing Taiji Industry Group Co (SHA: 600129) is engaged in the production and distribution of Chinese patent medicines and chemical drugs. It posted ¥5.99 billion in revenues and ¥161.59 million in net losses for 2010.
4. Lifan Industry Group Co (SHA: 601777) is engaged in the research, development, manufacture and distribution of motorcycles, automobiles and general gas engines. It posted ¥6.77 billion in revenues and ¥381.91 million in net profits for 2010.
5. Chongqing Brewery Co (SHA: 600132) is engaged in brewing and the distribution of beer. It posted ¥2.38 billion in revenues and ¥361.91 million in net profits for 2010.

Indicators for the ease of doing business

A. Starting a business

Procedures: 14
Time (days): 39
Cost (% of provincial GRP per capita): 9.5

B. Registering property

Procedures: 7
Time (days): 28
Cost (% of property value): 7

C. Getting credit – creating and registering collateral

Time (days): 15
Cost (% of loan value): 5

D. Enforcing contracts

Time (days): 286
Cost (% of claim): 14.8

Further reading

Andrews-Speed, Philip, Guo Ma, Bingjia Shao, Chenglin Liao (2005). "Economic responses to the closure of small-scale coal mines in Chongqing, China," *Resources Policy*, vol. 30, issue 1, March, pp. 39–54.

Cao, Guohua, et al. (2011). *China's Financial Development and Chongqing's Practice* (zhongguo de jinrong fazhan yu Chongqing de shijian). Chongqing: Chongqing University Press.

Chen, Aimin (1998). "Inertia in reforming China's state-owned enterprises: The case of Chongqing," *World Development*, vol. 26, issue 3, March, pp. 479–495.

Chongqing Municipal Government Legal Affairs Office (2006). "Basic situation of construction and implementation of the open government information system in Chongqing Municipality," *Government Information Quarterly*, vol. 23, issue 1, pp. 48–57.

Danielson, Eric N. (2005a). "Chongqing," in Danielson, Eric N. (ed.), *The Three Gorges and the Upper Yangzi: The Definitive Travel Guide* (New Yangzi River Trilogy). Singapore: Marshall Cavendish/Times Editions, pp. 325–362.

Danielson, Eric N. (2005b). "Revisiting Chongqing: China's Second World War temporary national capital," *Journal of the Royal Asiatic Society, Hong Kong Branch*, vol. 45. Hong Kong: Royal Asiatic Society, Hong Kong Branch.

Han, Sun Sheng, Yong Wang (2001). "Chongqing," *Cities*, vol. 18, issue 2, April, pp. 115–125.

He, Shizhong (1991). *Chongqing – The Mysterious Charm of the Three Gorges in Chongqing* (Panoramic China). Beijing: Foreign Languages Press.

Hong, Lijian (2002). "New Chongqing: Opportunities and challenges," in Fitzgerald, John (ed.), *Rethinking China's Provinces*. London and New York: Routledge, 2002, pp. 41–88.

Kapp, Robert A. (1974). "Chungking as a center of warlord power, 1926–1937," in Elvin, Mark, G. William Skinner (eds), *The Chinese City between Two Worlds*. Stanford, CA: Stanford University Press, pp.143–170.

Liu, Binfu (2010). *Designing Chongqing and Sichuan: Constructing the Fourth Growth Pole for the Chinese Economy* (cehua Chongqing, cehua Sichuan: gouzu zhongguo jingji de disi zengzhang ji). Beijing: Tsinbghua University Press.

McIsaac, Lee (2000). "The City as Nation: Creating a Wartime Capital in Chongqing," in Esherick, Joseph W. (ed.), *Remaking the Chinese City, 1900–1950*. Honolulu: University of Hawaii Press.

Okadera, Tomohiro, Masataka Watanabe, Kaiqin Xu (2006). "Analysis of water demand and water pollutant discharge using a regional input–output table: An application to the City of Chongqing, upstream of the Three Gorges Dam in China," *Ecological Economics*, vol. 58, issue 2, 15 June, pp. 221–237.

Ren, Hong, Liu Guiwen, et al. (2011). *New Thinking, New Exploration and New Model: The Practice of the Rural-Ruban Development in Chongqing* (xin sisuo, xin tansuo yu xin moshi: Chongqing tongchou chengxiang fazhan de shijian). Chongqing: Chongqing University Press.

Shu, Wei, Yang Fan, Liu Shiwen (2011). *The Chongqing Model* (chongqing moshi). Beijing: China Economics Press.

Wang, Hua, Jian Xie, Honglin Li (2010). "Water pricing with household surveys: A study of acceptability and willingness to pay in Chongqing, China," *China Economic Review*, vol. 21, issue 1, March, pp. 136–149.

Wang, Xu, Zhang Zongyi (2011). *Outward Patterns of Manufacturing and Trade: Chongqing's Exploration and Practice* (waixiangxing jiagong yu maoyi de moshi: Chongqing de tansuo yu shijian). Chongqing: Chongqing University Press.

Zhao, W., H. Ren, V.S. Rotter (2011). "A system dynamics model for evaluating the alternative of type in construction and demolition waste recycling center – The case of Chongqing, China," *Resources, Conservation and Recycling*, vol. 55, issue 11, September, pp. 933–944.

Zhao, W., R.B. Leeftink, V.S. Rotter (2010). "Evaluation of the economic feasibility for the recycling of construction and demolition waste in China – The case of Chongqing," *Resources, Conservation and Recycling*, vol. 54, issue 6, April, pp. 377–389.

Fujian

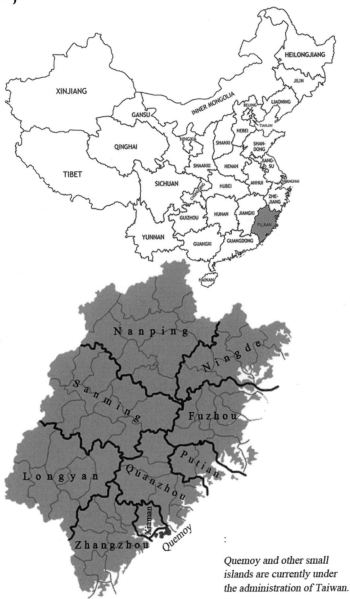

: Quemoy and other small islands are currently under the administration of Taiwan.

Source: The author, based on a file from the Wikimedia Commons.

Table A   The administrative divisions of Fujian

Name	Administrative seat	Population
Fuzhou PM	Gulou District	7,115,370
Longyan PM	Xinluo District	2,559,545
Nanping PM	Yanping District	2,645,549
Ningde PM	Jiaocheng District	2,821,996
Putian PM	Chengxiang District	2,778,508
Quanzhou PM	Fengze District	8,128,530
Sanming PM	Sanyuan District	2,503,388
Xiamen SPM	Siming District	3,531,347
Zhangzhou PM	Xiangcheng District	4,809,983

Notes: PM = prefectural level municipality; and SPM = sub-provincial level municipality. All data are as of 2010. Quemoy (Jinmen) County is nominally under the administration of Quanzhou Municipality, but it is administered in its entirety by the Republic of China. The PRC-administered Lianjiang County, under the jurisdiction of Fuzhou prefecture-level city, nominally includes the Matsu (Mazu) Islands, but Matsu (Mazu) is in reality controlled by the Republic of China, which administers Matsu as Lienchiang County (same name romanized differently). The Wuchiu (Wuqiu) Islands are nominally administered in the PRC by the Xiuyu District of the Putian prefecture, but are in reality controlled by the Republic of China, which administers Wuchiu (Wuqiu) as part of Quemoy (Jinmen) County.

Quick facts

Official name: Fujian Province
Abbreviated name: Min
Land area: 121,400 km^2
Population: 36,930,000
Population density: 291/km^2
GRP per capita of 2010: ¥40,025
HDI of 2008: 0.807
Capital: Fuzhou
Government office address: Hualin Road, Fuzhou
Tel: 0591–702–1333
Website: www.fj.gov.cn

Fujian is a province of the PRC. Located on the southeast coast of mainland China, it borders Zhejiang to the north, Jiangxi to the west and Guangdong to the south. Taiwan lies to the east, across the Taiwan Strait. Situated on the coast of the East China Sea, Fujian measures 540 km from east to west and 550 km from north to south. Its coastline stretches 3,324 km. Encompassing 1,401 islands of different sizes, it is a vital navigation hub between the East China Sea and the South China Sea.

The name comes from the combination of Fuzhou and Jianzhou (a former name for Jian'ou) – two important cities in Fujian during the Tang Dynasty. With a Han majority, it is one of the most culturally and linguistically diverse provinces in China. The province has the abbreviated name "Min" since it was the place for an ancient kingdom called Minyue. The word "Minyuè" was derived by combining "Min" (an ethnic name associated with the Chinese word for barbarians, *mán*) and "Yue" (after the State of Yue, a kingdom during the Spring and Autumn Period [771–221 BC] in Zhejiang Province to the north). This is because the royal family of Yuè fled to Fujian after their kingdom was annexed by the state of Chu in 306 BC. Min is also the name of the main river in this area.

Currently there are nine administrative divisions – at both prefectural and sub-provincial levels. These are divided into 85 county-level divisions (26 districts, 14 county-level cities and 45 counties). These are in turn divided into 1,107 township-level divisions (605 towns, 328 townships, 18 ethnic townships and 156 sub-districts). These are the official PRC numbers. Thus, Quemoy (Jinmen) is included as one of the 45 counties and Matsu (Mazu) as one of the 334 townships. Most of Fujian is administered by the PRC. However, the archipelagos of Quemoy and Matsu are under the control of the Republic of China.

Fujian Province is mostly mountainous and is traditionally described as "eight parts mountain, one part water, and one part farmland". The northwest is higher in altitude, with the Wuyi Mountains forming the border between Fujian and Jiangxi provinces. It is the most forested provincial-level administrative region in China, with 62.96% forest coverage in 2009. The highest point of Fujian is Huanggang Peak in the Wuyi Mountains with an altitude of 2,157 m.

The Min River and its tributaries cut through much of northern and central Fujian. Other rivers include the Jinjiang River and the Jiulong River. Due to its uneven topography, the region has many cliffs and rapids. It is separated from Taiwan by the 180 km wide Taiwan Strait. Some of the small islands in the strait are also part of the province. Small parts of the province, namely the islands of Quemoy and Matsu, are under the administration of the Republic of China.

Fujian Province has a sub-tropical humid monsoon climate, with annual temperatures averaging between 17 and 21 °C. The average temperatures in the coldest month (January) are 10–13 °C in the southeast coastal parts and 5–8 °C in the inland mountain areas. In the hottest month (July) the temperatures average 26–29 °C. The average annual precipitation is 1,000 mm and the frost-free period lasts 240–330 days a year.

Fujian possesses 86 kinds of minerals with verified reserves, including 34 kinds of metallic minerals and 47 non-metallic minerals. Among those with considerable reserves are gold, silver, lead, zinc, manganese, kaolin, limestone, granite, alunite, pyrophyllite and sulfur. Its reserve of quartz-sandstone ranks among the best nationally in both quantity and quality.

Farmland is sparse. Rice is the main crop, supplemented by sweet potatoes, wheat and barley. Cash crops include sugar cane and rapeseed. Fujian leads the provinces of China in longan production, and is also a major producer of lychees and tea. Seafood is another important product, with shellfish production especially prominent.

Mountains and hilly areas constitute over 80% of Fujian's land area while plains are concentrated in its southeast coastal areas. Forests cover 52.4% of Fujian's land area. Plant species are abundant. There are 1,943 kinds of woody plants, including 400 species of timber tree and 140 varieties of bamboo. Fujian has 400 million m³ of timber reserved, its timber production ranking third in China. There are several thousand species of terrestrial wild animals in Fujian. They include 100 species of mammals, 540 species of birds, 115 species of reptiles and 44 species of amphibians. There are also more than 5,000 kinds of insects. The Wuyi Mountain Nature Reserve is abundant in wildlife resources. It is also a world-renowned specimen base for new species of vertebrates and insects. The Meihua Mountain Nature Reserve in Longyan City is home to large numbers of animals. Fujian has five big fishing grounds which abound in marine resources. Among the more than 3,000 species of marine organisms, 750 are fish, accounting for 50% of the country's total marine fish species.

Fujian Province is rich in water resources, and its annual rainfall totals 201.1 billion m³. More than 500 rivers in the province each have a drainage area of more than 50 km². The volume of river runoff stands at 115 billion m³ a year on average. The province's theoretical water-power reserves total 10.46 million kw, which can generate 91.6 billion kw h of power annually. There are 1,000 places suitable for building a hydropower station with a generating capacity of over 500 kw. Their combined generating capacity can reach 7.05 million kw and their annual power generation 32 billion kw h, both ranking first in eastern China. The existing generating capacity accounts for only 30% of the province's total potential, leaving huge room for development. Fujian also has rich underground water resources. More than 100 hot springs have been discovered, with water temperatures of 40–60 °C.

There are many beautiful mountains in the province. Famous resorts include the Wuyi Mountain, the Gushan (Drum Hill) in Fuzhou, the Tailao Mountain in east Fujian and Wanshiyan in Xiamen. The province also has many beautiful beaches, such as the bathing beach on Gulangyu Islet of Xiamen, Luanwan Beach on Dongshan Island, Longwangtou Beach at Pingtan and Meizhou Island at Putian. Its numerous rivers offer many picturesque water spots, including the Jiuqu (nine-bend) Stream in Wuyi Mountain and Jinhu Lake, the largest artificial lake in Fujian. Northwest Fujian is noted for danxia and karst landforms, with countless grotesque rocks and fantastic caves. The Wuyi and Meihua mountain nature reserves preserve vast expanses of virgin forest, with rich fauna and flora resources. These reserves and other scenic resorts are ideal places for enjoying the charms of nature, taking holidays and conducting scientific explorations. In addition, Fujian has a lot of gardens and parks of different types.

Fujian Province is rich in tourist attractions, abounding with places of historical and cultural interest, and beautiful scenic spots. It has preserved many cultural sites from the Qin (221–207 BC), the Han (206 BC – AD 220), the Tang (AD 618–907), the Song (AD 960–1279), the Yuan (AD 1271–1368) and the Ming (AD 1368–1644) dynasties. There are numerous ancient temples, pagodas, bridges and castles, as well as former residences of celebrities. Fujian has a variety of navigation relics and religious legacies, thanks to its long history of navigation and frequent contact with the wider world.

Colorful ethnic customs, unique local cultures and rich products also add attraction to the province's tourism resources. Currently, Fujian encompasses 2 national tourist holiday resorts, 9 national scenic spots, 4 national nature reserves (forest parks), 4 national-level famous historic and cultural cities, 29 key cultural sites under state protection, 19 provincial-level scenic spots, 6 provincial tourist economic development areas and 204 cultural sites under provincial protection.

Hakka, a Han Chinese people with their own distinct identity, live in the southwestern parts of the province. Hui'an, also a Han branch with a distinct culture and fashion, populate Fujian's southeast coastline near Chongwu in Hui'an County. The She, scattered over mountainous regions in the north, are the largest minority ethnic group of the province. Many ethnic Chinese around the world, especially in Southeast Asia, trace their ancestry to Fujian. Descendants of the region's emigrants make up the majority ethnic Chinese populations of Taiwan, Singapore, Malaysia, Indonesia and the Philippines. Fujian, especially Fuzhou, is also the major source of Chinese immigrants in the US.

Fujian Province is located on China's southeastern coast and is the closet point in mainland China to Taiwan. Because of this close geographical proximity, Fujian was once considered the battlefield frontline in a potential war between mainland China and Taiwan. Today, although Fujian is one of the wealthier provinces of China, its GRP per capita is the lowest among the country's coastal administrative divisions. In 2010 Fujian's nominal GRP was ¥1.43 trillion (about US$212 billion), representing a rise of 12% from the previous year. It's GRP per capita was ¥33,051 (about US$4,890). The Minnan Golden Triangle, which includes Xiamen, Quanzhou and Zhangzhou, accounts for 40% of the GRP of Fujian Province.

Table B Demographic and socioeconomic profile: Fujian

Indicator	2000	2010
Population (thousands)	34,710	36,930
Illiteracy rate of population aged 15 or over (%)	7.20	2.44
GRP (¥ billions)	392.01	1,473.71
Composition of GRP (%)		
Primary sector	16.3	9.3
Secondary sector	43.7	51.0
Tertiary sector	40.0	39.7
Fixed asset investment (¥ billions)	111.22	819.91
Status of foreign-funded enterprises		
Number of registered enterprises	16,013	23,463
Total investment (US$ millions)	47,084	124,831
Registered capital (US$ millions)	27,585	69,358
Foreign trade (US$ millions)		
Export	13,623	66,619
Import	9,334	43,931
Sales of consumer goods (¥ billions)	137	531
Per capita annual disposable income of urban residents (¥)	7,432.26	21,781.31
Engle's coefficient (%)	44.66	39.26
Per capita annual net income of rural residents (¥)	3,230.49	7,426.86
Engle's coefficient (%)	41.19	46.14
Number of patent applications granted	3,003	18,063
Inventions	93	1,224
Utility models	1,074	9,664
Designs	1,836	7,175

Note: All monetary values are measured at current prices.
Source: *Fujian Statistical Yearbook*, 2001 and 2011.

In terms of spending power, retail sales for the province were roughly equivalent to that of Shanghai or Beijing. Fujian has been a major beneficiary of FDI, especially from overseas Fujianese and Taiwanese, but now that it is no longer the only point of access to Taiwan it is losing out on investment to Jiangsu and Guangdong. Major industries include petrochemicals, machinery and electronics. Its tourism sector has seen very strong growth and continues to be one of the brighter spots in its economy.

Fujian is one of the more affluent provinces with many industries, spanning tea production, clothing and sports equipment manufacturers (such as Anta, 361 Degrees, Xtep, Peak Sport Products and Septwolves). Many foreign firms have operations in Fujian. These include Boeing, Dell, GE, Kodak, Nokia, Siemens, Swire, TDK and Panasonic.

Fujian Province has been the major economic beneficiary of China's direct linkage scheme with Taiwan. Commenced on December 15, 2008, this scheme includes direct flights from Taiwan to major Fujian cities, such as Xiamen and Fuzhou. In addition, ports in Xiamen, Quanzhou and Fuzhou will be upgrading their port infrastructure to allow increased economic trade with Taiwan.

The province is host to the China International Fair for Investment and Trade. This is held annually in Xiamen to promote foreign investment for all of China.

Since 1978, when China opened to the world, Fujian Province has received a significant amount of FDI. The largest share comes from Hong Kong, followed by Singapore, the UK and Canada. Since Taiwan and China had not established direct links before 2008, most of the Taiwanese investments were counted as those from third sources (such as Hong Kong and other overseas sources). Since the late 2000s the region has benefited from China's direct links with Taiwan. Its FDI has been concentrated in Fuzhou, Xiamen, Quanzhou and Zhangzhou. Fujian's major foreign trade partners have been ASEAN, the US and Japan.

As of 2010, compared with those of other provinces, "manufacturing", "construction" and "real estate" were relatively strong, while "mining", "agriculture, forestry, animal husbandry and fishery" and "scientific research, technical services and geological prospecting" were relatively weak sectors (see Table C).

Fujian's economic and technological development zones include Dongshan Economic and Technology Development Zone, Fuzhou Economic & Technical Development Zone, Fuzhou Free Trade Zone, Fuzhou Hi-Tech Park, Fuzhou Taiwan Merchant Investment Area, Jimei

Table C   Fujian's comparative (dis)advantage index by sector, 2010

Sector	Index
Agriculture, forestry, animal husbandry and fishery	0.46
Mining	0.22
Manufacturing	1.71
Production and distribution of electricity, gas and water	0.77
Construction	1.27
Transport, storage and post	0.68
Information transmission, computer service and software	0.64
Wholesale and retail trades	0.67
Hotels and catering services	0.93
Financial intermediation	0.71
Real estate	1.10
Leasing and business services	1.02
Scientific research, technical services and geological prospecting	0.48
Management of water conservancy, environment and public facilities	0.52
Services to households and other services	0.61
Education	0.73
Health, social security and social welfare	0.64
Culture, sports and entertainment	0.72
Public management and social organization	0.55

Notes: All the sectors included in this table are determined according to China's official definitions and for urban areas only. Numerals greater than, equal to and less than 1 indicate that the province's sectors have advantages, no apparent (dis)advantages and disadvantages, respectively.
Sources: Calculated by author based on *China Statistical Yearbook*, 2011. See Appendix for a detailed methodological description.

Taiwan Merchant Investment Area, Meizhou Island National Tourist Holiday Resort, Pingtai Development Zone, Wuyi Mountain National Tourist Holiday Resort, Xiamen Export Processing Zone, Xiamen Free Trade Zone, Xiamen Haicang Economic and Technological Development Zone, Xiamen Torch New & Hi-Tech Industrial Development Zone and Xinglin Taiwan Merchant Investment Area.

As of 2010 the top five companies were as follows:

1. Industrial Bank Co (SHA: 601166) is a Fuzhou-based commercial lender that does business across the nation. It posted ¥43.46 billion in revenues and ¥18.52 billion in net profits for 2010.
2. Zijin Mining Group Co (SHA: 601899) is a gold and base metals explorer. It posted ¥28.54 billion in revenues and ¥4.83 billion in net profits for 2010.

3. Sanan Optoelectronics Co (SHA: 600703) is a leading producer of LEDs. It posted ¥862.61 million in revenues and ¥419.27 million in net profits for 2010.
4. Fuyao Glass Industry Group Co (SHA: 600660) is a manufacturer and distribution of automotive, decoration and industrial glass. It posted ¥8.51 billion in revenues and ¥1.79 billion in net profits for 2010.
5. Xiamen C&D Inc (SHA: 600153) is engaged in the operation of supply chains, property development and industrial investment. It posted ¥66.1 billion in revenues and ¥1.75 billion in net profits for 2010.

Indicators for the ease of doing business

A. Starting a business

Procedures: 12
Time (days): 40
Cost (% of provincial GRP per capita): 6.7

B. Registering property

Procedures: 7
Time (days): 37
Cost (% of property value): 4.1

C. Getting credit – creating and registering collateral

Time (days): 7
Cost (% of loan value): 2.3

D. Enforcing contracts

Time (days): 342
Cost (% of claim): 13.7

Further reading

Chen, Jian-fei, Su-qiong Wei, Kang-tsung Chang, Bor-wen Tsai (2007). "A comparative case study of cultivated land changes in Fujian and Taiwan," *Land Use Policy*, vol. 24, issue 2, April, pp. 386–395.
Chu, David K.Y., Yue-Man Yeung (2000, eds). *Fujian: A Coastal Province in Transition and Transformation* (Academic Monograph on China Studies). Hong Kong: The Chinese University Press.
Dai, Yifeng (2004). *Regional Economic Development and Social Transition: Studies in Modern Fujian* (quyuxing jingji fazhan yu shehui bianqian: yi jindai fujian diqu weizhongxin). Hunan: Yue Lu Publishing House.
Foreign Languages Press (2006, ed.). *Fujian, Mountain and Maritime Cultures* (Panoramic China). Beijing: Foreign Languages Press.

He, Donghang (2011). *Local Society, Government and Economic Development: Politcal and Social Sicence Research of a County-Level City in the Southern Fujian* (difang shehui, zhengzhi yu jingji fazhan: dui fujian nanbu yizuo xianjishi de zhengzhi shehui kexue kaocha). Beijing: China Social Science Publishing House.

Hook, Brian (1996). *Fujian: Gateway to Taiwan* (Regional Development in China). Oxford: Oxford University Press.

Hu, Xuwei, Hu Tianxin (1996). "Outward economy and urban system growth: Southeast Fujian case," *Asian Geographer*, vol. 15, issue 1–2, January, pp. 85–92.

Jin, Ling (2011). *On Sail: A Review of the Baisc Framework of Fujian's New Economic System* (qihang: fujiansheng jianli xinjingji tizhi jiben kuangjia de huigu). Xiamen: Strait Literature and Art Publishing House.

Lin, Xing, Chen Zhiping (2009). *Urban Development and Social Transition: Studies in the Fujian Modernizaion, 1843–1949* (chengshi fazhan yu shehui bianqian: fujian chengshi xiandaihua yanjiu, 1843–1949). Tianjin: Tianjin Ancient Books.

Liu, Rongzi, Wu Shanshan, Liu Ming, Liu Xiude (2008). *The Social Economic Influence Evaluation of the Fujian Filling-Sea Program* (fujiansheng haiwan tianhai guihua shehui jingji yingxiang pingjia). Beijing: Science Publishing House.

Long, Simon (1994). "Regionalism in Fujian," in Goodman, David S.G., Gerald Segal (eds), *China Deconstructs: Politics, Trade and Regionalism* (Routledge in Asia). London and New York: Routledge, pp. 202–223.

Luo, Dan, Haifeng Zheng, Yanhui Chen, Guo Wang, Ding Fenghua (2010). "Transfer characteristics of cobalt from soil to crops in the suburban areas of Fujian Province, southeast China," *Journal of Environmental Management*, vol. 91, issue 11, November, pp. 2248–2253.

Lyons, Thomas P. (1997). "Development in Fujian: A county-level perspective," *China Economic Review*, vol. 8, issue 2, Autumn, pp. 117–136.

Tang, Guozhong (2009). *The Western Strait Economic Zone* (haixia xi an jingjiqu duben). Fuzhou: Fujian People Publishing House.

Tang, Yonghong (2010). *The Research of Communication and Cooperation between Fujian and Taiwan* (fujian dui tai jiaoliu xianxing xianshi yanjiu). Beijing: Jiu Zhou Publishing House.

Wang, Bingan, Li Minrong (2007). *The Synthetical Competitiveness of the Fujian Economy* (fujiansheng jingji zonghe jingzhengli baogao). Beijing: The Social Science Reference Publishing House.

Wu, Changnan, et al. (2007). *Studies of Constructing Fujian as a Powerful Occean Province* (Fujian jianshe haiyang jingji qiangsheng yanjiu). Beijing: China Economics Publishing House.

Wu, Changnan, Huang Jiwei, et al. (2010). *Research of the Changing of Economic Development Model: The Case of Fujian Province* (zhuanbian jingji fazhan fashi yanjiu: yi Fujian weili). Beijing: China Economics Publishing House.

Wu, Changnan, Lin Changhua (2012). *The Studies of Industrial Transition and Upgrade in Fujian* (fujiansheng chanye zhuanxing shengji yanjiu). Beijing: China Economics Publishing House.

Wu, Changnan, Ma Xiaohong, Huang Jiwei (2009). *Regional Economic Development and the Western Strait Economic Zone* (haixia xi an jingji quyu fazhan yanjiu). Beijing: China Economics Publishing House.

Wu, Guopei, Yan Lurong (2010). *Financial Reform and Development and the Practice of the Western Strait Econimic Zone* (jinrong gaige fazhan yanjiu yu haixia xi an jingjiqu shijian). Beijing: China Finacial Economic Publishing House.

Ye, Wenzhen (2010). *The Western Strait Construction and the Cross-Strait Harmony and Coordination* (haixi jianshe yu liang'an hexie hudong yanjiu). Xiamen: Xiamen University Publishing House.

Zhang, Fan (2009). *Economic and Social Development: A Forecast of Fujian, 2008–2009* (2008 dao 2009 nian fujian jingji shehui fazhan yu yuce lanpishu). Fuzhou: Fujian People Publishing House.

Zhang, Ying, Lloyd Irland, Xiaohong Zhou, Yajie Song, Yali Wen, Junchang Liu, Weimin Song, Yang Qiu (2010). "Plantation development: Economic analysis of forest management in Fujian Province, China," *Forest Policy and Economics*, vol. 12, issue 3, March, pp. 223–230.

Zhang, Zhinan, Zheng Shanjie, Development and Reform Committee of Fujian Province (2011). *Planning the West Strait Economic Zone Development: 100 Questions and Answers* (haixia xi an jingjiqu fazhan guihua: jiedu baiwen baida). Fuzhou: Fujian People Publishing House.

Gansu

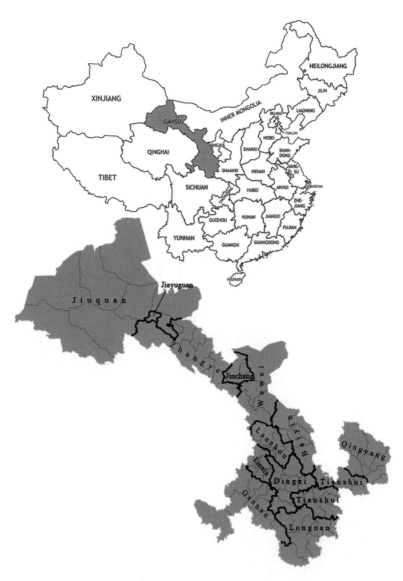

Table A   The administrative divisions of Gansu

Name	Administrative seat	Population
Baiyin PM	Baiyin District	1,708,751
Dingxi PM	Anding District	2,698,622
Gannan Tibetan AP	Hezuo	689,132
Jiayuguan PM	Jiayuguan	231,853
Jinchang PM	Jinchuan District	464,050
Jiuquan PM	Suzhou District	1,095,947
Lanzhou PM	Chengguan District	3,616,163
Linxia Hui AP	Linxia	1,946,677
Longnan PM	Wudu District	2,567,718
Pingliang PM	Kongtong District	2,068,033
Qingyang PM	Xifeng District	2,211,191
Tianshui PM	Qinzhou District	3,262,548
Wuwei PM	Liangzhou District	1,815,054
Zhangye PM	Ganzhou District	1,199,515

Notes: AP = autonomous prefecture; PM = prefectural level municipality. Data are as of 2010.

Quick facts

Official name: Gansu Province
Abbreviated name: Gan or Long
Land area: 454,000 km^2
Population: 25,575,000
Population density: 73/km^2
GRP per capita of 2010: ¥16,113
HDI of 2008: 0.705
Capital: Lanzhou
Government office address: 1 Central Square, Lanzhou
Tel: 0931-846-5941
Website: www.gu.gov.cn

Gansu is a province of the PRC. It lies in northwest China on the upper reaches of the Yellow River in China's western inland area, between the Tibetan Plateau, Inner Mongolia Autonomous Region and the Loess Plateau. It borders Shaanxi Province to the east, Ningxia Hui Autonomous Region to the northeast, Qinghai Province and Xinjiang Uygur Autonomous Region to the west and Inner Mongolia Autonomous Region and the People's Republic of Mongolia to the north. The Yellow River passes through the southern part of the province. Gansu contains the geographical center of China, marked at

35°50′40.9N and 103°27′7.5E. Part of the Gobi Desert is located here, as well as small parts of the Badain Jaran Desert and Tengger Desert. Lanzhou, its capital city, lies in the southeast.

Often abbreviated to "Gan" or "Long", Gansu is situated at the juncture of three highlands: the Qinghai–Tibet Plateau, the Inner Mongolia Plateau and the Huangtu (Loess) Plateau. The landscape is very mountainous in the south and flat in the north. The mountains in the south are part of the Qilian mountain range. At 5,547 m above the sea level, Qilian Mountain is Gansu's highest peak and is located at latitude 39°N and longitude 99°E. The Yellow River gets most of its water from the province. It also flows straight through Lanzhou. The area around Wuwei is part of Shiyang River Basin. A natural land passage known as Hexi Corridor, stretching some 1,000 km from Lanzhou to the Jade Gate, is situated within Gansu Province. It is bound on the north by the Gobi Desert and on the south by the Qilian Mountains.

With a land area of 455,000 km², Gansu has a large concentration of Hui Chinese and, along with Shaanxi, is the historical home to the dialect of the Dungans, who are Hui migrated to Central Asia. The southwestern corner of Gansu is home to a large Tibetan population.

The region is rich in mineral resources and 145 types of minerals have been discovered there. It boasts 94 types of reserves, including nickel, cobalt, platinum, selenium, gold and iridium. It also has large deposits of petroleum, natural gas, chromite and zinc. As a result of the 450 rivers (78 of which each have an annual runoff of over 100 million m³), water resources are abundant in Gansu. It has special advantages in tapping 15 kinds of minerals, such as nickel, zinc, cobalt, platinum, iridium, copper, stibium, barite and baudisserite. Along with its vast deposits of coal and rare earths, it is home to China's largest nickel deposits located around Jinchang City. Proven reserves of the metal there are in the neighborhood of 5.5 million tons, which is 90% of China's nickel reserves and the third largest in the world.

The water resources in Gansu are mainly distributed across nine river systems in the Yellow River, Yangtze River and inland river drainage basins with an annual discharge of 61.4 billion m³ and a combined hydropower potential of 17.24 million kw. Gansu ranks ninth among China's provinces and autonomous regions in terms of hydropower potential. To date, 29 hydropower stations have been constructed in the province with an installed generating capacity of 30 million kw and an annual output of 23.565 billion kw h. The Liujiaxia, Yanguoxia and Bapanxia hydropower stations on the upper reaches of the Yellow River, and the Bikou Hydropower Station on the Bailong River, have a total installed capacity of 2.125 million kw. The proven reserves of coal are 8.92 billion tons, and those of petroleum are between 600 and 700 million tons. There is also considerable potential for the development of wind and solar energies.

There are 659 species of wild animals (including the giant panda, the snub-nosed monkey, antelope, the snow leopard, musk deer and the bactrian camel), of which 24 first-class rare animals are under state protection. Gansu is home to 441 species of birds; it is a center of endemism and home to many species and subspecies which occur nowhere else in the world. The area holds second place among China's provinces and autonomous regions in terms of the variety of medicinal herbs. There are over 4,000 species of wild plants, including 951 of medical value. Among the latter, 450 species, such as angelica root, rhubarb, hairy asia-bell root, licorice root, fritillary bulb, marijuana, the bark of eucommia, glossy ganoderma and Chinese caterpillar fungus, have been found.

Gansu has many relics and places of interest. The Yangshao culture can be traced back about 6,000 years. The Silk Road, linking China with the western countries in ancient times, was built during the reign of Emperor Wu in the Western Han Dynasty (206 BC – AD 8). The historic Silk Road starts in Chang'an and stretches to Constantinople. On the way, merchants would go to Dunhuang in Gansu. Here they would get fresh camels, food and guards for the journey around the dangerous Taklamakan Desert. Before departing, they would pray to the Mogao Grottoes for a safe journey. These grottoes offer a collection of Buddhist art. There are 492 grottoes and 425 painted clay figures. Treated as the "Art Treasure House of China", the Dunhuang Mogao Grottoes are the largest and best-preserved Buddhist art museum. Each temple has a large statue of a Buddha or Bodhisattva and paintings of religious scenes.

Gansu has become a hot spot for tourism. Located about 5 km southwest of the city of Dunhuang, Yueyaquan (crescent lake) is an oasis and popular spot for tourists seeking respite from the heat of the desert. Bingling Temple (or Bingling Grottoes) is a Buddhist cave complex in a canyon along the Yellow River. Established in AD 420 during the Western Jin Dynasty, the site contains dozens of caves and caverns filled with outstanding examples of carvings, sculpture and frescoes. The great Maitreya Buddha is more than 27 m tall and is similar in style to the great Buddha that once lined the cliffs of Bamiyan in Afghanistan. Access to the site is by boat from Yongjing in the summer or fall.

Gansu's economy has been growing at an average rate of about 10% since 2000. The industrial and service sectors account for the majority of the province's GRP. Agriculture remains the lowest contributing sector. The region's consumption market is also expanding steadily. Despite recent growth in Gansu and the booming economy in the rest of China, the province is still considered to be one of the poorest. Tourism has been a bright spot in contributing to its economy. Gansu offers a variety of choices for national and international tourists.

Table B Demographic and socioeconomic profile: Gansu

Indicator	2000	2010
Population (thousands)	25,620	25,600
Illiteracy rate of population aged 15 or over (%)	14.34	8.69
GRP (¥ billions)	98.34	412.08
Composition of GRP (%)		
Primary sector	19.7	14.5
Secondary sector	44.7	48.2
Tertiary sector	35.6	37.3
Fixed asset investment (¥ billions)	39.54	315.83
Status of foreign-funded enterprises		
Number of registered enterprises	826	2,116
Total investment (US$ millions)	2,565	6,289
Registered capital (US$ millions)	1,817	2,766
Foreign trade (US$ millions)		
Export	421	1,275
Import	271	6,113
Sales of consumer goods (¥ billions)	36	139
Per capita annual disposable income of urban residents (¥)	4,916.25	13,188.55
Engle's coefficient (%)	37.63	37.41
Per capita annual net income of rural residents (¥)	1,428.68	3,424.65
Engle's coefficient (%)	28.60	44.71
Number of patent applications granted	493	1,868
Inventions	82	349
Utility models	326	1,131
Designs	85	388

Note: All monetary values are measured at current prices.
Source: *Gansu Statistical Yearbook*, 2001 and 2011.

As stipulated in the country's 12th five-year plan, the local government of Gansu hopes to increase the province's GRP by 10% annually by focusing investments on five pillar industries: coal and renewable energy, chemicals, non-ferrous metals, and pharmaceuticals and services.

Gansu is located on the western edge of central China. It is one of the country's poorest provinces and has one of the harshest climates.

While its climate is not favorable for attracting companies or individuals to work there, it is an optimal place for solar power stations as well as wind farms, and it is rich with mineral resources, including antimony, chromium, coal, cobalt, copper, fluorite, gypsum, iridium, iron and lead.

Most of Gansu's economy is based on mining and the extraction of minerals, especially rare-earth elements. The province has significant deposits of antimony, chromium, coal, cobalt, copper, fluorite, gypsum, iridium, iron, lead, limestone, mercury, mirabilite, nickel, crude oil, platinum, troilite, tungsten and zinc, among others. The oilfields at Yumen and Changqing are considered significant. Nickel production in Jinchang is exclusively controlled by the Jinchuan Group, one of the largest companies in the region.

Industries other than mining include electricity generation, petrochemicals, oil exploration machinery and building materials. In addition, Gansu is a center for China's nuclear industry. Thanks to the rich resources, petrochemicals, non-ferrous metals, electricity, metallurgy, food and equipment have become Gansu's five pillar industries. The province has relatively rich oil reserves. The two most important oilfields are the Yumen Oilfield and the Xifeng Oilfield. The former, located along the Silk Road, was the first found in China. The Xifeng Oilfield has more than 1 billion tons of oil and gas reserves. The Lanzhou Chemical Company, the Yumen Oilfield and the Qingyang Refinery and Petrochemical Co. Ltd – three units under the country's largest oil firm, China National Petroleum Corp (CNPC) – are the most important players in Gansu's petrochemical industry.

Thanks to ferrous and non-ferrous metals clustered in Lanzhou, Jinchang and Baiyin, state-level non-ferrous metal new material industrial bases have been formed. Major players in this industry include the Jinchuan Group, the Lanzhou Liancheng Aluminum Industrial Co. Ltd, the Lanzhou Aluminum Co. Ltd and the Baiyin Nonferrous Group. The booming non-ferrous metal sector has driven up the development of metallurgy. The Lanzhou Lanshi Group and the Spark Machine Tool Co. Ltd are two major equipment manufacturers in Gansu.

The province generally has a semi-arid to arid, continental climate with warm summers and very cold winters. Most of the precipitation is concentrated in the summers. Gansu was once an important agricultural base in ancient China. However, due to such ecological problems as severe water and soil losses and water shortage, the value-added output of farming, forestry and animal husbandry have been growing at a moderate pace. Agricultural production includes cotton, linseed oil, maize, melons, millet and wheat. Gansu is known as a source for the production of wild medicinal herbs which are used in Chinese medicine.

The turnover of foreign trade has hit a record high year after year over the past decade. The main exported products include equipment, chemicals and base metals, while the main imported goods are minerals, base metals and equipment. Australia is Gansu's largest foreign trade partner, followed by South Korea, Chile, the US and Germany.

Gansu has made various efforts to attract FDI. Foreign investors have chosen to set up ventures in the equipment and energy sectors. Much of the utilized FDI has been channeled into the manufacturing industry. Other industries with high utilized FDIs are energy, logistics, real estate and mining. Hong Kong remains the major FDI source for Gansu. Netzsch from Germany, Veolia from France, CIC Hightime Resources Limited from Hong Kong and Nuskin from the US have made their presence felt in the province.

As of 2010, compared with those of other provinces, "public management and social organization" "production and distribution of electricity, gas and water" and "education" and "Culture, sports and entertainment" were relatively strong, while "services to households and other services", "leasing and business services" and "real estate" were relatively weak sectors (see Table C).

Table C Gansu's comparative (dis)advantage index by sector, 2010

Sector	Index
Agriculture, forestry, animal husbandry and fishery	0.94
Mining	1.09
Manufacturing	0.65
Production and distribution of electricity, gas and water	1.47
Construction	0.82
Transport, storage and post	1.08
Information transmission, computer service and software	0.64
Wholesale and retail trades	0.71
Hotels and catering services	0.61
Financial intermediation	0.97
Real estate	0.55
Leasing and business services	0.40
Scientific research, technical services and geological prospecting	1.19
Management of water conservancy, environment and public facilities	1.04

Services to households and other services	0.26
Education	1.45
Health, social security and social welfare	1.06
Culture, sports and entertainment	1.45
Public management and social organization	1.73

Notes: All the sectors included in this table are determined according to China's official definitions and for urban areas only. Numerals greater than, equal to and less than 1 indicate that the province's sectors have advantages, no apparent (dis)advantages and disadvantages, respectively.
Sources: Calculated by author based on *China Statistical Yearbook*, 2011. See Appendix for a detailed methodological description.

Gansu has two state-level development zones, as described below.

- **Lanzhou Economic and Technological Development Zone** This was established in 1993, located in the center of Lanzhou Anning District. It has a planned area of 9.53 km². Some 17 colleges, 11 scientific research institutions, 21 large and medium-size companies and another 1,735 enterprises have been set up. The main industries include textiles, rubber, fertilizer, oil refinery, petrochemical, machinery and metallurgy.
- **Lanzhou New and High Technology Industrial Development Zone** This was one of the first 27 national hi-tech industrial development zones in China and was established in 1998. It covers more than 10 km². It is expected to expand another 19 km². The zone mainly focuses on biotechnology, chemicals, building decoration materials and IT.

In addition the province boasts province-level development zones that encourage investment in new materials, medicine, IT, biotech, new pharmaceutics and state-of-the-art manufacturing.

As of 2010 the top five companies were as follows:

1. Gansu Jiu Steel Group Hongxing Iron (SHA: 600307) is a steel and iron products manufacturer. It posted ¥39.52 billion in revenues and ¥939.44 million in net profits for 2010.
2. Fangda Carbon New Material Co (SHA: 600516) is a manufacturer and distributor of carbon products, including graphite electrodes, carbon bricks and ore concentrates. It posted ¥3.22 billion in revenues and ¥405.91 million in net profits for 2010.
3. Blue Star Cleaning Co (SHE: 000598) is engaged in the research, manufacture and distribution of industrial detergents, chemical

products and plastic modified materials. It posted ¥611.57 million in revenues and ¥235.95 million in net profits for 2010.
4. Gansu Yasheng Industrial Group Co (SHA: 600108) is a hi-tech agriculture company. It posted ¥1.41 billion in revenues and ¥130.14 million in net profits for 2010.
5. Gansu Qilianshan Cement Group Co (SHA: 600720) is a manufacturer and distributor of cement products. It posted ¥2.99 billion in revenues and ¥491.33 million in net profits for 2010.

Indicators for the ease of doing business

A. Starting a business

Procedures: 14
Time (days): 47
Cost (% of provincial GRP per capita): 14.1

B. Registering property

Procedures: 10
Time (days): 78
Cost (% of property value): 7.8

C. Getting credit – creating and registering collateral

Time (days): 20
Cost (% of loan value): 8

D. Enforcing contracts

Time (days): 440
Cost (% of claim): 29.9

Further reading

Atahan, Pia, John Dodson, Xiaoqiang Li, Xinying Zhou, Songmei Hu, Fiona Bertuch, Nan Sun (2011). "Subsistence and the isotopic signature of herding in the Bronze Age Hexi Corridor, NW Gansu, China," *Journal of Archaeological Science*, vol. 38, issue 7, July, pp. 1747–1753.
Bo, Wei (2005). *The Outstanding Theoretical and Innovative research Outcomes of Socio-Economic Development in Gansu, 2004* (2004 niandu gansu sheng shehui jingji kechixu fazhan lilun chuangxin youxiu yanjiu chengguo). Lanzhou: Gansu Cultural Publishing House.
Chen, Lixin (2004). *The Research of Ethnic Regional Economic Development in Gansu* (gansu minzu diqu jingji fazhan yanjiu). Beijing: China Social Science Publishing House.
Dong, Yuxiang (2007). *Gansu, Grottoes on the Ancient Silk Road* (Panoramic China). Beijing: Foreign Languages Press.

Gao, Xincai, Teng Tangwei (2008). *The Blue Cover Book of Northwest Region: Gansu* (xibeiquyu jingji fazhan lanpishu: gansujuan). Beijing: People Publishing House.

Gelek, Lopsang (2006). "Anthropological field survey on basic education development in the Tibetan nomadic community of Maqu, Gansu, China," *Asian Ethnicity*, vol. 7, issue 1, February, pp. 103–109.

Nie, Hualin, Gao kaishan, Bai Qirui (2006). *Studies of Economic issues in in the Smaller Northwest Region: Integrative Regional Economy and the Three-Agricultural Issues* (xiaoxibei jingji wenti yanjiu: diqu jingji yitihua chanye jiqun sannong wenti). Beijing: China Social Sicence Publishing House.

Qi, Yongan, Zhang Ping (2011). *The Regional Industrial Development in Gansu: Theory and Case Studies* (quyu chanye fazhan lun: yi gansu weili de lilun yu shili yanjiu). Beijing: Economic and Management Publishing House.

Qu, Wei, Li Shuji (2007). *The Methods and Roads to Rural Poverty Reduction in New Era: Studies in Whole-Village Advance of Gansu* (xinshiqi nongcun fupin kaifa fangshi yu fangfa: gansusheng zhengcun tuijan yanjiu). Lanzhou: Lanzhou University Publishing House.

Shi, Peiji, et al. (2004). *Ethnic Economic Development Research of the Gansu-Sichuan-Qinghai Border Area*. Beijing: Science Publishing House.

The Expert Inquiring Group of Asia Development Bank (2009). *The Research of Gansu Development* (gansusheng fazhan zhanlue yanjiu). Beijing: Science Publishing House.

Wagstaff, Adam, Shengchao Yu (2007). "Do health sector reforms have their intended impacts?: The World Bank's Health VIII project in Gansu Province, China," *Journal of Health Economics*, vol. 26, issue 3, 1 May, pp. 505–535.

Wang, Like, Yin Xiaoli (2010). *Technology Innovation Ability and Performance Evaluation in Gansu Province* (gansusheng keji chuangxin nengli jiqi jixiao pinggu yanjiu). Beijing: China Economics Publishing House.

Wu, Jiang (2001). *The Knowledge-Based Economy and the Development of North-West High-Tech Industry* (zhishi jingji yu xibei gaokeji chanye fazhan). Lanzhou: Gansu People Publishing House.

Yue, Dongxia, Xiaofeng Xu, Zizhen Li, Cang Hui, Wenlong Li, Hequn Yang, Jianping Ge (2006). "Spatiotemporal analysis of ecological footprint and biological capacity of Gansu, China 1991–2015: Down from the environmental cliff," *Ecological Economics*, vol. 58, issue 2, 15 June, pp. 393–406.

Zhang, Zhiqiang, Sun Chengquan, Wang Xueding (2001). *The Western Development and the Environment: Gansu's Environmental Protection and the Sustainable Development of Large Agriculture* (kaifa xibu shengtai xianxing: gansusheng shengtai jianshe yu danongye kechixu fazhan yanjiu). Beijing: China Environmental Science Publishing House.

Zhou, Duoming, Meng Chun (2010, eds). *A Study of Public Financial Policy for the Main Functional Area in Gansu* (ganchuanqing jiaojiequyu minzu jingji fazhan yanjiu). Beijing: China Financial Economic Publishing House.

Zhu, Qiang (2003). "Rainwater harvesting and poverty alleviation: A case study in Gansu, China," *International Journal of Water Resources Development*, vol. 19, issue 4, December, pp. 569–578.

Guangdong

1 = Zhongshan
2 = Dongguan

Source: The author, based on a file from the Wikimedia Commons.

Table A   The administrative divisions of Guangdong

Name	Administrative seat	Population
Chaozhou PM	Fengxi District	2,669,844
Dongguan PM	Dongguan	8,220,237
Foshan PM	Chancheng District	7,194,311
Guangzhou SPM	Yuexiu District	12,700,800
Heyuan PM	Yuancheng District	2,953,019
Huizhou PM	Huicheng District	4,597,002
Jiangmen PM	Pengjiang District	4,448,871
Jieyang PM	Rongcheng District	5,877,025
Maoming PM	Maonan District	5,817,753
Meizhou PM	Meijiang District	4,240,139
Qingyuan PM	Qingcheng District	3,698,394
Shantou PM	Jinping District	5,391,028
Shanwei PM	Chengqu District	2,935,717
Shaoguan PM	Zhenjiang District	2,826,612
Shenzhen SPM	Futian District	10,357,938
Yangjiang PM	Jiangcheng District	2,421,812
Yunfu PM	Yuncheng District	2,360,128
Zhanjiang PM	Chikan District	6,993,304
Zhaoqing PM	Duanzhou District	3,918,085
Zhongshan PM	Zhongshan	3,120,884
Zhuhai PM	Xiangzhou District	1,560,229

Notes: PM = prefectural level municipality; SPM = sub-provincial level municipality. All data are as of 2010.

Quick facts

Official name: Guangdong Province
Abbreviated name: Yue
Land area: 177,900 km^2
Population: 104,410,000
Population density: 536/km^2
GRP per capita of 2010: ¥44,736
HDI of 2008: 0.844
Capital: Guangzhou
Government office address: 305 Dongfeng Zhonglu, Guangzhou
Tel: 020–8313–2003
Website: www.gd.gov.cn

Guangdong is a province of the PRC. It is located on the northern coast of the South China Sea at the south end of mainland China, with a coastline of about 3,368 km. Its islands add a further 1,600 km^2. The Pearl River, which is 2,122 km long – the third largest river in the country – flows through Guangdong and forms a delta region. It is economically comparable to the Yangtze River Delta in eastern China where the region's economic hub is Shanghai.

Guangdong borders Fujian Province to the northeast, Jiangxi and Hunan provinces to the north, Guangxi Autonomous Region to the west, Hainan Province to the southwest and Hong Kong and Macau SARs to the south. Certain of the Pratas Islands, which are administered by the Republic of China, have traditionally been regarded as part of the province. The modern abbreviation of Guangdong is Yue, which is a shortened form of Baiyue – a collective name for various peoples who lived in southern China in ancient times.

Guangdong is officially China's most populous province. The massive influx of migrants from other areas, dubbed the "floating population", is due to the region's booming economy and high demand for labor. Guangdong is also the ancestral home of large numbers of overseas Chinese. Most of the railroad laborers in Canada, the western US and Panama in the 19th century came from Guangdong. The majority of the province's population is Han Chinese. Within this group, the largest sub-group in Guangdong are the Cantonese people. Two other major groups are the Teochew people in Chaoshan and the Hakka people in Huizhou, Meizhou, Heyuan, Shaoguan and Zhanjiang. There is a small Yao population in the north. Other smaller minority groups include the She, Miao, Li and Zhuang.

Guangdong has a humid sub-tropical climate, but with a near tropical climate in the far south. Winters are short, mild and relatively dry, while summers are long, hot and very wet. Its average annual temperature is 22 °C. The average daily highs in Guangzhou in January and July are 18 and 33 °C, respectively, although the humidity makes it feel much hotter in summer. Frost is rare on the coast but may occur a few days each winter well inland. Most areas enjoy a sub-tropical monsoon climate with adequate rainfall, long summers and warm winters. The annual precipitation in 2005 averaged 1,770 mm.

Guangdong boasts rich mineral resources. By the end of 2005 some 129 minerals had been discovered and the reserves of 92 minerals had been proven. The Tropic of Cancer runs through the center of this low-latitude province. The fertile Pearl River Delta is rich in fish and rice. Forests cover 57.5% of the province with standing timber reserves of 300 million m^3. Tree species include pine, Chinese catalpa, fir and eucalyptus. By the end of 2005, 237 forest, wetland and wildlife reserves had been established, covering an area of 1.07 million ha.

The province has extensive access to the sea together with a network of interconnected waterways with many reservoirs and fish ponds. It is rich in aquatic products. Its marine breeding areas cover 780,000 ha and it has a further 430,000 ha of freshwater breeding areas. The main crops are rice, vegetables and fruit. Zhanjiang is the main center for sisal hemp while fruit production is predominately based around Maoming. Among the 200 varieties of fruit grown in Guangdong are pineapples, bananas and lychees, together with longans and oranges.

Many of Guangdong's cities have been designated as "Excellent Tourist Cities". The province's scenic spots and scenic areas have been graded 4–A. Top-quality tourist areas in China include the Baiyun Hill in Guangzhou, the Xiangjiang Wildlife Park in Guangzhou, the Overseas Chinese Town in Shenzhen, the Guanlan Golf Course in Shenzhen, the Yuanming New Park in Zhuhai, Dr Sun Yat-sen's birthplace in Zhongshan, Lake Star in Zhaoqing, Mount Sijiao in Foshan, Mount Danxia in Shaoguan, the Qingxin Hot Springs in Qingyuan and Hailing Island's Dajiao Bay in Yangjiang. Development of the tourism triangle based on Guangdong, Hong Kong and Macau has now taken off. The State Council has approved the introduction of a 144-hour visa-endorsement service in the ten abovementioned cities on the Zhujiang River Delta and Shantou City.

Guangdong Province surpassed Henan and Sichuan provinces to become the most populous province in China in January 2005, with 79 million permanent residents and 31 million migrants who lived there for at least six months of the year. Since 1989 it has topped the total GRP rankings among all provincial-level divisions, with Jiangsu and Shandong being second and third in rank. According to provincial annual preliminary statistics, Guangdong's GRP in 2010 reached ¥4,601 billion, or US$689.02 billion. It has the third highest GRP per capita among all provinces of mainland China after Jiangsu and Zhejiang.

Table B Demographic and socioeconomic profile: Guangdong

Indicator	2000	2010
Population (thousands)	86,420	104,410
Illiteracy rate of population aged 15 or over (%)	3.84	1.96
GRP (¥ billions)	966.22	4,601.31
Composition of GRP (%)		
Primary sector	10.4	5.0
Secondary sector	50.4	50.0
Tertiary sector	39.3	45.0
Fixed asset investment (¥ billions)	314.51	1,562.37

Table B   (Continued)

Indicator	2000	2010
Status of foreign-funded enterprises		
Number of registered enterprises	49,865	93,756
Total investment (US$ millions)	216,510	421,260
Registered capital (US$ millions)	128,086	249,493
Foreign trade (US$ millions)		
Export	93,428	467,177
Import	82,060	366,829
Sales of consumer goods (¥ billions)	407	1,746
Per capita annual disposable income of urban residents (¥)	9,761.57	23,897.80
Engle's coefficient (%)	38.62	36.49
Per capita annual net income of rural residents (¥)	3,654.48	7,890.25
Engle's coefficient (%)	41.34	47.68
Number of patent applications granted	15,799	119,343
Inventions	261	13,691
Utility models	4,797	43,900
Designs	10,741	61,752

Note: All monetary values are measured at current prices.
Source: *Guangdong Statistical Yearbook*, 2001 and 2011.

Guangdong Province is home to the production facilities and offices of a wide-ranging set of multinational and Chinese corporations. It hosts the largest import and export fair in China called the Canton Fair in its capital city, Guangzhou. It is not only China's largest exporter of goods but also the largest importer. Its annual fair is the largest trade fair in China. The region's largely private manufacturing base is one of the main engines which have made its economy so dynamic. Guangdong has also led the way in moving up the manufacturing value chain from light industry production of textiles, toys and shoes to high-end manufacturing of things like IT products and power equipment.

The province is now one of the richest in the nation with the most billionaires in mainland China and the highest GRP per capita among all the provinces. In addition there is an overconcentration of wealth in the Pearl River Delta cities of Guangzhou, Huizhou, Jiangmen and Shenzhen, and there are large swaths of rural Guangdong which still remain relatively poor in comparison.

The region has played a pioneering role in China's economic reforms ever since the country's implementation of opening policies in the late 1970s. Three of China's "special economic zones", namely, Shenzhen, Zhuhai and Shantou, are located in Guangdong. In recent years, the province's leading economic position has been challenged by Shandong and Jiangsu, which are the second and third largest economies in China, respectively. Despite this threat, the industrial output of the area is on the rise. Its robust manufacturing sector has also greatly benefited from foreign investments.

Guangdong is a major export processing base for Hong Kong and Taiwan investors. Major industrial production bases are clustered in Guangzhou, Shenzhen, Dongguan, Foshan, Huizhou, Jiangmen and Zhuhai. In addition, the province has a robust manufacturing base. The traditionally strong light industries, such as textiles and garments, food and beverages, and toys formerly accounted for more than half of its total industry output. These products still rank near the top of China's export market. The nine pillar industries in Guangdong currently include three new leading industries (electronic information, electric machinery and special purpose equipment, and petroleum chemicals), three traditional industries (textiles and garments, food and beverages, and construction materials) and three potential leading industries (paper making, pharmaceuticals and automobiles).

Guangdong is China's electronics industry base. The electronics enterprises in the province, which are mainly located in Shenzhen and Guangzhou, account for about one-third of China's total. Other important production bases include Zhuhai, Foshan, Dongguan and Shantou. Examples of major products produced in Guangdong are telecommunications equipment, personal computers, video/audio products, consumer electronic products, electronic parts and components, and optical information storage. Currently, the province has quite a large number of successful domestic enterprises whose products are also well known on the global market. Major domestic brands include Huawei, ZTE, TCL, Midea, Konka and Galanz.

A newly developed industry in Guangdong Province is petroleum and chemicals. Major enterprises in this area include Sinopec Maoming Refining and Chemical, Sinopec Guangzhou Petrochemical, CNOOC Shenzhen Ltd, CNOOC and Shell Petrochemicals Company Ltd.

Guangdong is the largest textile and garment production and export base in China. By the end of 2006 it had more than 6,000 textile and garment enterprises with major production bases in Dongguan, Foshan, Zhongshan, Guangzhou, Shantou and Zhuhai. Key players in this industry are the Guangdong Yida Textile, Yishion and Foshan Shunde Qianjin Industry Co. As the first area in China to open up to foreign investors, Guangdong has attracted a large number of foreign garment makers and exporters. These companies have facilitated the transfer of technology that helped local enterprises to grow quickly. In recent years, however,

Guangdong has faced the problem of rising labor and land costs. Most private enterprises are labor-intensive and they focus on mass production and export of low-end products. All of these challenge the sustainable growth of local enterprises.

Guangdong has a vibrant service sector with enormous growth potential. Its service sector is characterized by the presence of diverse channels, a high level of maturity, a strong clustering and radiation effect, and brisk trading.

The province has one of the most developed retail markets in China. In 2006 the added value of the retail and wholesale sector amounted to ¥254.2 billion, up 11.2% from the previous year. The sector accounted for 22.7% of the province's services sector and contributed 9.7% to the GRP. Large foreign retail enterprises have established a presence there. These include Wal-Mart from the US, Carrefour from France, Jusco from Japan and Park'N Shop, Watsons and Mannings from Hong Kong.

Guangdong has always been the logistics hub of southern China. Logistics and its related services, such as road transportation, warehousing, loading and unloading, processing, packaging, delivery, and related information and consultancy service for ordinary goods have developed quickly. Demand for large-scale, third-party logistics companies is also expected to increase.

The province is the largest foreign trade center in China. Among the major export products are machinery, and garments and textiles. Foreign-invested enterprises are the largest contributors to the province's exports. Exports from private enterprises have also expanded quickly. Major trading partners of the Guangdong Province include Hong Kong, the US, countries in the EU and the ASEAN, and Japan.

The booming Yangtze Delta region has recently threatened the leading position of the Pearl River Delta, with foreign investment momentum in Guangdong being weakened. The largest FDI destination has also shifted to Jiangsu since 2003. Most funds were invested in Guangdong's manufacturing sector. Major industries include computers and accessories, machinery and electrical products, refined chemicals and some traditional industries, such as toys, garments and textiles. The service sector has also seen rapid growth, with real estate being one of the most attractive industries.

As of 2010, compared with other provinces, "real estate", "manufacturing" and "hotels and catering services" were relatively strong, while "mining", "agriculture, forestry, animal husbandry and fishery" and "construction" were relatively weak sectors (see Table C).

Table C Guangdong's comparative (dis)advantage index by sector, 2010

Sector	Index
Agriculture, forestry, animal husbandry and fishery	0.27
Mining	0.07
Manufacturing	1.53
Production and distribution of electricity, gas and water	0.70
Construction	0.59
Transport, storage and post	1.04
Information transmission, computer service and software	1.10
Wholesale and retail trades	0.93
Hotels and catering services	1.41
Financial intermediation	1.02
Real estate	1.60
Leasing and business services	1.13
Scientific research, technical services and geological prospecting	0.72
Management of water conservancy, environment and public facilities	0.75
Services to households and other services	1.24
Education	0.83
Health, social security and social welfare	0.93
Culture, sports and entertainment	0.84
Public management and social organization	0.77

Notes: All the sectors included in this table are determined according to China's official definitions and for urban areas only. Numerals greater than, equal to and less than 1 indicate that the province's sectors have advantages, no apparent (dis)advantages and disadvantages, respectively.
Sources: Calculated by author based on *China Statistical Yearbook*, 2011. See Appendix for a detailed methodological description.

There are several major development zones in Guangdong. These include Guangdong Province Economic and Technological Development Zones, Foshan National New and Hi-Tech Industrial Development Zone, Guangzhou Development District, Guangzhou Export Processing Zone, Guangzhou Free Trade Zone, Guangzhou Nansha Economic and Technical Development Zone, Guangzhou Nanhu Lake Tourist Holiday Resort, Guangzhou New and Hi-Tech Industrial Development Zone, Huizhou Dayawan Economic and Technological Development Zone, Huizhou Export Processing Zone, Huizhou Zhongkai Hi-Tech Development Zone, Shantou Free Trade Zone, Shatoujiao Free Trade Zone, Shenzhen Export Processing Zone, Shenzhen Futian Free Trade Zone, Shenzhen Hi-Tech Industrial Park, Yantian Port Free Trade Zone, Zhanjiang Economic and Technological Development Zone, Zhuhai National Hi-Tech Industrial Development

Zone, Zhuhai Free Trade Zone and Zhongshan Torch High-Tech Industrial Development Zone. Below are two examples.

- **Guangzhou Development District** (GDD) GDD is the only one in China that has four kinds of industrial parks under a single administrative committee. It is one of the cornerstones of Guangzhou. In 2006, the district's GRP reached ¥78.9 billion, 20.9% higher than in 2005. GDD accounted for 13% of the economy of Guangzhou and had substantially contributed to Guangzhou's growth. The six pillar industries have a total industrial output of ¥166.6 billion, up 29% from 2005, accounting for 83.15% of the district's total. In 2006, GDD approved 197 foreign investment projects with contracted investments of US$1.8 billion, an increase of 34.9%. The utilized FDI reached US$792 million, accounting for 26.8% of Guangzhou's total. Most of the funds were invested in the manufacturing sector with a total utilized FDI of US$305 million, up 40% from 2005. Major invested industries include communication equipment and electronics, chemicals and pharmaceuticals. Hong Kong is the largest investor in the district with a utilized FDI of US$326 million, an increase of 1.95 times from 2005. In 2006, the export value of GDD amounted to US$7.5 billion, accounting for 23.2% of Guangzhou's total.
- **Shenzhen High-Tech Industrial Park** Located in western Shenzhen, the park is a major contributor to Shenzhen's economic growth. In 2006, industrial output of the park amounted to ¥160.2 billion, up 17.1% from 2005. From this amount, high-tech products comprised ¥155.2 billion, accounting for 97% of the park's total. In 2006, the value-added industrial output amounted to ¥32.7 billion, up 25.1% year on year. The park contributed 11.4% to the city's value-added industrial output while the land area only accounted for 0.6%. Currently, a number of famous enterprises have set up business in the park. Domestic brands include Huawei, ZTE, Lenovo and TCL, and foreign brands include IBM, Compaq, Epson and Philips.

As of 2010 the top five companies were as follows:

1. Ping an Insurance Group Co of China (SHA: 601318, HKG: 2318) is the nation's top privately owned insurer. It posted ¥189.44 billion in revenues and ¥17.31 billion in net profits for 2010.

2. China Merchants Bank Co (SHA: 600036) is a Shenzhen-based commercial lender that operates across the nation. It posted ¥71.38 billion in revenues and ¥25.77 billion in net profits for 2010.
3. China Vanke Co (SHE: 000002) is the nation's largest property developer. It posted ¥50.71 billion in revenues and ¥7.28 billion in net profits for 2010.
4. China Merchants Securities Co (SHA: 600999) offers services in trading of stocks, funds, bonds, asset management, investment banking and securities investment. It posted ¥6.49 billion in revenues and ¥3.23 billion in net profits for 2010.
5. ZTE Corporation (SHE: 000063, HKG: 0763) is a leading telecommunications equipment manufacturer. It posted ¥70.26 billion in revenues and ¥3.25 billion in net profits for 2010.

Indicators for the ease of doing business

A. Starting a business

Procedures: 13
Time (days): 28
Cost (% of provincial GRP per capita): 6.3

B. Registering property

Procedures: 8
Time (days): 35
Cost (% of property value): 3.7

C. Getting credit – creating and registering collateral

Time (days): 11
Cost (% of loan value): 2.4

D. Enforcing contracts

Time (days): 120
Cost (% of claim): 9.7

Further reading

Andrews-Speed, Philip, Stephen Dow, Andreas Oberheitmann, Bruce Ramsay, Victor Smith, Bin Wei (2003). "First steps in power sector reform: The case of China's Guangdong Province," *Utilities Policy*, vol. 11, issue 3, September, pp. 169–183.

Brinkmann, Peter C. (1985). "Towards decentralization: Energy planning in Guangdong, PR China," *Energy Policy*, vol. 13, issue 3, June, pp. 204–214.

Bui, Tung X., David C. Yang, Wayne D. Jones, Joanna Z. Li (2003). *China's Economic Powerhouse: Economic Reform in Guangdong Province*. London: Palgrave Macmillan.

Chen, Jiajian, Robert D. Retherford, Minja Kim Choe, Li Xiru, Cui Hongyan (2010). "Effects of population policy and economic reform on the trend in fertility in Guangdong Province, China, 1975–2005," *Population Studies*, vol. 64, issue 1, March, pp. 43–60.

Cheng, Joseph Y.S., Kinglun Ngok, Heng Qu (2008). "NGOs and Migrant Workers' Rights Protection – A Case Study of the Document Management Service Center for Migrant Workers in Panyu, Guangdong," *The Journal of Comparative Asian Development*, vol. 7, issue 1, March 2008, pp. 109–128.

Cheung, Kui-yin, Chengze Simon Fan (1998). "Post-reform productivity performance in Guangdong: 1978–94," *Journal of the Asia Pacific Economy*, vol. 3, issue 3, January, pp. 379–387.

Cheung, Peter (2002). "Guangdong under reform: Social and political trends and challenges," in Fitzgerald, John (ed.), *Rethinking China's Provinces*. London and New York: Routledge, pp. 125–152.

Fan, C. Cindy (1996). "Economic opportunities and internal migration: A case study of Guangdong Province, China," *The Professional Geographer*, vol. 48, issue 1, February, pp. 28–45.

Fitzgerald, John (1996). "Autonomy and growth in China: County experience in Guangdong Province," *Journal of Contemporary China*, vol. 5, issue 11, March, pp. 7–22.

Fu, Wenying, Javier Revilla Diez (2010). "Knowledge spillover and technological upgrading: The case of Guangdong Province, China," *Asian Journal of Technology Innovation*, vol. 18, issue 2, January, pp. 187–217.

Goodman, David S.G., Feng Chongyi (1994). "Guangdong: Greater Hong Kong and the new regionalist future," in Goodman, David S.G., Gerald Segal (eds), *China Deconstructs: Politics, Trade and Regionalism* (Routledge in Asia). London and New York: Routledge, pp. 177–201.

Hook, Brian (1997). *Guangdong: China's Promised Land* (Regional Development in China). Oxford: Oxford University Press.

Jiang, BinBin, Chen Wenying, Yu Yuefeng, Zeng Lemin, David Victor (2008). "The future of natural gas consumption in Beijing, Guangdong and Shanghai: An assessment utilizing MARKAL," *Energy Policy*, vol. 36, issue 9, September, pp. 3286–3299.

Johnson, Graham E. (2002). "50 years on, 20 years on: Revolution and reform in Guangdong," *Asian Geographer*, vol. 21, issue 1–2, January, pp. 125–144.

Kroll, Henning, Ulrike Tagscherer (2009). "Chinese regional innovation systems in times of crisis: The case of Guangdong," *Asian Journal of Technology Innovation*, vol. 17, issue 2, January, pp. 101–128.

Li, Linda Chelan (1998a). "Investment in Guangdong: Central policy and provincial implementation," in Li, Linda Chelan (ed.), *Center and Provinces: China 1978–1993: Power as Non-Zero-Sum* (Studies on Contemporary China). Oxford: Oxford University Press, pp. 80–113.

Li, Linda Chelan (1998b). "Discretion and strategies in Guangdong," in Li, Linda Chelan (ed.), *Center and Provinces: China 1978–1993: Power as Non-Zero-Sum* (Studies on Contemporary China). Oxford: Oxford University Press, pp. 150–217.

Liu, Kam-biu, Caiming Shen, Kin-sheun Louie (2001). "A 1,000-year history of typhoon landfalls in Guangdong, Southern China, reconstructed from Chinese historical documentary Records," *Annals of the Association of American Geographers*, vol. 91, issue 3, September, pp. 453–464.

Lo, Carlos Wing-Hung, Shui-Yan Tang (2006). "Institutional reform, economic changes, and local environmental management in China: The case of Guangdong Province," *Environmental Politics*, vol. 15, issue 2, April, pp. 190–210.

Loo, Becky P.Y. (1999). "Development of a regional transport infrastructure: Some lessons from the Zhujiang Delta, Guangdong, China," *Journal of Transport Geography*, vol. 7, issue 1, March, pp. 43–63.

Mu, Qing (2006). *Guangdong, Forerunner of an Era* (Panoramic China). Beijing: Foreign Languages Press.

Sharif, Naubahar, Can Huang (2012). "Innovation strategy, firm survival and relocation: The case of Hong Kong-owned manufacturing in Guangdong Province, China," *Research Policy*, vol. 41, issue 1, February, pp. 69–78.

Tang, Shui-Yan, Carlos Wing-Hung Lo, Gerald E. Fryxell (2010). "Governance reform, external support, and environmental regulation enforcement in rural China: The case of Guangdong Province," *Journal of Environmental Management*, vol. 91, issue 10, October, pp. 2008–2018.

Tian, Gang (1997). "China's post 1979 uneven regional policy: Shanghai and Guangdong," *Journal of Contemporary China*, vol. 6, issue 14, March, pp. 61–78.

Tsui, Kai-yuen (1998). "Trends and inequalities of rural welfare in China: Evidence from rural households in Guangdong and Sichuan," *Journal of Comparative Economics*, vol. 26, issue 4, December, pp. 783–804.

Wang, Yuan-Kang (2001). "Toward a Synthesis of the Theories of Peripheral Nationalism: A Comparative Study of China's Xinjiang and Guangdong," *Asian Ethnicity*, vol. 2, issue 2, September, pp. 177–195.

World Bank (2010). *Reducing Inequality for Shared Growth in China: Strategy and Policy Options for Guangdong Province* (Directions in Development). Washington, DC: The World Bank.

Yeung, Godfrey (2002). "WTO accession, the changing competitiveness of foreign-financed firms and regional development in Guangdong of Southern China," *Regional Studies*, vol. 36, issue 6, August, pp. 627–642.

Zhang, Chi, Michael M. May, Thomas C. Heller (2001). "Impact on global warming of development and structural changes in the electricity sector of Guangdong Province, China," *Energy Policy*, vol. 29, issue 3, February, pp. 179–203.

Zhao, Simon X.B., Chun-Shing Chow (1998). "Disparities between social and economic development in Guangdong," *Journal of Contemporary China*, vol. 7, issue 19, November, pp. 477–492.

Guangxi

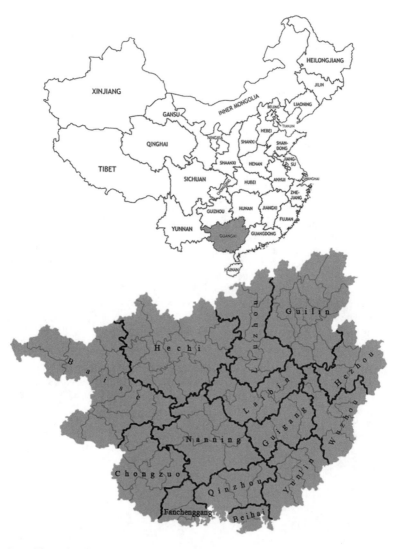

Source: The author, based on a file from the Wikimedia Commons.

Table A The administrative divisions of Guangxi

Name	Administrative seat	Population
Baise PM	Youjiang District	3,466,800
Beihai PM	Haicheng District	1,539,300
Chongzuo PM	Jiangzhou District	1,994,300
Fangchenggang PM	Gangkou District	866,900
Guigang PM	Gangbei District	4,118,800
Guilin PM	Xiangshan District	4,748,000
Hechi PM	Jinchengjiang District	3,369,200
Hezhou PM	Babu District	1,954,100
Laibin PM	Xingbin District	2,099,700
Liuzhou PM	Chengzhong District	3,758,700
Nanning PM	Qingxiu District	6,661,600
Qinzhou PM	Qinnan District	3,079,700
Wuzhou PM	Wanxiu District	2,882,200
Yulin PM	Yuzhou District	5,487,400

Notes: PM = prefectural level municipality. All data are as of 2010.

Quick facts

Official name: Guangxi Zhuang Autonomous Region
Abbreviated name: Gui
Land area: 236,700 km^2
Population: 46,100,000
Population density: 207/km^2
GRP per capita of 2010: ¥20,219
HDI of 2008: 0.776
Capital: Nanning
Government office address: 1 Minyue Road, Nanning
Tel: 0771–280–7778
Website: www.gx.gov.cn

Guangxi is an autonomous region (officially called Guangxi Zhuang Autonomous Region) of the PRC, a region with special privileges created specifically for the Zhuang people. Guangxi's location in the far south of China has placed it on the frontier of Chinese civilization throughout much of China's history. The current name "Guang" means "expanse" and has been associated with the regions of Guangdong and Guangxi since the creation of the Guang Prefecture in AD 226.

One of China's five autonomous regions, Guangxi Zhuang Autonomous Region lies on the southeastern part of the Yunnan-Guizhou

Plateau, with a mountain area in its north. It is bordered by Yunnan Province to the west, Guizhou Province to the north, Hunan Province to the northeast and Guangdong Province to the east and southeast. It is also bounded by Vietnam in the southwest and the Gulf of Tonkin in the south. The abbreviated name for Guangxi Zhuang Autonomous Region is Gui, which derives from Guilin, the former capital of, and currently a major city in, the autonomous region.

Guangxi is a mountainous region. The Nanling Mountains form the northeast border, with the Yuecheng and Haiyang mountains branching from them. Also in the north are the Duyao and Fenghuang mountains. Near the center of the region are the Dayao and Daming mountains. On the southeastern border are the Yunkai Mountains. The highest point is Mount Mao'er in the Yuecheng, at 2,141 m. Many rivers cut valleys through the mountains. Most form the tributary basin of the West River. Guangxi has a short coastline on the Gulf of Tonkin (Beibu Wan). Important seaports include Beihai, Qinzhou and Fangchenggang. Along the border with Vietnam is Detian Waterfall.

Situated in a low-latitude region, Guangxi borders the tropic sea to the south and has mountain ranges in the north. Yunnan-Guizhou Plateau extends into the western part of the province. Under the joint action of the sun's radiation and atmospheric circulation, the climate is characterized as having short winters and long summers with an annual average temperature of 16–23 °C. The annual rainfall is between 1,000 mm and 2,800 mm, with the level growing gradually southward from the north. The rainfall from April through September makes up 75% of the annual rainfall. The rainy season just coincides with the hot season. The sub-tropical monsoon climate with plenty of rainfall brings with it an abundance of plant species. About 8,000 tree species, including the Cathay silver fir, have been found in this province. It is also rich in mineral resources, such as silver, aluminum, antimony and vanadium.

The southern section of Guangxi is ringed by seacoast. Beibu Bay, a natural semi-enclosed bay in the northwest of the South China Sea, covers an area of 129,300 km^2, with the depth of water averaging 38 m, the deepest point being at 100 m. Due to the abnormal advances and retreats of monsoon, the area often sees changes in precipitation and temperature. Drought, floods, typhoons and hailstorms frequently hit the area. Crossed by a number of rivers, Guangxi is rich in water resources. Because of the abundance of water, it has the potential to generate significant hydropower.

Guangxi is known for having various mineral deposits, and it serves as one of the ten most important production bases of non-ferrous metals in the country. The number of proven mineral resources is 96, including 53 for which the deposits rank tenth or above among the provinces. The region has especially abundant reserves of manganese and tin, which account for one-third of the national reserves of each. In addition, Guangxi has sizeable reserves of vanadium, tungsten, antimony, silver, aluminum, talcum and others. What makes the province a favorite place for mineral development and production is the fact that the mineral resources are relatively concentrated.

Located in the tropic zone, Beibu Bay provides a favorable environment for breeding various fish species. It is home to over 500 types of fish and shellfish. Among them more than 50 are of economic value. These include red snapper, grouper, Spanish mackerel, butterfish and red coat. The fish resources amount to 750,000 tons. By now, 929 kinds of land-based vertebrates are found in Guangxi, accounting for 43.3% of those found in China. Among these, 149 are rare species.

Guangxi ranks first among the Chinese provinces and autonomous regions in terms of its rare species of plants. About 8,354 wild plants have been found in the region, including 122 that are close to extinction and need special protection. Among the 670 species of fruits growing in China, 110 are found there. As the tropical or sub-tropical fruits account for 80% of the total growing there, Guangxi is regarded as a leading province in China for the production and export of these delicacies. The region is well known for high-quality shaddock, banana, pineapple and orange.

The favorable climate and geographical location enable Guangxi to have as many as 8,000 tree species, including more than 1,000 kinds of arbor. Most of the precious forest resources are concentrated in the northeastern and Baise areas. By the end of 2005, 72 nature reserves had been established across the region, covering an area of 1.515 million ha. The picturesque scenic spots in Guangxi are famous worldwide, symbolized by Guilin, a natural beauty spot produced by unique karst geology. The province has established several tourist attractions, including 3 state-level natural scenic spots, 11 state-level forest parks, 30 regional natural scenic spots, 15 state-level cultural and historical relics, 221 regional cultural and historical relics and 1 state-level tourist resort in Beihai City.

The Han Chinese are the largest ethnic group in the province. Of these the main sub-groups are those that speak the Southwestern Mandarin and Cantonese varieties of Chinese. The region has over 14 million Zhuang, the largest minority ethnicity of China. More than 90% of Zhuang in China live in Guangxi, especially in the central and western regions. There are also a significant number of both Dong and Miao minority peoples. Other ethnic groups include Yao, Hui, Yi (Lolo), Shui and Gin (Vietnamese). There is a minor Christian population, which is subject to rigorous official regulations. Given its large population of ethnic minorities and beautiful scenery, cultural tourism is Guangxi's major industry.

With picturesque scenery, Guangxi is a hot tourism spot in China. Guilin and Yangsuo along the Li River, Hezhou Stone Forest and Behai Silver Bay attract a large number of domestic and overseas tourists. The major tourist attraction of Guangxi is Guilin, a town famed across China and the world for its spectacular setting by the Li Jiang (Li River) among striking karst peaks. It also used to be the capital of Guangxi, and Jingjiang Princes' City, the old princes' residence, is open to the public. South of Guilin down the river is the town of Yangshuo, which has become another favorite destination for foreign tourists. Ethnic minorities in Guangxi, such as the Zhuang and Dong, are also interesting for tourists. The northern part of the province, bordering with Guizhou, is home to the Longsheng Rice Terraces, some of the steepest in the world. Nearby is Sanjiang Dong Autonomous County.

During the past decade, Guangxi Zhuang Autonomous Region has achieved a fast economic growth. Its industrial and service sectors have attracted a large proportion of fixed asset investments. Manufacturing and real estate represent the largest portion of fixed asset investments, followed by energy, logistics, water conservancy, and environmental and public facility management. The economy has languished behind that of its wealthy neighbor and twin, Guangdong. Due to its lack of major manufacturing industry in comparison with other provinces, despite its proximity to Guangdong and low wages, Guangxi is the fourth most energy-efficient province in China, helping to boost its green image further.

Table B   Demographic and socioeconomic profile: Guangxi

Indicator	2000	2010
Population (thousands)	44,890	46,100
Illiteracy rate of population aged 15 or over (%)	3.79	2.71
GRP (¥ billions)	205.01	956.99
Composition of GRP (%)		
Primary sector	26.3	17.5
Secondary sector	36.5	47.1
Tertiary sector	37.2	35.4
Fixed asset investment (¥ billions)	58.33	705.76

Status of foreign-funded enterprises		
Number of registered enterprises	2,705	5,327
Total investment (US$ millions)	10,850	27,973
Registered capital (US$ millions)	6,268	15,478
Foreign trade (US$ millions)		
Export	1,640	6,525
Import	644	13,024
Sales of consumer goods (¥ billions)	86	331
Per capita annual disposable income of urban residents (¥)	5,834.43	17,063.89
Engle's coefficient (%)	39.90	38.06
Per capita annual net income of rural residents (¥)	1,864.51	4,543.41
Engle's coefficient (%)	40.20	48.49
Number of patent applications granted	1,191	3,647
Inventions	99	426
Utility models	730	2,167
Designs	362	1,054

Note: All monetary values are measured at current prices.
Source: Guangxi Statistical Yearbook, 2001 and 2011.

Local government has embarked on a major infrastructure upgrade in the hope of bringing more business and industry into the province. In particular, the Beibu Gulf Economic Zone has been a major priority for development because of its land and water access to Southeast Asia. Growth in exports from this region has helped to boost confidence in the economy and as a result increase real-estate investment.

Liuzhou is the main industrial center and is a major motor vehicle manufacturing area. General Motors has a manufacturing base here in a joint venture as SAIC-GM-Wuling Automobile. The city also has a large steel factory and several related industries. Local government hopes to expand the province's manufacturing sector, and during the drafting of China's five-year plan in 2011 it earmarked ¥2.6 trillion for investment in the province's Beibu Gulf Economic Zone.

With its suitable weather and geographic location, Guangxi is one of China's most important sugarcane, vegetable and fruit bases. The increasing production of vegetables, fruit and crops has brought about the large growth in its food-processing industry. As a large production base for sugarcane in China, it has also gained two-thirds of the value-added output from the food-processing sector. Nanning Sugar Industry Co. Ltd, Guangxi Guitang Group and Guangxi Funan East Asia Sugar Co. Ltd are the top three sugar makers in the province. In the automobile industry, major players include Liuzhou Wuling Motors Co.

Ltd, SAIC-GM-Wuling Automobile Co. Ltd, Dongfeng Liuzhou Motor Co. Ltd and Yucai Group.

Equipment manufacturing, metallurgy, food processing, electrical power and automobile manufacturing form the major industries in the industrial sector. Guangxi Liugong Machinery Co. Ltd, set up in 1958, is China's top construction equipment manufacturer and the first listed company in the domestic industry. Rich resources in the province have aided the strong development of its metallurgy industry. Guangxi Liuzhou Steel Corp, with annual production capacity of steel and iron both surpassing 5 million tons, is a major player in Guangxi.

Due to the many scenic locations in Guangxi, tourism contributes significantly to the development of the service sector. The finance sector, though not as strong as others in China's coastal regions, has been emerging as another important industry.

Major imported products include soybeans, mechanical and electrical products, spinning fibers, coal and high-tech products. Mechanical and electrical products remain the most important export products for the province. Other important export products include travel goods, boxes and bags, rolled steel, porcelain and pottery wares, and high-tech products. Guangxi's largest foreign trade partner is Vietnam (for both export and import). The other major trade partners are the US, Hong Kong, Japan and Taiwan (for export), and Australia, Japan, the US and Germany (for import).

Guangxi has also strengthened its effort to attract foreign investors. Hong Kong was the largest foreign investment source, followed by the British Virgin Islands, Singapore, Japan and the US. The industrial sector has received the largest proportion of foreign investment, followed by the real-estate and public service sectors, which are followed by the agricultural sector and logistics.

As of 2010, compared with those of other provinces, "education" "health, social security and social welfare" and "management of water conservancy, environment and public facilities" were relatively strong, while "mining", "services to households and other services" and "manufacturing" were relatively weak sectors (see Table C).

Guangxi Zhuang Autonomous Region has various economic and technological development zones, including 4 state-level development zones and 23 provincial-level development zones. The state-level development zones include Nanning Economic and Technological Development Area, Nanning New and High-Tech Industrial Development Zone, Beihai Export Processing Zone and Dongxing Border Trade Development Zone. Six of the zones are described in pages 83 and 84.

Table C   Guangxi's comparative (dis)advantage index by sector, 2010

Sector	Index
Agriculture, forestry, animal husbandry and fishery	1.18
Mining	0.32
Manufacturing	0.71
Production and distribution of electricity, gas and water	1.19
Construction	0.99
Transport, storage and post	1.18
Information transmission, computer service and software	0.79
Wholesale and retail trades	0.92
Hotels and catering services	0.85
Financial intermediation	0.86
Real estate	0.83
Leasing and business services	1.18
Scientific research, technical services and geological prospecting	0.98
Management of water conservancy, environment and public facilities	1.40
Services to households and other services	0.57
Education	1.51
Health, social security and social welfare	1.49
Culture, sports and entertainment	1.00
Public management and social organization	1.14

Notes: All the sectors included in this table are determined according to China's official definitions and for urban areas only. Numerals greater than, equal to and less than 1 indicate that the province's sectors have advantages, no apparent (dis)advantages and disadvantages, respectively.
Sources: Calculated by author based on *China Statistical Yearbook*, 2011. See Appendix for a detailed methodological description.

- **Beihai Export Processing Zone** Approved by the State Council, this was established in March 2003. The planned area is 1.454 km². The first phase of developed area is 1.135 km². It was verified and accepted by the Customs General Administration and eight ministries of the state on December 26, 2003. It is the export processing zone nearest to ASEAN in China and also the only one bordering the sea in western China. It is situated next to Beihai Port.
- **Guilin Hi-Tech Industrial Development Zone** This was established in May 1988. In 1991 it was approved as a national-level industrial zone. It has an area of 12.07 km². Encouraged industries include electronic information, biomedical, new materials and environmental protection.
- **Nanning Economic and Technological Development Area** Established in 1992, this was approved as a national level zone in May 2001. Its total planned area is 10.796 km². It is located in the south

of Nanning. It has become a new developing zone with fine chemical engineering, auto parts, aluminum processing, biological medicine and other industries.

- **Nanning National Hi-Tech Industrial Development Zone** This was established in 1988 and approved as a national-level industrial zone in 1992. It has a planned area of 43.7 km² and it encourages industries dealing with electronic information, bioengineering and pharmaceuticals, mechanical and electrical integration, and new materials.
- **Pingxiang Border Economic Cooperation Zone** This was established in 1992. It has an area of 7.2 km². It focuses on the development of hardware mechanical and electrical products, daily-use chemical processing, the services, and the international logistics-based storage and information industry.
- **Beibu Gulf Economic Zone (BGEZ)** This covers six coastal cities along the Beibu Gulf. It integrates Nanning, the region's capital, Beihai, Qinzhou, Fangchenggang, Chongzuo and Yulin. The state will adopt policies and measures to support mechanism innovation, rational industry layout and infrastructure construction in the zone. In late February 2008, central government approved China's first international and regional economic cooperation zone in Guangxi. The construction of BGEZ began in 2006. It will serve as the logistics base, business base, processing and manufacturing base and information exchange center for China–ASEAN cooperation. Regional government is also working on speeding up key cooperation projects, including transportation, the marine industry, agriculture, forestry, fisheries, energy development, cross-border tourism and environmental protection. BGEZ has already attracted a number of major projects, such as Qinzhou oil refinery projects and Stora Enso, a Fortune 500 forest products company based in Finland.

As of 2010 the top five companies were as follows:

1. Guangxi Liugong Machinery Co (SHE: 000528) is an engineering, machinery and accessories manufacturer.
2. Liuzhou Iron & Steel Co (SHA: 601003) is a leading Chinese steelmaker.
3. Guilin Sanjin Pharmaceutical Co (SHE: 002275) is a leading pharmaceutical company specializing in herbal lozenges.
4. Guangxi Guiguan Electric Power Co (SHA: 600236) is a power generator and distributor.

5. Guangxi Wuzhou Zhongheng Group Co (SHA: 600252) is a drug maker and property developer.

Indicators for the ease of doing business

A. Starting a business

Procedures: 14
Time (days): 46
Cost (% of provincial GRP per capita): 16.5

B. Registering property

Procedures: 12
Time (days): 68
Cost (% of property value): 6.8

C. Getting credit – creating and registering collateral

Time (days): 47
Cost (% of loan value): 3.9

D. Enforcing contracts

Time (days): 397
Cost (% of claim): 17.1

Further reading

Augustin-Jean, Lours (2009). "Which market economy for China? Decision making and bureaucracy in the Guangxi sugar market," *Canadian Journal of Development Studies/Revue canadienne d'études du développement*, vol. 28, issue 3–4, January, pp. 567–588.

Chen, Linjie, Zhang Jiashou, Zhao Yuhua (2011). *The Optimization of Industrial Distribution in the Beibu Bay Economic Zone, Guangxi* (guangxi beibuwan jingjiqu chanye buju youhua yanjiu). Beijing: People Publishing House.

Chen, Wei (2008). *The Urban and Rural Business Network and the Ethnic Economic Development in the Mordern Era of Guangxi* (jindai guangxi chengzhen shangye wangluo yu minzu jingji kaifa). Sichuan: Bashu Publishing House and Sichuan Publication Ltd.

Chen, Zhao, Ming Lu, Junzhi He (2008). "Power and political participation of entrepreneurs: Evidence from Liuzhou, Guangxi, China," *Journal of the Asia Pacific Economy*, vol. 13, issue 3, June, pp. 298–312.

Committee of the Beibu Bay Construction and Management (2008). *The Beibu Bay Economic Zone Development Programming in Guangxi* (guangxi beibuwan jingjiqu fazhan guihua). Nanning: Guangxi People Publishing House.

Fan, Jie (2011). *The Sustainable Development Research in the Jiangxi Economic Area (Guangxi): Function, Progress and Structure* (jiangxi jingjidai [guangxiduan] kechixu fazhan yanjiu: gongneng, guocheng he geju). Beijing: Science Publishing House.

Fan, Ruicheng (2010). *The Research of Tranistion of Guangxi's Agriculture Economic Structure in Mordern Era* (jinxiandai guangxi nongye jingji jiegou de yanbian yanjiu). Beijing: Ethnological Publishing House.

Fan, Zuojun (2011). *Regional Development and Finaincal Support: The Case of the Beibu Bay Circle Economic Zone Development* (quyu kaifa yu jinrong zhicheng: yi huan beibuwan jingjiqu kaifa weili). Beijing: People Publishing House.

Feng, Jing (1995). "Guangxi: Southwest China's access to the Sea," *Beijing Review*, vol. 38, issue 30, 24 July, pp. 14–18.

Hendrischke, Hans (1997). "Guangxi: Towards Southwest China and Southeast Asia," in Goodman, David S.G. (ed.), *China's Provinces in Reform: Class, Community and Political Culture*. London and New York: Routledge, pp. 21–52.

Huang, Suxin, Wang Chunlei (2012). *The Research of Manage and Promote the Income Gap of Guangxi Urban-Rural Area* (guangxi chengxiang shouru chaju zhili fanglue yanjiu). Beijing: Economy and Science Publishing House.

Hutchings, Graham (2009). "A Province at War: Guangxi during the Sino-Japanese Conflict, 1937–45," *The China Quarterly*, vol. 108, February, pp. 652–679.

Jiang, Yongpu, Yang Guoliang (2011). *Regional Public Management in the China-ASEAN Cooperation Framework: Cases Studies of the Beibu Bay in Guangxi* (zhongguo-dongmeng hezuo kuangjia zhong de quyu gonggong guanli: jiyu guangxi beibuwan jingjiqu de shizhengyanjiu). Beijing: China Social Science Publishing House.

Ke, Tizu (2009). *The Scientific Road of Guangxi's Industrialization* (guangxi gongyehua kexue zhilu). Beijing: China Economics Publishing House.

Lai, Ma (2009). *A Study of the Port Logistical Development in the Beibu Bay, Guangxi* (guangxi beibuwan gangkou wuliu fazhan zhanlue yanjiu). Beijing: China Economics Publishing House.

Levich, Eugene William (1993). *The Kwangsi Way in Kuomintang China*. Armonk, NY: M.E. Sharpe.

Li, Shaoyou, Yuan Ze (2009). *Studies of Regional Economic Development in Guangxi* (guangxi quyu jingji fazhan yanjiu). Beijing: China Forestry Publishing House.

Li, Wei, Xu Wanli, Gao Fang (2009). *The Environmental Impact and Evaluation of the Guangxi Beibu Bay Economic Zone Development*. Beijing: Science Publishing House.

Long, Yuwei (2011). *Studies in Regional Economic Cooperation of Guangxi* (guangxi quyu jingji hezuo yanjiu). Beijing: China Book Publishing House.

Qin, Qun, Geoffrey Wall, Xiaohang Liu (2011). "Government roles in stimulating tourism development: A case from Guangxi, China," *Asia Pacific Journal of Tourism Research*, vol. 16, issue 5, October, pp. 471–487.

Qin, Yong, Shi Yongjiu (2012). *The Rise of the Beibu Bay* (beibuwan queqi). Beijing: China Economics Publishing House.

Research Team of the Guangxi Academy of Social Sciences (2012). *The Choice of Regional Development in Jiangxi* (xijiang quyu fazhan de xuanze). Beijing: Social Science Reference Publishing House.

Shou, Sihua, et al. (2011). *The New Thinking of Speeding Up Guangxi Industrialization* (jiakuai tuijian guangxi gongyehua zhanlue xinsilu). Beijing: China Economics Publishing House.

Tan, Zhuyuan (2008). *The Auspicious Village in the Dashi Mountain Area: The Social, Economic and Cultural Transition of Bunuyao in Guangxi Province* (dashishanqu de xianghe cunluo: guangxi bunuyao shehui jingji wenhua bianqian). Beijing: Ethnological Publishing House.

Wang, Ronghua (2009). *Guangxi's Development of Beibu Bay and the New Development of Beihai: Strateges and Choices* (guangxi beibuwan fazhan yu beihai xinyilun fazhan: zhanlue yu xuanze). Shanghai: Shanghai Academy of Social Sciences Publishing House.

Wei, Haiming (2009). *Economic Integration in the Beibu Bay Economic Zone of Gungxi* (guangxi beibuwan jingjiqu jingji zhenghe yanjiu). Beijing: China Economics Publishing House.

Wu, Xiaorong (2010). *Outward Push and Endogeneity: Economic Production Manner Transition and Social Cultural Changing in the Southwest Ethnic Area* (waitui yu neisheng: xinan minzu diqu jingji shengchan fangshi zhuanbian yu shenghui wenhua bianqian). Nanning: Guangxi Normal University Publishing House.

Zhang, Hongwei (2006). *Guangxi, Land of Wonders and Beauty* (Panoramic China). Beijing: Foreign Languages Press.

Zhao, Weibing (2009). "The nature and roles of small tourism businesses in poverty alleviation: Evidence from Guangxi, China," *Asia Pacific Journal of Tourism Research*, vol. 14, issue 2, June, pp. 169–182.

Guizhou

Source: The author, based on a file from the Wikimedia Commons.

Table A   The administrative divisions of Guizhou

Name	Administrative seat	Population
Anshun PM	Xixiu District	2,297,339
Bijie PM	Qixingguan District	6,536,370
Guiyang PM	Yunyan District	4,324,561
Liupanshui PM	Zhongshan District	2,851,180
Qiandongnan Miao & Dong AP	Kaili	3,480,626
Qiannan Buyei & Miao AP	Duyun	3,231,161
Qianxinan Buyei & Miao AP	Xingyi	2,805,857
Tongren PM	Bijiang District	3,092,365
Zunyi PM	Honghuagang District	6,127,009

Notes: AP = autonomous prefecture; PM = prefectural level municipality. Data are as of 2010.

Quick facts

Official name: Guizhou Province
Abbreviated name: Qian
Land area: 176,100 km^2
Population: 34,746,468
Population density: 222/km^2
GRP per capita of 2010: ¥13,119
HDI of 2008: 0.690
Capital: Guiyang
Government office address: 242 North Zhonghua Road, Guiyang
Tel: 0851–682–5445
Website: www.gz.gov.cn

Guizhou is a province of the PRC located in the southwestern part of the country. Its provincial capital city is Guiyang. Guizhou (often abbreviated to "Gui" or "Qian") is located on the eastern slope of the Yunnan-Guizhou Plateau in the southeastern part of China. It borders Hunan Province to the east, Guangxi Autonomous Region to the south, Yunnan Province to the west and Sichuan Province and Chongqing Municipality to the north.

Overall Guizhou is a mountainous province. However, it is more hilly in the west while the eastern and southern portions are relatively flat. About 92.5% of the province's area is blanketed by mountains and hills and 61.9% of this land is dominated by karst landforms. Its average altitude is 1,100 m. Unique natural landscapes, such as Huangguoshu (yellow fruit tree) Waterfall, the Limestone Cave and the Stone Woods are major tourist attractions.

In the province there are over 300 basins which are wide in the middle and narrow at both ends, and each covers over 160 ha. The average annual temperature is 14–16 °C. High in the east and low in the west, Guizhou lies over 1,000 m above sea level. It enjoys ample precipitation. Rivers flow through steep terrain, resulting in a hydropower generating resource of 18.74 million kw, placing the province at sixth place in the country. It is also rich in gas stored in coal reserves. The abundant water and coal reserves allow the province to have a strategy of developing water and coal energy at the same time.

As one of the resource-rich provinces, Guizhou boasts more than 110 kinds of minerals, of which the amount of reserves of 76 of them is already known. It is among the top ten sites in the nation in terms of reserves of 42 kinds of minerals and the top three for 22 of these. The province is particularly strong in reserves of coal, phosphorus, mercury, aluminum, manganese, antimony, gold, barite, raw materials for cement and bricks, dolomite, sandstone and limestone.

The province also has the largest bauxite reserves in China, accounting for 28.1% of the country's total. With a reserve of 241.9 billion tons of coal, it has the largest reserves in south China. Guizhou has been known as the "home of coal in south China". Its phosphorus reserve accounts for 44% of the national total while the mercury reserve, after long years of tapping, still makes up 38% of the total amount in the country. The newly discovered gold reserve of 150 tons offers the country another gold production base.

Guizhou has a sub-tropical humid climate with few seasonal changes. Its annual average temperature is roughly 10–20 °C, with January temperatures of 1–10 °C and July temperatures of 17–28 °C. The climate and abundant rainfall mean that the province is home to over 3,800 species of wild animals. Out of this figure, over 1,000 are rare species under state protection. More than 3,700 kinds of medicinal herbs (80% of the total in China) are found in Guizhou. There are 130 nature reserves covering an area of 961,000 ha and accounting for 5.5% of the province's territory.

Guizhou is a newly flourishing tourist destination. Unique natural scenery, rich ethnic traditions, splendid culture and history, and a pleasant climate draw tourists to the province. Now over 120 tourist sites have been opened up, including national scenic areas of Huangguoshu Waterfalls, the Dragon Palace, the Golden Brocade Cave, the Red Maple Lake, the Maling River Valley, the Shizhang Cave on the Chishui River, four national nature reserves (the Fanjing Mountain Botanic Garden, the Maolan Karst Primeval Forest, the Chishui Primeval Forest and the bird reserve at Caohai), eight national cultural relic sites and many villages with distinctive ethnic minority customs and ways of life.

Demographically, Guizhou is one of China's most diverse provinces. Minority groups comprise 37.8% of the total population. These groups, such as the Miao, Bouyei, Dong, Yi, Shui, Hui, Gelao, Zhuang, Yao, Bai and Tujia, have brought rich and varied folk customs, culture, architecture and festivals to the province, offering another important tourism resource. The rich population of minorities in Guizhou allows for a great number of ethnic festivals throughout the calendar. During the first lunar month (usually February), the early festival in Kaili (in the east of Guiyang) celebrates local culture with acts of bullfighting, horse racing, pipe playing and comedy works. The southeastern corner of the province is known for its unique Dong minority culture. Towns such as Rongjiang, Liping, Diping and Zhaoxing are scattered among the hills along the border with Guangxi.

Guizhou is a relatively poor and economically undeveloped province but is rich in natural, cultural and environmental resources. Its nominal GRP for 2010 was ¥460.22 billion. Its per capita GRP of ¥10,258 (US$1,502) ranks last in all provinces of the PRC.

Table B   Demographic and socioeconomic profile: Guizhou

Indicator	2000	2010
Population (thousands)	35,250	34,789
Illiteracy rate of population aged 15 or over (%)	13.89	8.74
GRP (¥ billions)	99.35	460.22
Composition of GRP (%)		
Primary sector	27.3	13.6
Secondary sector	39.0	39.1
Tertiary sector	33.7	47.3
Fixed asset investment (¥ billions)	39.70	310.49
Status of foreign-funded enterprises		
Number of registered enterprises	715	1,936
Total investment (US$ millions)	1,493	4,132
Registered capital (US$ millions)	1,166	2,510
Foreign trade (US$ millions)		
Export	482	2,016
Import	375	1,443
Sales of consumer goods (¥ billions)	34	148
Per capita annual disposable income of urban residents (¥)	5,122.21	14,142.74
Engle's coefficient (%)	42.95	39.90

Table B   (Continued)

Indicator	2000	2010
Per capita annual net income of rural residents (¥)	1,374.16	3,471.93
Engle's coefficient (%)	36.13	46.26
Number of patent applications granted	710	3,086
Inventions	65	441
Utility models	377	1,936
Designs	268	709

Note: All monetary values are measured at current prices.
Source: *Guizhou Statistical Yearbook*, 2001 and 2011.

Guizhou relies heavily on agriculture and tourism to prop up its economy. It is China's third largest grower of tobacco and home to the Guizhou Tobacco, a well-known consumer brand. Its natural industry includes timber and forestry. Other important industries in the province include energy (especially electricity) and mining (especially in coal, limestone, arsenic, gypsum and oil shale). A target of investments, the province's significant coal reserves and power generation industry allow the export of a large amount of produced energy to Guangdong and other provinces.

Poor infrastructure has limited the development of a manufacturing industry and hinders tourism. A high-speed rail line from Guiyang to Guangzhou and other projects meant to expand the province's transportation links with neighboring provinces are planned in the hope of spurring on economic growth.

The structure of the region's industrial output reflects the province's natural resources. The production and distribution of electricity, gas and water, metallurgy, tobacco manufacturing, coal, raw chemical materials and chemical products, beverage manufacturing, coal, and medical and pharmaceutical products form the pillar industries of the province. Guizhou is known as "coal home of South China". Guizhou Shuicheng Coal Mining Co. Ltd is the largest coal miner in the province.

Guizhou has high altitudes in the east and low altitudes in the west. The dramatic downward flow of water offers vast hydropower generating resources, making the region a major base for supplying electricity from the western part of China to the eastern regions. Guizhou Power Grid is the largest state-owned electricity power operator in the province. During the past decade, smelting and pressing of non-ferrous metal has yielded a sharp increase in industrial value-added output. Shuicheng Steel Group and Guizhou Branch of Aluminum Corp of China (Chalco) are the two largest companies in Guizhou's metallurgical sector.

In 2006 the province produced 297,300 tons of tobacco, 13.7% less than 2005, due to the government's control over land use for the tobacco industry. It produced 10.6 billion cigarettes, accounting for over 5.2% of the country's total. The industrial value-added output from tobacco manufacturing amounted to ¥7.9 billion by the end of 2006, up 5.8% year on year. Guizhou Huangguoshu Tobacco Group is the largest tobacco maker in the province. The industrial value-added output from the beverage-manufacturing industry surpassed ¥5 billion, representing an increase of 23.5% year on year, while the industrial value-added output from alcohol production jumped 23.1% year on year to ¥4.9 billion, making up 98% of the total generated by the province's beverage manufacturing sector. The China Kweichow Moutai Distillery Group is one of China's largest and most ancient alcohol makers.

The ample number of medicinal herbs have favored the development of the medical and pharmaceutical industry there. In 2006 this sector generated ¥3.7 billion of industrial value-added output, up 9.9% compared with the previous year. Large pharmaceutical producers include Guizhou Yibai Pharmaceutical Corp, Guizhou Eakan Pharma Group and Guizhou Baixiang Pharmaceutical Group.

Wholesale and retail trade, and tourism are the two most important industries in Guizhou's service sector. By the end of 2006 there were 1,801 wholesale marts, 23 of which had annual transaction volumes of more than ¥100 million. Hualian from Beijing and Wal-Mart from the US have made their presence felt. As a popular tourist destination, Guizhou attracted 321,400 foreign tourists and 47 million domestic tourists in 2006, which brought in US$115 million and ¥38 billion revenue.

The top export products include chemicals and related products, followed by base metal and related products, mechanical and electrical products, rubber and related products and metal and related products. Major import products are iron ore, sulfur, rubber, ribbed smoke sheets and manganese. Major export destinations are the US, Vietnam, Hong Kong, Japan and South Korea, while key import sources are India, Australia, Canada, Thailand and Brazil.

Among the foreign-funded projects approved by provincial government, manufacturing and real estate received the greatest amount of FDI. A substantial portion of this has also been channeled into other industries, such as logistics, accommodation and catering, research and technical service. Foreign investors are encouraged to invest in auto parts, tourism, textiles, food processing, medicines, health products and other high-tech industries.

As of 2010, compared with those of other provinces, "public management and social organization", "education" and "production and distribution of electricity, gas and water" were relatively strong, while "agriculture, forestry, animal husbandry and fishery", "manufacturing" and "leasing and business services" were relatively weak sectors (see Table C).

Table C　Guizhou's comparative (dis)advantage index by sector, 2010

Sector	Index
Agriculture, forestry, animal husbandry and fishery	0.32
Mining	1.22
Manufacturing	0.59
Production and distribution of electricity, gas and water	1.31
Construction	1.07
Transport, storage and post	0.88
Information transmission, computer service and software	0.85
Wholesale and retail trades	1.12
Hotels and catering services	0.71
Financial intermediation	0.80
Real estate	1.06
Leasing and business services	0.62
Scientific research, technical services and geological prospecting	0.86
Management of water conservancy, environment and public facilities	0.89
Services to households and other services	0.98
Education	1.54
Health, social security and social welfare	1.09
Culture, sports and entertainment	0.81
Public management and social organization	1.64

Notes: All the sectors included in this table are determined according to China's official definitions and for urban areas only. Numerals greater than, equal to and less than 1 indicate that the province's sectors have advantages, no apparent (dis)advantages and disadvantages, respectively.
Sources: Calculated by author based on *China Statistical Yearbook*, 2011. See Appendix for a detailed methodological description.

Guizhou has 13 provincial-level development zones and 2 state-level development zones, as described below.

- **Guiyang Economic and Technological Development Zone** Established in 1993, this covers an area of 63.1 km². Investments in equipment and machine manufacturing, plane parts, auto (including motorcycle) parts and basic industrial fittings are encouraged. CJ from South Korea and China's leading electric home appliance maker, Hisence, have already established their presence here.

- **Guiyang National New and Hi-Tech Industrial Development Zone**
  Approved in 1992, this covers an area of 6.5 km². It consists of
  Xintian Park and Jinyang New Area in Guiyang. Investments in IT,
  software, medicine and pharmaceuticals, and other high-tech indus-
  tries are encouraged. Snecma from France, AMC from Singapore and
  OSG from Japan entered the zone in 2006.

As of 2010 the top five companies were as follows:

1. Guizhou Maotai Co (SHA: 600519) is the distiller of China's most
   famous white liquor. It posted ¥11.63 billion in revenues and
   ¥5.05 billion in net profits for 2010.
2. Guizhou Panjiang Refined Coal Co (SHA: 600395) is a coal miner,
   processor and distributor. It posted ¥5.47 billion in revenues and
   ¥1.35 billion in net profits for 2010.
3. AVIC Heavy Machinery Co (SHA: 600765) is engaged in cast and
   forge, hydraulic and new energy business. It posted ¥4.19 billion in
   revenues and ¥230.19 million in net profits for 2010.
4. Zhongtian Urban Development Group Co (SHE: 000540) is engaged
   in real estate, mineral resource exploration, tourism, and convention
   and exhibition businesses. It posted ¥3.33 billion in revenues and
   ¥554.77 million in net profits for 2010.
5. Guizhou Chitianhua Co (SHA: 600227) is a urea manufacturer and
   distributor. It posted ¥1.33 billion in revenues and ¥125.3 million
   in net profits for 2010.

Indicators for the ease of doing business

A. Starting a business

Procedures: 14
Time (days): 50
Cost (% of provincial GRP per capita): 26.6

B. Registering property

Procedures: 9
Time (days): 77
Cost (% of property value): 12.6

C. Getting credit – creating and registering collateral

Time (days): 17

D. Enforcing contracts

Time (days): 397
Cost (% of claim): 23

Further reading

Economic Development Research Center of Less-Developed Area, Guizhou University of Economics and Finance (2009). *The Collection Papers of International Conference of Poor Area Development and Harmonious Society Building* (pinkun diqu fazhan yu hexie shehui goujian guoji xueshu yantaohui lunwenji). Chengdu: Sichuan University Publishing House.

Goodman, David S.G. (1998). *Center and Province in the People's Republic of China: Sichuan and Guizhou, 1955–1965* (Contemporary China Institute Publications). Cambridge: Cambridge University Press.

He, Guangyu (2006). *Guizhou* (Panoramic China). Beijing: Foreign Languages Press.

Hong, Mingyong (2010). *Development and Assessment of Karst Area*, vol.1 (kasite diqu fazhan pinglun diyiji). Beijing: China Economics Publishing House.

Institution of Less-Development Area, Guizhou Financial College (2011). *Economic Development Research in the Less-Development Area, vol. 2: Future of the Guizhou Industry Structure* (qianfada diqu jingji fazhan yanjiu 2: zouxiang weilai de guizhou chanye jiegou). Beijing: China Economics Publishing House.

Li, Xiaozhu (2011*). Sixty Years of Guizhou Ethnic Economic Works: Theory and Practice* (guizhou minzu jingji gongzuo 60 nian de lilun yu shijian). Beijing: China University of Electronical Sicence and Technology Press.

Li, Xing, Shenggen Fan, Xiaopeng Luo, Xiaobo Zhang (2009). "Community poverty and inequality in western China: A tale of three villages in Guizhou Province," *China Economic Review*, vol. 20, issue 2, June, pp. 338–349.

Liu, Jing (2010). *The Development Issues of Great Western Development in Guizhou* (xibudakaifa zhongde guizhou fazhan wenti yanjiu). Beijing: China Agriculture Publishing House.

Liu, Zhaojun (2011). *Research of Desertification Prevention and Control and the Economic Transition in Guizhou Province* (guizhou shimohua fangzhi yu jingji zhuanxing yanjiu). Beijing: China Social Science Publishing House.

Martin, Michael F. (1991). "Urban demand and free market inflation in Guizhou Province, P.R.C.: 1984–1987," *Journal of Rural Studies*, vol. 7, issue 4, pp. 423–431.

Oakes, Tim (1999). "Selling Guihou: Cultural development in an era of marketization," in Hendrischke, Hans (ed.), *The Political Economy of China's Provinces: Competitive and Comparative Advantage*. London and New York: Routledge, pp. 31–72.

Wang, Feiyue (2008). *The Research of Public Policies and the Overall Urban-Rural Management of Ethnic Area: The Case of Guizhou Province* (gonggong zhengce yu minzu diqu chengxiang tongchou fazhan duice yanjiu: yi guizhou weili). Beijing: Economy and Science Publishing House.

Wu, Yanbing, Liu Shucheng, Wu Taichang (2008). *Economic and Social Development Report of Qingyan Town Guiyang City, Guizhou Province* (guizhousheng guiyangshi qingyanzhen jingji yu shehui fazhan diaoyan baogao). Beijing: China Social Sciences Publishing House.

Xu, Dayou (2011). *The Evolution of Green-Market Pattern and Green Economic Development: The Case in Guizhou Market* (luse yingxiao moshi yu luse jingji fazhan: jiyu guizhou shichang de shizheng yanjiu). Beijing: Science Publishing House.

Xu, W., Y. Yin, S. Zhou (2007). "Social and economic impacts of carbon sequestration and land use change on peasant households in rural China: A case study of Liping, Guizhou Province," *Journal of Environmental Management*, vol. 85, issue 3, November, pp. 736–745.

Yang, Yong (2010). *Sixty Years of Guizhou Development: Selected Works of the 7th Guizhou Economic Forum* (guizhou jingji fazhan 60 nian yanjiu: diqijie guizhou jingji luntan wenji). Beijing: China Economics Publishing House.

Yu, Fan, Dai Jianwei (2010). *Planning Guizhou* (cehua guizhou). Guiyang: Guizhou People Publishing House.

Yuan, Juanwen, Anke Niehof (2011). "Agricultural Technology Extension and Adoption in China: A Case from Kaizuo Township, Guizhou Province," *The China Quarterly*, vol. 206, June, pp. 412–425.

Zhou, S., Y. Yin, W. Xu, Z. Ji, I. Caldwell, J. Ren (2007). "The costs and benefits of reforestation in Liping County, Guizhou Province, China," *Journal of Environmental Management*, vol. 85, issue 3, November, pp. 722–735.

Hainan

Source: The author, based on a file from the Wikimedia Commons.

Table A   The administrative divisions of Hainan

Name	Administrative seat	Population
Baisha Li AC	Yacha	167,918
Baoting Li & Miao AC	Baocheng	146,684
Changjiang Li AC	Shilv	223,839
Chengmai C	Jinjiang	467,161
Danzhou CM	Nada	932,362
Ding'an C	Dingcheng	284,616
Dongfang CM	Basuo	408,309
Haikou PM	Meilan District	2,046,189
Ledong Li AC	Baoyou	458,876
Lingao C	Lincheng	427,873
Lingshui Li AC	Yelin	320,468
Qionghai CM	Jiaji	483,217
Qiongzhong Li & Miao AC	Yinggen	174,076
Sansha PM	Yongxing Island	444
Sanya PM	Hedong District	685,408
Tunchang C	Tuncheng	256,931
Wanning CM	Wancheng	545,597
Wenchang CM	Wencheng	537,428
Wuzhishan CM	Chongshan	104,122
Yangpu EDZ	Xinganchong District	37,000

Notes: AC = autonomous county; C = county; CM = county-level municipality; EDZ = economic development zone; PM = prefectural level municipality. Sovereignty over Sansha (including the Xisha [Paracel], the Nansha [Spratly] and the Zhongsha Islands) is in disputes. Population data are as of 2010.

Quick facts

Official name: Hainan Province
Abbreviated name: Qiong
Land area: 33,920 km^2
Population: 8,671,518
Population density: 241/km^2
GRP per capita of 2010: ¥23,831
HDI of 2008: 0.784
Capital: Haikou
Government office address: 59 Haifu Road, Haikou
Tel: 0898–6534–2277/6537–9204
Website: www.hainan.gov.cn

Hainan is a province of the PRC. The name also refers to Hainan Island, the main island of the province, which measures 155 km long and 169 km wide. The province lies at the southernmost tip of China, facing Guangdong in the north across the shallow and narrow Qiongzhou Strait, Vietnam in the west across the Beibu Gulf (Gulf of Tonkin) and Taiwan in the east across the South China Sea. To the south and southeast it is bounded in the South China Sea by the Philippines, Brunei and Malaysia.

For centuries Hainan Island was part of Guangdong Province. In 1988 this resource-rich tropical island became part of the newly created Hainan Province, which has an area of 33,920 km² and is China's southernmost province. Although it comprises some 200 islands scattered among three archipelagos off the southern coast, 32,900 km² (97%) of its land mass is Hainan Island.

There are 8 major cities and 10 counties in Hainan Province. Haikou on the northern coast of Hainan Island is the capital, while Sanya is a well-known tourist destination on the south coast. The other major cities are Wenchang, Qionghai, Wanning, Wuzhishan, Dongfang and Danzhou.

Hainan Province uses a slightly different administrative system than the other provinces. Most others are divided into prefecture-level divisions, while county-level divisions generally do not come directly under the province. In Hainan, however, nearly all county-level divisions (the four districts are the only exceptions) come directly under the province. The Paracel Islands and Spratly Islands, south of Sanya, are claimed by the PRC and are thus considered to form an administrative division of Hainan Province by them. Sovereignty of the islands is disputed, however.

With Mount Wuzhi (five fingers) and Mount Yingge (parrot) standing at its very heart, Hainan Island has a staircase-like topography descending step by step from towering mountains to flat tablelands and plains at its periphery. Most mountains on the island are 500–800 m high. Among those rising 1,500 m or higher above sea level are Mount Wuzhi, Mount Yingge, Mount Ezong, Mount Houmi, Yajiada Ridge and Mount Diaoluo. The inland has 154 streams flowing directly into the sea. Most rivers on the island originate from the central mountain area, forming a radiating river system. The drainage area covered by the three major rivers of Nandu, Changhua and Wanquan accounts for 47% of the island's territory.

Hainan is rich in mineral resources. Among the 148 minerals with verified workable reserves nationwide, 57 (or 65 if classified based on their potential industrial purposes) are of certain mining value in Hainan. In addition, 126 mineral deposits (including six large groundwater sources) have had their reserves verified. More than ten varieties of superior minerals produced here hold a very important position in China's mining industry, including glass-quality quartz sand, natural gas, titanium, zircon, sapphire, crystal, gibbsite, oil shale and zeolite. The reserves of iron ore accounts for roughly 70% of the country's high-grade iron ore. Those of titanium and zircon make up 70% and 60% those of China as a whole, respectively. In addition, gold, granite and mineral water are of significant developmental value in the region.

Hainan abounds with oil and natural gas. General survey and exploration have targeted three large sedimentation basins – the Beibu Gulf, Yingge Sea and southeast Hainan – with a total area of around 120,000 km^2, of which 60,000 km^2 prospect well with oil-gas mines. The potential reserves of hydroelectricity on the island amount to 1 million kw, of which 650,000 kw are expected to generate 2.6 billion kw h of electricity annually. The volume of groundwater is about 7.5 billion m^3, making up about 20% of Hainan's water reserves, of which approximately 2.53 billion m^3 is potentially exploitable. Its untapped energy sources with great potential include ocean energy, solar energy and bio-electricity. In addition, Hainan Island is one of China's ideal natural saltworks. Salt can be made by evaporating brine in the sun along its coast, which stretches for hundreds of miles from Sanya to Dongfang. At present, several large saltworks, including Yinggehai, Dongfang and Yuya, have been developed.

A tropical maritime climate prevails in Hainan, bringing it all-year-round windy but warm days, abundant rainfall, clearly divided dry and wet seasons, frequent tropical storms and typhoons, and diverse climatic resources. Winterless Hainan Island has annual sunshine of 1,750–2,650 hours, a yearly average temperature of 23–25 °C and an average annual rainfall of more than 1,600 mm. The wet central part and east coast receive more rainfall than the semi-dry southwest coast and other semi-wet areas. Winter and spring are usually dry while summer and autumn produce the wettest seasons.

Hainan Island makes up 42.5% of the nation's tropical land, with an average per capita possession of 0.48 ha of land used for agriculture, forestry, animal husbandry and fishery. As a result of such excellent conditions of sunlight, heat and water, the farmlands here can be cultivated anytime of the year, and many plants can yield two or three crops annually. Based on tits suitability the land on Hainan Island can be assigned to seven major categories: that suitable for farming, rubber planting, tropical crop growing, forestation, livestock breeding, aquaculture and other purposes. Currently, 3.152 million ha of land on the island have been cultivated, while 260,000 ha remain virgin soil, around 90% of which is potential farmland.

Grain crops, which have the widest distribution and highest yield in Hainan, mainly comprise rice, upland rice, shanlanpo rice, wheat, sweet potato, cassava, taro, maize, Chinese sorghum, millet and beans. Among the industrial crops are sugarcane, hemp, peanuts, sesame and tea. There also exist a great variety of both cultivated and wild fruits that fall into 29 families and 53 genera. Cultivated commodity fruits consist of pineapple, lychees, longan, banana, plantain, citrus, mango, watermelon, parambola, jackfruit and others. In addition, over 120 kinds of vegetables are grown here. Hainan Island is rich in tropical crop resources. Major tropical crops with a large growing area and of high economic value include rubber plant, coconut palm, oil palm, betel palm, pepper, sisal hemp, lemongrass, cashew and cocoa.

More than 4,000 kinds of plants have been found in Hainan – roughly one-seventh of the nation's total. Hainan's tropical forests, characterized by conspicuous vertical zoning and mixed growth of trees of different species and ages, and with high trunks and broad crowns, are mainly distributed over the mountains of Wuzhi, Jianfeng, Bawang, Diaoluo and Limu, with those on Wuzhi Mountain belonging to rainforests. Hainan is home to over 500 species of terrestrial vertebrates, including 37 kinds of amphibians (of which 11 are only found in Hainan, and 8 are listed as unique to China), 104 kinds of reptiles, 344 kinds of birds and 82 varieties of mammals (21 of which are peculiar to Hainan). In addition to black-crested gibbon – one of the four anthropoid apes living on earth – and slope deer, which are among the rarest species in the world, there are such treasured animals as sambar, macaque and cloud-leopard. By the end of 2005, 15 kinds of wild animals were under first-class state protection and 87 under second-class state protection.

Farms of tropical crops on the island also present charming pictures of unique rural scenery. As a result of Hainan's tropical climate, the province is an important source of paddy rice, coconuts, palm oil, tropical fruit and fish. Tourist-related services and agriculture are the main economic drivers. Secondary industries, such as automobile equipment, constitute a small portion. Hainan is rich in medicinal herbs. Of the 4,000 or so kinds of plants growing there, about 2,500 can be used as medicinal herbs. About 50 kinds of animals and marine products can be used to serve medicinal purposes too.

Vast offshore fishing grounds with an area of nearly 300,000 km², great variety of aquatic products with a short growth period, and a long fishing season form the characteristics of Hainan's aquatic and marine resources. This makes Hainan an ideal place to develop tropical marine fishing. There are more than 800 kinds of aquatic products, including over 600 fish, of which over 40 are cash fish. The province's coastal beaches that can be used for sea farming totals 25,700 ha.

As Hainan Island is not heavily industrialized, its greenery, together with its beautiful beaches, hot springs, clean air and other attractions, make it popular with tourists. In 2000 the province initiated a visa-upon-arrival policy for foreign tourist groups. This is available to citizens of 26 different countries and was established to attract visitors. The top scenic sites include the Yalong Bay National Resort, the Dadonghai Tourist Resort, the Qizhi Shan (Seven Finger Mountain), the Nuilin Mountain Tropical Botanical Reserve in Lingshui County, the Guantang Hot Spring Resort, the Shishan Volcanic Garden, the Wanquan River, the Baishi Ridge Scenic Zone and the Baihua Ridge.

Hainan Island is densely crossed by rivers. Winding streams, deep pools, fantastic waterfalls and mirror-like reservoirs dotted through the mountains and virgin forests add beauty to the landscapes and attract tourists. Hainan is noted for its singularly shaped mountains, of which many are summer resorts. Densely spread tropical primeval forests are characteristic of Hainan's lofty mountains, such as the four most well-known virgin forest regions of Mount Jianfeng in Ledong County, Mount Bawang in Changjiang County, Mount Diaoluo in Lingshui County and Mount Wuzhi in Qiongzhong County.

To protect rare birds and animals, several wildlife reserves and have been established in Hainan, including the Bawangling Black-Crested Gibbon Reserve in Changjiang County, the Datian Slope Deer Reserve in Dongfang County, the Dazhou Isle Esculent Swift Reserve in Wanning City and the Macaque Reserve on the Nanwan Peninsula in Lingshui County.

Hainan is the home of the Li as well as many other ethnic groups who still hold to their unsophisticated folk customs and unique living habits, which have made the island even more valuable to tourism.

Its province's GRP for 2010 was ¥206.45 billion (about US$30 billion), making it the fourth smallest in the PRC, and it contributes just 0.5% to the country's economy. In December 2009 the government of China announced that it plans to establish Hainan as an "international tourist destination" by 2020. This announcement contributed to a surge in the province's economy.

Table B   Demographic and socioeconomic profile: Hainan

Indicator	2000	2010
Population (thousands)	7,870	8,686
Illiteracy rate of population aged 15 or over (%)	6.98	4.08
GRP (¥ billions)	51.85	206.45
Composition of GRP (%)		
Primary sector	37.9	26.1
Secondary sector	19.8	27.7
Tertiary sector	42.3	46.2
Fixed asset investment (¥ billions)	19.89	131.70
Status of foreign-funded enterprises		
Number of registered enterprises	7,248	4,171
Total investment (US$ millions)	23,436	25,886
Registered capital (US$ millions)	13,926	14,545
Foreign trade (US$ millions)		
Export	609	2,162
Import	486	8,209
Sales of consumer goods (¥ billions)	17	64
Per capita annual disposable income of urban residents (¥)	5,358.32	15,581.05
Engle's coefficient (%)	49.31	44.81
Per capita annual net income of rural residents (¥)	2,182.26	5,275.37
Engle's coefficient (%)	45.75	50.04
Number of patent applications granted	320	714
Inventions	15	190
Utility models	90	305
Designs	215	219

Note: All monetary values are measured at current prices.
Source: *Hainan Statistical Yearbook*, 2001 and 2011.

Hainan's economy is predominantly agricultural, and more than a half of the island's exports are agricultural products. Its elevation to province-level status in 1988, however, was accompanied by its designation as China's largest special economic zone, the intent being to hasten the development of the island's plentiful resources. Prior to this, the province had a reputation for being a "Wild West" area. Even today there are relatively few factories in the province. Tourism plays an important part in Hainan's economy, thanks largely to its tropical beaches and lush forests.

Central government has encouraged foreign investment in Hainan and has allowed the island to rely to a large extent on market forces. Hainan's industrial development has been limited largely to the processing of its mineral and agricultural products, particularly rubber and iron ore. Since the 1950s, machinery, farm equipment and textiles have been manufactured in the Haikou area for local consumption. A major constraint on industrial expansion has been an inadequate supply of electricity. Much of the island's generating capacity is hydroelectric, and this is subject to seasonal fluctuations in stream and river flows.

The largest share of Hainan's FDI is Hong Kong, which concentrates mainly on Haikou, Sanya and Wanning. The EU is now Hainan's largest export partner, while Oman, Angola, the US, Russia, Malaysia and Japan are the major import partners.

As of 2010, compared with those of other provinces, "agriculture, forestry, animal husbandry and fishery", "hotels and catering services" and "real estate" were relatively strong, while "mining", "manufacturing" and "information transmission, computer service and software" were relatively weak sectors (see Table C).

Hainan's economic and technological development zones include Haikou Free Trade Zone, Haikou New and Hi-Tech Industrial Development Zone, Sanya Yalong Bay National Resort and Yangpu Economic Development Zone.

As of 2010 the top five companies were as follows:

1. Hainan Airlines Co (SHA: 600221) is an integrated travel and financial services provider. It posted ¥21.71 billion in revenues and ¥3.01 billion in net profits for 2010.
2. Huawen Media Investment Co (SHE: 000793) is engaged in cultural dissemination, production and distribution of coal gas, and wholesale of energy and chemical products and electrical equipment. It posted ¥3.48 billion in revenues and ¥231.86 million in net profits for 2010.
3. Hainan Strait Shipping Co (SHE: 002320) is an operator of passenger and transport business in the South China Sea. It posted ¥600.43 million in revenues and ¥187.75 million in net profits for 2010.
4. Hainan Zhenghe Industrial Group Co (SHA: 600759) is a property manager and developer. It posted ¥902 million in revenues and ¥183.56 million in net profits for 2010.
5. Rising Nonferrous Metals Share Co (SHA: 600259) is a non-ferrous metal miner, processor and distributor. It posted ¥1.12 billion in revenues and ¥38.12 million in net profits for 2010.

Table C   Hainan's comparative (dis)advantage index by sector, 2010

Sector	Index
Agriculture, forestry, animal husbandry and fishery	5.24
Mining	0.26
Manufacturing	0.36
Production and distribution of electricity, gas and water	1.01
Construction	0.86
Transport, storage and post	1.09
Information transmission, computer service and software	0.63
Wholesale and retail trades	1.06
Hotels and catering services	3.35
Financial intermediation	0.72
Real estate	2.41
Leasing and business services	1.13
Scientific research, technical services and geological prospecting	0.92
Management of water conservancy, environment and public facilities	1.63
Services to households and other services	0.83
Education	1.19
Health, social security and social welfare	1.05
Culture, sports and entertainment	1.45
Public management and social organization	1.09

Notes: All the sectors included in this table are determined according to China's official definitions and for urban areas only. Numerals greater than, equal to and less than 1 indicate that the province's sectors have advantages, no apparent (dis)advantages and disadvantages, respectively.
Sources: Calculated by author based on *China Statistical Yearbook,* 2011. See Appendix for a detailed methodological description.

Indicators for the ease of doing business

A. Starting a business

Procedures: 13
Time (days): 38
Cost (% of provincial GRP per capita): 12.1

B. Registering property

Procedures: 16
Time (days): 76
Cost (% of property value): 4.8

C. Getting credit – creating and registering collateral

Time (days): 14
Cost (% of loan value): 5.1

D. Enforcing contracts

Time (days): 310
Cost (% of claim): 14.5

Further reading

Brødsgaard, Kjeld Erik (2008). *Hainan State, Society, and Business in a Chinese Province* (China Policy Series), London and New York: Routledge.
Chen, Guangliang (2004). *Studies in the Economic History of Hainan* (hainan jingjishi yanjiu). Guangdong: ZhongShan University Publishing House.
China (Hainan) Academy of Reform Development (2011a). *Hainan in 2020* (2020 nian de hainian). Beijing: China Economics Publishing House.
China (Hainan) Academy of Reform Development (2011b). Opening Hainan (zouxiang kaifang de hainan). Beijing: China Economics Publishing House.
Feng, Chongyi, David S.G. Goodman (1995). China's Hainan Province: Economic Development and Investment Environment (Asia Papers, 5). Perth: University of Western Australia Press.
Feng, Chongyi, David S.G. Goodman, (1997). "Hainan: Communal politics and struggle for identity," in Goodman, David S.G. (ed.), *China's Provinces in Reform: Class, Community and Political Culture*. London and New York: Routledge, pp. 53–92.
Feng, Chongyi, David S.G. Goodman (1999). "Hainan Province in reform: Political dependence and economic interdependence," in Cheung, Peter, Jae Ho Chung, Zhimin Lin (eds), *Provincial Strategies of Economic Reform in Post-Mao China: Leadership, Politics, and Implementation* (Studies on Contemporary China). Armonk, NY: M.E. Sharpe.
Foreign Languages Press (2005, ed.). *Hainan: China's Island Paradise* (Panoramic China). Beijing: Foreign Languages Press.
Hunter, I., C.-G. von Hahn, Zhu Zhaohua, Zhou Yanhua (2003). "Stabilizing forest margins by growing non-timber forest products: A novel example from Hainan Island, China," *Land Use Policy*, vol. 20, issue 3, July, pp. 225–230.
Liu, Renwu (2006). *The Report of Southeast Asia Economic Work, 2006* (dongnanya jingji yunxing baogao, 2006). Beijing: Social Science Reference Publishing House.
Tan, Chia-Zhi, Henry Wai-chung Yeung (2000). "The regionalization of Chinese business networks: A study of Singaporean firms in Hainan, China," *The Professional Geographer*, vol. 52, issue 3, August, pp. 437–454.
Wang, Yang, Geoffrey Wall (2007). "Administrative arrangements and displacement compensation in top-down tourism planning – A case from Hainan Province, China," *Tourism Management*, vol. 28, issue 1, February, pp. 70–82.
Yu, Jie (2010). *Destroying Desolation: Building Hainan Special Economic Zone and the Yangpo Incident* (Dapo tianhuang: jianli Hainan jingji tequ yu yangbu fengbo). Changchun: Jilin Publication Ltd.
Zhai, De-Li, Charles H. Cannon, J.W. Ferry Slik, Cui-Ping Zhang, Zhi-Cong Dai (2012). "Rubber and pulp plantations represent a double threat to Hainan's natural tropical forests," *Journal of Environmental Management*, vol. 96, issue 1, 15 April, pp. 64–73.

Hebei

Source: The author, based on a file from the Wikimedia Commons.

Table A   The administrative divisions of Hebei

Name	Administrative seat	Population
Baoding PM	Xinshi District	11,194,379
Cangzhou PM	Yunhe District	7,134,053
Chengde PM	Shuangqiao District	3,473,197
Handan PM	Hanshan District	9,174,679
Hengshui PM	Taocheng District	4,340,773
Langfang PM	Anci District	4,358,839
Qinhuangdao PM	Haigang District	2,987,605
Shijiazhuang PM	Chang'an District	10,163,788
Tangshan PM	Lunan District	7,577,284
Xingtai PM	Qiaodong District	7,104,114
Zhangjiakou PM	Qiaoxi District	4,345,491

Notes: PM = prefectural level municipality. All data are as of 2010.

Quick facts

Official name: Hebei Province
Abbreviated name: Ji
Land area: 187,700 km^2
Population: 71,854,202
Population density: 372/km^2
GRP per capita of 2010: ¥28,668
HDI of 2008: 0.810
Capital: Shijiazhuang
Government office address: 10 Weimingjie, Shijiazhuang City
Tel: 0311–709–2680
Website: www.hebei.gov.cn

Hebei is a province of the PRC in north China. The name means "north of the river", referring to its location completely above the Yellow River. Its abbreviated name is Ji after the ancient prefecture "Ji" (Jizhou), which included the southern part of present-day Hebei. A common (unofficial) alternate name is "Yanzhao," which is after the Yan and the Zhao – two kingdoms that existed during the Eastern Zhou Dynasty (771–221 BC). In 1928, Hebei was formed after central government dissolved the province of Zhili (which means "directly ruled by the Imperial Court").

Hebei Province is located in the northern part of the North China Plain extending into the Inner Mongolian Plateau. The Bohai Bay of the Yellow Sea lies to the east of Hebei, which represents a 487 km coastline.

Beijing, the capital of China, and Tianjin, an important trading port in north China, are situated at the center of the province but are not part of it. It adjoins Liaoning and Inner Mongolia to the north, Shanxi to the west, Shandong to the southeast and Henan to the south. A small part of Hebei, an exclave disjointed from the rest of the province, is wedged between the municipalities of Beijing and Tianjin.

Most of central and southern Hebei lies within the North China Plain. The western part rises into the Taihang Mountains (Taihang Shan), while the Yan Mountains (Yan Shan) run through northern Hebei, beyond which lie the grasslands of Inner Mongolia. The Great Wall of China cuts through northern Hebei from east to west as well, briefly entering the border of Beijing Municipality, and terminates at the seacoast of Shanhaiguan in northeastern Hebei. The highest peak is Mount Xiaowutai in northwestern Hebei, with an altitude of 2,882 m above sea level.

Hebei borders Bohai Sea to the east. The Hai He watershed covers most of the province's central and southern parts, and the Luan He watershed covers the northeast. Among the numerous reservoirs found in the hills and mountains, the largest lake is Baiyangdian, located mostly in Anxin County.

Ancient Hebei has been ruled by a multitude of dynasties. Situated in the north of China, it sits at the mouth of the Yellow River at the Bohai Sea and spans a land area of 187,700 km^2, completely surrounding the Beijing and Tianjin municipalities. Made up of 11 cities, it houses a population of 69 million. The major ethnic group within the province is the Han, and the minority ethnic groups are the Manchus, the Hui and the Mongols. These are subdivided into 172 county-level divisions (22 county-level cities, 108 counties, 6 autonomous counties and 36 districts). These are, in turn, divided into 2,207 township-level divisions (1 district public office, 937 towns, 979 townships, 55 ethnic townships and 235 sub-districts).

The topography of Hebei Province is composed of three major geomorphic features, of which the average height of the Bashang highland is 1,200–1,500 m above sea level, making up 8.5% of the total area. Meanwhile, Mount Yanshan and Mount Taihangshan, including hilly land and basins, mostly lie within an elevation below 2,000 m, accounting for 48.1% of the total area. The Hebei Plain is part of the North China Plain, with an elevation mostly below 50 m, accounting for 43.4% of the provincial area.

Hebei has a continental monsoon climate, with cold, dry winters and hot, humid summers. In most areas the change of season is distinct, with yearly sunshine averaging 2,500–3,100 hours. The annual frost-free period lasts about 120–200 days. The annual rainfall averages 300–800 mm, concentrated heavily in summer. The monthly mean temperature is 3 °C or below. The mean temperature in July is 18–27 °C.

The province has a coastline of 487.3 km, covering an area of 1 million ha. As a result the province can develop such industries as offshore petroleum oil drilling, marine chemicals, marine transportation and marine tourism. Qinhuangdao is a well-known ice-free port in north China. The Yellow River, the Haihe River and the Luanhe River run across the province where an offshore aquatic breeding industry could easily be developed.

So far 116 varieties of mineral ores have been discovered, the deposits of 74 of which have been surveyed. There are 45 mines whose reserves are among the nation's top ten. The province boasts two large coal mines at Kailuan and Fengfeng, in addition to the North China oilfield.

In the province there are more than 3,000 species of plants, of which more than 140 are fiber plants, more than 1,000 are medicinal herbs and plants and more than 100 are sources of timber. There are 300 or more kinds of forage grass, 140 kinds of oily plants and more than 450 varieties of cultivated plants. Of these, the output of cotton makes up one-seventh of the nation's total and that of maize and fruits each makes up one-tenth. There are 215 varieties of farming products in 12 major categories that can be listed as brand name and best products, or native or rare products. There are more than 20 varieties of medicinal herbs and materials for export.

The province is the only one in the country that boasts highlands, mountainous and hilly areas, plains, lakes and a coastline. Across the region there are 304 ancient ruins and groups of ancient buildings, including 58 key relics under state protection. The number of historical and cultural relics in the province ranks first in the country along with Shaanxi Province. The number of natural and human cultural scenic sites ranks second nationally. These include the Chengde Summer Resort, Shanhaiguan Pass at the head of the Great Wall of China, Beidaihe Holiday Resort and the Eastern and Western Tombs of the emperors of the Qing Dynasty (AD 1644–1911).

The Great Wall of China crosses the northern part of Hebei. The eastern end is located on the coast at Shanhaiguan (Shanhai Pass) near Qinhuangdao. The Shanhaiguan is known as the "First Pass of The World". Beidaihe, near Shanhaiguan, is a popular beach resort well known as a former meeting place for top governmental officials.

The Qing Dynasty's imperial tombs are located in Zunhua and Yi counties, which are called the Eastern Qing Tombs and the West Qing Tombs, respectively. The Eastern Qing Tombs are the resting place of 161 Qing emperors, empresses and other members of the Qing imperial family, while the West Qing Tombs number 76. They are also part of a World Heritage Site. The Zhaozhou, or Anji Bridge, built by Li Chun during the Sui Dynasty (AD 581–618), is the oldest stone arch bridge in China and one of the most significant examples of pre-modern Chinese civil engineering.

The Chengde Mountain Resort and its outlying temples are a UNESCO World Heritage Site. Also known as the Rehe Palace, this was the summer resort of the Manchu Qing Dynasty emperors. The Chengde Resort was built between 1703 and 1792. It consists of a palace complex, a large park area consisting of lakes, pavilions, causeways, bridges and so on, and a number of Tibetan Buddhist and Han Chinese temples in the surrounding area.

Thanks to its favorable geographical location, Hebei's GRP reached ¥2.04 trillion (about US$303 billion) in 2010, an increase of 10.1% over the previous year, and ranked sixth in all the Chinese provinces. Meanwhile, its per capita GRP reached ¥24,428. More than half of its GRP comes from the industry sector and approximately a third from the service sector.

Table B   Demographic and socioeconomic profile: Hebei

Indicator	2000	2010
Population (thousands)	67,440	71,936
Illiteracy rate of population aged 15 or over (%)	6.65	2.61
GRP (¥ billions)	508.90	2,039.43
Composition of GRP (%)		
Primary sector	16.2	12.6
Secondary sector	50.3	52.5
Tertiary sector	33.5	34.9
Fixed asset investment (¥ billions)	181.68	1,508.34
Status of foreign-funded enterprises		
Number of registered enterprises	3,812	9,531
Total investment (US$ millions)	14,010	40,348
Registered capital (US$ millions)	8,290	21,663
Foreign trade (US$ millions)		
Export	3,278	27,974
Import	2,209	34,079
Sales of consumer goods (¥ billion)	161	682

Per capita annual disposable income of urban residents (¥)	5,661.16	16,263.43
Engle's coefficient (%)	34.91	32.32
Per capita annual net income of rural residents (¥)	2,478.86	5,957.98
Engle's coefficient (%)	28.62	35.15
Number of patent applications granted	2,812	10,061
Inventions	221	954
Utility models	1,917	6,838
Designs	674	2,269

Note: All monetary values are measured at current prices.
Source: *Hebei Statistical Yearbook*, 2001 and 2011.

Hebei's economy is largely dominated by iron and steel manufacturing, as consolidation of the province's steel industry continues.

Going forward, tighter integration of Beijing, Tianjin and 13 municipalities from Hebei into an economic zone will help to promote growth in Hebei, particularly in the areas of high-tech manufacturing, logistics and tourism. Currently, a large amount of transportation infrastructure construction is underway to make this a reality. Along with helping to promote the province's economy, this is also likely to create strong growth in the region's real-estate market.

Hebei's industries include textiles, coal, steel, iron, engineering, chemical production, petroleum, power, ceramics and food. Kailuan, with a history of over 100 years, is one of China's first modern coal mines and remains a major operation with annual production of over 20 million metric tons. Much of the North China Oilfield is situated in Hebei, and there are also major iron mines at Handan and Qian'an.

With a large area of cultivated land, Hebei is a major agricultural base in China. Some 40% of the labor force work in the agriculture, forestry and animal husbandry sectors, with the majority of production from these industries going to Beijing and Tianjin. Hebei's main agricultural products are cereal crops, including wheat, maize, millet and sorghum. Cash crops like cotton, peanuts, soya beans and sesame are also produced.

Rich in resources, Hebei's iron and steel industry is one of the key industries within the province. In 2006 it was the largest producer of iron and steel in China. Tangshan Iron and Steel Group and the Handan Iron and Steel Group are among the largest enterprises within the national industry. Meanwhile, Shougang Iron and Steel Group closed its plants, which were responsible for much pollution in Beijing. It relocated to a new facility in Hebei, built with an annual capacity of 9.7 million tons. In addition to iron and steel, Hebei is also the largest producer of cement among all the other municipalities and provinces.

Boasting a large quantity of mineral reserves, Hebei offers rich energy resources, such as coal, natural gas and petroleum. Within the province, the supply of petroleum and natural gases comes mainly from the Jidong, Jizong and Dagang oilfields. Other leading industries within the sector are the pharmaceutical and electronics industries. Two established pharmaceutical enterprises within the province are North China Pharmaceutical Group and Shijiazhuang Pharmaceutical Group.

Thanks to its strategic location, Hebei serves as a convenient distribution center for northern China. The major retail and commercial centers are the cities of Shijiazhuang, Tangshan, Handan and Cangzhou. Besides Chinese departmental chains, many foreign supermarkets, such as Carrefour and Trust-Mart, have penetrated the growing retail market. The US, Australia, Japan, South Korea and Taiwan serve as Hebei's major export destinations. Primary exports include iron and steel, crude oil, fabrics and food. Meanwhile, the major import markets are Australia, Brazil, the US, Germany and India.

Most of Hebei's FDI has been channeled into the manufacturing industry, followed by real estate, transport, storage and postal services, farming, forestry, animal husbandry and fishery, and rental and business services. Within its overall foreign investment climate, Hong Kong was Hebei's largest source of FDI. Cities such as Shijiazhuang, Tangshan, Qinhuangdao and Langfang continue to receive large amount of foreign investments, while a growing number of investments are pouring into Handan and Chengde. Foreign investments that have established their presence within the provinces include Microsoft, GM and Siemens.

As of 2010, compared with those of other provinces, "production and distribution of electricity, gas and water", "education" and "public management and social organization" were relatively strong, while "leasing and business services", "agriculture, forestry, animal husbandry and fishery" and "real estate" were relatively weak sectors (see Table C).

There are several economic and technological development zones in Hebei Province. They are Baoding Hi-Tech Industry Development Zone, Langfang Export Processing Zone, Qinhuangdao Economic and Technological Development Zone, Qinhuangdao Export Processing Zone and Shijiazhuang Hi-Tech Industrial Development Zone. Examples of these zones are described in the following page.

Table A   Hebei's comparative (dis)advantage index by sector, 2010

Sector	Index
Agriculture, forestry, animal husbandry and fishery	0.44
Mining	1.24
Manufacturing	0.83
Production and distribution of electricity, gas and water	1.61
Construction	0.72
Transport, storage and post	1.00
Information transmission, computer service and software	0.85
Wholesale and retail trades	1.06
Hotels and catering services	0.54
Financial intermediation	1.30
Real estate	0.49
Leasing and business services	0.40
Scientific research, technical services and geological prospecting	0.76
Management of water conservancy, environment and public facilities	1.16
Services to households and other services	0.85
Education	1.37
Health, social security and social welfare	1.10
Culture, sports and entertainment	0.95
Public management and social organization	1.36

Notes: All the sectors included in this table are determined according to China's official definitions and for urban areas only. Numerals greater than, equal to and less than 1 indicate that the province's sectors have advantages, no apparent (dis)advantages and disadvantages, respectively.
Sources: Calculated by author based on *China Statistical Yearbook*, 2011. See Appendix for a detailed methodological description.

- **Qinhuangdao Economic and Technological Development Zone**
  This is one of the state-level development zones within the province. Established in 1984, it comprises east and west districts, spanning an area of 56.72 km². Key industries include metallurgy, machinery, electronics, chemicals and food processing. LG and Fujitsu are two of the major investors within the zone.
- **Shijiazhuang Hi-Tech Industrial Development Zone** Located in the northeast of Shijiazhuang, this was designated as a state-level development zone in 1991. Spanning a development area of about 18 km², major industries within it include IT, pharmaceuticals, electronics and new materials.
- **Baoding Hi-Tech Industry Development Zone** This is the other state-level development zone. Established in 1992, it spans an area of about 12 km² with key industries including IT, electronics, new energy, new materials and biological engineering.

As of 2010 the top five companies were as follows:

1. Hebei Jinniui Energy Resources Co (SHE: 000937) is a coal miner, processor and distributor. It posted ¥30.29 billion in revenues and ¥2.4 billion in net profits for 2010.
2. Tangshan Iron & Steel Co (SHE: 000709) is a leading smelter, processor and distributor of steel products. It posted ¥116.92 billion in revenues and ¥1.41 billion in net profits for 2010.
3. Baoding Tianwei Baobian Electric Co (SHA: 600550) is a generator transformer manufacturer and distributor. It posted ¥7.63 billion in revenues and ¥618.81 million in net profits for 2010.
4. Tangshan Jidong Cement Co (SHE: 000401) is a leading manufacturer and distributor of construction materials. It posted ¥11.06 billion in revenues and ¥1.4 billion in net profits for 2010.
5. Kailuan Energy Chemical Co (SHA: 600997) is a coal miner, processor and distributor. It posted ¥15.15 billion in revenues and ¥868.85 million in net profits for 2010.

Indicators for the ease of doing business

A. Starting a business

Procedures: 14
Time (days): 42
Cost (% of provincial GRP per capita): 9.8

B. Registering property

Procedures: 10
Time (days): 58
Cost (% of property value): 3.2

C. Getting credit – creating and registering collateral

Time (days): 15
Cost (% of loan value): 2.8

D. Enforcing contracts

Time (days): 397
Cost (% of claim): 12.2

Further reading

Anson, Ofra (2005). *Healthcare in Rural China: Lessons from Hebei Province.* Aldershot, Hampshire: Ashgate Pub Ltd.

Anson, Ofra, Shifang Sun (2004). "Health inequalities in rural China: Evidence from Hebei Province," *Health and Place*, vol. 10, issue 1, March, pp. 75–84.

Chen, Lu (2008). *The Rise of the Bohai Circle: Studies of Constructing Hebei as a Powerful Occean Province* (Bosanjiao jueqi: hebei dazao yanhai qiangsheng yanjiu). Beijing: China Social Science Publishing House.

Gao, Shulin, Liu Qiugen (2011). *The Research of Economic History in Ancient Society* (gudai shehui jingji shitan). Shijiazhuang: Hebei University Publishing House.

Hsiung, Bingyuang, Louis Putterman (1989). "Pre- and post-reform income distribution in a Chinese commune: The case of dahe township in Hebei Province," *Journal of Comparative Economics*, vol. 13, issue 3, September, pp. 406–445.

Lan, Guoliang, Zhao Guojie (2005). *The Multilateral Perspectives of Sustainable Economic Development in County-level Area* (kechixu fazhan xianyu jingji de duowei shijiao). Shijiazhuang: Hebei People Publishing House.

Li, Wenjun, Hu jie, Lü Jun (2008). *Economic and Social Development Research of Santunying Town, Qianxi County, Hebei Province* (hebeisheng qianxixian santuiyingzhen jingji shehui fazhan diaocha baogao). Beijing: China Social Science Publishing House.

Research Division of the CCP History of Hebei Province (2004). *The National Economic Situation and Development of Hebei* (hebei guomin jingji de zhuangkuang he fazhan). Beijing: Central Compilation and Translation Press.

Tan, Minghong, Xiubin Li, Hui Xie, Changhe Lu (2005). "Urban land expansion and arable land loss in China – A case study of Beijing–Tianjin–Hebei region," *Land Use Policy*, vol. 22, issue 3, July, pp. 187–196.

Wiemer, Calla (1994). "State policy and rural resource allocation in China as seen through a Hebei Province township, 1970–1985," *World Development*, vol. 22, issue 6, June, pp. 935–947.

Xiang Jinke (2006). *Hebei, the Great Wall Legacy* (Panoramic China). Beijing: Foreign Languages Press.

Xin, Hong (2010). *Theory and Case Studies of Modern Rural Circulation System Construction in the New Era, Hebei Province* (xinshiqi hebeisheng nongcun xiandailiutong tixi jianshe de lilun yu shizheng yanjiu). Beijing: China Social Science Publishing House.

Xing, Tie (2011). *The Hebei Economy in the Song, Liao, Jin Era* (songliaojin shiqi de hebei jingji). Beijing: Science Publishing House.

Yang, Shaomei (2010). *Studies of Regional Economic Difference and Coordinated Development in Rural Area: A Case of the Rural Economic Situation in Hebei Province* (nongcun jingji quyu chayi yu Proverty yanjiu). Beijing: Intellectual Property Publishing House.

Yu, Rengang, Dai Hongwei (2006). *Regional Economic Cooperation and Development in The Beijing-Hebei-Tianjin Area: The Case of Hebei Province* (jing jin Yi quyu jingji xiezuo yu fazhan). Beijing: China Marketing Publishing House.

Zhang, Weiguo (2002). "Changing nature of family relations in a Hebei village in China," *Journal of Contemporary Asia*, vol. 32, issue 2, January, pp. 147–170.

Heilongjiang

Source: The author, based on a file from the Wikimedia Commons.

Table A   The administrative divisions of Heilongjiang

Name	Administrative seat	Population
Da Hinggan Ling P	Jiagedaqi District	511,564
Daqing PM	Sartu District	2,904,532
Harbin SPM	Nangang District	10,635,971
Hegang PM	Xingshan District	1,058,665
Heihe PM	Aihui District	1,673,898
Jiamusi PM	Qianjin District	2,552,097
Jixi PM	Jiguan District	1,862,161
Mudanjiang PM	Aimin District	2,798,723
Qiqihar PM	Longsha District	5,367,003
Qitaihe PM	Taoshan District	920,419
Shuangyashan PM	Jianshan District	1,462,626
Suihua PM	Beilin District	5,416,439
Yichun PM	Yichun District	1,148,126

Notes: P = prefecture; PM = prefectural level municipality; SPM = sub-provincial level municipality. All data are as of 2010.

Quick facts

Official name: Heilongjiang Province
Abbreviated name: Hei
Land area: 460,000 km^2
Population: 38,334,000
Population density: 83 km^2
GRP per capita of 2010: ¥27,076
HDI of 2008: 0.808
Capital: Harbin
Government office address: Zhongshan Road, Nangang District, Harbin
Tel: 0451–262–7188/262–7194
Postcode: 150001
Website: www.hlj.gov.cn

Heilongjiang is a province of the PRC, located in the northeastern part of the country. The name literally means "black dragon river," the Chinese name for the Amur. The province is located at the highest latitudes. It neighbors Russia across the Amur and Wusuli rivers running in its north and east, respectively. In the west it adjoins Inner Mongolia Autonomous Region and to its south is Jilin Province. The one-character abbreviation of Heilongjiang Province is "Hei".

Much of province is dominated by mountain ranges, such as the Greater Khingan Range, the Lesser Khingan Range, the Zhangguangcai

Mountains, the Laoye Mountains and the Wanda Mountains. The highest peak is Mount Datudingzi at 1,690 m, located on the border with Jilin Province. The Greater Khingan Range contains China's largest remaining virgin forest and is an important area for China's forestry industry. The interior of the province, which is relatively flat and low in altitude, contains the Muling River, the Naoli River, the Songhua River, the Nen River and the Mudan River, all of which are tributaries of the Amur's basin, while the northern border forms part of the Amur Valley. Xingkai Lake (or Khanka Lake) is found on the border with Russia's Primorsky Krai. It covers an area of 454,000 km², accounting for 4.7% of the nation's total. Under its jurisdiction are 13 prefectures and cities, 66 counties (cities), 1,211 townships (towns) and 14,488 villages.

Heilongjiang Province has a sub-arctic climate. The winters are long and cold with an average temperature of −31 to −15 °C in January, while summers are short and cool with an average temperature of 18–23 °C in July. The annual average rainfall is 500–600 mm and is concentrated in summer. Clear weather is prevalent throughout the year. In the spring the Songnen Plain and the Sanpingjiang Plain provide abundant sources of wind energy. The warm summer with plentiful rainfall and sun is good for crops.

The province's topography is higher in the northwest, the north and the southeast, and lower in the northeast and the southwest. In the northwest are the Greater Hinggan Mountains and in the north the Lesser Hinggan Mountains. In the southeast there are the ridges of Zhangguangcai, Laoye and Taiping, in addition to Wanda Mountain. The Nenjiang River and Songhua River run across the province from south to north, forming the Sanjiang (three-river) Plain in the northeast and the Songnen Plain in the southwest. Also in the southeast is Xingkai Lake. Hilly land and mountain areas account for 70% of the province's land, with heights ranging from 300 to 1,780 m above sea level. Plains, 50–250 m above sea level, make up about 30% of the province's total area.

The province has 44.37 million ha of soiled land with rich organics, of which 40% is suitable for farming. Heilongjiang is one of the world's three major black soil zones, with 67.6% of its farmland being cultivated on black soiled land, marshland or black calcium soil. Furthermore, the province ranks first in terms of farmland and forest area, seventh in area of pasture, fourth in land to be developed and second in land reserved for farming. Both its farmland area and the reserved land resources account for one-tenth or more of the nation's total. The average per head area of farmland operated by individual farmers is three times the nation's average.

The province has the largest forestry industry in the country, occupying an important position in China's forest ecology. The area involved is 68.9% of the province's total land area. Its forests cover 19.19 million ha of land, with a reserve of 1.5 billion m^3 of live timber. With 41.9% of its land covered with forest, Heilongjiang ranks first among all China's provinces in afforested area, reserve of forest resources and timber output. It is the most important state-owned forest area and the largest timber center in the country. In its forests are more than 100 species of trees, including 30 of high use-value. Natural forests, which constitute the principal part of its forest resources, are mainly distributed in the Greater Hinggan Mountains, the Lesser Hinggan Mountains and the Changbai Mountains.

Some 131 minerals have been discovered in the province and reserves of 74 of them have been surveyed. The deposits of ten minerals lead the country: petroleum, graphite, sillimanite, cast basalt, asbestos-use basalt, cement-use marble, colorant loess, lava ash, glass-use marble and orthoclase. Its coal deposit is the largest among the three northeast China provinces. Some 39 minerals have been mined and the annual output value of various minerals ranks second in the country.

Heilongjiang is one of China's water-rich provinces. Its numerous rivers form five water systems: those of the Amur River, the Wusuli River, the Songhua River, the Nenjiang River and the Suifeng River. There are about 6,000 lakes and reservoirs covering a surface area of more than 800,000 ha. About 70% of the area's rainfall is concentrated in the warm season, providing an ideal environment for plants and crops to grow.

The province also has a rich resource of wildlife. There are 86 species of vertebrates in 20 families of 6 orders, accounting for 21.6% of the nation's total species. Of them, five are under first-class state protection, including sable, glutton, leopard, tiger and sika deer. There are 343 bird species in 57 families of 19 orders, making up 29% of the nation's total, of which 12 species are under first-class state protection, including white cranes, Chinese goosanders, stocks and golden eagles. There are 2,100 species of wild plants, 17 of which are gymnosperms in 8 genera of 4 families; 1,747 species of angiosperms of 636 genera in 107 families; and 1,764 species of seed plants in 644 genera of 111 families. There are 2.5 million tons of reserved wild plants of economic value, including more than 250,000 tons of edible plants, over 1 million tons of wild grasses for paper making and 1.25 million tons of medicinal herbs. The province's major agricultural products include soybeans, wheat, maize, potato, rice, beet, flax and tobacco. At the end of 2005 the province had 170 nature reserves covering an area of 4.689 million ha.

The majority of Heilongjiang's population is Han Chinese, while the major ethnic minorities include the Manchus, Koreans, Mongols, Hui, Daur, Xibe, Oroqin, Hezhen and Russians. Harbin, the provincial capital, is a city of contrasts, with Chinese, Russian and eclectic worldwide influences clearly apparent. Bukui Mosque, a national heritage site, is the largest glazed tile building in the province. Eastern Orthodox, Roman Catholic and Protestant churches dot the city.

Heilongjiang has abundant tourism resources. Its resorts for ice and snow activities are the best in China. The snow-skiing period in the province lasts 120–140 days a year. In the mountain area, snow on the ground can be 100–300 cm deep and it's of good quality. Among its smooth mountain slopes, 100 have been chosen for building large-scale skiing grounds. The area's beautiful landscape, forests, grasslands, wetlands, rivers and lakes provide rich resources for developing eco-tourism. The province's unique history has also left it a rich cultural legacy and colorful customs. In addition, there are the Zoo of Northeast China Tigers, the Reserve of Red-Crowned Cranes, a site for admiring the northern lights and a number of large-scale enterprises relating to mining, farming and oilfields open to tourists. The province has set up 84 nature reserves (including 7 at state-level and 17 at provincial level), which cover an area of 2.30 million ha, or 5.05% of the province's land area.

In 2010, Heilongjiang's nominal GRP was ¥1,036.86 billion (about US$140 billion). The industry and service sectors take up more than 40% of the overall GRP each. Agriculture contributes significantly less to the economy, comprising only one-tenth of the GRP.

Table B   Demographic and socioeconomic profile: Heilongjiang

Indicator	2000	2010
Population (thousands)	36,890	38,334
Illiteracy rate of population aged 15 or over (%)	5.10	2.06
GRP (¥ billions)	325.30	1,036.86
Composition of GRP (%)		
Primary sector	11.0	12.6
Secondary sector	57.4	50.2
Tertiary sector	31.6	37.2
Fixed asset investment (¥ billion)	83.26	681.26

Status of foreign-funded enterprises		
Number of registered enterprises	3,318	5,814
Total investment (US$ millions)	8,344	19,617
Registered capital (US$ millions)	5,606	12,046
Foreign trade (US$ millions)		
Export	2,424	8,506
Import	1,569	9,833
Sales of consumer goods (¥ billion)	109	404
Per capita annual disposable income of urban residents (¥)	4,912.88	13,856.51
Engle's coefficient (%)	38.42	35.42
Per capita annual net income of rural residents (¥)	2,148.22	6,210.72
Engle's coefficient (%)	38.30	33.79
Number of patent applications granted	2,252	6,780
Inventions	208	1,512
Utility models	1,663	4,391
Designs	381	877

Note: All monetary values are measured at current prices.
Source: *Heilongjiang Statistical Yearbook*, 2001 and 2011.

The agriculture of Heilongjiang, heavily defined by the region's cold climate, is based on crops such as soybeans, maize and wheat. As one of the country's most important commodity grain production bases, it occupies first place in terms of both the volume and storage of commodity grains. Commercial crops grown include beets, flax and sunflowers. Heilongjiang is also an important source of lumber for China. Pine, especially Korean pine and larch, are the most important forms of lumber produced there. Forests are mostly to be found in the Daxingan Mountains and Xiaoxingan Mountains, which are also home to protected animal species, such as the Siberian Tiger, the red-crowned crane and the lynx. Herding in Heilongjiang is centered upon horses and cattle. The area has the greatest number of milking cows and the highest production of milk among all the provinces of China.

Heilongjiang is the traditional base of industry for the PRC. Industry is focused on coal, petroleum, lumber, machinery and food. Petroleum is of great importance there and the Daqing oilfields are a key source of petroleum for the country. Coal, gold and graphite are other important minerals to be found there. Heilongjiang also has great potential for wind power, with an average wind energy density of 200 watts per m^2. In line with central government's policy to revitalize the northeast, it is now restructuring its six pillar industries, namely equipment manufacturing, petrochemicals, food processing, energy, pharmaceuticals, and forestry and timber processing.

Heilongjiang has rich energy resources. The Daqing Oilfield is not only the biggest in the nation but also in the world. The region also has the fifth largest gas field and the seventh largest coal mine in the country. However, like the other two provinces with energy resources in northeast China, it is facing a major resource depletion problem after decades of energy production. Oil production has dropped in recent decades. As a result, the province has moved down the industrial chain to producing petrochemicals.

Heilongjiang has become one of China's most important equipment manufacturing bases. Large-scale enterprises have been set up there. Examples of these are Qiqihar Heavy CNC Equipment Corp, Qier Machine Tool Group Corp, Harbin Power Equipment Corp and China First Heavy Industries. The province is the nation's largest organic food-processing base. It has the largest organic food production output as well as the largest crop area. Harbin Beer, Wandashan and Red Star are among the better-known brands.

The service sector in Heilongjiang contributes more than 40% to the region's overall GRP. However, it still contributes less in GRP than the service industry in other developed areas in China. Traditional service industries are still the focus, and the newly emerging service industries are in need of development. To improve this situation, Heilongjiang has been encouraging the development of the computer, software, exhibition, sports and entertainment industries, while at the same time continuing the development of traditional service industries, such as real estate, transportation, warehousing and resident services.

Large foreign investors in Heilongjiang include Lane Crawford and New World from Hong Kong, Wal-Mart and Coca-Cola from the US and Mitsubishi and Kirin from Japan. Mechanical and electrical products comprise the major portion of imports. Given its geographical location, the province is an important gateway for trade with Russia, so Russia is the main trading partner, with trade between the two areas amounting to more than half of Heilongjiang's overall trade. Other major trading partners include Hong Kong, the US, Japan and Saudi Arabia.

In terms of FDI, the Virgin Islands and Hong Kong have injected the most into Heilongjiang. The Cayman Islands is also a key source of FDI. Of all the various sectors, manufacturing has received the most. Other noteworthy sectors are real estate and energy.

As of 2010, compared with those of other provinces, "agriculture, forestry, animal husbandry and fishery", "services to households and

Table C Heilongjiang's comparative (dis)advantage index by sector, 2010

Sector	Index
Agriculture, forestry, animal husbandry and fishery	7.02
Mining	2.13
Manufacturing	0.52
Production and distribution of electricity, gas and water	1.31
Construction	0.60
Transport, storage and post	1.13
Information transmission, computer service and software	0.85
Wholesale and retail trades	0.94
Hotels and catering services	0.50
Financial intermediation	0.86
Real estate	0.66
Leasing and business services	0.54
Scientific research, technical services and geological prospecting	1.17
Management of water conservancy, environment and public facilities	1.26
Services to households and other services	3.06
Education	0.83
Health, social security and social welfare	0.88
Culture, sports and entertainment	0.85
Public management and social organization	0.83

Notes: All the sectors included in this table are determined according to China's official definitions and for urban areas only. Numerals greater than, equal to and less than 1 indicate that the province's sectors have advantages, no apparent (dis)advantages and disadvantages, respectively.
Sources: Calculated by author based on *China Statistical Yearbook*, 2011. See Appendix for a detailed methodological description.

other services" and "mining" were relatively strong, while "hotels and catering services", "manufacturing" and "leasing and business services" were relatively weak sectors (see Table C).

There are several major economic and technological development zones in Heilongjiang Province. They are the Daqing New and Hi-Tech Industrial Development Zone, the Heihe Border Economic Cooperation Area, the Harbin Economic and Technological Development Zone, the Harbin New and Hi-Tech Industrial Development Zone the Sino-Russia Dongning-Piurtaphca Trade Zone and the Suifenhe Border Economic Cooperation Area. Some examples are described below.

- **Daqing New and Hi-Tech Industrial Development Zone** This was constructed in April 1992 and then approved as a national high-tech zone by the State Council later that year. Its initial zone area was 208.54 km^2 but it recently expanded by 32.45 km^2. By the end of 2006, 1,860 enterprises had been set up there, with 74,000 people employed. Their gross output value was ¥41.3 billion with a profit of ¥4.73 billion. Based on Daqing's resource advantage, six major industries have been set up in the zone: petrochemicals, new materials, electronic information, machinery manufacturing, intensive processing of agricultural and pastoral products, and pharmaceuticals.

- **Harbin Development Zone** This consists of the Harbin Economic and Technological Development Zone and Harbin High and New Technological Development Zone (HHNTDZ) (both at a national level). It was modeled after the ideal concept of having one zone comprising various parks with various functions. These parks include centralized, university, and administrative, scientific and technological parks. HHNTDZ was set up in 1988 and was approved by the State Council as a national development zone in 1991. It has an area of $34\,km^2$ in the centralized parks, subdivided into Nangang Centralized Park, Haping Road Centralized Park and Yingbin Road Centralized Park. Nangang Centralized Park is designated for the incubation of high-tech projects and an R&D base of enterprises as well as tertiary industries, such as finance, insurance, services, catering, tourism, culture, recreation and entertainment, where the headquarters of large, well-known companies and their branches in Harbin are located. Haping Road Centralized Park is a comprehensive industrial base for investment projects of automobile and automobile parts manufacturing, medicines, foodstuffs, electronics and textiles. Yingbin Road Centralized Park is mainly for high-tech incubation projects and high-tech industrial development.

- **Sino-Russia Dongning-Piurtaphca Trade Zone** This was approved by the State Council in 2000 and was completed in 2005. It has a planned area of 275.4 ha. The Chinese part has a 22 ha trade center with four subsidiary areas (A, B, C and D), in which more than 6,000 stalls are already set up, mainly dealing with clothes, household appliances, food and construction materials

- **Suifenhe Border Economic Cooperation Area** This is located in the north of Suifenhe City and borders Russia to the east. It is the largest among the three state-level border-trade zones of Heilongjiang in terms of investor numbers. It has a convenient transport network. The Binzhou–Suifenhe Railway, which connects the Russian Far East Railway, is an important port for export. The railway distance between Suifenhe and Harbin is 548 km. Buguranikinai, the corresponding Russian port city, is 21 km away.

As of 2010 the top five companies were as follows:

1. China First Heavy Industries (SHA: 601106) is a machinery designer and manufacturer established in 1954. It posted ¥8.59 billion in revenues and ¥789.81 million in net profits for 2010.
2. Harbin Pharmaceutical Group Co (SHA: 600664) is a leading drug maker and distributor. It posted ¥12.54 billion in revenues and ¥1.13 billion in net profits for 2010.
3. Heilongjiang Agriculture Co (SHA: 600598) is a grain and fertilizer producer and distributor. It posted ¥9.23 billion in revenues and ¥356.68 million in net profits for 2010.
4. Orient Group Inc (SHA: 600811) is a retailer of construction materials and household decoration materials. It is also involved in industrial and mining production, as well as being a leasing services provider. It posted ¥2.96 billion in revenues and ¥283.61 million in net profits for 2010.
5. Hafei Aviation Industry Co (SHA: 600038) is an aerospace producer and distributor. It posted ¥2.27 billion in revenues and ¥119.65 million in net profits for 2010.

Indicators for the ease of doing business

A. Starting a business

Procedures: 14
Time (days): 42
Cost (% of provincial GRP per capita): 11.9

B. Registering property

Procedures: 8
Time (days): 55
Cost (% of property value): 6.1

C. Getting credit – creating and registering collateral

Time (days): 13
Cost (% of loan value): 3.1

D. Enforcing contracts

Time (days): 290
Cost (% of claim): 31.5

Further reading

Chai, Fangying, Yu Hongxian (2011). *The Research of Low-Carbon Economic Development in Heilongjiang* (heilongjiangsheng ditanjingji fazha duice yanjiu). Beijing: China Agriculture Publishing House.

Christoffersen, Gaye (2002). "The political implications of Heilongjiang's industrial structure," in Fitzgerald, John (ed.), *Rethinking China's Provinces*. London and New York: Routledge, pp. 221–246.

Financial Institution of Heilongjiang (2008). *Regional Finance and Local Economic Development: The Case Study of Heilongjiang's Financial Institutaion, 2007* (quyu jinrong yu difang jingji fazhan: heilongjiangsheng jinrong xuehui jinrong yanjiu huojiang keti huibian, 2007). Beijing: China Financial Publishing House.

Foreign Languages Press (2005, ed.). *Heilongjiang, World of Ice and Snow and Green Home* (Panoramic China). Beijing: Foreign Languages Press.

Gao, Jay, Yansui Liu (2011). "Climate warming and land use change in Heilongjiang Province, Northeast China," *Applied Geography*, vol. 31, issue 2, April, pp. 476–482.

Guo, Li (2008). *Studies of the New Model of Regional Industrial Modernization: A Case in the Qi-Da-Ha Industrial Belt and the Northeast Asian Cooperation* (xinxing quyu gongyu xiandaihua yanjiu: yi qidaha gongye zoulang yu dongbeiya geguo chanye hezuo weili). Beijing: Economy and Science Publishing House.

Huang, Yanzhong, L. Yang Dali (1996). "The northeast phenomenon in China: Heilongjiang and the dilemmas of industrial adjustment," Zhejiang University, October 20–24, 1996.

Joshua, S.S. Muldavin (1997). "Environmental degradation in Heilongjiang: Policy reform and agrarian dynamics in China's new hybrid economy," *Annals of the Association of American Geographers*, vol. 87, issue 4, December, pp. 579–613.

Li, Gang, Chen Zhi (2010). *China's Inland Area Development: Case Studies of Changwu Town Zhaodong City Heilongjiang Province* (zhongguo neilu jizhen de neishengxing fazhan: heilongjiang zhaodongshi changwuzhen de anli yanjiu). Beijing: China Social Science Publishing House.

Li, Yufeng (2010). *Structural Optimization and Simulation of Heilongjiang's Industries*. Beijing: China Agriculture Publishing House.

Liu, Yuming (2008). *The Scaled Agriculture Business and Agricultural Industrialization: The Case in Kenqu, Heilongjiang Province* (nongye huimo jingyi yu nongye chanye yanjiu: yi heilongjiang kenqu weili). Beijing: Economy and Science Publishing House.

Qu, Wei (2012). *The Economic Development Report of Heilongjiang in 2012* (2012 ban Heilongjiang jingji fazhan baogao). Beijing: Social Science Reference Publishing House.

Shan, Patrick Fuliang (2006). "Ethnicity, nationalism and race relations: The Chinese treatment of the solon tribes in Heilongjiang frontier society, 1900–1931," *Asian Ethnicity*, vol. 7, issue 2, June 206, pp. 183–193.

Wang, Zhanguo, Liu Xiaoning (2006). *Theory and Practice of the County-level Area Development in Heilongjiang* (Heilongjiang sheng xianyu jingji fazhan lilun yu shijian tansuo). Beijing: China Agriculture Publishing House.

Xu, Shuqin, Sun Xujing (2009). *The Strategic Research in the Qi-Da-Ha Industrial Belt Economic Development* (qidaha gongye zoulang jingji fazhan de celue yanjiu). Beijing: China Agriculture Publishing House.

Zhang, Xiaoshan, Du Zhixiong, Qin Qingwu, et al. (2010). *The Overall Urban-Rural Management and County Economic Development* (chengxiang tongchou yu xianyu jingji fazhan). Heilongjiang: Heilongjiang People Publishing House.

Zhang, Xinying (2007). *The Hot Economic Issues Studies* (heilongjiang jingji redian wenti yanjiu). Harbin: Heilongjiang People Publishing House.

Zhuang, Yan (2012). *The Studies of Core Competitiveness of Newly Build Universities in the Less-Developed Area* (jingji qianfada diqu xinjian benke xuanxiao hexin jingzhengli yanjiu). Harbin: Heilongjiang University Publishing House.

Henan

Source: The author, based on a file from the Wikimedia Commons.

Table A The administrative divisions of Henan

Name	Administrative seat	Population
Anyang PM	Beiguan District	5,172,834
Hebi PM	Qibin District	1,569,100
Jiaozuo PM	Jiefang District	3,539,860
Jiyuan SPM	Jiyuan	675,710
Kaifeng PM	Gulou District	4,676,159
Luohe PM	Yancheng District	2,544,103
Luoyang PM	Xigong District	6,549,486
Nanyang PM	Wolong District	10,263,006
Pingdingshan PM	Xinhua District	4,904,367
Puyang PM	Hualong District	3,598,494
Sanmenxia PM	Hubin District	2,233,872
Shangqiu PM	Liangyuan District	7,362,472
Xinxiang PM	Weibin District	5,707,801
Xinyang PM	Shihe District	6,108,683
Xuchang PM	Weidu District	4,307,199
Zhengzhou PM	Zhongyuan District	8,626,505
Zhoukou PM	Chuanhui District	8,953,172
Zhumadian PM	Yicheng District	7,230,744

Notes: PM = prefectural level municipality; SPM = sub-prefectural-level municipality. All data are as of 2010.

Quick facts

Official name: Henan Province
Abbreviated name: Yu
Land area: 167,100 km^2
Population: 94,023,567
Population density: 591/km^2
GRP per capita of 2010: ¥24,446
HDI of 2008: 0.787
Capital: Zhengzhou
Government office address: 10 Wei'er Road, Zhengzhou
Tel: 0371–590–8241
Postcode: 450003
Website: www.henan.gov.cn

Henan is a province of the PRC located in the center of the country. Henan means "south of the river" in Chinese, and it received this name due to its location to the south of the Yellow River, which runs more than 700 km across the region. At present, however, approximately one-quarter of the province lies north of the Yellow River. The name is abbreviated to "Yu," after Yuzhou, an ancient prefecture that used to include parts of present-day Henan. The Chinese character "Yu" is closely related to that for "elephant," probably indicating that Henan had a tropical climate in ancient times.

Situated on the plain between the Yellow River and the Huai River, Henan is often referred to as Zhongyuan, which literally means "central plain" or "mid-land", although the name is also applied to the entirety of China proper. The province shares borders with six other provinces, including Shaanxi to the west, Hubei to the south, Shanxi to the north-west, Hebei to the northeast, Shandong to the northeast and Anhui to the southeast. The 17 prefecture-level divisions and 1 directly adminis-tered county-level city of Henan are subdivided into 159 county-level divisions (50 districts, 21 county-level cities and 88 counties; Jiyuan is counted as a county-level city here). These are in turn divided into 2,440 township-level divisions (866 towns, 1,234 townships, 12 ethnic townships and 328 sub-districts).

Henan Province is in the transitional area between the second and third steps of China's four-step terrain rising from east to west, with rolling mountains over 1,000 m above sea level in its western part and a plain area of 100 m or lower in its east. Laoyacha in Lingbao City, 2,413.8 m above sea level, is the highest peak. The lowest point, at 23.2 m, is found at the place where the Huaihe River leaves the province. High in the west and low in the east, even in the north and concave in the south, Henan is surrounded by four mountain ranges (Taihang in the north, Funiu in the west and Tongbai and Dabie in the south), leaving subsidence basins here and there. In its middle and eastern parts there is a vast fluvial plain created by the Yellow, Huaihe and Haihe rivers. Mountainous regions comprise 44.3% of its area and the plains 55.7%.

Four rivers run across Henan, the Yellow River, the Huaihe River, the Weihe River and the Hanshui River. The Yellow River passes through central Henan. It enters from the northwest via the Sanmenxia Reser-voir. After it passes Luoyang, the mountains give way to plains. Excessive amounts of sediments are formed due to the silt it picks up from the Loess Plateau, raising the riverbed and causing frequent floods, which have shaped the region. More recently, however, the construction of dams and levees, as well as the depletion of water resources, has ended the floods. The Huai River in southern Henan is also important and has been recognized as part of the boundary dividing the northern and southern Chinese climate and culture.

Henan has a temperate climate that is humid sub-tropical to the south of the Yellow River and bordering on humid continental to the north. Located between the northern sub-tropical zone and warm temperate zone, it has four distinctive seasons with complicated weather conditions characterized with a hot and rainy summer and generally cool to cold, windy, dry winter. Southern Henan is in the northern sub-tropical zone. The province's average temperature of the year is 13–15 °C, with around freezing in January and 27–28 °C in July. The average annual rainfall is 807 mm, the great majority of which occurs during the summer. The frost-free period lasts 275–308 days.

Henan is also rich in minerals and natural resources. Some 126 kinds of minerals are found, of which the reserves of 74 have been confirmed. Some 61 have been mined and utilized. With considerable reserves of petroleum and natural gas, the region includes Zhongyuan Oilfields and Henan Oilfields and it is the fifth largest petroleum and natural gas producer in China. Some 121 of the 150 kinds of minerals found on earth are available in the province. It is also home to over 3,800 species of plants and more than 400 kinds of animals. This territory is an important production base for wheat, corn, cotton, tobacco and oil plants. Some 32 nature reserves have been established in the province covering an area of 748,400 ha.

Henan has water reserves of 40.6 billion m^3 or about 410 m^3 per capita. The average annual precipitation stands at 797.7 mm. The key water-conservation project at Xiaolangdi on the Yellow River, supported by a loan from the World Bank, has a total installed capacity of 1.8 million kw.

With a population of approximately 93.6 million, Henan is the second most populous Chinese province after Guangdong. Although the population is highly homogeneous with 98.8% being Han, Henan has the largest Muslim Hui population in eastern China, which constitute approximately 1% and lives mostly in Muslim enclaves in the Guancheng District (in Zhengzhou), the Chanhe District (in Luoyang) and the Shunhe District (in Kaifeng). Small populations of Mongols and Manchus exist in scattered rural communities as well as major urban centers. Kaifeng is also known for its historical Jewish communities, although, after centuries of integration, few are aware of their ancestry and Jews are not an officially recognized ethnic minority in China.

Henan has a diverse landscape with floodplains in the east and mountains in the west. Much of the province forms part of the densely populated North China Plain, an area known as the "breadbasket" of China. The Taihang Mountains intrude partially into Henan's northwestern borders from Shanxi, forming the eastern edge of Loess Plateau. To the west the Xionger and Funiu mountains form an extensive network of mountain ranges and plateaus, supporting one of the few remaining temperate deciduous forests which once covered all of Henan. The famous Mount Song and its Shaolin Temple is located in the far east of the region, near the capital city of Zhengzhou. To the far south the Dabie Mountains divide Hubei from Henan. The Nanyang Basin, separated from the North China Plain by these mountains, is another important agricultural and population center, with culture and history distinct from the rest of Henan and closer to that of Hubei. Unlike the rest of northern China, desertification is not a problem in Henan, though sand storms are common in cities near the Yellow River due to the large amount of sand present there.

Henan plays an important role in China's history, including as it does four of the country's ancient capitals (Anyang, Kaifeng, Luoyang and Zhengzhou). More than ten ancient dynasties have established their capitals in Henan. This has contributed to the vast number of ruins and relics found throughout the province. As one of the major birthplaces of Chinese civilization, the area offers several epoch-making archeological discoveries, including the Peiligang Culture Site dating back 7,000 years, Yanshao Culture Site of some 6,000 years ago and Dahe Culture Site of more than 5,000 years ago. In ancient China, more than 20 dynasties established their capitals there. Three of China's seven great ancient capitals are located in Henan: Anyang of the Shang Dynasty, Luoyang of nine dynasties and Kaifeng of seven dynasties. Three of ancient China's four great inventions – the compass, paper making and gunpowder – were made in Henan. The province comes first place in the country in terms of underground cultural relics, and second with regard to existing cultural relics on the ground. The Yellow River, with numerous ancient relics and scenic attractions, also provides a rich tourist trap. There are 16 key national units of protected historical relics and 267 provincial units. The over-ground historical relics of the province take second place. Historical relics in museums represent one-eighth of those in China, and the underground historical relics are the greatest in number in the country. In Henan Museum there are 120,000 historical relics, including more than 40,000 classified as rare.

The province has seen rapid development in its economy over the past two decades, and this has expanded at an even faster rate than the national average. This rapid growth has transformed Henan from one of the poorest provinces to one that matches other central provinces, though it is still relatively impoverished on a national scale. In 2010 its nominal GRP was ¥2.31 trillion (about US$339 billion), making it the

Table B Demographic and socioeconomic profile: Henan

Indicator	2000	2010
Population (thousands)	92,560	94,055
Illiteracy rate of population aged 15 or over (%)	5.87	4.25
GRP (¥ billions)	513.77	2,309.24
Composition of GRP (%)		
Primary sector	22.6	14.1
Secondary sector	47.0	57.3
Tertiary sector	30.4	28.6
Fixed asset investment (¥ billion)	137.77	1,658.59
Status of foreign-funded enterprises		
Number of registered enterprises	3,004	10,254
Total investment (US$ millions)	11,359	37,866
Registered capital (US$ millions)	7,337	20,535
Foreign trade (US$ millions)		
Export	1,587	12,194
Import	1,537	7,821
Sales of consumer goods (¥ billions)	179	800
Per capita annual disposable income of urban residents (¥)	4,766.26	15,930.26
Engle's coefficient (%)	36.20	32.99
Per capita annual net income of rural residents (¥)	1,985.82	5,523.73
Engle's coefficient (%)	32.21	37.24
Number of patent applications granted	2,766	16,539
Inventions	209	1,498
Utility models	2,113	11,048
Designs	444	3,993

Note: All monetary values are measured at current prices.
Source: *Henan Statistical Yearbook*, 2001 and 2011.

fifth largest economy in China, although it ranks 19th in terms of GRP per capita.

Henan is the fifth largest provincial economy of China and the largest among inland provinces. However, the per capita GRP is low compared with other eastern and central provinces, and Henan is considered to be one of the more backward areas in China. The economy continues to depend on its dwindling aluminum and coal reserves, as well as agriculture, heavy industry, tourism and retail. High-tech industry and the service sector are underdeveloped and are concentrated around Zhengzhou and Luoyang.

Agriculture has traditionally been a pillar of the region's economy, with the nation's highest wheat and sesame output and second highest rice output, earning its reputation as the breadbasket of China. Henan is also an important producer of beef, cotton, maize, pork, animal oil and corn. Food production and processing make up more than 14% of the output from the province's secondary industry, and it is said that 90% of Chinese McDonald's and KFC ingredients come from Henan.

Although Henan's industry has traditionally been based on light textiles and food processing, recent developments have diversified the industry sector to metallurgy, petrol, cement, chemical industry, machinery and electronics. It has the second largest molybdenum reserves in the world. Coal, aluminum, alkaline metals and tungsten are also present in large amounts in the west of the province. Export and processing of these materials is one of the main sources of revenues.

Henan is actively trying to build its economy around the provincial capital of Zhengzhou, and it is hoped that it may become an important transportation and manufacturing hub in the future. Foreign exchanges are increasing continuously. Friendly provincial relationships have been established with 16 states (districts) in the US, Japan, Russia, France, Germany and other countries. Some cities of Henan have established friendly relationships (sister city) with 32 foreign cities.

The service sector is rather small and underdeveloped. Finance and commerce are largely concentrated in urban centers, such as Zhengzhou and Luoyang, where the economy is fueled by a large and relatively affluent consumer base. In order to make the economy more knowledge and technology based, government established a number of development zones in all of the major cities, promoting industries such as software, information technologies, new materials, bio-pharmaceuticals and photo-machinery-electronics. Henan is a major destination for tourists, with places such as Shaolin Temple and Longmen Grottoes attracting millions each year.

With the vast amount of cultivated land and sown area, Henan is a large and well-known agricultural region in China. It is the largest production base for grain, oil-bearing crops and fruits. Rich agricultural products (such as wheat, corn, oil-bearing crops, fruit and vegetables) and a large number of livestock ensure sufficient supply for its food-processing industries. As a result, the region has developed into a major food-processing base, producing foodstuffs such as meat, frozen food, instant noodles, biscuits and seasoning. Henan is the second largest food-processing base in China, after Shandong. Sanquan Corp, the country's largest frozen food-processing firm, is located in Henan. It is also home to Shineway Group, China's biggest meat-processing enterprise. Zhengzhou Commodity Exchange, set up in 1990, is one of three commodity futures markets in the country. The trading items of futures contracts include wheat, cotton, white sugar, pure terephthalic acid, rapeseed oil and green beans.

With the advantages of cheap labor and low land prices, Henan's prospects appear to be found in its development as a major transportation hub, which may benefit other industries and pave the way for Henan to become a manufacturing hub as well.

The province's pillar industries include food processing, equipment manufacturing, metallurgy, coal and textiles. Equipment manufacturing is the second largest industry in terms of value-added industrial output in the area. A key player in this industry is CITIC Heavy Machine Inc, located in Luoyang. It is one of China's largest mining equipment manufacturers.

Henan is China's third largest coal production base, after Shanxi and Inner Mongolia. The main coal producers include Pingdingshan Coal Group, Yima Coal Industry Group and Yongmei Group. Thanks to the abundance of mineral resources, the metallurgy industry plays an important role in the province's industrial sector. Anyang Iron & Steel Group and the Henan branch of China Aluminum Corp are the two major players in the metallurgy sector.

Tourism plays an important role in Henan's service sector, thanks to its great number of historical ruins and relics.

The province conducts international trade with various countries. Major export destinations are the US, South Korea, Hong Kong, Taiwan and India, while key import sources are Japan, the US, India, Germany and Brazil. Henan's main import products are minerals, including vanadium ore, unsintered iron ore, cathodes and alumina. All these account for more than half of the imported products. In terms of exports, Henan mainly exports wigs, unwrought and non-alloyed aluminum, and unwrought and refined lead. The province has also seen an increase in the export of machinery and electrical appliances.

The primary sources of foreign investment are from Hong Kong and Latin American countries. Henan attracts many foreign investors, such as Coca-Cola, GE, Metro and Toshiba. The manufacturing sector receives the highest amount of FDI among all the sectors. Other noteworthy recipients are the production and distribution of electricity, gas and water, real estate, mining, and tenancy and business services.

As of 2010, compared with those of other provinces, "mining", "public management and social organization" and "construction" were

Table C   Henan's comparative (dis)advantage index by sector, 2010

Sector	Index
Agriculture, forestry, animal husbandry and fishery	0.33
Mining	1.63
Manufacturing	0.76
Production and distribution of electricity, gas and water	1.18
Construction	1.28
Transport, storage and post	0.80
Information transmission, computer service and software	0.45
Wholesale and retail trades	1.24
Hotels and catering services	0.83
Financial intermediation	0.83
Real estate	0.74
Leasing and business services	0.63
Scientific research, technical services and geological prospecting	0.68
Management of water conservancy, environment and public facilities	0.97
Services to households and other services	0.56
Education	1.25
Health, social security and social welfare	1.12
Culture, sports and entertainment	0.92
Public management and social organization	1.29

Notes: All the sectors included in this table are determined according to China's official definitions and for urban areas only. Numerals greater than, equal to and less than 1 indicate that the province's sectors have advantages, no apparent (dis)advantages and disadvantages, respectively.
Sources: Calculated by author based on *China Statistical Yearbook*, 2011. See Appendix for a detailed methodological description.

relatively strong, while "agriculture, forestry, animal husbandry and fishery", "information transmission, computer service and software" and "services to households and other services" were relatively weak sectors (see Table C).

Henan has 4 state-level development zones, 23 province-level development zones and 73 city-level development zones. The 4 state-level development zones are the Zhengzhou Economic and Technological Development Zone, Zhengzhou Export Processing Zone, Zhengzhou Hi-Tech Development Zone and Luoyang Hi-Tech Development Zone. These achieved a combined value-added output and industrial output of ¥295.3 billion and ¥112.6 billion in 2006, accounting for 23.7% of Henan's GRP and 18.5% of Henan's industrial output, respectively. Together the zones received US$2.89 billion worth of foreign investment – that is, 85.66% of the province's foreign investment. Combined exports of these zones also amounted to US$2.31 billion, contributing to 34.5% of the province's exports.

As of 2010 the top five companies were as follows:

1. Pingdingshan Tianan Coal Mining Co (SHA: 601666) is a leading coal miner, processor and distributor. It posted ¥22.9 billion in revenues and ¥1.85 billion in net profits for 2010.
2. Henan Shuanghui Investment & Development Co (SHE: 000895) is a leading processor of various pork products. It posted ¥36.75 billion in revenues and ¥1.09 billion in net profits for 2010.
3. Hualan Biological Engineering Inc (SHE: 002007) is engaged in research, production and the sale of blood-related products and vaccines. It posted ¥1.26 billion in revenues and ¥612.36 million in net profits for 2010.
4. Zhengzhou Coal Mining Machinery Group Co (SHA: 601717) is a mining machinery manufacturer. It posted ¥6.75 billion in revenues and ¥882.57 million in net profits for 2010.
5. Henan Shenhuo Coal & Power Co (SHE: 000933) is a processor and distributor of coal and aluminum products. It posted ¥16.9 billion in revenues and ¥1.16 billion in net profits for 2010.

Indicators for the ease of doing business

A. Starting a business

Procedures: 13
Time (days): 41
Cost (% of provincial GRP per capita): 11.6

B. Registering property

Procedures: 11
Time (days): 60
Cost (% of property value): 5.1

C. Getting credit – creating and registering collateral

Time (days): 16
Cost (% of loan value): 3.3

D. Enforcing contracts

Time (days): 285
Cost (% of claim): 31.5

Further reading

Chang, Li (2008). *Administrative Division and Regional Economic Development: An Analysis of Henan Province* (xingzheng quhua yu quyu jingji fazhan: henansheng anli fenxi). Beijing: Science Publishing House.

Di, Jiaping, Yujiang Li (2008). "Rural labor transfer mode and regional nonequilibrium degree comparative study in Shandong and Henan provinces," *China Population, Resources and Environment*, vol. 18, issue 5, October, pp. 189–193.

Fan, Xinsheng (2007). *The Multilateral Research of Regional Economic Space Structure Transition: The Case of Henan Province* (quyu jingji kongjian jiegou yanbian de duochidu yanjiu: yi henansheng weili). Beijing: Science Publication Pte, Ltd.

Heberer, Thomas, Sabine Jakobi (2002). "Henan as a model: From hegemonism to fragmentation," in Fitzgerald, John (ed.), *Rethinking China's Provinces*. London and New York: Routledge, pp. 89–124.

Jia, Junsong, Hongbing Deng, Jing Duan, Jingzhu Zhao (2009). "Analysis of the major drivers of the ecological footprint using the STIRPAT model and the PLS method – A case study in Henan Province, China," *Ecological Economics*, vol. 68, issue 11, 15 September, pp. 2818–2824.

Li, Dongsheng, Hu Xining, Shao Chengshan (2008). *The Countermeasure of Circulated Economic Development in Coal Resource Based Cities: A Case Study of Circulated Economic Development in Hebi City, Henan Province* (meitan ziyuan chengshi xunhuan jingji fazhan duice: jiyu henansheng hebishi xunhuan jingji fazhan de shizheng yanjiu). Beijing: China Economics Publishing House.

Li, Yanyan (2007). *Cultural and Economic Transformations: Analysis of Zhongyuan Development Experiences* (wenhua yu jingji zhanxing: jiyu zhongyuan fazhan jingyan de fenxi). Beijing: Social Science Referencs Publishing House.

Lin, Xianzhai (2011). *The Strategic Adjustment of Economic Stucture in the Post-Crisis Era, Henan Province* (houweiji shiqi henan jingji jiegou de zhanluexing tiaozheng). Beijing: Social Science Reference Publishing House.

Lin, Xianzhai, Yu Xinan (2011). *Henan Urban Development Report, 2011: Changing the Direction of Urban Development* (henan chengshi fazhan baogao, 2011: zhuanbian chengshi fazhan fangxiang). Beijing: Social Science Reference Publishing House.

Liu, Fuheng (2011). *The Strategies and Planning of Cities in Central China* (zhongyuan chengshiqun zhanlue yu guihua). Beijing: Economy and Science Publishing House.

Liu, Shiwei (2009). *Coal Economic Studies in Henan*, vol.4 (henan meitan jingji yanjiu, 4). Henan: Huang River Water Conservancy Publishing House.

Liu, Shiwei (2010). *The Strategic Thinking of Coal Economic Harmonious Development in Henan* (henan meitan jingji hexie fazhan zhanlue gousi). Zhengzhou: Yellow River Water Conservancy Publishing House.

Liu, Yungang, Guanwen Yin, Laurence J.C. Ma (2012). "Local state and administrative urbanization in post-reform China: A case study of Hebi City, Henan Province," *Cities*, vol. 29, issue 2, April, pp. 107–117.

Lu, Dongxie, Li Jie, Gao Chunping (2011). *Coal Chemistry, Mining Indusrty and Resource and Environment Issues Studies in Henan Province* (henansheng meihua gongye chanye fazhan ziyuan huanjing wenti yanjiu). Beijing: China Environment Science Studies.

Qin, Yaochen, Miao Changhong (2011). *The Studies of Scientific Development of the Zhongyuan Economic Zone* (zhongyuan jingjiqu kexue fazhan yanjiu). Beijing: Science Publishing House.

Wang, Jianguo (2012a). *Henan Urban Development Report: The Practice of Pushing New City Model in 2012* (henan chengshi fazhan baogao: 2012 tuijin xinxing chengzhenhua de shijian yu tansuo). Beijing: Social Science Reference Publishing House.

Wang, Shaohua (2012b). *Environmental Optimization in Henan* (youhua huanjing kan henan). Beijing: Enterprise Management Publishing House.

Wang, Weiguang (2010). *The Central China Economic Growth Pole: Development Research in the Great Zhengzhou* (zhongyuan jingji hexin zengzhangji: dazhengzhou dushiqu fazhan zhanlue yanjiu). Beijing: Economic Management Publishing House.

Wang, Yanling, Yang Dedong, Zhang Dongping (2009). *Modern Agricultural Development Studies: The Case of Henan Province* (xiandai nongye fazhan yanjiu: yi henan weili). Beijing: China Agriculture Publishing House.

Wou, Odoric Y.K. (1994). *Mobilizing the Masses: Building Revolution in Henan.* Stanford, CA: Stanford University Press.

Yang, Changchun (2006). *Henan, the Central Plains of Chinese Culture* (Panoramic China). Beijing: Foreign Languages Press.

Yano, Go, Maho Shiraishi, Xohrat Mahmut (2011). "What caused the 'marginal-products-of-labor wage gap' in state-owned enterprises in China during the early-reform era? A reconsideration based on a case study in Henan," *Journal of Chinese Economic and Business Studies*, vol. 9, issue 3, August, pp. 217–238.

Yong, Xinan, Gu Yongdong (2011). *The Strategy of Developing the Zhongyuan Economic Zone* (zhongyuan jingjiqu celue). Beijing: Economic Management Publishing House.

Zhang, Rui, Gu Jianquan (2011). *Henan Economic Development Report, 2011* (henan jingji fazhan baogao, 2011). Beijing: Social Science Reference Publishing House.

Zhao, Baozuo (2009). *Henan's Outward Eonomy* (henan kaifang jingji). Beijing: Social Science Reference Publishing House.

Zhao, Peng, Wang Yanling (2007). *A Systemic Analysis of Elements in Henan's New Rural Construction* (henan xinnongcun jianshe yaosu xitong fenxi). Beijing: China Agriculture Publishing House.

Zhu, Shanli, Gong Liutang (2010). *Studies of Agricultural Industralization in Luohe, Henan Province* (henan luohe nongye chanyehua yanjiu). Beijing: Economy and Science Publishing House.

Hubei

Source: The author, based on a file from the Wikimedia Commons.

Table A　The administrative divisions of Hubei

Name	Administrative seat	Population
Enshi Tujia & Miao AP	Enshi	3,290,294
Ezhou PM	Echeng District	1,048,672
Huanggang PM	Huangzhou District	6,162,072
Huangshi PM	Huangshigang District	2,429,318
Jingmen PM	Dongbao District	2,873,687
Jingzhou PM	Shashi District	5,691,707
Qianjiang CM	Qianjiang	946,277
Shennongjia FD	Shennongjia	76,140
Shiyan PM	Zhangwan District	3,340,843
Suizhou PM	Zengdu District	2,162,222
Tianmen CM	Tianmen	1,418,913
Wuhan SPM	Jiang'an District	9,785,392
Xiangyang PM	Xiangcheng District	5,500,307
Xianning PM	Xian'an District	2,462,583
Xiantao CM	Xiantao	1,175,085
Xiaogan PM	Xiaonan District	4,814,542
Yichang PM	Xiling District	4,059,686

Notes: AP = autonomous prefecture; CM = county-level municipality; FD = forestry district; PM = prefectural level municipality; SPM = sub-provincial level municipality. All data are as of 2010.

Quick facts

Official name: Hubei Province
Abbreviated name: È
Land area: 185,900 km^2
Population: 57,237,740
Population density: 324/km^2
GRP per capita of 2010: ¥27,906
HDI of 2008: 0.784
Capital: Wuhan
Government office address: Shuiguohu, Wuchang, Wuhan City
Tel: 027–8723–5544/8723–5552
Postcode: 430071
Website: www.hubei.gov.cn

Hubei is a province of the PRC, situated in central China. Extending across two major river systems – the Yangtze and its largest tributary, the Han – the region adjoins Henan Province to the north, Anhui Province to the east, Jiangxi Province to the southeast, Hunan Province to the south, Chongqing Municipality to the west and Shaanxi Province to the northwest. Hubei means "north of the lake" in Chinese, referring to its position north of Lake Dongting. It is officially abbreviated to "È", an ancient name associated with the eastern part of the province since the Qin Dynasty (221–206 BC), while a popular, though unofficial, name for it is "Chu" after the powerful state of Chu that existed there during the Eastern Zhou Dynasty (771–221 BC).

About 10% of the province consists of lakes, lending it the nickname "province of a thousand lakes." The 13 prefecture-level divisions and 4 directly administered county-level divisions of Hubei are subdivided into 102 county-level divisions (38 districts, 24 county-level cities, 37 counties, 2 autonomous counties, 1 forestry area; the directly administered county-level divisions are included here). These are in turn divided into 1,234 township-level divisions (737 towns, 215 townships, 9 ethnic townships and 273 sub-districts).

The major rivers of Hubei are the Yangtze (Chang-jiang) and its tributary Han-shui, which give their names to the Jianghan Plain. The Yangtze River enters Hubei from the west via the Three Gorges. The eastern half of the Three Gorges (the Xiling Gorge and part of the Wu Gorge) lies in western Hubei, while the western half is in neighboring Chongqing Municipality. The Han-shui enters the province from the northwest. After crossing most of the province, the two rivers meet at Wuhan, the provincial capital. The Jianghan Plain takes up most of central and eastern Hubei, while the west and the peripheries are more mountainous, with ranges such as the Wudang Mountains, the Jingshan Mountains, the Daba Mountains and the Wu Mountains (in rough north-to-south order). The Dabie Mountains lie to the northeast of the Janghan Plain, on the border with Henan and Anhui; the Tongbai Mountains lie to the north on the border with Henan; and to the southeast, the Mufu Mountains form the border with Jiangxi. The highest point in Hubei is Shennong Peak.

Hubei is located in the transitional region from the second to the third terrace in the terrain of China, thus having a variety of landforms. It is surrounded by the mountains of Wuling, Wushan, Daba, Wudang, Tongbai, Dabie and Mufu on the west, north and east. Lying in the central and southern parts is the Jianghan Plain, which extends to Hunan Province to link with Lake Dongting Plain. Except for the hills on the fringes of the plain, the altitude there is 35 m or less above sea level. The various geographical features of the province include 55.5% of mountains, 24.5% of hills and hillocks and 20% of plain and lake areas. The elevation of different parts varies greatly. The Shennong Summit, the highest peak of Shennongjia in west Hubei, which is known as the "Roof of Central China", is 3,105 m above sea level, while the Tanjiayuan of Jianli County on the eastern plain has an elevation of zero.

Hubei has a sub-tropical monsoon climate. It enjoys abundant sunlight, with the annual amount of solar radiation totaling 85–114 kilocalories per cm^2 and the annual duration averaging 1,200–2,200 hours. The temperature is on the high side, with the annual temperature averaging 13–18 °C. It can reach 41 °C at its highest, while the lowest can be −14.9 °C. The short frost period and abundant precipitation are favorable for agriculture. There are 230–300 days free of frost in a year and the annual rainfall has stood at 1,180 mm for many years. The rainfall is unevenly distributed. The amount of precipitation in the Wuling Mountain area is as high as 1,600–1,700 mm, while that in west Hubei is as low as 700–800 mm.

To date 138 kinds of minerals have been discovered, 89 of which have had their reserves verified. The reserves of phosphorus ore, hongshiite, wollastonite, garnet and marlstone rank fifth in China, and several others, including iron, phosphorus, copper, gypsum, rock salt, gold amalgam, manganese and vanadium, rank seventh. However, the province lacks energy resources, with limited verified reserves of coal, petroleum and natural gas. Its proven reserves of coal stand at 548 million tons.

Hubei is rich in underground water resources. Of its estimated 265 billion m^3 of underground water reserves, 35.57 billion m^3 are ready for annual extraction, amounting to approximately 36% of the province's average annual surface runoff. There are 58 large reservoirs in the province with water storage of 43.75 billion m^3. The area boasts a number of large and medium-sized hydropower stations – the Gezhouba, Danjiangkou, Geheyan, Hanjiang, Duhe, Huanglongtan, Bailianhe, Lushui and Fushui. In addition, some thermal power stations have been built in Wuhan, Jingmen, Huangshi and at other sites in recent years.

There are 570 species of terrestrial vertebrates in Hubei. Dozens of them have been listed as rare animals under state protection. These include the golden-haired monkey, serow, leopard, white bear, white musk, white deer, white snake, white-crowned king pheasant and red-bellied tragopan. There are also 175 kinds of fish, accounting for about one-quarter of the country's freshwater fish species. Rare species under key state protection include the Chinese sturgeon, Chinese paddlefish, mullet and giant salamander.

Hubei boasts both large numbers of broad-leaved deciduous species, which are typical of northern China, and many broad-leaved evergreen species, which are well known in southern China. There are more than

2,000 species of wild plants, including some 1,300 kinds of medicinal plants and over 30 species that are either rare in the world or peculiar to China. The well-preserved Shennongjia virgin forest is a natural park of sub-tropical fauna and flora. By the end of 2005 the number of nature reserves in the province had reached 62, covering an area of 1.086 million ha.

Thanks to its geographic location, the province enjoys favorable environmental conditions and diversified natural resources suitable for different crops. It is a main production base for rice, cotton, tea and oil crops, and as such it has long been known as "the land of rice and fish" in China. Some potential problems include the long-term effects of the Three Gorges Dam: while the project provides power and significantly reduces the risk of potential losses from Yangtze River floods, environmental impacts of the project are becoming apparent. Additionally, Hubei has yet to show that its large economy can maintain growth without depending on influxes of fixed asset investment.

Hubei has rich tourism resources that feature both beautiful landscapes and abundant places of historic and cultural interest. It was once the capital for the Chu Kingdom during the Warring States Period (475–221 BC). It also played an important strategic role in the Three Kingdoms Period (AD 190–280). There are 6 national-level scenic spots, 13 national forest parks and 3 national nature reserves. Shennongjia has been listed in UNESCO's program of Man and Biosphere, and Wudang Mountain is on the list of World Cultural and Natural Heritage Sites. The Three Gorges of the Yangtze River, the Yellow Crane Tower and the Gezhouba Dam have been listed among China's top 40 tourist scenic spots. Hubei encompasses 5 famous historical and cultural cites designated by the state, 20 cultural sites under state protection, 365 cultural sites under provincial protection, 5 sites of Chu City ruins, 73 Chu cultural sites and over 140 sites relating to the Three Kingdoms.

The province's most famous natural attraction (shared with the adjacent Chongqing Municipality) is the scenic area of the Three Gorges of the Yangtze. Located in the far west, the gorges can be conveniently visited by one of the numerous tourist boats (or regular passenger boats) that travel up the Yangtze from Yichang through the Three Gorges and into the neighboring Chongqing municipality.

The mountains of western Hubei, in particular in Shennongjia District, offer a welcome respite from Wuhan's and Yichang's summer heat, as well as skiing opportunities in winter. The tourist facilities in that area are concentrated around Muyu in the southern part of Shennongjia, the gateway to Shennongjia National Nature Reserve. Closer to the provincial capital, Wuhan, is Mount Jiugong (Jiugongshan) National Park in Tongshan County near the border with Jiangxi.

Hubei's economy ranks 11th in the country and its nominal GRP for 2010 was ¥1.60 trillion (about 233.4 billion US$) with a per capita of 21,566 ¥ (about US$2,863).

Table B Demographic and socioeconomic profile: Hubei

Indicator	2000	2010
Population (thousands)	60,280	57,279
Illiteracy rate of population aged 15 or over (%)	7.15	4.58
GRP (¥ billions)	427.63	1,596.76
Composition of GRP (%)		
Primary sector	15.5	13.4
Secondary sector	49.7	48.6
Tertiary sector	34.9	37.9
Fixed asset investment (¥ billions)	133.92	1,026.27
Status of foreign-funded enterprises		
Number of registered enterprises	5,123	7,486
Total investment (US$ millions)	16,670	42,864
Registered capital (US$ millions)	10,348	24,314
Foreign trade (US$ millions)		
Export	1,900	13,910
Import	1,993	12,119
Sales of consumer goods (¥ billions)	179	701
Per capita annual disposable income of urban residents (¥)	5,524.54	16,058.37
Engle's coefficient (%)	38.31	38.68
Per capita annual net income of rural residents (¥)	2,268.59	5,832.27
Engle's coefficient (%)	33.86	43.10
Number of patent applications granted	2,198	17,362
Inventions	156	2,025
Utility models	1,573	10,431
Designs	469	4,906

Note: All monetary values are measured at current prices.
Source: *Hubei Statistical Yearbook*, 2001 and 2011.

Hubei has witnessed rapid economic development since the opening up of the Yangtze Economic Belt and the construction of the Three Gorges Dam project. The soaring investment, consumption and exports have helped the regional economy to grow. Industry and service lead the economy, while agriculture remains a moderately significant contributor.

The province has developed into an important industrial production base in central China with major industries including automobiles, iron and steel production, machinery, power generation, textiles, food and beverage, electronics, shipbuilding and chemical raw materials, and Hubei is one of the major automobile production centers in China. The concentration of the automobile industry there has resulted in the rapid growth of the auto accessories industry. The Dongfeng Motor Corporation, which was launched in 1969, is one of the Big Three Auto Groups in China. Its subsidiaries in the area include the Dongfeng Peugeot Citroen Automobile, a joint venture with French car maker Peugeot, and the Dongfeng Honda Automobile Co. Ltd, a joint venture with Japanese car giant Honda.

Since the launch of China's first iron plant (Hanyang Iron Plant) in Wuhan in 1891, Hubei has developed into a comprehensive iron and steel production base in China. A key player in this industry is Wuhan Iron and Steel Group. It has an annual production capacity of 20 million tons and is ranked the third largest iron and steel consortium in China after nearly 50 years of development. Steel products are the key export of Hubei. Wuhan Iron & Steel Group and the Hubei Xinyegang Co. Ltd are the two major exporters in the province.

Hubei's service sector is developing rapidly and steadily. Retail and tourism are the key industries that have helped the sector's growth. Many overseas retail enterprises, such as the New World Development Group, the Tak Shun Group, Carrefour, Wal-Mart and Metro, have invested in the region.

Like other provinces in China, Hubei conducts a great deal of trade with many other countries. The main export destinations (in terms of trade volume) include the US, Hong Kong, South Korea, Japan and Germany. Major import sources are Japan, France, Germany, Australia and Taiwan. Among all the exports, those of machinery and electrical appliances have expanded the most. Major imports include iron ore, auto accessories, copper ore and piston engine components.

FDI sources include Hong Kong, Japan, the Virgin Islands, the UK and France. The manufacturing sector accounts for the majority of the total actualized FDI, followed by the service sector, with a focus on the hotel, retail, logistics and real-estate industries.

As of 2010, compared with those of other provinces, "construction" and "health, social security and social welfare" were relatively strong, while "leasing and business services", "mining" and "services to households and other services" were relatively weak sectors (see Table C).

Table C Hubei's comparative (dis)advantage index by sector, 2010

Sector	Index
Agriculture, forestry, animal husbandry and fishery	0.94
Mining	0.45
Manufacturing	0.97
Production and distribution of electricity, gas and water	0.98
Construction	1.46
Transport, storage and post	1.03
Information transmission, computer service and software	0.62
Wholesale and retail trades	1.03
Hotels and catering services	0.94
Financial intermediation	0.88
Real estate	0.80
Leasing and business services	0.42
Scientific research, technical services and geological prospecting	0.95
Management of water conservancy, environment and public facilities	1.04
Services to households and other services	0.51
Education	1.06
Health, social security and social welfare	1.22
Culture, sports and entertainment	0.99
Public management and social organization	0.98

Notes: All the sectors included in this table are determined according to China's official definitions and for urban areas only. Numerals greater than, equal to and less than 1 indicate that the province's sectors have advantages, no apparent (dis)advantages and disadvantages, respectively.
Sources: Calculated by author based on *China Statistical Yearbook*, 2011. See Appendix for a detailed methodological description.

Hubei has 3 development zones at the state level, 24 at the provincial level and 38 others at the city level. Some examples are described below.

- **Jingzhou Chengnan Economic Development Zone** This was established in 1992 under the approval of local government. Three major industries include textile, petroleum and chemical processing, which account for 90% of output. The zone also enjoys a well-developed transportation network – only 6 km to the airport and 4 km to the railway station.
- **Wuhan East Lake High-Tech Development Zone (WELHTDZ)** This is a national level high-tech development zone. Optical-electronics, telecommunications and equipment manufacturing are the core industries, while software outsourcing and electronics are also encouraged. It is China's largest production center for optical-electronic products with key players like Changfei Fiber-optic Cables (the largest fiber-optic cable maker in China),

Fenghuo Telecommunications and Wuhan Research Institute of Post and Telecommunications (the largest research institute in optical telecommunications in China). Wuhan WELHTDZ also represents the development center for China's laser industry with key players such as HUST Technologies and Chutian Laser being based there. It is the smallest state-level development zone in Hubei but it has the largest industrial output among all the state-level development zones. Pillar industries in the zone include optoelectronics, IT, energy, environmental protection, software and biotechnology.

- **Wuhan Economic and Technological Development Zone (WETDZ)** This national level industrial zone was incorporated in 1993. Its current area is about 10–25 km^2 and it plans to expand to 25–50 km^2. Industries encouraged there include the automobile industry, electronics, food and beverage processing, pharmaceuticals and biotechnology.
- **Wuhan Export Processing Zone** This was established in 2000. It is located in WETDZ and planned to cover an area of 2.7 km^2. The first 0.7 km^2 has been launched.
- **Wuhan Optical Valley (Guanggu) Software Park** This is located in WELHTDZ where it is jointly developed by Dalian Software Park Co. Ltd. The planned area is 0.67 km^2 with a floor area of 600,000 m^2. The zone is 8.5 km from the 316 national highway and is 46.7 km from Wuhan Tianhe Airport.
- **Xiangyang New and Hi-Tech Industrial Development Zone** This is the largest state-level development zone in the province. Its pillar industries are the automobile and auto parts, high-technology and textiles industries. Its industrial output in 2006 reached ¥37.0 billion, accounting for 20.5% of the combined state-level development zones' output.

As of 2010 the top five companies were as follows:

1. Wuhan Iron & Steel Co (SHA: 600005) is a leading steelmaker. It posted ¥75.6 billion in revenues and ¥1.7 billion in net profits for 2010.
2. China Gezhouba Group Co (SHA: 600068) is an infrastructure and engineering contractor. It posted ¥36.58 billion in revenues and ¥1.38 billion in net profits for 2010.
3. Changjiang Securities Co (SHE: 000783) offers services in securities broking, securities underwriting, asset management, stock index futures and financial derivatives. It posted ¥35.77 billion in revenues and ¥3.2 billion in net profits for 2010.

4. SDIC Huajing Power Holdings Co (SHA: 600886) is engaged in investment, construction, operation and management of power plants. It posted ¥15.95 billion in revenues and ¥494.49 million in net profits for 2010.
5. Fiberhom Telecommunication Technology Co (SHA: 600498) is engaged in the manufacture and sale of communication equipment, and the provision of network solutions. It posted ¥5.68 billion in revenues and ¥377.36 million in net profits for 2010.

Indicators for the ease of doing business

A. Starting a business

Procedures: 13
Time (days): 36
Cost (% of provincial GRP per capita): 13.6

B. Registering property

Procedures: 9
Time (days): 60
Cost (% of property value): 6.2

C. Getting credit – creating and registering collateral

Time (days): 13
Cost (% of loan value): 3.3

D. Enforcing contracts

Time (days): 277
Cost (% of claim): 33.1

Further reading

Brown, Melissa J. (2001). "Ethnic classification and culture: The case of the Tujia in Hubei, China," *Asian Ethnicity*, vol. 2, issue 1, March, pp. 55–72.

Cai, Jiayuan (2006). *Hubei* (Panoramic China) (Chinese Edition). Beijing: Foreign Languages Press.

Hubei Academy of Social Sciences (2010). *The Annual Report of Social Economic Development in Hubei Province* (hubei jingji shehui fazhan niandu baogao, 2010). Wuhan: Hubei People Publishing House.

Li, Tieqiang (2009). *Land, Nation and Farmer: A Case Study of Land Tax Issue in Hubei* (tudi, guojia yu nongmin: jiyu hubei tianfu wenti de shizhengyanjiu). Beijing: People Publishing House.

Lü, Dongsheng (2011). *Accelerating the Transformation of Economic Development Pattern* (jiakuai zhuanbian jingji fazhan fangshi gailun). Wuhan: Hubei People Publishing House.

Qian, Jin, Jiang Congjin, Li Shuqing, Liu Shucheng (2009). *The Economic Development Report of Xincheng Town, Dawu County, Wuhan Province* (hubeisheng dawuxian xinchengzhen jingji fazhan diaoyan baogao). Beijing: China Social Science Publishing House.

Tang, Shangying, He Sheng, Song Shengbang (2011). *A Comparison of the Economic Development: Hubei and Other Five Provinces in the Central China* (hubei yu zhongbu wusheng jingji fazhan yanjiu). Beijing: China University of Geosciences Publishing House.

The Development Institute of Wuhan University (2008, ed.). *Hubei Development Report, 2008* (hubei fazhan yanjiu baogao, 2008). Wuhan: Wuhan University Publishing House.

Wang, Kan, Cheng Guoping, Cheng Binwu, et al. (2011). *The Studies of State-Owned Enterprise Reform model and Innovation in Hubei Province* (hubei guoqi gaige moshi yu chuangxin yanjiu). Beijing: Economic Management Publishing House.

Wang, Ximing, and Translated by Matthew A. Hale (2009). "Seniors' organizations in China's new rural reconstruction: Experiments in Hubei and Henan," *Inter-Asia Cultural Studies*, vol. 10, issue 1, March, pp. 138–153.

Wu, Handong (2005). *An Economic Analysis of Hubei Province* (hubei shengqing diaocha yu fenxi). Beijing: China Economic and Finance Publishing House.

Wu, Shaoxin, Xu Chuanhua (2006). *Financial Development, Financial Market, and Financial Security: The 2005 Research Project on the Institution of Financial Development and Financial Security* (jinrongfazhan, jinrongshichang, jinronganquan: hubei jingrong fazhan yu jinrong anquan yanjiu zhongxin 2005 niandu kexue yanjiu xiangmu). Beijing: China Economics and Finance Publishing House.

Xia, Chunping (2006). *The Studies of Overall Rural-Urban Management and Economic Development* (hubeisheng tongchou chengxiang jingji fazhan yanjiu). Beijing: China Agricultural Publishing House.

Xu, Chuanhua, et al. (2008). *The Harmonious Development of Hubei's Economy and Finance* (hubei jingji yu jinrong hexie fazhan yanjiu). Wuhan: Hubei People Publishing House.

Yang, Youwang, Shi Zhongchuan (2007). *The Research of Comprehensive Well-Off Society in Hubei Province* (hubeisheng quanmian jianshe xiaokang shehui renkou fazhan zhanlue yanjiu). Wuhan: Wuhan University Publishing House.

Yang, Yunyan, et al. (2011). *The South-North Water Diversion and Regional Sustainable Development in Hubei* (nanshuibeidiao yu hubei quyu kechixu fazhan). Wuhan: Wuhan University of Technology.

Yu, Guangming, Jing Feng, Yi Che, Xiaowei Lin, Limei Hu, Shan Yang (2010). "The identification and assessment of ecological risks for land consolidation based on the anticipation of ecosystem stabilization: A case study in Hubei Province, China," *Land Use Policy*, vol. 27, issue 2, April, pp. 293–303.

Zhao, Lingyun (1999). "Hubei: Rising abruptly over central China?" in Hendrischke, Hans (ed.), *The Political Economy of China's Provinces: Competitive and Comparative Advantage*. London and New York: Routledge, pp. 155–182.

Zhong, Xinqiao (2011). *The Research of Hubei Industry and County Economic Development* (hubei chanye yu xianyu jingji fazhan yanjiu). Wuhan: Hubei People Publishing House.

Hunan

Source: The author, based on a file from the Wikimedia Commons.

Table A   The administrative divisions of Hunan

Name	Administrative seat	Population
Changde PM	Wuling District	5,747,218
Changsha PM	Yuelu District	7,044,118
Chenzhou PM	Beihu District	4,581,778
Hengyang PM	Yanfeng District	7,141,462
Huaihua PM	Hecheng District	4,741,948
Loudi PM	Louxing District	3,785,627
Shaoyang PM	Shuangqing District	7,071,826
Xiangtan PM	Yuetang District	2,748,552
Xiangxi Tujia & Miao AP	Jishou	2,547,833
Yiyang PM	Heshan District	4,313,084
Yongzhou PM	Lengshuitan District	5,180,235
Yueyang PM	Yueyanglou District	5,477,911
Zhangjiajie PM	Yongding District	1,476,521
Zhuzhou PM	Tianyuan District	3,855,609

Notes: AP = autonomous prefecture; PM = prefectural level municipality. All data are as of 2010.

Quick facts

Official name: Hunan Province
Abbreviated name: Xiang
Land area: 211,800 km²
Population: 65,683,722
Population density: 316/km²
GRP per capita of 2010: ¥24,719
HDI of 2008: 0.781
Capital: Changsha
Government office address: Wuyi Zhonglu, Changsha
Tel: 0731–221–7781
Postcode: 410000
Website: www.hunan.gov.cn

Hunan is a province of the PRC. It is located to the south of the middle reaches of the Yangtze River and south of Lake Dongting. Its name means "south of the lake". The province borders Hubei Province to the north, Jiangxi Province to the east, Guangdong Province to the south, Guangxi Zhuang Autonomous Region to the southwest, Guizhou Province to the west and Chongqing Municipality to the northwest. It is sometimes called and officially abbreviated to "Xiang", after the Xiang River, which runs through the area.

Hunan is located on the south bank of the Yangtze River, about mid-way along its length. Shanghai lies 1,000 km away, Beijing 1,200 km away and Guangzhou 500 km away. It is situated between 109°–114° east longitude and 20°–30° north latitude. The east, south and west sides of the province are surrounded by mountains and hills, with the Wuling Mountains to the northwest, the Xuefeng Mountains to the west, the Nanling Mountains to the south and the Luoxiao Mountains to the east. The mountains and hills occupy more than 80% of the area and the plains comprise less than 20%. The land in the province generally slopes from the east, south and west toward the north in the shape of a horse's hoof. The majority of Hunan Province lies at altitudes between 100 m and 800 m.

Hunan is 667 km wide and 774 km long. As an inland province adjacent to coastal areas, it has an area of 211,800 km², 2.2% of the national total, ranking as the 11th largest in China. The 14 prefecture-level divisions of Hunan are subdivided into 122 county-level divisions (34 districts, 16 county-level cities, 65 counties and 7 autonomous counties). These are in turn divided into 2,587 township-level divisions (1,098 towns, 1,158 townships, 98 ethnic townships, 225 sub-districts and 8 district public offices).

The Xiangjiang, Zijiang, Yuanjiang and Lishui rivers converge on the Yangtze River at Lake Dongting in the north of Hunan. The center and northern parts are somewhat low and form a U-shaped basin, open in the north and with Lake Dongting as its center. Most of Hunan Province lies in the basins of four major tributaries of the Yangtze River. Lake Dongting is the largest lake in the province and the second largest freshwater lake of China. Due to the reclamation of land for agriculture, the lake has been subdivided into many smaller lakes, though there is now a trend to reverse some of the reclamation, which has damaged wetland habitats surrounding the lake.

Hunan Province has a humid continental and sub-tropical monsoon climate with average annual sunshine of 1,300–1,800 hours. The annual average temperature is 16–18 °C (average 3–8 °C in January and 27–30 °C in July), with a frost-free period of 260–310 days and mean annual precipitation of 1,200–1,700 mm. Its climate has three characteristics. First, it has abundant sunshine, heat and water resources, and they reach their peak synchronously. During the period from April to October, the total radiation is 70–76% of the whole year, and rainfall accounts for 68–84% of the total. Second, there are distinct seasons, with cold winters and hot summers. The temperature always changes in spring and then declines abruptly in autumn. There is much rainfall in spring and summer, with drought every autumn and winter. Third, areas with an abruptly changeable climate are surrounded by mountains in three directions, especially in the mountainous regions in west and south Hunan.

The province has an extensive water system. Dongting Lake in northern Hunan, the second largest freshwater lake in China, has an area of 2,691 km². It takes the waters of the Xiangjiang, Zishui, Yuanjiang and Lishui rivers (a total waterway length of 2,200 km in Hunan, with nearly 5,000 tributaries) from the southwest and then flows into the Yangtze River at Chenglingji.

The region has rich mineral reserves. A land and geological survey conducted within the province in 2005 found 11 new mines with six minerals having proven reserves. The lead and zinc deposits amounted to 64,100 tons and the coal deposits to 6.54 million tons. The reserves of tungsten, antimony, zinc and bauxite are among the largest in China. Other major mineral deposits include lead, tin, barite and graphite. Because of this the province has often been called "the country of non-ferrous metals" and "the country of non-metal minerals". The Lengshuijiang area is noted for its stibnite mines and is one of the major centers of antimony extraction in the country.

The province's traditional crops are rice and cotton. The Lake Dongting area is an important center of ramie production, and Hunan is also an important center for tea cultivation. Aside from agricultural products, in recent years it has grown to become an important center for steel, machinery and electronics, especially as China's manufacturing sector moves away from coastal areas such as the Guangdong and Zhejiang provinces.

Incomplete statistics show that Hunan has 70 kinds of mammals, 310 kinds of birds, and over 160 kinds of fish. It has 44 rare and state-protected species, of which 18 are under Class A protection, such as the white-flag dolphin and the south China tiger, and 19 are under Class B protection, such as the macaque and the short-tail monkey. By the end of 2005 the province had set up 92 nature reserves to ensure protection for 1.1 million ha.

The region offers many beautiful landscapes and numerous historic sites. It now has over 20,000 cultural remains, including 22 national-level key protection units and 211 provincial-level key protection units. There are 4 state-class natural reserves, 22 provincial-class natural reserves and 21 national forest parks. The total area of nature reserves is 7,260 km², which is 3.43% of the province's total area.

Hunan Province has developed 43 scenic areas. There are 3 national-level key scenic areas covering Mount Hengshan, WulingYuan, Yueyang Tower, Dongting Lake and Shaoshan, and 27 provincial-class scenic areas. WulingYuan tourist area (including Zhangjiajie, Suoxi Valley,

Tianzi Mountain and Mengdong River), with its unique limestone caves, brooks, hot springs, ancient trees and rare animals, has been placed by UNESCO on the World Natural Heritage Site list. Mount Hengshan is the famous sacred mountain of Buddhism and a summer resort. Yueyang Tower is also well known at home and abroad for its long history, folklore and grand architecture. Changsha, the provincial capital, is a historic and cultural city. Tourist sites there include Han Dynasty Tombs at Mawangdui, Yuelu Hill, Loving Youth Pavilion (Aiwanting), Orange Isle (Juzizhou) and Yuelu Academy of Classical Learning.

Located in southern China, the province is traditionally a rice and cotton grower in China but machinery, steel, tobacco, food processing and electronics are now also major contributors to its economy. As manufacturing industries begin moving from coastal provinces like Guangdong and Zhejiang to inland China, Hunan is a desirable destination due to its low wages, low real-estate costs and one of the largest populations of migrant workers.

Hunan Province had a nominal GRP of ¥1.60 trillion (about US$234.9 billion) in 2010. Its per capita GRP is ¥20,226 (about US$2,961). Thanks to its fertile soil, the output of major farm and sideline products occupies a leading position in China. It has the highest output of rice and the second highest output of ramie in China. The output of rapeseed, cured tobacco and freshwater fish is also among the top five in the country.

Table B   Demographic and socioeconomic profile: Hunan

Indicator	2000	2010
Population (thousands)	64,400	65,701
Illiteracy rate of population aged 15 or over (%)	4.65	2.67
GRP (¥ billions)	369.19	1,603.80
Composition of GRP (%)		
Primary sector	21.3	14.5
Secondary sector	39.6	45.8
Tertiary sector	39.1	39.7
Fixed asset investment (¥ billions)	101.22	966.36
Status of foreign-funded enterprises		
Number of registered enterprises	2,316	5,410
Total investment (US$ millions)	7,306	32,406
Registered capital (US$ millions)	4,338	16,111
Foreign trade (US$ millions)		
Export	1,632	8,578
Import	1,360	7,031
Sales of consumer goods (¥ billions)	136	584

Table B (Continued)

Indicator	2000	2010
Per capita annual disposable income of urban residents (¥)	6,218.73	16,565.70
Engle's coefficient (%)	37.24	36.55
Per capita annual net income of rural residents (¥)	2,197.16	5,621.96
Engle's coefficient (%)	40.21	48.44
Number of patent applications granted	2,555	13,873
Inventions	197	1,920
Utility models	1,759	7,861
Designs	599	4,092

Note: All monetary values are measured at current prices.
Source: *Hunan Statistical Yearbook*, 2001 and 2011.

Metallurgy, equipment manufacturing and tobacco manufacturing are the three pillar industries of the region. After many years of development, metallurgy is the top industry. This has an optimized structure and is strongly competitive. At present, fine products with high value-add and high technology are the focus of the industry. Major companies include the Valin Steel Group Corp, the Lengshuijiang Steel Group Corp and the Hunan Nonferrous Metals Holding Group Corp.

In recent years the region has also focused on several categories of products in the equipment manufacturing industry. These are primarily engineering machinery (the province has the second largest base in China), electrical appliances, automobiles and rail transportation equipment. The Sany Group Corp, the Tebian Electric Apparatus Stock Company, the Chang Feng Group Corp and the CSR Zhuzhou Electric Locomotive Works are the top players in these fields. Hunan's tobacco industry ranks second in the nation and its brand competitiveness ranks first.

The province's major import sources are Japan, Australia, Germany, the US and South Korea while key export destinations include Hong Kong, the US, Japan, South Korea and the Netherlands. Its major export products are rolled steel, textiles, manganese, clothing and fireworks, and major import products are iron ore, rolled steel, machine tool, paper pulp and liquid pumps.

Several dozens of the world's top 500 enterprises have invested in Hunan, including Pepsi, NEC, Hutchison Whampoa, Mitsubishi and Time Warner. Hong Kong is the largest investor, making up half of the province's FDI sources. Its investment has further accelerated since the Closer Economic Partnership Arrangement was implemented in 2004.

Other noteworthy FDI sources are Taiwan, the US and the Virgin Islands. In terms of sectors, industry has received the most FDI at 61.0%, while agriculture accounts for only 2.8%. The service sector has also received a fairly substantial portion of FDI, making up 36.2% of the total.

As of 2010, compared with those of other provinces, "construction", "public management and social organization" and "health, social security and social welfare" were relatively strong, while "agriculture, forestry, animal husbandry and fishery", "services to households and other services", "mining" and "leasing and business services" were relatively weak sectors (see Table C).

Table C   Hunan's comparative (dis)advantage index by sector, 2010

Sector	Index
Agriculture, forestry, animal husbandry and fishery	0.36
Mining	0.70
Manufacturing	0.75
Production and distribution of electricity, gas and water	1.01
Construction	1.54
Transport, storage and post	0.86
Information transmission, computer service and software	0.79
Wholesale and retail trades	0.78
Hotels and catering services	1.12
Financial intermediation	1.02
Real estate	1.18
Leasing and business services	0.70
Scientific research, technical services and geological prospecting	0.74
Management of water conservancy, environment and public facilities	1.02
Services to households and other services	0.64
Education	1.14
Health, social security and social welfare	1.27
Culture, sports and entertainment	0.90
Public management and social organization	1.41

Notes: All the sectors included in this table are determined according to China's official definitions and for urban areas only. Numerals greater than, equal to and less than 1 indicate that the province's sectors have advantages, no apparent (dis)advantages and disadvantages, respectively.
Sources: Calculated by author based on *China Statistical Yearbook*, 2011. See Appendix for a detailed methodological description.

Hunan Province has four major development zones. These are described below.

- **Changsha National Economic and Technical Development Zone**
  This was founded in 1992 and is located east of Changsha. The planned area is 38.6 km^2 and the current area is 14 km^2. Nearby

are national highways G319 and G107 as well as Jingzhu Highway. In addition the zone is close to downtown and the railway station. The distance between the zone and the airport is 8 km. Changsha also has a river port with an annual throughput of 40,000 TEUs. Major industries there include high-tech industry, biology project technology and new material industry. With an average annual growth of 40%, its industrial production value and its import and export values account for one-third and half of those of Changsha City, respectively. Its overall investment environment ranks second among all the national development zones in central and west China.

- **Changsha National New and Hi-Tech Industrial Development Zone** This is divided into four parks. More than 400 enterprises have invested there. It is 28 km from the airport, 10 km from the train station and 10 km from the river port.
- **Chenzhou Export Processing Zone** Approved by the State Council, this was established in 2005 and is the only export processing zone in the province. The scheduled production area covers 3 km². Its industrial strategy is to concentrate on developing export-oriented hi-tech industries, including electronic information, precision machinery and new-type materials. The zone has good infrastructure and the enterprises there enjoy preferential policies of tax-exemption, tax-guarantee and tax-refunding. By the end of 2010 the zone had achieved a total export and import volume of over US$1 billion and provided more than 50,000 jobs. It aims to be one of the first-class export processing zones in China.
- **Zhuzhou National New and Hi-Tech Industrial Development Zone** This was founded in 1992. Its total planned area is 35 km². It is very close to national highway G320. Its major industries include biotechnology, food processing and heavy industry. In 2007 it signed a cooperation contract with Beijing Automobile Industry, one of the largest auto makers in China, which plans to set up a manufacturing base there.

As of 2010 the top five companies were as follows:

1. Sany Heavy Industry Co (SHA: 600031) is an engineering machinery and accessories maker. It posted ¥33.95 billion in revenues and ¥5.62 billion in net profits for 2010.
2. Changsha Zoomlion Heavy Industry Co (SHE: 000157) is a producer and leaser of heavy industrial equipment. It posted ¥32.19 billion in revenues and ¥4.67 billion in net profits for 2010.

3. Hunan AVA Holdings Co (SHE: 000918) is a property developer and restaurant operator. It posted ¥9.18 billion in revenues and ¥1.12 billion in net profits for 2010.
4. Hunan Valin Steel Co (SHE: 000932) is a steel and non-ferrous metal smelter. It posted ¥60.6 billion in revenues and ¥2.64 billion in net losses for 2010.
5. AVIC Aeroengine Controls Co (SHE: 000738) is an aeroengine control system manufacturer. It posted ¥1.51 billion in revenues and ¥169.06 million in net profits for 2010.

Indicators for the ease of doing business

A. Starting a business

Procedures: 14
Time (days): 42
Cost (% of provincial GRP per capita): 14.6

B. Registering property

Procedures: 10
Time (days): 53
Cost (% of property value): 6.9

C. Getting credit – creating and registering collateral

Time (days): 20
Cost (% of loan value): 3.7

D. Enforcing contracts

Time (days): 382
Cost (% of claim): 26.6

Further reading

Chen, Xiaohong, Yu Cao, Fuqiang Wang (2010). "A life cycle analysis of Hunan's enterprises and their determinants," *China Economic Review*, vol. 21, issue 3, September, pp. 470–481.
Grosvenor, W. Clayton (1928). "The province of Hunan: Some characteristics and peculiarities," *Scottish Geographical Magazine*, vol. 44, issue 3, May, pp. 144–150.
Huang, Yao, et al. (2008). *The Social and Economic Development of Yuanling County, Hunan Province* (hunan yuanlingxian shehui jingji fazhan yanjiu baogao). Beijing: Economics and Science Publishing House.
Li, Kangyang, Chen Xiaohong (2008). *The Development Road of Zhejiang and the Rise of Hunan* (zhejaing fazhan zhilu yu hunan jueqi) Changsha: Hunan Normal University Publishing House.

Ljungwall, Christer (2004). "Guangdong: A catalyst for economic growth and exports in Hunan Province," *Journal of Chinese Economic and Business Studies*, vol. 2, issue 3, September, pp. 249–265.

Sue, Duncan, Huang Youyi, Sun Lei (2006). *Hunan – Home of Chinese Celebrities* (Panoramic China), Beijing: Foreign Language Press.

Tian, Jinxia, Yu Yong, Jiang Hongying (2008). *The Ethnic Cultural and Tourism Development in the Northeast Hunan Area* (xiangxibei shaoshuminzu wenhua yu lüyou fazhan yanjiu). Changsha: Hunan University Publishing House.

Wang, Haiyan (2002). "Assessment and prediction of overall environmental quality of Zhuzhou City, Hunan Province, China," *Journal of Environmental Management*, vol. 66, issue 3, November, pp. 329–340.

Zeng, Saifeng, Cao Youpeng (2009). *An Economic History of Hunan in the ROC Era* (hunan minguo jingjishiliao xuankan). Changsha: Hunan People Publishing House.

Zhang, Ping (2009). *Changsha-Zhuzhou-Xiangtan Cities: Two Social Model Construction and the Low-Carbon Economic Development* (changzhutan chengshiqun fazhan baogao, 2009: "liangxing shehui" jianshe yu fazhan ditan jingji). Beijing: Social Science Reference Publishing House.

Zhang, Yanchun (2009). *The Studies of Financial Policy in Hunan's Circular Economic Development* (hunan xunhuan jingji fazhan de caizheng zhengce yanjiu). Changsha: Hunan University Publishing House.

Zheng, Yangwen (2007). "Hunan: Laboratory of reform and land of revolution: Hunanese in the Making of Modern China," *Modern Asian Studies*, vol. 42, issue 6, September, pp. 1113–1136.

Zhong, Yunxiang (2008). *Circular Economy and the Transformation of Economic Development Model* (xunhuan jingji yu hunan jingji fazhan fangshi zhuanbian yanjiu). Changsha: Hunan University Publishing House.

Zhu, Shanli, Liang Hongfei (2008). *Labour Transfer and Economic Development: A Study of Migrant Worker Model in You County, Hunan Province* (laodongli zhanyi yu jingji fazhan: hunansheng youxian waichu wugong moushi yanjiu). Beijing: Economics and Science Publishing House.

Zhu, Youzhi, Guo Yong (2011). *Let the World Enter into Hunan and Hunan Go to the World: Promote Newly Industrialization in Hunan* (rang shjie zouxiang hunan rang hunan zouxiang shijie: hunan tuijin xinxing gongyehua huimou). Changsha: Hunan People Publishing House.

Zhu, Youzhi, Ou Yanghuang, Luo Boyang (2007). *Hunan Economic and Social Development Report, 2006* (hunan jingji shehui fazhan baogao, 2006). Changsha: Hunan People Publishing House.

Zhu, Youzhi, Zhou Xiaomao, He Peiyu (2009). *Overtaking around the Curve: Opportunities and Challenges of the Leap Development in Hunan* (wandao chaoche: hunan kuayueshi fazhan de jiyu he tiaozhan). Changsha: Hunan People Publishing House.

Inner Mongolia

Source: The author, based on a file from the Wikimedia Commons.

Table A   The administrative divisions of Inner Mongolia

Name	Administrative seat	Population
Alxa PL	Alxa Left Banner	231,334
Baotou PM	Kundulun District	2,650,364
Bayannur PM	Linhe District	1,669,915
Chifeng PM	Hongshan District	4,341,245
Hinggan PL	Ulanhot	1,613,250
Hohhot PM	Huimin District	2,866,615
Hulunbuir PM	Hailar District	2,549,278
Ordos PM	Dongsheng District	1,940,653
Tongliao PM	Horqin District	3,139,153
Ulanqab PM	Jining District	2,143,590
Wuhai PM	Haibowan District	532,902
Xilingol PL	Xilinhot	1,028,022

Notes: PL = prefectural level league; PM = prefectural level municipality. All data are as of 2010.

Quick facts

Official name: Inner Mongolia Autonomous Region
Abbreviated name: Meng
Land area: 1,183,000 km^2
Population: 24,706,321
Population density: 20/km^2
GRP per capita of 2010: ¥47,347
HDI of 2008: 0.803
Capital: Hohhot
Government office address: 1 Xinhua Dajie, Hohhot City
Tel: 0471–694–4404
Postcode: 010055
Website: www.nmg.gov.cn

Inner Mongolia (also officially called Nei Mongol) is an autonomous region of the PRC, located in the northern frontier of the country. It lies along the northern border of China, neighboring Heilongjiang, Liaoning, Jilin, Hebei, Shanxi, Shaanxi and Gansu provinces and Ningxia Hui Autonomous Region to the east, south and west, as well as Russia and Mongolia to the north. The region is a long, narrow strip of land sloping from north to south, spanning 2,400 km from west to east and 1,700 km from north to south.

The region was established in 1947 on the area of the former provinces of Suiyuan, Chahar, Rehe, Liaobei and Xing'an, all of which were established during the period of the Republic of China. It is the third largest subdivision of China and covers about 12% of the country's total land area. The majority of its population are Han Chinese, with a substantial Mongol minority. The official languages are Chinese and Mongolian, the latter written in Mongolian script as opposed to the Mongolian Cyrillic alphabet used in the state of Mongolia.

The region is divided into 12 prefecture-level divisions. Until the late 1990s, most of these were known as leagues (*meng* in Chinese), a usage retained from Mongol divisions of the Qing Dynasty (AD 1644–1911). Similarly, county-level divisions are often known as banners (*qi* in Chinese). The prefecture-level divisions are further subdivided into 101 county-level divisions, including 21 districts, 11 county-level cities, 17 counties, 49 banners and 3 autonomous banners. These are in turn divided into 1,425 township-level divisions, including 532 towns, 407 townships, 277 sumu, 18 ethnic townships, 1 ethnic sumu and 190 sub-districts.

Due to its elongated shape, Inner Mongolia experiences a variety of climates. Officially, most of the region is classified as either a cold arid or steppe regime. A small portion is classified as humid continental in the northeast, or subartic in the far north near Hulunbuir. Spring is warm and windy; summer is short and hot with many rainy days; autumn usually sees an early frost and plummeting temperature; and winter is long and bitter cold with frequent polar outbreaks and blizzards. Dangerous sand storms can occur between spring and autumn. The region has an annual precipitation of 100–500 mm, 80–150 frost-free days and around 2,700 hours of sunshine. The Greater Xing'an and the Yinshan mountains divide the regions into areas with different climates. That east of the Greater Xing'an Mountains and north of the Yinshan Mountains has a lower temperature and less precipitation than the area to the west.

More than 120 kinds of minerals of the world's 140 have been found in the region, 5 of which have the largest deposits in China and 65 of which rank among the top ten in the country. The reserves of rare-earth metals amount to 84.59 million tons, or 80% of the world's total and over 90% of the country's total. The proven deposits of coal are 224.75 billion tons, the second largest in the country. The region has large reserves of ferrous metals, non-ferrous metals, precious metals, industrial chemicals and non-metal minerals. It also has abundant oil and natural gas – 13 large oil and gas fields have been discovered with expected oil reserves of 2–3 billion tons and gas reserves of 1,000 billion m³. The minerals (excluding oil and natural gas) in the region have a potential value of ¥13,000 billion (about US$1,570 billion), accounting for 10% of the country's total volume and ranking as the third largest in the country.

Inner Mongolia has an abundance of resources, especially coal, cashmere, natural gas and rare-earth elements, and it has greater deposits of niobium, zirconium and beryllium than any other province-level region in China. It boasts almost one-quarter of the world's total coal reserves. However, due to its reliance on coal and energy resources, the province is susceptible to economic slowdowns and sluggish demand; additionally, its major industries are environmentally harmful and energy intensive. With the largest usable wind power capacity in China, there is potential for the development of new energy industries based on natural resources.

The region has 7.22 million ha of cultivated land (6.11% of the country's total), 86.67 million ha of grasslands (73.3% of the total) and 18.67 million ha of forests (15.8% of the total). With a continental monsoon climate, vast grassland plateaus with a flat surface and mountains along its fringe, the region is home to 362 species of birds, 117 species of animals and 2,351 species of plants.

The region is also rich in water, especially mineral water and springs with medicinal value. It has a total water area of 984,300 ha including 655,000 ha of freshwater, which accounts for 10.68% of the country's total freshwater area. Nearly 1,000 rivers flow through the area, 107 averaging a valley area of more than $1,000\,km^2$ each. Moreover, 1,000 lakes dot the region, 8 of them with an area of over $100\,km^2$ each. Inner Mongolia has water resources of 90.3 billion m^3, of which 67.5 billion is surface water.

Mongols are the second largest ethnic group. They include many diverse Mongolian-speaking groups, such as the Buryats and the Oirats. Many of the traditional nomadic Mongols have settled in permanent homes as their pastoral economy was collectivized during the Maoist Era. Other ethnic groups include the Daur, the Evenks, the Oroqen, the Hui, the Manchus and the Koreans.

Besides hills, plains, deserts, rivers and lakes, Inner Mongolia has plateau landforms, mostly over 1,000 m above sea level, including the Inner Mongolia Plateau, the second largest among the four major plateaus in the country. The region is rich in tourist attractions, including colorful ethnic culture, grassland scenery, the virgin forests in the Greater Xing'an Mountains, grand views along the Yellow River, the majestic Xiangsha Gulf, rivers, lakes and springs. It is home to the Mausoleum of Genghis Khan, the Zhaojun Tomb, the ancient Great Wall of China, Wudang Monastery at the bottom of the Yinshan Mountains,

Wuta Monastery, Bailing Temple and tomb murals dating back to the Eastern Han Dynasty (AD 25–220).

The nominal GRP of Inner Mongolia in 2010 was ¥1.16 trillion (about US$172.1 billion), with an average annual increase of 20% from the year 2003 onwards. Its per capita GRP reached ¥47,347 in 2010. The industrial sector contributes more than 50% of the total GRP, while the service and agricultural sectors contribute 36.1% and 9.4%, respectively. As with much of China, economic growth has led to a boom in construction, including new commercial development and large apartment complexes.

Table B   Demographic and socioeconomic profile: Inner Mongolia

Indicator	2000	2010
Population (thousands)	23,760	24,722
Illiteracy rate of population aged 15 or over (%)	9.12	4.07
GRP (¥ billions)	140.10	1,167.20
Composition of GRP (%)		
Primary sector	25.0	9.4
Secondary sector	39.7	54.6
Tertiary sector	35.3	36.1
Fixed asset investment (¥ billions)	42.36	892.65
Status of foreign-funded enterprises		
Number of registered enterprises	874	3,693
Total investment (US$ millions)	2,536	23,243
Registered capital (US$ millions)	1,718	12,240
Foreign trade (US$ millions)		
Export	1,114	4,357
Import	1,272	7,325
Sales of consumer goods (¥ billions)	48	338
Per capita annual disposable income of urban residents (¥)	5,129.05	17,698.15
Engle's coefficient (%)	41.14	36.52
Per capita annual net income of rural residents (¥)	2,038.21	5,529.59
Engle's coefficient (%)	28.85	37.55
Number of patent applications granted	775	2,096
Inventions	60	262
Utility models	530	1,276
Designs	185	558

Note: All monetary values are measured at current prices.
Source: *Inner Mongolia Statistical Yearbook*, 2001 and 2011.

Inner Mongolia has a strong agricultural industry. It is China's largest livestock producer, including cashmere, milk and meat. Farming of crops, such as wheat, takes precedence along the river valleys. In the more arid grasslands, herding of goats, sheep and other animals is a traditional method of subsistence. Forestry and hunting are important in the Greater Khingan ranges in the east. Reindeer herding is carried out in the Evenk Autonomous Banner. More recently, growing grapes and winemaking have become an economic factor in the Wuhai area.

The province's economic growth has surged as a result of coal and huge discoveries of other energy and metal resources. In the past, the exploitation and utilization of resources were rather inefficient, which resulted in poor returns from rich resources. Inner Mongolia is also an important coal production base. Industry in Inner Mongolia has grown up mainly around coal, power generation, forestry-related industries, and related industries. Well-known Inner Mongolian enterprises include ERDOS, Yili and Mengniu.

In addition to its large reserves of natural resources, Inner Mongolia has the largest usable wind power capacity in China (thanks to strong winds which develop in the province's grasslands). Some private companies have set up wind parks in areas such as Bailingmiao, Hutengliang and Zhouzi.

The pillar industries include metallurgy, coal mining and processing, food processing, equipment manufacturing, petrochemicals and chemicals, and energy, which make up more than 80% of the region's total gross output. The region has rich chromite ore and zinc reserves, both ranking the second largest in China. It is also rich in iron ore, with its reserves ranking the fourth largest in the country. The rich mineral resources contribute to the steady development of the region's metallurgy industry, which includes the production of steel and steel products, pig iron and ten major non-ferrous metals. Baotou Iron & Steel (Group) Co. Ltd, with total assets amounting to ¥29.5 billion, is the largest industrial enterprise in Inner Mongolia. Other major players in this sector include Inner Mongolia Baotou Steel Union Co. Ltd, Baotou Aluminum Industry Group, HongJun Aluminum and Power Co. Ltd, and East Hope Baotou Rare-Earth and Al Industry Co. Ltd.

Rich solar power and wind power resources, together with large coal reserves, make the region one of the key power suppliers for China's Northeast Power Grid, the Beijing–Tianjin–Tangshan Power Grid and China's neighbor, Mongolia. Many solar power plants, wind power plants and coal power plants are clustered in the region. The key players include Datang Tuoketuo Power Generation Company, Shenhua Group Zhungeer Energy Industry Co. Ltd and Yimin Huaneng Coal and Electricity Co. Ltd. Its coal reserves are the second largest in the country.

Similarly, the great variety of farming products and large amount of livestock contribute to the development of the food-processing industry in the region. Inner Mongolia is thus known as China's largest dairy product manufacturing base. In 2006 nearly 3.5 million tons of dairy products were produced in the region, 12.4% more than the previous year. Mengniu Milk Industry Group and Inner Mongolia Yili Industrial Group Co. Ltd, China's two leading milk product manufacturers, have established their headquarters there.

There have been hundreds of enterprises specializing in petrochemical and chemical products in Inner Mongolia. The most profitable industries include petroleum processing, raw chemical and chemical products, coke products and nuclear fuel processing. Leading enterprises in this sector include the Tianye Chemical Industry (Group) Co. Ltd, the Inner Mongolia Jinhe Industry Group and the Lan Tai Industrial Co. Ltd.

Major import goods include minerals, wood and wooden products, charcoal, cork and related products, straws, plaited products, baskets and wickerwork, chemicals and related products, and electronics. The main export goods include base metals and related products, textile materials and related products, chemicals and related products, electronic products, and vegetables, fruit and cereals. Major export destinations are Japan, the US, South Korea, Italy and Mongolia.

Most of the FDI has been channeled into manufacturing, energy, real estate and resident services and other services. The investments have mainly come from Hong Kong, Taiwan, Japan, the US and Australia.

As of 2010, compared with those of other provinces, "agriculture, forestry, animal husbandry and fishery", "services to households and other services", "management of water conservancy, environment and public facilities" and "mining" were relatively strong, while "real estate", "leasing and business services", "manufacturing" and "construction" were relatively weak sectors (see Table C).

Table C   Inner Mongolia's comparative (dis)advantage index by sector, 2010

Sector	Index
Agriculture, forestry, animal husbandry and fishery	3.72
Mining	1.72
Manufacturing	0.54
Production and distribution of electricity, gas and water	1.71
Construction	0.56
Transport, storage and post	1.35

Table C   (Continued)

Sector	Index
Information transmission, computer service and software	1.10
Wholesale and retail trades	0.66
Hotels and catering services	0.59
Financial intermediation	1.13
Real estate	0.38
Leasing and business services	0.48
Scientific research, technical services and geological prospecting	0.78
Management of water conservancy, environment and public facilities	1.74
Services to households and other services	1.78
Education	1.15
Health, social security and social welfare	1.02
Culture, sports and entertainment	1.33
Public management and social organization	1.29

Notes: All the sectors included in this table are determined according to China's official definitions and for urban areas only. Numerals greater than, equal to and less than 1 indicate that the province's sectors have advantages, no apparent (dis)advantages and disadvantages, respectively.
Sources: Calculated by author based on *China Statistical Yearbook*, 2011. See Appendix for a detailed methodological description.

There are 5 state-level and 37 provincial-level development zones in Inner Mongolia. The state-level development zones are Baotou Rare-Earth High-Tech Industrial Development Zone, Erenhot Border Economic Cooperative Area, Huhhot Economic and Technological Development Zone, Huhhot Export Processing Zone and Manzhouli Border Economic Cooperative Area. One of these is described below.

• **Huhhot Export Processing Zone** This was established on June 21, 2002 by the State Council, which is located in the west of the Hohhot, with a planning area of $2.2 \, \text{km}^2$. Industries encouraged in the export processing zone include electronics assembly and manufacturing, telecommunications equipment, garment and textiles production, trading and distribution, biotechnology/pharmaceuticals, food/beverage processing, instruments and industrial equipment production, medical equipment and supplies, shipping, warehousing, logistics and heavy industry.

As of 2010 the top five companies were as follows:

1. Inner Mongolia Baotou Steel Rare Earth (SHA: 600111) is a producer and distributor of refined, deep processed and new rare-earth

products. It posted ¥5.26 billion in revenues and ¥750.74 million in net profits for 2010.

2. Huolinhe Opencut Coal Industry Corp (SHE: 002128) is a coal miner, processor and distributor. It posted ¥5.67 billion in revenues and ¥1.46 billion in net profits for 2010.
3. Inner Mongolia Yili Industrial Group Co (SHA: 600887) is a producer and distributor of dairy products and mixed foodstuffs. It posted ¥29.67 billion in revenues and ¥777.2 million in net profits for 2010.
4. Inner Mongolia Baotou Steel Union Co (SHA: 600010) is a supplier of steel pipes, steel plates, steel profiles, steel wires, steel rods and steel billets. It posted ¥40.55 billion in revenues and ¥194.1 million in net profits for 2010.
5. Inner Mongolia Mengdian Huaneng Thermal Co (SHA: 600863) is an electric power and heat generator and distributor. It posted ¥6.74 billion in revenues and ¥653.67 million in net profits for 2010.

Indicators for the ease of doing business

A. Starting a business

Procedures: 14
Time (days): 45
Cost (% of provincial GRP per capita): 7.9

B. Registering property

Procedures: 11
Time (days): 47
Cost (% of property value): 4.6

C. Getting credit – creating and registering collateral

Time (days): 15
Cost (% of loan value): 3.3

D. Enforcing contracts

Time (days): 330
Cost (% of claim): 23.7

Further reading

Alessandro Casella (1968). "A visit to inner Mongolia," *Journal of the Royal Central Asian Society*, vol. 55, issue 2, June, pp. 152–157.
Bijoor, N., W.J. Li, Q. Zhang, G. Huang (2006). "Small-scale co-management for the sustainable use of Xilingol Biosphere Reserve, Inner Mongolia," *AMBIO*, vol. 35, pp. 25–29.

Chen, Jun, Daming Huang, Masae Shiyomi, Yoshimichi Hori, Yasuo Yamamura, Yiruhan (2007). "Spatial heterogeneity and diversity of vegetation at the landscape level in inner Mongolia, China, with special reference to water resources," *Landscape and Urban Planning*, vol. 82, issue 4, 17 October, pp. 222–232.

Clark II, Woodrow W., William Isherwood (2010). "Report on energy strategies for inner Mongolia autonomous region," *Utilities Policy*, vol. 18, issue 1, March, pp. 3–10.

Clark II, Woodrow W., William Isherwood (2010). "Inner Mongolia must 'Leapfrog' the energy mistakes of the Western Developed Nations," *Utilities Policy*, vol. 18, issue 1, March, pp. 29–45.

Dickinson, Debbie, Michael Webber (2007). "Environmental resettlement and development, on the Steppes of Inner Mongolia, PRC," *Journal of Development Studies*, vol. 43, issue 3, April, pp. 537–561.

Fernandez-Gimenez, M.E. (1999). "Reconsidering the role of absentee herd owners: A view from Mongolia," *Human Ecology*, vol. 27, issue 1, pp. 1–27.

Fernandez-Gimenez, M.E (2002). "Spatial and social boundaries and the paradox of pastoral land tenure: A case study from postsocialist Mongolia," *Human Ecology*, vol. 30, issue 1, pp. 49–78.

Fish, M.Steven (2001). "The inner Asian anomaly: Mongolia's democratization in comparative perspective," *Communist and Post-Communist Studies*, vol. 34, issue 3, September, pp. 323–338.

Foreign Languages Press (2005, ed.). *Inter Mongolia* (Panoramic China) (Chinese Edition). Beijing: Foreign Languages Press.

Hong Jiang (2006). "Decentralization, ecological construction, and the environment in post-reform China: Case study from Uxin Banner, Inner Mongolia," *World Development*, vol. 34, issue 11, November, pp. 1907–1921.

Jiang, Hong (2005). "Grassland management and views of nature in China since 1949: Regional policies and local changes in Uxin Ju, inner Mongolia," *Geoforum*, vol. 36, issue 5, September, pp. 641–653.

Kwan, Calvin Lee (2010). "The inner Mongolia autonomous region: A major role in China's renewable energy future," *Utilities Policy*, vol. 18, issue 1, March, pp. 46–52.

Li, W.J., S. Ali, Q. Zhang (2007). "Property rights and grassland degradation: A study of the Xilingol Pasture, Inner Mongolia, China," *Journal of Environmental Management*, vol. 85, issue 2, October, pp. 461–470.

Li, Wenjun, Lynn Huntsinger (2011). "China's grassland contract policy and its impacts on herder ability to benefit in inner Mongolia: Tragic feedbacks," *Ecology and Society*, vol. 16, issue 2. Available at http://www.ecologyandsociety.org/vol16/iss2/art1/.

Sneath, D. (2000). *Changing Inner Mongolia: Pastoral Mongolian Society and the Chinese State*. New York: Oxford University Press.

Taylor, J.L. (2006). "Negotiating the grassland: The policy of pasture enclosures and contested resource use in inner Mongolia," *Human Organization*, vol. 65, issue 4, pp. 374–386.

Wang, Zhi-Ping, Xing-Guo Han, Ling-Hao Li (2008). "Effects of grassland conversion to croplands on soil organic carbon in the temperate inner Mongolia," *Journal of Environmental Management*, vol. 86, issue 3, February, pp. 529–534.

Williams, D.M. (2002). *Beyond Great Walls: Environment, Identity and Development on the Chinese Grasslands of Inner Mongolia.* Palo Alto, CA: Stanford University Press.

Wilske, Burkhard, et al. (2009). "Poplar plantation has the potential to alter the water balance in semiarid inner Mongolia," *Journal of Environmental Management*, vol. 90, issue 8, June, pp. 2762–2770.

Xie, Y., W.J. Li (2008). "Why do herders insist on otor? Maintaining mobility in inner Mongolia," *Nomadic Peoples*, vol. 12, issue 2, pp. 35–52.

Zhang, L.X., Z.F. Yang, G.Q. Chen (2007). "Energy analysis of cropping–grazing system in inner Mongolia autonomous region, China," *Energy Policy*, vol. 35, issue 7, July, pp. 3843–3855.

Zhang, Q., W.J. Li (2009). "Hierarchical framework for rangeland management: A case study in inner Mongolia," *Journal of Arid Lands Studies*, vol. 19, issue 1, pp. 81–84.

Jiangsu

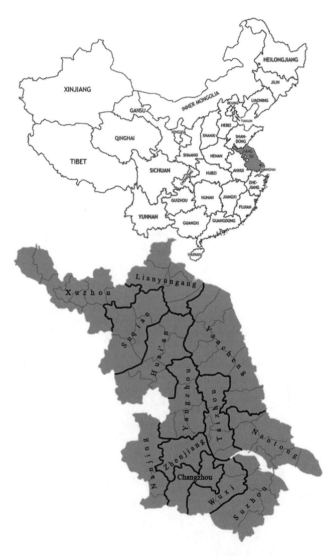

Source: The author, based on a file from the Wikimedia Commons.

Table A   The administrative divisions of Jiangsu

Name	Administrative seat	Population
Changzhou PM	Zhonglou District	4,591,972
Huai'an PM	Qinghe District	4,799,889
Lianyungang PM	Xinpu District	4,393,914
Nanjing SPM	Xuanwu District	8,004,680
Nantong PM	Chongchuan District	7,282,835
Suqian PM	Sucheng District	4,715,553
Suzhou PM	Jinchang District	10,465,994
Taizhou PM	Hailing District	4,618,558
Wuxi PM	Chong'an District	6,372,624
Xuzhou PM	Yunlong District	8,580,500
Yancheng PM	Tinghu District	7,260,240
Yangzhou PM	Guangling District	4,459,760
Zhenjiang PM	Jingkou District	3,113,384

Notes: PM = prefectural level municipality; SPM = sub-provincial level municipality. Data are as of 2010.

Quick facts

Official name: Jiangsu Province
Abbreviated name: Su
Land area: 102,600 km^2
Population: 78,659,903
Population density: 767/km^2
GRP per capita of 2010: ¥52,840
HDI of 2008: 0.837
Capital: Nanjing
Government office address: 70 West Beijing Road, Nanjing City
Postcode: 210013
Website: www.jiangsu.gov.cn

Jiangsu is a province of the PRC, located along the east coast of the country. It lies at the center of China's east coast. It borders Shandong Province to the north, Anhui Province to the west, and Zhejiang Province and Shanghai Municipality to the south. It has a coastline of over 1,000 km along the Yellow Sea, and the Yangtze River passes through its southern parts. The name "Jiangsu" comes from Jiang, which is short for the city of Jiangning (now called Nanjing), and Su, short for the city of Suzhou. The abbreviation for this province is "Su", the second character of its name.

Although there is no official definition of the boundary, the province is divided into Su Nan (or southern Jiangsu) and Su Bei (or northern Jiangsu). The Yangtze River lies along the line that roughly divides the two regions. The cities of Nanjing, Zhenjiang, Suzhou, Wuxi, Changzhou, Yangzhou, Taizhou and Nantong (the province's economic hub) lie within the Su Nan region and the cities of Xuzhou, Lianyungang, Huaiyin, Xiancheng and Shuqian lie within Su Bei.

The region comprises mainly plains, abundant rivers and numerous lakes. The Yangtze River cuts through the province in the south before flowing into the East China Sea. The 13 prefecture-level divisions of Jiangsu are subdivided into 106 county-level divisions (54 districts, 27 county-level cities and 25 counties). These are in turn divided into 1,488 township-level divisions (1,078 towns, 122 townships, 1 ethnic township and 287 sub-districts).

Located in a transit belt from the sub-tropics to a warm temperate zone, Jiangsu features a distinctive monsoon climate. Generally speaking, the area south of the Huaihe River and the Northern Jiangsu General Irrigation Canal enjoys a sub-tropical humid monsoon climate, while the area to the north enjoys a warm temperate humid monsoon climate. It is warm with moderate rainfall and clear-cut seasons in the province. The annual average temperature is 13–16 °C, with temperatures at an average of −2 to 4 °C in January and 26–30 °C in July. The annual rainfall is 724–1,210 mm. The rainfall in summer accounts for 50% of the annual rainfall. The province has clear-cut seasonals.

Jiangsu is very flat and low-lying, with plains covering 68% of its area and waters another 18%. It is located in the fertile land of the Yangtze River Delta. Most of its land is flat. On its southwestern and northern borders are hilly lands. Jiangsu also borders the Yellow Sea. The main cash crops are cotton, soybeans, peanuts, rape, sesame, ambary hemp and tea. Other products include peppermint, spearmint, bamboo, medicinal herbs, apples, pears, peaches, loquats and ginkgo. Silkworms also form an important part of Jiangsu's agriculture, with the Lake Taihu region to the south a major base of silk production.

Jiangsu Province boasts a network of rivers and lakes. The Yangtze River, China's longest river, runs over 400 km through the province from west to east while the Beijing–Hangzhou Grand Canal runs 690 km from north to south, traversing all the east–west river systems. There is the Qinhuai River in its southwest and the Northern Jiangsu General Irrigation Canal, Xinmu River and Nantong–Yanzhou Canal in the north. The province also boasts more than 290 lakes, including the third and fourth largest freshwater lakes in China, Lake Taihu and Lake Hongze.

Jiangsu has abundant aquatic resources. The area of fish farms in the east coast reaches 154,000 km². The four most notable farms, including Lusi and Haizhou Bay, teem with yellow croaker, cutlass fish, butterfish, shrimps, crabs, shellfish and algae. The province is also the major producer of freshwater crabs and eel fry. The inland waters within the province cover a total area of 1.73 million ha.

Jiangsu has a wide distribution and rich variety of mineral resources. The number discovered so far is 120. Major energy resources include coal, petroleum and natural gas. Non-metallic resources include sulfur, phosphorus, sodium salt, crystal, cyanite, sapphire, diamond, kaolin, limestone, quartz sand, marble and pottery clay. The metallic resources include copper, lead, zinc, silver, gold, strontium and manganese. The province is particularly rich in clay, building materials, chemical raw materials, metallurgic auxiliary materials, minerals for special uses and non-ferrous metals.

The province originated in the 17th century with the splitting of the defunct and erroneously named Jiangnan Province ("south of the river") into Jiangsu and Anhui. Before then the northern and southern parts of Jiangsu had less connection with each other than they later did. Traditionally, South Jiangsu is referred to as the three more prosperous southern cities: Suzhou, Wuxi and Changzhou. Their culture (the "Jiangnan" culture shared with Shanghai and Zhejiang) is often referred to as the Wu. All the other parts of the province are dominated by the so-called Jianghuai culture, which means the culture in the area between the Yangtze River (Jiang) and the Huaihe River (Huai), though not all of them lie within the district defined by the term.

Jiangsu has a long history of a relatively developed economy and culture. Rich in landscape gardens, scenic attractions and historical sites, it is noted for having the largest number of historical cities in the country. Such cities include Nanjing, Suzhou, Yangzhou, Zhenjiang, Changshu, Xuzhou and Huai'an. There are 20 scenic spots, 23 forest parks, 6 holiday resorts and 416 cultural heritage sites under state- and provincial-level protection. Classical gardens in Suzhou have been added to the World Cultural Heritage Site list by UNESCO.

In 2010, Jiangsu's nominal GRP was ¥4.14 trillion (about US$612 billion), making it the second largest GRP of all the provinces after Guangdong Province. Its per capita GRP was ¥52,448 (about US$7,945). Since the inception of economic reforms in 1978, Jiangsu has been a hot spot for economic development and it now has the highest GRP per capita of all Chinese provinces. The wealth divide between the rich southern and the poor northern regions, however, remains a prominent issue there. Cities like Nanjing, Suzhou and Wuxi have GRP per capita around twice the provincial average, making south Jiangsu one of the most prosperous regions in China.

Table B   Demographic and socioeconomic profile: Jiangsu

Indicator	2000	2010
Population (thousands)	74,380	78,693
Illiteracy rate of population aged 15 or over (%)	6.31	3.81
GRP (¥ billions)	858.27	4,142.55
Composition of GRP (%)		
Primary sector	12.0	6.1
Secondary sector	51.7	52.5
Tertiary sector	36.3	41.4
Fixed asset investment (¥ billions)	257.00	2,318.43
Status of foreign-funded enterprises		
Number of registered enterprises	18,060	51,666
Total investment (US$ millions)	75,004	508,106
Registered capital (US$ millions)	40,657	273,899
Foreign trade (US$ millions)		
Export	26,377	281,449
Import	22,817	217,334
Sales of consumer goods (¥ billions)	260	1,361
Per capita annual disposable income of urban residents (¥)	6,800.23	22,944.26
Engle's coefficient (%)	43.04	39.51
Per capita annual net income of rural residents (¥)	3,595.09	9,118.24
Engle's coefficient (%)	33.09	38.08
Number of patent applications granted	6,432	138,382
Inventions	341	7,210
Utility models	4,095	41,161
Designs	1,996	90,011

Note: All monetary values are measured at current prices.
Source: *Jiangsu Statistical Yearbook*, 2001 and 2011.

The agricultural sector is based on rice, wheat, peanuts and cotton. Although the province has some petro-carbon deposits, more significant deposits include rock salt, sulfur, phosphorus and marble.

The region is historically oriented toward light industries, such as textiles and food. Since 1949 it has also developed heavy industries, such as chemicals and construction materials. Its important industries include machinery, electronics, chemicals and automobiles. Recently, government has worked hard to promote the solar industry. Economic reform and the opening-up policies of China have greatly benefited the southern cities, especially Suzhou and Wuxi, which outstrip the provincial capital Nanjing in total output. In the eastern outskirts of Suzhou, Singapore has built the Suzhou Industrial Park, a flagship of Sino-Singapore cooperation and the only industrial park in China that is in its entirety the investment of a single foreign country.

Jiangsu is known for its "Su'nan" (or southern Jiangsu) Model, which developed many booming collective and township enterprises in the 1980s and 1990s. These are government-funded enterprises that were set up by rural farmers and the remaining workforce after the government made appeals for them to do so. They started to prosper as a result of reforms carried out by government. Until the mid-1990s, the township enterprises were a fast-growing sector and were the main contributors to the economy. Today, however they are slowly losing their importance as industrial parks bring in large revenues from Chinese state and foreign investors.

The north lags behind the south of Jiangsu. The three main reasons for this are the underdeveloped transportation system of the north, its immature industries and its immense distance from Shanghai compared with the south. Also, in the past, northern Jiangsu was frequently affected by heavy floods from the Hai River. The uneven development of economies on either side of the Yangtze River poses an issue for the continued sustainability of the province as a whole.

The pillar industries in Jiangsu are electronics, chemicals, textiles, metallurgy, electrical equipment manufacturing and general purpose equipment manufacturing. Electronics is the leading industry. The region also has a well-established industry cluster which has set up various types of production models, such as export-oriented (in Jintan), market-oriented (in Changshu) and brand-oriented (in Ganjiang). Most of the electronic enterprises in Jiangsu are jointly set up by Chinese and foreign companies. Major investors include Philips Semiconductor, Hejian Technology (Suzhou), Infineon, Samsung, Hitachi Display, Sumitomo Bakelite and Seagate. Moreover, Jiangsu has developed a number of famous domestic brands, such as Bosideng Corp, Jiangsu AB Group, Hongdou Group and Jiangsu Sunshine Group.

The chemical industry is another important sector. Major producers include Nanjing Jinling Chemical Plant, Lianyungang Taisheng Chemical, Yancheng City Longgang Perfume Chemical Factory and Yangzhou Aokang Chemical. It should be noted that Nanjing Jinling Chemical is one of the largest PVC plastic stabilizer producers in China. In 2000, BASF, the largest chemical producer in the world, and Sinopec (a Chinese petroleum giant) jointly set up an integrated petrochemical site in Nanjing. The core business is the supply of steam crackers to nine world-scale downstream plants, and the production of chemicals and polymers for the domestic market.

The province is a leading textile and garment production base in China. It is also a major export market for textiles and garments. In recent years the rapid growth of the Yangtze River Delta has gradually threatened Guangdong's leading position in the industry. This growth is partially due to the fact that the delta has more available land and a larger labor supply from less developed neighboring provinces, such as Anhui and Jiangxi.

Jiangsu Province has strong trade ties with more than 200 countries and regions. Its foreign trade ranks second in China (after Guangdong Province). Foreign-invested enterprises are the main contributors to the area's exports, followed by private enterprises. Major export destinations include the EU, the US and Japan, while the import regions are Taiwan, Japan and Korea. To a great extent the rapid growth of the economy is the result of surging foreign investment in the province. In 2003, Jiangsu displaced Guangdong as the largest FDI recipient. Since then it has remained at the top position.

As of 2010, compared with those of other provinces, "manufacturing" was relatively strong, while "services to households and other services", "mining", "agriculture, forestry, animal husbandry and fishery" and "real estate" were relatively weak sectors (see Table C).

Table C   Jiangsu's comparative (dis)advantage index by sector, 2010

Sector	Index
Agriculture, forestry, animal husbandry and fishery	0.45
Mining	0.38
Manufacturing	1.58
Production and distribution of electricity, gas and water	0.71
Construction	0.71
Transport, storage and post	0.85
Information transmission, computer service and software	0.80
Wholesale and retail trades	0.93
Hotels and catering services	0.87
Financial intermediation	0.98
Real estate	0.59
Leasing and business services	0.66
Scientific research, technical services and geological prospecting	0.63
Management of water conservancy, environment and public facilities	0.96

Services to households and other services	0.30
Education	0.92
Health, social security and social welfare	0.98
Culture, sports and entertainment	0.74
Public management and social organization	0.75

Notes: All the sectors included in this table are determined according to China's official definitions and for urban areas only. Numerals greater than, equal to and less than 1 indicate that the province's sectors have advantages, no apparent (dis)advantages and disadvantages, respectively.
Sources: Calculated by author based on *China Statistical Yearbook*, 2011. See Appendix for a detailed methodological description.

Jiangsu has had more than 20 state-level economic and technology development zones and high-tech parks, and 1 free trade zone. Selected examples are described below.

- **Changzhou National Hi-Tech District** This is a state-level high-tech industrial development zone. It is located in the northern part of Changzhou city. With a population of 500,000 and an area of 439 km², it is 160 km from Shanghai to the east and 110 km from Nanjing to the west. It represents the highest-level and most sophisticated industrial park in Changzhou, and more than 1,300 foreign companies and over 5,000 local industrial enterprises have been registered there. Among these investments, around 40% are from Europe and the US. Industries encouraged include engineering machinery, transformer and transmission equipment, automotive, locomotive and its components, parts, precision machinery, biotechnology/pharmaceuticals, photovoltaics (PV) and new materials, chemicals, garment and textile production, computer software and R&D. Some major investors include Terex, Komatsu, Ashland Chemical, Johnson, Caltex Oil Corp, Disa, +GF+, Rieter and General Electronics.
- **Kunshan Economic and Technological Development Zone (KETDZ)** Established in 1985, this is situated to the east of Kunshan City, 50 km to the west of Shanghai and 37 km east of Suzhou. It is 45 km from Shanghai Hongqiao Airport and 100 km from Shanghai Pudong Airport. Fuelled by foreign investment, the zone has been enjoying robust growth for the past ten years. Taiwanese companies have invested in about 65% of enterprises in Kunshan. There are many reasons for the zone's success. The most obvious is its geographic location – specifically, its proximity to Shanghai. Moreover, its main competitive advantage lies in its pro-business environment and the encouraging attitude of the local authorities.

The electronic and information industries are the largest contributors to the zone's growth.

- **Kunshan Export Processing Zone** This was established in April 2000 upon approval from state government. It is located in KETDZ and has a planned area of 2.86 km². In the zone there are electronic information, optical, precision machinery industry and bonded logistics industry clusters. It enjoys convenient transportation, being located 45 km from Shanghai Pudong Airport and 60 km from Shanghai Port.
- **Nanjing Economic and Technological Development Zone** Established in 1992, this is a national-level zone surrounded by convenient transportation network. Nanjing is the capital of Jiangsu Province. Situated in the downstream of the Yangtze River Drainage Basin and the Yangtze River Delta Economic Zone, Nanjing has always been a national center of commerce, education, research, transportation and tourism in the east China region, preceded only by Shanghai. It is only 20 km from Nanjing Port and 40 km from Nanjing Lukou Airport. It is well equipped with basic facilities such as electricity, water, communication, gas and steam. It has formed four specialized industries: electronic information, bio-pharmaceutical, machinery and new materials.
- **Nanjing New and High-Tech Industry Development Zone** this was founded jointly by Jiangsu Provincial People's Government and Nanjing Municipal Government, and its construction began on September 1, 1988. It was established as a national high-tech industry development zone by the State Council on March 6, 1991. The zone is next to national highways 104 and 312. Its pillar industries include electronic information, bio-engineering and pharmaceuticals.
- **Nantong Economic and Technological Development Area (NETDA)** Established in 1984, this was one of the first state-level development zones approved by central government and it has been certified as an ISO14000 National Demonstration Zone. It benefits from superior transportation facilities by both rail and road. The zone has direct links to two railways – the Xinyi–Changxing Railway and the Nanjing–Qidong Railway. The Su-Tong Yangtze River Bridge feeds into the center and connects the Nanjing–Nantong and Yancheng–Nantong expressways to the north, and Shanghai–Nanjiang and Suzhou–Jiaxing–Hangzhou expressways and Riverside Expressways to the south.
- **Suzhou Industrial Park** This is a high-profile bilateral cooperative project between the governments of China and Singapore. Established in 1994, it is 80 km from Shanghai Hongqiao Airport and

120 km from Shanghai Pudong Airport. The Shanghai Port is an important transportation hub for the park as 70% of goods produced in there are imported or exported via this port. It has adapted Singapore's experience in urban planning, trade promotion, human resource management and other fields. Today the concept of the park has become the model for others in China.

- **Suzhou Industrial Park Export Processing Zone** This was approved by government in April 2000 with a planning area of 2.9 km². It is located in Suzhou Industrial Park, which was set up by China and Singapore. Inside the export processing zone the infrastructure is of a high standard. With the information platform and electronic methods, customs declaration and all other procedures can be handled on line. Investors benefit from many preferential policies.
- **Suzhou Hi-Tech Industrial Development Zone** This was established in 1990. In November 1992 it was approved as the national-level hi-tech industrial zone. By the end of 2007, foreign-invested companies had total registered capital of US$13 billion, of which US$6.8 billion was paid in. The zone now hosts more than 1,500 foreign companies. Some 40 Fortune 500 companies set up 67 projects in the district.
- **Wuxi New District** Since it was established in 1992, this has evolved into one of the major industrial parks in China. A variety of components, sub-systems and original equipment are made in the district. Approximately 1,200 enterprises had been registered there by the end of 2008. It provides strong support for international manufacturing operations. It is focussing on the formation of the five pillar industries of electronic information, precision machinery and mechanical and electrical integration, bio-pharmaceuticals, fine chemicals and new materials.

As of 2010 the top five companies were as follows:

1. Suning Appliance Co (SHE: 002024) is China's largest electronics and household appliances retailer. It posted ¥75.5 billion in revenues and ¥4.01 billion in net profits for 2010.
2. Huatai Securities Co (SHA: 601688) is engaged in investment banking, brokerage and asset management. It posted ¥8.9 billion in revenues and ¥3.43 billion in net profits for 2010.
3. Jiangsu Yanghe Brewery JSC Ltd (SHE: 002304) is liquor producer. It posted ¥7.62 billion in revenues and ¥2.2 billion in net profits for 2010.

4. Jiangsu Expressway Co (SHA: 600377) is engaged in investment, construction, operation and management of the Jiangsu section of the Shanghai–Nanjing Expressway and other toll roads within Jiangsu. It posted ¥6.76 billion in revenues and ¥2.48 billion in net profits for 2010.
5. Sinopec Yizheng Chemical Fibre Co (SHA: 600871) is a manufacturer and distributor of polyester chips and polyester fibers. It posted ¥16.35 billion in revenues and ¥1.23 billion in net profits for 2010.

Indicators for the ease of doing business

A. Starting a business
Procedures: 12
Time (days): 31
Cost (% of provincial GRP per capita): 5.8

B. Registering property
Procedures: 7
Time (days): 31
Cost (% of property value): 4.6

C. Getting credit – creating and registering collateral
Time (days): 10
Cost (% of loan value): 2.1

D. Enforcing contracts
Time (days): 112
Cost (% of claim): 13.6

Further reading

Ash, Robert (2006). "The high tide in Jiangsu: A perspective from local sources of the time," *The China Quarterly*, vol. 187, September, pp. 743–753.

Dennis, Yehua Wei, C. Cindy Fan (2000). "Regional inequality in China: A case study of Jiangsu Province," *The Professional Geographer*, vol. 52, issue 3, August, pp. 455–469.

Gu, Shan (2006). *Jiangsu, Water Town Journeys* (Panoramic China). Beijing: Foreign Languages Press.

Hendrischke, Hans (2003). "How local are local enterprises? Privatisation and translocality of small firms in Zhejiang and Jiangsu," *Provincial China*, vol. 8, issue 1, April, pp. 27–39.

Huang, Yefang (2002). "Decomposition of regional inequalities in Jiangsu since 1978," *Asian Geographer*, vol. 21, issue 1–2, January, pp. 145–158.

Jacobs, J. Bruce (1999). "Uneven development: Prosperity and poverty in Jiangsu," in Hendrischke, Hans (ed.), *The Political Economy of China's Provinces: Competitive and Comparative Advantage*. London and New York: Routledge, pp. 113–154.

Liang, Sai, Tianzhu Zhang (2011). "What is driving CO2 emissions in a typical manufacturing center of South China? The case of Jiangsu Province," *Energy Policy*, vol. 39, issue 11, November, pp. 7078–7083.

Liu, Y.S., J.Y. Wang, H.L. Long (2010). "Analysis of arable land loss and its impact on rural sustainability in southern Jiangsu Province of China," *Journal of Environmental Management*, vol. 91, issue 3, January–February, pp. 646–653.

Liu, Yunhua, Chew Soon Beng, Li Wenzhi (1998). "Education, experience and productivity of labor in China's township and village enterprises: The case of Jiangsu Province," *China Economic Review*, vol. 9, issue 1, Spring, pp. 47–58.

Long, Guoying, Mee Kam Ng (2001). "The political economy of intra-provincial disparities in post-reform China: A case study of Jiangsu Province," *Geoforum*, vol. 32, issue 2, May, pp. 215–234.

Lu, Zhiji (1987). "A quantitative method of dialect subgrouping: The case of dialects in Jiangsu and Shanghai," *Language Sciences*, vol. 9, issue 2, October, pp. 217–229.

Schoolman, Ethan D., Chunbo Ma (2012). "Migration, class and environmental inequality: Exposure to pollution in China's Jiangsu Province," *Ecological Economics*, vol. 75, March, pp. 140–151.

Shen, Xiaoping, Laurence J.C. Ma (2005). "Privatization of rural industry and de facto urbanization from below in southern Jiangsu, China," *Geoforum*, vol. 36, issue 6, November, pp. 761–777.

Shi, Zulin, Bi Liangliang (2007). "Trans-jurisdictional river basin water pollution management and cooperation in China: Case study of Jiangsu/Zhejiang Province in Comparative Global Context," *China Population, Resources and Environment*, vol. 17, issue 3, May, pp. 3–9.

Sun, Yifei, Hongyang Wang (2005a). "Does internet access matter for rural industry? A case study of Jiangsu, China," *Journal of Rural Studies*, vol. 21, issue 2, April, pp. 247–258.

Sun, Yifei, Hongyang Wanf (2005b). "Does Innovation Matter for Export in China's Rural Enterprises? Empirical Evidence from Jiangsu," *Asian Geographer*, vol. 24, issue 1–2, January, pp. 1–15.

Veeck,Gregory, Clifton W. Pannell (1989). "Rural economic restructuring and farm household income in Jiangsu, People's Republic of China," *Annals of the Association of American Geographers*, vol. 79, issue 2, June, pp. 275–292.

Wang, Longmian, Zheng Zheng, Xingzhang Luo, Jibiao Zhang (2010). "The current pollution status and control technology of the Taihu Lake Basin, Jiangsu Province, China," *International Journal of Environmental Studies*, vol. 67, issue 2, April, pp. 195–205.

Wang, Xiaohua, Zhenmin Feng (2003). "Energy consumption with sustainable development in developing country: A case in Jiangsu, China," *Energy Policy*, vol. 31, issue 15, December, pp. 1679–1684.

Wei, Y.D., S. Kim (2002). "Widening inter-county inequality in Jiangsu Province, China, 1950–95," *Journal of Development Studies*, vol. 38, issue 6, August, pp. 142–164.

Zhang, Mingqiong, Chris Nyland, Cherrie Jiuhua Zhu (2010). "Hukou-based HRM in Contemporary China: The Case of Jiangsu and Shanghai," *Asia Pacific Business Review*, vol. 16, issue 3, July, pp. 377–393.

Zhao, Yuan, Li-Sha Hao, Yu-Ping Wang (2009). "Development strategies for wind power industry in Jiangsu Province, China: Based on the evaluation of resource capacity," *Energy Policy*, vol. 37, issue 5, May, pp. 1736–1744.

Zheng, Zhenzhen, Yong Cai, Wang Feng, Gu Baochang (2009). "Below-replacement fertility and childbearing intention in Jiangsu Province, China," *Asian Population Studies*, vol. 5, issue 3, November, pp. 329–347.

Jiangxi

Source: The author, based on a file from the Wikimedia Commons.

Table A   The administrative divisions of Jiangxi

Name	Administrative seat	Population
Fuzhou PM	Linchuan District	3,912,312
Ganzhou PM	Zhanggong District	8,368,440
Ji'an PM	Jizhou District	4,810,340
Jingdezhen PM	Zhushan District	1,587,477
Jiujiang PM	Xunyang District	4,728,763
Nanchang PM	Donghu District	5,042,565
Pingxiang PM	Anyuan District	1,854,510
Shangrao PM	Xinzhou District	6,579,714
Xinyu PM	Yushui District	1,138,873
Yichun PM	Yuanzhou District	5,419,575
Yingtan PM	Yuehu District	1,124,906

Notes: PM = prefectural level municipality. Data are as of 2010.

Quick facts

Official name: Jiangxi Province
Abbreviated name: Gan
Land area: 166,900 km^2
Population: 44,567,500
Population density: 264/km^2
GRP per capita of 2010: ¥21,253
HDI of 2008: 0.760
Capital: Nanchang
Government office address: 69 West Beijing Road, Nanchang City
Tel: 0791–622–4166/622–4110
Website: www.jiangxi.gov.cn

Jiangxi is a province of the PRC, situated in the middle and lower reaches of the Yangtze River. Spanning from the banks of the Yangtze River in the north into hillier areas in the south, and locked in on all sides by the neighboring provinces of China, Jiangxi Province shares a border with Anhui Province to the north, Zhejiang Province to the northeast, Fujian Province to the east, Guangdong Province to the south, Hunan Province to the west and Hubei Province to the northwest.

The name "Jiangxi" derives from the Jiangnan xidao (Western Jiangnan Lu – a provincial administration under the Tang Dynasty in AD 733). Jiangxi is also called "Gan" for short after the Gan River, which runs from the south to the north and flows into the Yangtze

River. The 11 prefecture-level divisions of Jiangxi are subdivided into 99 county-level divisions (19 districts, 10 county-level cities and 70 counties). These in turn are divided into 1,548 township-level divisions (770 towns, 651 townships, 7 ethnic townships and 120 sub-districts).

Mountains surround Jiangxi on three sides, with the Mufu Mountains, Jiuling Mountains and Luoxiao Mountains on the west; the Huaiyu Mountains and Wuyi Mountains on the east; and the Jiulian Mountains and Dayu Mountains in the south. The southern half of the province is hilly with ranges and valleys interspersed, while the northern half is flatter and lower in altitude. The highest point in Jiangxi is Mount Huanggang in the Wuyi Mountains, on the border with Fujian Province.

The Gan River dominates the province, flowing the entire length of the region from south to north. It enters Lake Poyang in the north, the largest freshwater lake of China, which in turn empties into the Yangtze River, which forms part of the northern border of Jiangxi. Important reservoirs include the Xiushui Tuolin Reservoir in the northwest on the Xiushui River and the Wan'an Reservoir in the upper section of the Gan River.

The topographies of Jiangxi are dominated by mountainous and hilly land, with mountains covering 36% of the province's total territory and hills 42%. The remaining 22% comprises plains and waters. Most of the mountains lie on the provincial borders. Mount Huaiyu in the northeast has the province's largest copper reserve; Wuyi Mountain, a World Cultural Heritage Site, lies in the east; the Dageng Ridge and Jiulian Mountain in the south are known as the "capital of tungsten"; in the west there is the Luoxiao Mountain; and in the northwest lie the mountains of Mufu and Jiuling.

The climate is sub-tropical. Jiangxi's annual average temperature is around 18 °C, with temperatures of 3–9 °C in January and 27–31 °C in July. Temperatures in the northeastern and northwestern areas and along the Yangtze River are lower, at 16–17 °C. Other parts of the province are warmer, with temperatures of 18–20 °C. Rainfall is plentiful. The average annual rainfall is 1,341–1,940 mm. It is greater in the southern, eastern and mountainous regions and less in the northern, western and basin areas. The average annual rainfall in the mountains of Wuyi, Huaiyu and Jiuling can be as high as 1,800–2,000 mm, while that of the area along the Yangtze River, the Poyang Lake and the Jitai Basin is 1,350–1,400 mm. Other parts of the province have average annual rainfall of 1,500–1,700 mm.

Like many other provinces in China, Jiangxi is rich in mineral deposits. In particular, it has huge reserves of copper, tungsten, lead, zinc and rock salt. It is also famous for local traditional products, such as China produced in Jingdezhen. Jiangxi has abundant mineral resources. Of the 150 known minerals, more than 140 have been found in Jiangxi. Among these, the deposits of 89 have been verified, with 33 of them ranking among the top five in the country. Ferrous metals include iron, manganese, titanium and vanadium. Among the 13 non-ferrous and precious metals are copper, lead, zinc, gold and silver. Noted centers of mining include Dexing (copper) and Dayu County (tungsten). There are also 29 rare and rare-earth minerals, such as niobium and tantalum. The province has developed the largest copper mine in Asia and its copper-smelting base is the largest in China.

The mountainous terrain and large forest coverage of Jiangxi has made it one of the wilder areas in central China. South China Tigers have been seen as recently as 15 or 20 years ago and projects are underway to document evidence of any that remain. Several mountain areas along the northern border with Hunan and Hubei are potential sites for "wilderness" preserves, specifically for protecting or even reintroducing tigers. Other wildlife, though not plentiful, are more numerous in Jiangxi than in many other developed areas of China. Numerous species of birds are common, especially around the marshes of Lake Poyang in the north. Though protected, mammals such as muntjak, wild boar, civet cats and pangolins are still common enough that they'll even occasionally be seen in markets for sale as game meat, or possibly even in a forest.

Some 59% of the territory is covered in forest. Its timber reserve amounts to 250 million m³, in addition to 1 billion plants of bamboo, both figures taking leading positions in the country. Most of the forests are natural secondary forests. Coniferous forests occupy a larger proportion, with pine and masson pine being the major species. Tea-oil tree, tung tree and Chinese tallow tree are the major economic species scattered across the province, which also boasts more than 4,000 species of seed plants, some 470 types of pteridophyte and over 100 types of bryophyte. Among the lower plants, the varieties of large fungus alone are as many as 500. There are more than 2,000 species of woody plants, including over 400 kinds of arbor. Jiangxi is also home to many ancient trees, such as ginkgo, known as the "living fossil" of plants.

The good ecological environment characterized by a rich water resource, changing topographies and wide coverage of vegetation ensures an abundance of wildlife. The 30 nature reserves cover a total area of 9,016 km², accounting for 5.4% of the province. Jiangxi now has over 600 kinds of vertebrates, including more than 170 species of fish, which account for 21.4% of the national total of freshwater fish.

There are more than 40 species of amphibians accounting for 20.4% of the national total; some 70 species of reptiles, accounting for 23.5%; 270 species of birds, accounting for 23.2%; and 50 species of mammals, accounting for 13.3%.

Jiangxi boasts more than 2,400 rivers and streams, some 160 of which, totaling 18,400 km in length, having water running all year round. Ganjiang, Fuhe, Xinjiang, Xiuhe and Raohe are the five largest rivers in the province. Jiangxi's total water reserve is 150.5 billion m³, with the per capita figure standing at 3,491 m³, which is 1,393 m³ more than the national average. Fish and birds have great economic value and therefore take priority for protection. Lake Poyang offers an ideal winter shelter for migratory birds.

Jiangxi has beautiful landscapes with green mountains and clear waters. It has 11 cultural relics under state protection and 2,406 of its scenic spots and tourism areas have been registered as major provincial projects. The key scenic spots include Mount Lushan, Jinggang Mountain, Longhu (dragon and tiger) Mountain, Sanqing Mountain, Poyang Lake and the cities of Nanchang and Jingdezhen. Near the northern port city of Jiujiang lies the well-known resort area of Mount Lushan – one of the 14 major international tourist routes in China. Also near the city are the Donglin (East Wood) Temple and the Tiefo (iron Buddha) Temple, two important Buddhist temples. Mount Lushan has been listed as a World Heritage Site by UNESCO and, together with Jinggang and Sanqing mountains, offers charming peaks and quiet valleys.

Guifeng Peak and Dragon Palace are noted for their precipitous cliffs and deep caves. The landscapes of Poyang Lake and Ganjiang River are attractive, while ancient temples at Longhu Mountain, Qingyuan and Donglin attract visitors with their unique religious architectures. Other attractions include Tengwang Tower, Bajing Terrace, the former residences of historical nobilities in Linchuan and Jiujiang, headquarters of the Red Army on Jinggang Mountain, the Memorial Museum of the Nanchang Uprising, and Ruijin, the first capital of the Communist administration in China.

The province is rather poor area compared with its neighbors. It is located near some of the richest provinces of China (Guangdong, Zhejiang, Fujian), which are sometimes blamed for taking away talents and capital from the area. Jiangxi has the lowest wages and third lowest property prices in China and, as a result of wages and labor, the economy sits at the low end of the value chain. As Guangdong and Zhejiang draw away skilled labor with higher wages, Jiangxi has been victim to a brain drain and finds itself trapped in a combination of low skill, low value-added, low innovation and low energy efficiency. Thus, without meaningful structural changes, its rich mineral resources may be at risk. The province plans to expand railways and develop new energy projects, including nuclear.

Table B   Demographic and socioeconomic profile: Jiangxi

Indicator	2000	2010
Population (thousands)	41,400	44,622
Illiteracy rate of population aged 15 or over (%)	5.16	3.13
GRP (¥ billion)	200.31	945.13
Composition of GRP (%)		
Primary sector	24.2	12.8
Secondary sector	35.0	54.2
Tertiary sector	40.8	33.0
Fixed asset investment (¥ billion)	51.61	877.23
Status of foreign-funded enterprises		
Number of registered enterprises	2,246	7,574
Total investment (US$ millions)	6,876	43,917
Registered capital (US$ millions)	3,301	28,136
Foreign trade (US$ millions)		
Export	1,188	11,807
Import	864	9,146
Sales of consumer goods (¥ billions)	70	296
Per capita annual disposable income of urban residents (¥)	5,103.58	15,481.12
Engle's coefficient (%)	39.36	32.26
Per capita annual net income of rural residents (¥)	2,135.30	5,788.56
Engle's coefficient (%)	39.82	46.34
Number of patent applications granted	1,072	4,349
Inventions	67	411
Utility models	690	2,588
Designs	315	1,350

Note: All monetary values are measured at current prices.
Source: *Jiangxi Statistical Yearbook*, 2001 and 2011.

Jiangxi's consumer market lags behind that of other provinces, ranking 21st in terms of retail sales of consumer goods. Most of the goods consumed are food, clothing and household articles. Its major consumer centers are located in Nanchang, Jiujiang and Jingdezhen.

The province is a major producer of rice, freshwater products, timber and bamboo. Rich in minerals, its reserves of copper, gold, silver and rare earths are among the largest in the country. As such, metal-related mining, smelting and pressing dominate its secondary industry. Jiangxi has the lowest average wage and third lowest property prices in China, allowing the province to lure manufacturing from its neighbors, Guangdong and Zhejiang provinces. While agriculture lags behind industry and services, it is one of the third largest rice-producing provinces in China in terms of output. In addition, its output of freshwater fish is among the highest. Cash crops commonly grown include cotton and rapeseed. Jiangxi is the leading producer of kumquats in China, particularly in Suichuan County.

The region's pillar industries are in metallurgy, chemicals, food processing, automobiles, electrical appliances and pharmaceuticals. The metallurgy industry has grown rapidly in terms of output volume and revenue. Metals processed include iron, steel and copper. Home to the biggest copper mine in Asia (located in Dexing), the province is a major source of copper for most copper companies. Key players in this industry are Jiangxi Copper Corp and Xinyu Iron & Steel Corp. Starting in the 1960s, automobile manufacturing there is focussed on the development of light and compact cars. Most of the automobile technologies are introduced from outside the province owing to its limited R&D capability. Famous companies in the automobile industry are Jiangling Motors Corp and Jiangxi Changhe Motor Corp.

Another key industry is in electrical appliance manufacturing. Appliances made there are mainly digital audiovisual products and home air-conditioners. AUX (Nanchang) Corp is one of the key manufacturers of air-conditioners. The food-processing industry is also growing in the province.

Jiangxi's pharmaceutical industry concentrates on the development of Chinese medicine. It has a high concentration of industrial groups, such as Huiren Group and Jiangzhong Medical Corp. As for the chemical industry, this focuses on the development of petrochemicals, silicone and dry cement. A major company in this industry is Jiujiang Petrochemical Corp.

Major export products include clothing, mechanical and electrical products, rolled steel, textiles and copper, while major import products include mechanical and electrical products, copper ore, hi-tech products, iron ore and copper. A substantial share of trade has been conducted with the US and Japan. The US is the province's fifth largest import source as well as the top export destination, while Japan is the province's third largest import source and export destination. Other key trading partners are Chile, Taiwan, Australia, Hong Kong, the Netherlands and South Korea. While Hong Kong may not be a key source of imports, it is the main source of FDI for Jiangxi. The US, Taiwan, Singapore and Japan are the other key sources.

As of 2010, compared with those of other provinces, "agriculture, forestry, animal husbandry and fishery", "production and distribution of electricity, gas and water", "public management and social organization" and "education" were relatively strong, while "Hotels and catering services", "services to households and other services", "leasing and business services" and "real estate" were relatively weak sectors (see Table C).

Table C   Jiangxi's comparative (dis)advantage index by sector, 2010

Sector	Index
Agriculture, forestry, animal husbandry and fishery	1.41
Mining	0.70
Manufacturing	0.86
Production and distribution of electricity, gas and water	1.34
Construction	1.02
Transport, storage and post	1.06
Information transmission, computer service and software	0.78
Wholesale and retail trades	0.65
Hotels and catering services	0.34
Financial intermediation	0.98
Real estate	0.44
Leasing and business services	0.41
Scientific research, technical services and geological prospecting	0.76
Management of water conservancy, environment and public facilities	1.12
Services to households and other services	0.37
Education	1.32
Health, social security and social welfare	1.16
Culture, sports and entertainment	1.06
Public management and social organization	1.34

Notes: All the sectors included in this table are determined according to China's official definitions and for urban areas only. Numerals greater than, equal to and less than 1 indicate that the province's sectors have advantages, no apparent (dis)advantages and disadvantages, respectively.
Sources: Calculated by author based on *China Statistical Yearbook*, 2011. See Appendix for a detailed methodological description.

Major development zones in Jiangxi are Jiangxi Province Economic and Technological Development Zone, Nanchang Export Processing Zone, Nanchang National Hi-Tech Industrial Development Zone and Nanchang Economic and Technological Development Zone. Some examples are described in the following page.

- **Nanchang National Export Processing Zone** Located within the Nanchang National Hi-Tech Industrial Development Zone, this was approved by the State Council on May 8, 2006, and passed the national acceptance inspection on September 7, 2007. It has a planning area of 1 km². It enjoys simple and convenient customs clearances and special preferential policies.
- **Nanchang National High-Tech Industrial Development Zone** Established in March 1991, this is located 10 km from the nearest river port, 3 km from the train station and 25 km from the airport. It is the only national grade high-tech zone in Jiangxi. At present there are more than 200 foreign enterprises there, such as Microsoft, Kohler and ABB. The zone covers an area of 231 km², in which 32 km² have been completed. The zone has brought 25% industrial added value and 50% industrial benefit and tax to Nanchang City by using only 0.4% of the land area.
- **Nanchang Economic and Technological Development Zone** This has a land area of 118 km². Pillar industries there include the manufacturing of electrical appliances and automobiles, food processing and pharmaceuticals. It has good transport infrastructure, with an international container terminal, bonded warehouse center, international airport, freight terminal and transportation hubs of four highways linking the cities all over the country.

As of 2010 the top five companies were as follows:

1. Jiangxi Copper Co (SHA: 600362) is a leading copper producer. It posted ¥76.44 billion in revenues and ¥4.91 billion in net profits for 2010.
2. Jiangling Motors Corp (SHE: 000550) is a manufacturer of compact and light cars and spare parts. It posted ¥15.77 billion in revenues and ¥1.71 billion in net profits for 2010.
3. Jiangxi Hongdu Aviation Industry Co (SHA: 600316) is engaged in research, development, manufacture and distribution of aerospace products. It posted ¥1.72 billion in revenues and ¥146.19 million in net profits for 2010.
4. Telling Telecom Holding Co (SHE: 000829) is a manufacturer and repairer of communication products. It posted ¥20.88 billion in revenues and ¥310.72 million in net profits for 2010.
5. Jiangxi Ganyue Expressway Co (SHA: 600269) is engaged in construction, maintenance and operation of expressways, as well as toll collection. It posted ¥3.98 billion in revenues and ¥1.26 billion in net profits for 2010.

Indicators for the ease of doing business

A. Starting a business

Procedures: 14
Time (days): 46
Cost (% of provincial GRP per capita): 14.6

B. Registering property

Procedures: 10
Time (days): 50
Cost (% of property value): 6.1

C. Getting credit – creating and registering collateral

Time (days): 17
Cost (% of loan value): 5.9

D. Enforcing contracts

Time (days): 365
Cost (% of claim): 16.5

Further reading

Chen, Le, Nico Heerink, Marrit van den Berg (2006). "Energy consumption in rural China: A household model for three villages in Jiangxi Province," *Ecological Economics*, vol. 58, issue 2, 15 June, pp. 407–420.

Chen, Ronghua, Yu Boliu, Zou Gengsheng (2004). *An History of the Jiangxi Economy* (Jiangxi jingji shi). Nanning: Jiangxi People Publishing House.

Chen, Xinhua, Li Wanping (2004). *Economic World Thinking: A Case of Jiangxi's Economic Development* (jingji shijie sikaolu: yi jiangxi jingji fazhan weili). Beijing: Economic Management Publishing House.

Chi, Zexin, Zhu Shubin (2009). *Research Report of Rural Economic and Social Development in Jiangxi* (jiangxi nongcun jingji yu shehui fazhan yanjiu baogao). Beijing: China Agriculture Publishing House.

Feng, Chongyi (1999). "Jiangxi in reform: The fear of exclusion and the search of new identity," in Hendrischke, Hans (ed.), *The Political Economy of China's Provinces: Competitive and Comparative Advantage*. London and New York: Routledge, pp. 249–276.

Foreign Languages Press (2006, ed.). *Jiangxi, Cradle of Red China* (Panoramic China). Beijing: Foreign Languages Press.

Huang, Guoqin (2009). *The Developing Ecological Economy of Jiangxi Province* (fazhanzhong de jiangxi shengtai jingji). Beijing: China Environment Science Publishing House.

Huang, Guoqin (2010). *Exploring Jiangxi's Low-Carbon Economy* (tansuozhong de Jiangxi ditan jingji). Beijing: China Environment Science Publishing House.

Liu, Moyan (2006). *The Modern Change of Traditional Rural Economy: Theory and Case Studies of Jiangxi* (chuantong nongcun jingji de xiandai zhuanbian: lilun yu jiangxi shizheng yanjiu). Nanning: Jiangxi People Publishing House.

Luo, Laiwu, Wang Dehe (2004). *Regional Development and Institutional Innovation: Collected Papers of the First Jiangxi Development Conference* (diqufazhan yu zhidu chuangxin: shoujie jiangxi fazhan luntan weiji). Beijing: Economy and Science Publishing House.

Murphy, Rachel (2007). "Return migration, entrepreneurship and local state corporatism in rural China: The experience of two counties in South Jiangxi," *Journal of Contemporary China*, vol. 9, issue 24, pp. 231–247.

Rao, Aijing (2010). *A Study of Private High-Education in Less-Developed Regions: A Case of Jiangxi* (jingji qianfada diqu minban gaodeng jiaoyu yanjiu). Nanning: Jiangxi People Publishing House.

Shi, Xiaoping, Nico Heerink, Futian Qu (2007). "Choices between different off-farm employment sub-categories: An empirical analysis for Jiangxi Province, China," *China Economic Review*, vol. 18, issue 4, pp. 438–455.

Shi, Xiaoping, Nico Heerink, Futian Qu (2009). "The role of off-farm employment in the rural energy consumption transition – A village-level analysis in Jiangxi Province, China," *China Economic Review*, vol. 20, issue 2, June, pp. 350–359.

Shi, Xiaoping, Nico Heerink, Futian Qu (2011). "Does off-farm employment contribute to agriculture-based environmental pollution? New insights from a village-level analysis in Jiangxi Province, China," *China Economic Review*, vol. 22, issue 4, December, pp. 524–533.

Shuhao Tan, Nico Heerink, Gideon Kruseman, Futian Qu (2008). "Do fragmented landholdings have higher production costs? Evidence from rice farmers in northeastern Jiangxi Province, P.R. China," *China Economic Review*, vol. 19, issue 3, September, pp. 347–358.

Wang, Wanshan, Huang Jianjun (2008). *A Study of the Eco-Economic Zone in Lake Boyang* (boyanghu shengtai jingjiqu kaifangxing jingji yanjiu). Nanning: Jiangxi People Publishing House.

Wu, Chaoyang (2007). *The Organizational Analysis of Regional Economic Integration* (quyu jingji yitihua de zuzhi jingjixue fenxi). Beijing: Economic Management Publishing House.

Yang, Liqiong, Wang Zhenzhong, Wu Li, Liu Shucheng (2011). *The Rise of New Towns in the Revolution Old District: Economic and Social Development in Laicun Town, Ningdu County, Jiangxi Province* (queqizhong de geming laiqu xinzheng: jiangxisheng ningduxian laicunzhen jingji shehui fazhan diaoyan). Beijing: China Social Science Publishing House.

Yao, Mugen, Fu Xiuyan (2006). *The Analysis and the Forecast of Jiangxi's Economic Situation* (jingji lanpishu, 2006: jiangxi jingji xingshi fenxi yu yuce). Nanning: Jingxi People Publishing House.

Yi, Yongchun (2009). *Constructing Fengcheng: A Study of Social and Economic History in County-Level Area* (jianchufengcheng: xianyu shehui jingjishi gean yanjiu). Nanning: Jiangxi People Publishing House.

Yin, Jidong, et al. (2002). *The Strategy of Jiangxi Development in Central-Western Area* (jiangxi zhongxibu diqu jueqi fanglue). Nanning: Jiangxi People Publishing House.

Zheng, Keqiang (2009). *The New Theory of Industrial Structure Evolution in Less-Developed Area: A Case Study in Jiangxi* (fazhanzhong diqu chanye jiegou fuwuhua yanjin xinlun: Jiangxi fazhan xiandai fuwuye wenti yanjiu). Beijing: Social Science Reference Publishing House.

Zhou, Shaosen, Wang Jiannong (2003). *The Rise of Jiangxi: A Comparison of Economic and Social Developments in Six Central Provinces* (zailun jiangxi jueqi: zhongbu diqu liusheng jingji shehui fazhan taishi bijiao). Nanning: Jiangxi People Publishing House.

Jilin

Source: The author, based on a file from the Wikimedia Commons.

Table A   The administrative divisions of Jilin

Name	Administrative seat	Population
Baicheng PM	Taobei District	2,033,058
Baishan PM	Badaojiang District	1,295,750
Changchun SPM	Chaoyang District	7,677,089
Jilin PM	Chuanying District	4,414,681
Liaoyuan PM	Longshan District	1,176,645
Siping PM	Tiexi District	3,386,325
Songyuan PM	Ningjiang District	2,881,082
Tonghua PM	Dongchang District	2,325,242
Yanbian Korean AP	Yanji	2,271,600

Notes: AP = autonomous prefecture; PM = prefectural level municipality; SPM = sub-provincial level municipality. All Data are as of 2010.

Quick facts

Official name: Jilin Province
Abbreviated name: Ji
Land area: 187,400 km^2
Population: 27,462,297
Population density: 145/km^2
GRP per capita of 2010: ¥31,599
HDI of 2008: 0.815
Capital: Changchun
Government office address: 11 Xinfa Road, Changchun City
Tel: 0431–891–9971
Website: www.jl.gov.cn

Jilin is a province of the PRC, located in the central area of northeast China. It borders Heilongjiang Province to the north, Liaoning Province to the south, Inner Mongolia Autonomous Region to the west, Russia to the east and North Korea to the southeast across the Tumen and the Yalu – two rivers serving as the boundary between China and North Korea.

The region is drained by various river systems, including the Yalu and Tumen rivers, tributaries of the Liao River along the southern border, and the Songhua and Nen rivers (both of the latter eventually flowing into the Amur). The literal meaning of the Chinese characters for "Jilin" is "auspicious forest". The name "Jilin" probably originates from "Girin Ula", a Manchu term meaning "along the river", which was then shortened to Jilin in Chinese.

The land is high in the southeast and low in the northwest, with a vast plain lying in its mid-west. The eastern part of the province includes the mountain area of the Changbai Mountains with an elevation of over 1,000 m and the Jidong hilly land of 500 m above sea level or lower. The western part of the province is the Songliao Plain, whose low and level western section is the grain base of the province.

Jilin is located in the middle latitudes of the northern hemisphere, east of the Euro-Asian continent, the northernmost section of the temperate zone in China, near the sub-frigid zone. The eastern part of the province is close to the Yellow Sea and the Sea of Japan, where the atmosphere is moist and often accompanied by much rain. The climate of its western part, which is far from the sea and approaches the arid Mongolian Plateau, is dry. As a whole, the area has a distinct temperate continental monsoon climate with four clear-cut seasons. The yearly average temperature of most parts is 3–5 °C. The annual precipitation is 550–910 mm and the frost-free period lasts 120–160 days (beginning in the last ten days of September and lasting until the end of April or early May). With hot and rainy days in the same season, it is good for farming.

There is an abundance of minerals, with a total of 136 varieties of ores discovered. The number of surveyed mineral deposits is 93, of which 75 have been explored. The reserves of 22 minerals rank as the top five in the country. The main minerals include coal, with a reserve of nearly 2.1 billion tons; petroleum, with a remaining potential reserve of 113.99 million tons; iron ores, with a reserve of 460 million tons; gold, with a reserve ranking 13th in the country; reserves of ten other minerals, such as oil shale, diatomite and wollastonite, ranking first; veneer gabbro and carbon dioxide gas, ranking second; molybdenum and germanium, ranking third; and the remaining potential reserve of petroleum, ranking sixth. Jilin is favored with non-metallic mineral products and most of its exports are crude non-metallic minerals and their products. The reserves of wollastonite, diatomite, bentonite and refractory clay are rich enough for mining. Those of petroleum, natural gas and coal are also abundant.

The province is one of China's six major forestry areas. The Changbai Mountains stretching about 500 km are known as the "Changbai Sea of Forest". Forests cover 7.98 million ha, accounting for 82.04% of the total land used for forestry, ranking eighth in the country. The province's storage of live limber is 840 million m^3, ranking sixth in the country. The province's forest coverage is 42.4%. Timber production by Jilin is ranked sixth in the nation. Trees of quality timber for industrial use include Korean pine, Changbai pine, yeddo spruce, northeast China ash, yellow pineapple, Manchurian walnut catalpa and linden. Chinese grapes, the fruit of Chinese magnolia vine, cowberry and haw are all used for brewing wine. There are 300 varieties of wild plants that provide a rich source for honey-making.

The prairie in western Jilin is situated in the center of the Songhuajiang-Nenjiang Prairie, one of the famous grasslands in China. It is known for its rich forage grasses for sheep, most of which are perennial rootstock and bushy grasses. It is also one of the breeding bases for commercial cattle and fine-wool sheep in northern China. There are 4.379 million ha of grassland available in the province, mainly in its western and eastern parts.

There is a rich wildlife in the area, particularly in the Changbai Mountains. Jilin is the original producer of the world-famous Three Northeast China Treasures – ginseng, marten fur and pilose antler. Its other products, such as glossy ganoderma, the tuber of elevated gastrodia, astragali, pine mushroom, hedgehog fungus and frog fat are all well known at home and abroad.

Jilin has an abundance of traditional Chinese medicinal resources, with approximately 27,000 kinds of wild plants and 9,000 kinds of medicinal herbs. Among its 437 species of wild animals, there are precious fur animals and feather fowls, such as sables, otters, lynx, Manchurian tigers, leopards and flowery-tail pheasants. Precious animals that can be used as medicinal materials include red deer, musk deer, brown bears, badgers, frogs and wood frogs. Animals of high economic value include wild boars, roe deer and grouse.

The province's soil is fertile and thus suitable for growing grains, beans, oil crops, beetroot, tobacco, jute, potato, ginseng, traditional Chinese medicinal herbs and fruits. It has 55,760 km² of arable land area, accounting for 4.3% of the nation's total arable land area. The arable land area per capita in Jilin is 134% higher than the country's average level. The province's sown area is 3.96 million ha. The Song-Liao Plain is an important grain base of the country and a well-known corn-growing zone. It has been called one of the "Golden Corn Belts" of the world. As the largest granary of China, the province's grain output accounts for 5.5% of the country's total output. It also produces soybeans, rice, maize and sorghum. Rice is mostly cultivated in the eastern parts, such as Yanbian Korean Prefecture. The region's per capita consumption of grain, the commodity rate of grain, the volume of grains shipped to other provinces and the export of corn have been the highest in the country for many years.

The province boasts rich tourism resources. In the provincial capital, Changchun, are the former government office of the Manchurian State, established by Japanese invaders during World War II, the Jingyuetan Forest Park, the Automobile Town and the Changchun Film Studio. The Changbaishan Nature Reserve covers a vast area in the three counties of Changbei, Antu and Fusong, and boasts scenic spots such as the Heavenly Pond, waterfalls, and groups of hot springs and grand canyons. The Goguryeo sites and tombs found in Ji'an and Jilin, including Wandu, Gungnae Fortress and the pyramidal General's Tomb, have been listed as World Heritage Sites by UNESCO. The Baekdu Mountain, especially Heaven Lake on the border with North Korea, is another popular tourist destination.

In 2010 the nominal GRP of Jilin Province totaled ¥866.76 billion (about US$120 billion). It has been rising at more than 10% since 2003.

Table B   Demographic and socioeconomic profile: Jilin

Indicator	2000	2010
Population (thousands)	27,280	27,466
Illiteracy rate of population aged 15 or over (%)	4.57	1.92
GRP (¥ billions)	182.12	866.76
Composition of GRP (%)		
Primary sector	21.9	12.1
Secondary sector	43.9	52.0
Tertiary sector	34.2	35.9
Fixed asset investment (¥ billions)	60.35	787.04
Status of foreign-funded enterprises		
Number of registered enterprises	2,747	4,309
Total investment (US$ millions)	7,661	22,259
Registered capital (US$ millions)	5,277	12,299
Foreign trade (US$ millions)		
Export	1,487	4,507
Import	1,498	12,517
Sales of consumer goods (¥ billions)	81	350
Per capita annual disposable income of urban residents (¥)	4,810.00	15,411.47
Engle's coefficient (%)	40.68	35.08
Per capita annual net income of rural residents (¥)	2,022.50	6,237.44
Engle's coefficient (%)	37.05	36.73
Number of patent applications granted	1,650	4,343
Inventions	154	785
Utility models	1,142	2,806
Designs	354	752

Note: All monetary values are measured at current prices.
Source: *Jilin Statistical Yearbook*, 2001 and 2011.

The Changbai Mountains are a key source of lumber. Herding of sheep is an important activity in the western parts, such as Baicheng. Traditionally, Jilin has been known as a major pharmaceutical center, with yields of ginseng and deer antlers among the largest in China, being used extensively in traditional Chinese medicine.

While agriculture still counts as one of Jilin's largest industries, since the reforms of the 1980s, the ever-expanding secondary and tertiary sectors have driven economic growth. A significant automobile industry as well as important petroleum and chemical industries continue to underpin the economy, and future sights are set on nurturing a high-tech industry centered on photoelectron products. Ongoing reforms to modernize traditional heavy industries increase the efficiency of state-owned enterprises and develop foreign trade aim to widen the province's economic achievements.

Industry is the leading contributor making up near a half of the GRP, followed by the service sector and agriculture. Jilin has four pillar industries: automobile manufacturing, petrochemicals, food processing and pharmaceuticals. The province was once the center of the nation's industrial base. First Auto Works, China's second largest carmaker after Shanghai Automotive Industry Corp, is the pioneer of the country's automobile industry. The petrochemical industry is the second pillar industry of Jilin. Since China's first petrochemical company, Jilin Petrochemical Corp, was founded in 1957, the petrochemical industry in this region has been the strongest in the nation due to its rich mineral resources, such as oil, oil shale and natural gas.

Benefitting from the advantages of rich agricultural resources, Jilin's food-processing industry has grown substantially in recent years. Three major categories have been formed: corn processing led by Dacheng Corp, meat processing led by the Aoyue Corp and mineral water processing led by Quanyang Corp. Jilin also has the largest biofuel project in China.

Jilin is China's primary base for modern Chinese traditional medicine. Today there are 317 pharmaceuticals manufacturers there. Tonghua Dongbao, Jilin Aodong and Changchun Haiwang are well-known brands in China.

The logistics industry has also developed very quickly in the region. The province has sped up the construction of infrastructure such as railways and highways to connect the far east of Russia with coastal cities like Dalian and Dandong. In addition, several large-scale logistics enterprises have been set up, such as Jilin Materials Group Corp.

There are more than 150 countries and areas that have trade relationships with Jilin. The province has 12 national open ports and 6 provincial open ports. Jilin has organized different trade fairs in recent years to boost trade. Examples include those held for automobile and auto parts (China Changchun International Automobile Fair), optical goods (China International Optoelectronic Expo), agricultural products and the China Jilin-Northeast Asia Investment and Trade Expo.

The province's FDI comes mainly from the industries of manufacturing of transportation equipment, food processing, computer applications and software, production and supply of gas, and pharmaceutical products. Changchun and Jilin City are the two leading cities in attracting foreign investment. Local government encourages investment in auto parts, pharmaceuticals, agricultural products, optical and electronic products, infrastructure and public utilities. Germany is Jilin's largest foreign investor, followed by the US, Hong Kong, South Korea and Japan. Well-known international enterprises that have invested there include Pepsi-Cola, Ford and Chrysler from the US; Pilkington from the UK; Siemens and Volkswagen AG from Germany; and Nissan from Japan.

The region's major trading partners are Germany, Japan, South Korea, the US and Russia. Its major exports are clothing, corn, steel, plywood and automobiles, while its major imports are auto parts, automobiles, ores, measuring instruments and engine parts.

As of 2010, compared with those of other provinces, "agriculture, forestry, animal husbandry and fishery", "management of water conservancy, environment and public facilities" and "culture, sports and entertainment" were relatively strong, while "construction", "leasing and business services" and "hotels and catering services" were relatively weak sectors (see Table C).

Table C   Jilin's comparative (dis)advantage index by sector, 2010

Sector	Index
Agriculture, forestry, animal husbandry and fishery	2.17
Mining	1.35
Manufacturing	0.81
Production and distribution of electricity, gas and water	1.29
Construction	0.52
Transport, storage and post	1.12

Table C   (Continued)

Sector	Index
Information transmission, computer service and software	1.37
Wholesale and retail trades	0.81
Hotels and catering services	0.71
Financial intermediation	1.06
Real estate	0.83
Leasing and business services	0.70
Scientific research, technical services and geological prospecting	1.11
Management of water conservancy, environment and public facilities	1.81
Services to households and other services	0.89
Education	1.13
Health, social security and social welfare	1.18
Culture, sports and entertainment	1.38
Public management and social organization	1.07

Notes: All the sectors included in this table are determined according to China's official definitions and for urban areas only. Numerals greater than, equal to and less than 1 indicate that the province's sectors have advantages, no apparent (dis)advantages and disadvantages, respectively.
Sources: Calculated by author based on *China Statistical Yearbook*, 2011. See Appendix for a detailed methodological description.

There are several development zones in the province. These are Jilin New and Hi-Tech Industry Development Zone, Jilin Economic and Technological Development Zone, Changchun Economic and Technological Development Zone, Changchun Hi-Tech Industrial Development Area, Hunchun Border Economic Cooperation Zone and Hunchun Export Processing Zone. Some examples are described below.

- **Jilin New and Hi-tech Industry Development Zone** This was founded in 1992 and is located in Jilin City, covering 818 km² of planned area with 242 km² already established. The leading industries are new materials, refined chemical products, photoelectron, electronics, medicine and bioengineering. It is 14 km from Songhua Lake and the nearest bus and train stations are within 3 km.
- **Jilin Economic and Technological Development Zone** This was founded in May 1998 and is situated in the northeast of Jilin City. It has a total planned area of 28 km². It is located 90 km from Changchun, 5 km from Jilin Airport and 8 km from Jilin Railway Station. Major industries include refined chemicals, bioengineering, fine processing of chemical fiber, and farm products. It is divided into

four parts, namely the Chemical Industrial Park, the Food Industrial Park, the Textile Industrial Park and the Medical Industrial Park. The latter specializes in the development of traditional Chinese pharmaceuticals, mini molecule medicine, bio-pharmaceuticals and health products.

- **Changchun Economic and Technological Development Zone** In 1993, this became a state-level economic and technological development zone. It is in the east area of Changchun, 2 km from a freight train station, 26 km from Changchun Longjia Airport and about a 6-hour drive from Dalian Port. The three major highways of Northeastern China all pass through this zone. The total area is 112.72 km², of which 30 km² has been set aside for development and utilization. It enjoys all the preferential policies stipulated for the economic and technological development zones of open coastal cities. By the end of 2006, the total fixed assets investment of the zone reached ¥38.4 billion. There are 1,656 registered enterprises there including 179 foreign-funded enterprises. The GRP of the zone is ¥101.8 billion, the industrial output value is ¥233.0 billion and the overall financial revenue is ¥15.7 billion.

- **Changchun High-Tech Industrial Development Area** This is located in the southwest of Changchun within the Changchun International Automobile City (a planned area of 100 km²) and is adjacent to the First Auto Works and the government's new administrative center. It is connected by four roads and one light rail to the downtown area. The nearest train station, Changchun Station, is 20 minutes away by light rail. In 2002 it became the first park in northeast China to qualify for the environmental certification of ISO14001. Its landscaping ratio reaches 38%.

- **Hunchun Border Economic Cooperation Zone (HBECZ)** This was approved as a national-level border economic cooperation zone in 1992, with a planning area of 24 km². In 2001 and 2002, Hunchun Export Processing Zone and Hunchun Sino-Russia Trade Zone were set up in the area. Being situated at the junction of China, Russia and Korea, it enjoys a strategic location. Plenty of infrastructure is available. The zone focuses on the development of seafood processing, electronic product manufacture, bio-pharmaceuticals, textiles and other industry.

- **Hunchun Export Processing Zone** This is located in a 5 km² area in HBECZ. Its planned area is 2.44 km². It enjoys good infrastructure and the same policies as its parent zone.

As of 2010 the top five companies were as follows:

1. Yan Bian Road Construction Co (SHE: 000776) is a transport infrastructure services provider. It posted ¥10.22 billion in revenues and ¥4.03 billion in net profits for 2010.
2. FAW Car Co (SHE: 000800) is a leading auto and accessories maker under the brands of Benteng, Hongqi, Mazda6 and Wagon. It posted ¥37.3 billion in revenues and ¥1.86 billion in net profits for 2010.
3. Suning Universal Co (SHE: 000718) is engaged in investing, developing, selling and leasing properties as well as selling construction materials. It posted ¥3.47 billion in revenues and ¥771.61 million in net profits for 2010.
4. Jilin Aodong Medicine Industry Group Co (SHE: 000623) is a supplier of capsules, granules, oral liquids, tablets, ointments, powders, syrups, pills, medicated wines, injections and prepared slices of Chinese crude drugs, among others. It posted ¥1.11 billion in revenues and ¥1.24 billion in net profits for 2010, thanks to negative financial fees.
5. Jilin Ji En Nickel Industry Co (SHA: 600432) is a manufacturer and distributor of nickel sulfate, high-copper nickel, electrolytic nickel, nickel hydroxide, nickel chloride, copper sulfate, copper concentrate and sulfuric acid. It posted ¥2.25 billion in revenues and ¥107.2 million in net profits for 2010.

Indicators for the ease of doing business

A. Starting a business

Procedures: 14
Time (days): 37
Cost (% of provincial GRP per capita): 9.5

B. Registering property

Procedures: 8
Time (days): 55
Cost (% of property value): 4.2

C. Getting credit – creating and registering collateral

Time (days): 22
Cost (% of loan value): 3.3

D. Enforcing contracts

Time (days): 540
Cost (% of claim): 18.4

Further reading

Fischer, Susan L., Catherine P. Koshland, John A. Young (2005). "Social, economic, and environmental impacts assessment of a village-scale modern biomass energy project in Jilin Province, China: Local outcomes and lessons learned," *Energy for Sustainable Development*, vol. 9, issue 4, December, pp. 50–59.

Fischer, Susan L., John A. Young, Catherine P. Koshland (2008). "Producer gas projects in Jilin Province, China: Technical hurdles and the need for project assessment," *Energy for Sustainable Development*, vol. 12, issue 1, March, pp. 68–71.

Han, Xinghai (2010). *The Free Road-Port Zone of the Tumen River* (tumenjiang ziyou lugangqu yanjiu). Changchun: Jilin People Publishing House.

Liu, Lee (1999). "Labor location, conservation, and land quality: The case of West Jilin, China," *Annals of the Association of American Geographers*, vol. 89, issue 4, December, pp. 633–657.

Liu, Lee (2000). "Labor location and agricultural land use in Jilin, China," *The Professional Geographer*, vol. 52, issue 1, February, pp. 74–83.

Liu, Shuying, Wang Guocai, Pat DeLaquil (2001). "Biomass gasification for combined heat and power in Jilin Province, People's Republic of China," *Energy for Sustainable Development*, vol. 5, issue 1, March, pp. 47–53.

Liu, Zijun (2011). *Developing New Industries in the Liaoshen Old Industry Base* (liaoshen laogongye jidi xinxing chanye peiyu). Changchun: Jilin University Publishing House.

Miao, Miao, Tian Yanfen (2010). *The Research of the Regional Economic Growth Based on Local Government Payment* (jiyu difang zhengfu zhichi de quyu jingji zengzhang yanjiu). Changchun: Jilin University Publishing House.

Qiu, Guijie (2010). *The Coordinated Regional Development and Environmental Protection: Driving Forces and Mechanism* (quyu kaifa yu huanjing xietiao fazhan). Changchun: Jilin University Publishing House.

Steven, H., Cao Hanjun, Liu Yi, Zhu Tianbiao (2009). *Leaving the Margin: Politics of the New Industrial Economic Growth* (zouchubianyuan: xinxing gongyuehua jingjiti chengzhang de zhengzhi). Changchun: Jilin Publications Ltd.

Sun, Yuhong (2010). *An Introduction to the Circulation Economy: The Path Choice in Sustainable Development* (xunhuan jingji yinlun: kechixu fazhan de lujing xuanze). Changchun: Jilin University Publishing House.

Wang, Ying (Jan 2007). *Jinlin, Tales of Changbei Mountain* (Panoramic China). Beijing: Foreign Languages Press.

Zheng, Shi, Zhigang Wang, Shunfeng Song (2011). "Farmers' behaviors and performance in cooperatives in Jilin Province of China: A case study," *The Social Science Journal*, vol. 48, issue 3, September, pp. 449–457.

Zheng, Xiaoliang, Wang Yongjun (2008). *Theory and Practice of Promoting Dongbei Old Industrial Bases* (zhenxing dongbei lao gongye jidi de lilun yu shijian). Changchun: Jilin People Publishing House.

Liaoning

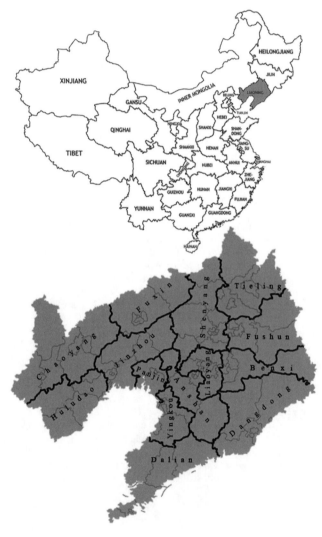

Source: The author, based on a file from the Wikimedia Commons.

Table A The administrative divisions of Liaoning

Name	Administrative seat	Population
Anshan PM	Tiedong District	3,645,884
Benxi PM	Pingshan District	1,709,538
Chaoyang PM	Shuangta District	3,044,641
Dalian SPM	Xigang District	6,690,432
Dandong PM	Zhenxing District	2,444,697
Fushun PM	Shuncheng District	2,138,090
Fuxin PM	Haizhou District	1,819,339
Huludao PM	Longgang District	2,623,541
Jinzhou PM	Taihe District	3,126,463
Liaoyang PM	Baita District	1,858,768
Panjin PM	Xinglongtai District	1,392,493
Shenyang SPM	Shenhe District	8,106,171
Tieling PM	Yinzhou District	2,717,732
Yingkou PM	Zhanqian District	2,428,534

Notes: PM = prefectural level municipality; SPM = sub-provincial level municipality. All data are as of 2010.

Quick facts

Official name: Liaoning Province
Abbreviated name: Liao
Land area: 145,900 km^2
Population: 43,746,000
Population density: 289/km^2
GRP per capita of 2010: ¥42,355
HDI of 2008: 0.835
Capital: Shenyang
Government office address: 45 Beiling Street, Huanggu District, Shenyang
Tel: 024–8689–3032
Postcode: 110032
Website: www.ln.gov.cn

Liaoning is a province of the PRC, located in the southern part of China's northeast. It adjoins Jilin Province to the northeast, Hebei Province to the west and Inner Mongolia Autonomous Region to the northwest. On the south and southeast sides it is surrounded by the Yellow Sea (Korea Bay) and the Bohai Sea to the south, and is bordered along the Yalu River by the Democratic People's Republic of Korea.

The name "Liaoning" is taken from the Liao River that flows through the province; "ning" means "peace". Its one-character abbreviation is "Liao".

The coastline of the province is 2,178 km long – nearly 12% of China's total. The hilly regions in the east are the main areas of forest. Adjoining the long, narrow coastal plains (called the Liaoxi Corridor) is the main road for northeast China, linking with the north of the country. The Liaohe Plain in central Liaoning, as part of the Northeastern China Plain, has sedimentary deposits from the Liaohe River and other tributaries. It has abundant water and fertile soil, and it is the main farming area and commodity grain base in the province.

The modern provincial administration of Liaoning was first established in 1907 as Fengtian Province and the name was changed to Liaoning in 1929. Under the Japanese puppet Manchukuo regime, the province reverted to its 1907 name, but the name Liaoning was restored in 1945. It is split administratively into 100 county-level divisions (17 county-level cities, 19 counties, 8 autonomous counties and 56 districts), which are then further subdivided into 1,511 township-level divisions (613 towns, 301 townships, 77 ethnic townships and 520 sub-districts).

The area can be approximately divided into three geographical regions: the highlands in the west, the plains in the middle and the hills in the east. The highlands are dominated by the Nulu'erhu Mountains, which roughly follow the border between Liaoning and Inner Mongolia. The entire region has many low hills. The central part consists of the watersheds of rivers such as the Liao, the Daliao and their tributaries. This region is mostly flat and low altitude. The eastern part of Liaoning is dominated by the Changbai Shan and Qianshan ranges, which extends into the sea to form the Liaodong Peninsula. The highest point (1,336 m above sea level) is Mount Huabozi.

The province has a continental monsoon climate with distinct seasonal variations. It has an annual rainfall of 714.9 mm and an annual average temperature of 4–10 °C with a frost-free period of 140–200 days. Liaoning features a temperate continental monsoon climate with a long winter, a warm summer and a short spring and fall. The summer is rainy while the other seasons are dry.

There are 392 rivers of 160,000 km total length and a drainage area of 145,000 km^2 within the province. Liaohe River, one of the seven longest rivers in China, is 512 km long and has a drainage area of 69,000 km^2 within the province. The average runoff of rivers there is 32.5 billion m^3

(or a 223 mm runoff depth). The province has a total water resource of 36.3 billion m³. Liaoning has plentiful fishing resources with its marine life area ranking second in China.

Nearly 115 minerals have been found in Liaoning, including reserves of 64 of these. Its deposits of iron, boron, magnesite, diamonds and talcum are some of the largest in China. The region is also an important source of petroleum (especially in Liaohe Oilfield) and natural gas. Salt is produced along the coast.

The main agricultural products there are maize, sorghum and soybeans. The region also grows a lot of fruit trees. It has the third largest total area of fruit in the defoliated zone and the second largest production in the area. The region around Dalian produces three-quarters of China's exported apples (from Dalian and Yingkou) and peaches (from Dalian). Liaoning also grows pears (from Beizhen of Jinzhou), white pears (from Huludao and Suizhong) and apricots and plums (from Gushan of Dandong). Cotton is also produced. The total forestry area measures 4.185 million ha with 28.7% forest cover.

The province has more than 11,300 cultural remains, including 19 national-level key protection units and 159 provincial-level key protection units. There are seven state-class natural reserves and seven provincial-class natural reserves. Some of the folk festivals attract the attention of both domestic and foreign visitors, such as the Dalian Costume Festival.

The Mukden Palace was the palace of the Qing Dynasty emperors before they conquered the rest of China and moved their capital to Beijing. It is significant for its representation of palace architecture at the time and has recently been included on the UNESCO World Heritage Site as an extension of the Imperial Palace site in Beijing. In addition, three imperial tombs dating from the Qing Dynasty are located in Liaoning. Wunu Mountain City, a Goguryeo site found in Huanren Manchu Autonomous County, is part of a combined UNESCO World Heritage Site. Liaoyang City, one of the oldest continuously inhabited cities in northeast China, has a number of historical sites, including the White Pagoda (Baita), which dates to the Yuan Dynasty (AD 1279–1368). The port city of Dalian, located at the tip of the Liaodong Peninsula, is a tourist destination in its own right, with beaches, resorts, zoos, seafood, shopping, Russian- and Japanese-era architecture, and streetcars – a rare sight in China.

The province has the largest economy of northeast China. Its nominal GRP for 2010 was ¥1.85 trillion (about US$270 billion), making it the seventh largest in China. Its per capita GRP was ¥41,782 (about

Table B   Demographic and socioeconomic profile: Liaoning

Indicator	2000	2010
Population (thousands)	42,380	43,749
Illiteracy rate of population aged 15 or over (%)	4.76	1.93
GRP (¥ billions)	466.91	1,845.73
Composition of GRP (%)		
Primary sector	10.8	8.8
Secondary sector	50.2	54.1
Tertiary sector	39.0	37.1
Fixed asset investment (¥ billions)	126.77	1,604.30
Status of foreign-funded enterprises		
Number of registered enterprises	13,146	18,377
Total investment (US$ millions)	65,543	147,615
Registered capital (US$ millions)	39,626	97,535
Foreign trade (US$ millions)		
Export	10,589	42,943
Import	9,478	52,349
Sales of consumer goods (¥ billions)	185	689
Per capita annual disposable income of urban residents (¥)	5,357.79	17,712.58
Engle's coefficient (%)	35.73	33.24
Per capita annual net income of rural residents (¥)	2,355.58	6,907.93
Engle's coefficient (%)	34.90	38.18
Number of patent applications granted	4,842	17,093
Inventions	458	2,357
Utility models	3,703	12,067
Designs	681	2,669

Note: All monetary values are measured at current prices.
Source: *Liaoning Statistical Yearbook*, 2001 and 2011.

US$6,172). Among the three provinces of northeast China, Liaoning is the largest in terms of GRP.

Leading industries include petrochemicals, metallurgy, electronics, telecommunications and machinery. On a national level, Liaoning is a major producer of pig iron, steel and metal-cutting machine tools, all of whose production rank among the top three in the nation. The province is one of the most important raw materials production bases in China. Industries such as mining, quarrying, smelting and pressing of ferrous metals, petroleum and natural gas extraction are all of great significance.

Meanwhile, Liaoning is an important production base of equipment and machinery manufacturing, with Shenyang and Dalian being the industrial centers. Enterprises such as Shenyang Jinbei Co. Ltd, Daxian

Group Co. Ltd and Shenyang Machine Tool Co. Ltd are leaders in their sectors. The province's light industry mainly focuses on textiles and clothing industries, which include cotton and wool spinning, chemical fiber production, knitting, silk production and the manufacturing of both garments and textile machinery. Meanwhile, the province is concentrating on developing its four pillar industries: petrochemicals, metallurgy, machinery and electronics.

Liaoning is an important transportation hub as it is home to Dalian Port.

Liaoning is one of China's most important industrial bases, covering a wide range of industries, such as machinery, electronics, metal refining, petroleum, chemical industries, construction materials and coal. The sea off Dalian abounds with quality seafood, such as abalones, sea cucumbers, scallops, prawns, crabs and sea urchins. The big fish of Dandong, the jellyfish of Yingkou and the clams of Panjin are known worldwide for their good taste right from the sea, and seafood products are made in Liaoning for export domestically and internationally. Dependence on heavy industry and the province's energy inefficiency are signs that Liaoning is still at the lower end of the value chain. To stimulate economic growth, the province aims to nurture the private sector and specifically help small and medium-sized enterprises by raising funds from equity and debt markets.

Equipment manufacturing is the top industry in Liaoning. The industry focuses on the manufacture of general equipment, special use equipment and transport equipment. Famous companies include Shenyang Machine Tool Works, Dalian Machine Tool Works, Shenyang SIASUN Robot Corp, Dalian Locomotive and Roll Stock Works, Brilliance Auto (which has a joint venture with BMW to produce 3 and 5 series BMW sedans in Shenyang), Daxian Group Corp, Northeast Electric Transmission and Transformation Equipment Group Corp.

The metallurgy industry is Liaoning's traditional pillar industry. The region has the advantage of having rich mineral resources, a central location and a strong talent pool. The industry mainly focuses on the development of ferrous metallurgy as the province has the biggest iron ore reserve in China. The Anshan and Benxi Iron and Steel Group is the leading steel maker in Liaoning.

The petrochemical industry is the third pillar industry of Liaoning, focusing on the development of fine chemical, rubber products and newly emerging petrochemical technologies. PetroChina (Liaohe) Corp and Jinhua Chemical Group are the leading companies in this industry.

The development of new service industries, such as logistics, IT and commercial services, is currently being encouraged by government. The cities of Dalian, Dandong and Yingkou have been developed as major ports and economic gateways to the rest of northeast China. Liaoning ranks fifth in China and first in the northeast in terms of retail sales of consumer goods. The major consumer centers in the province are located in Shenyang and Dalian.

The major export products are steel, refined oil, water products and tires, while the major import products are machine tools, automobiles, steel, rubber and copper. The major import sources are Japan, South Korea, Germany, the US and Australia. Its major export destinations are Japan, the US, South Korea, Singapore and Hong Kong.

The province has attracted the largest amount of FDI among all the three provinces in northeast China. Dalian and Shenyang are the most popular destinations for FDI. Hong Kong is the largest source of FDI, followed by the US, Singapore, Japan and South Korea.

Apart from Dalian and Shenyang, Anshan, Dandong and Yingkou have become destinations of foreign companies. Leading Hong Kong enterprises such as Cheung Kong, Hang Lung and New World, and MNCs such as General Electric, Siemens, Mitsubishi, Toshiba and Sanyo, have invested in the province. The manufacturing industry has attracted the largest share of FDI, in terms of both contracted amount and utilized amount. Government has placed emphasis on equipment manufacturing, raw materials, new technology and high-tech endeavors, food processing and service industries. To re-vitalize the old industrial base, government has begun selling off stakes in state-owned enterprises to foreign acquirers.

As of 2010, compared with those of other provinces, "agriculture, forestry, animal husbandry and fishery", "mining" and "management of water conservancy, environment and public facilities" were relatively strong, while "construction", "hotels and catering services" and "wholesale and retail trades" were relatively weak sectors (see Table C).

Table C Liaoning's comparative (dis)advantage index by sector, 2010

Sector	Index
Agriculture, forestry, animal husbandry and fishery	1.87
Mining	1.58
Manufacturing	1.00
Production and distribution of electricity, gas and water	1.35
Construction	0.62

Transport, storage and post	1.21
Information transmission, computer service and software	0.95
Wholesale and retail trades	0.80
Hotels and catering services	0.77
Financial intermediation	1.11
Real estate	1.05
Leasing and business services	0.99
Scientific research, technical services and geological prospecting	1.03
Management of water conservancy, environment and public facilities	1.48
Services to households and other services	1.20
Education	0.83
Health, social security and social welfare	1.02
Culture, sports and entertainment	0.98
Public management and social organization	0.87

Notes: All the sectors included in this table are determined according to China's official definitions and for urban areas only. Numerals greater than, equal to and less than 1 indicate that the province's sectors have advantages, no apparent (dis)advantages and disadvantages, respectively.
Sources: Calculated by author based on *China Statistical Yearbook*, 2011. See Appendix for a detailed methodological description.

Of the development zones formally recognized by the PRC State Council, 56 are located in Liaoning, including 14 on the national level and 42 on the provincial level. These are further grouped into economic development zones, high-tech zones free trade and export processing zones and special development zones. Some examples are described below.

- **Shenyang Cross-Strait Science Industrial Zone** In October 1995, this was approved by the State Council. It is the only zone established in Shenyang Hi-Tech Industrial Development Zone and has a total area of 5 km². It welcomes investors from around the world, especially Taiwan, and they enjoy many preferential policies. It focuses on the development of instrument manufacturing, telecommunication, bio-pharmaceuticals, electronics and new materials.
- **Shenyang Economic and Technological Development Zone** This is located in the southwest of Shenyang. By the end of 2006 there were enterprises from 41 countries investing in 1,837 projects, with an accumulated utilized FDI of US$2.2 billion. Some 83 MNCs have invested in the zone, including 25 Fortune 500 companies.
- **Shenyang Export Processing Zone** This was approved by state government in June 2005. It is located in National-Level Shenyang Economic and Technological Development Zone, with a planned area of 62 km² and a current area of 14.1 km². It encourages and focuses

on the development of automobiles and auto parts, electronics, precision machinery, new energy, new materials and chemicals.

- **Shenyang Hunnan Hi-Tech Industrial Development Zone** This used to be called Shenyang Hi-Tech Industrial Development Zone. Established in 1988, it was approved by the State Council. It is located in the west of Shenyang city with 32 km². Its encouraged industries include electronic information, new materials, biological engineering, energy saving and environmental protection.
- **Dalian Economic and Technological Development Zone** This was established in September 1984 as one of the first of the China National Economic and Technological Development Zones. It is located at the southeastern edge of the Liaodong Peninsula, which comprises both an economic development zone and an export processing zone. It is ranked fourth and sixth, respectively, in terms of GRP and utilized FDI among all the national economic and technological development zones in China. There are 2,185 foreign-invested projects in the area, including 43 from Fortune 500 companies. Most of the enterprises are foreign funded, especially those from Japan, South Korea and the US, such as Canon, Pfizer, Toshiba, Intel, IBM, GE, Dell, SAP and HP.
- **Dalian Export Processing Zone** This was approved by the State Council in April 2000. With a planned area of 2.95 km², it is divided into two parts: A and B. A zone has a construction area of 1.5 km², and started operation in May 2001. All the basic infrastructure is available, which includes road, water, gas, power supply and telecommunications. The zone encourages several leading industries, such as home appliances, light industry, machinery, construction materials and medicine instruments.
- **Dalian Free Trade Zone** This was approved by government in May 1992. Investors can enjoy preferential policies, including duty-free. All necessary infrastructure is available within the zone and it enjoys a strategic location and convenient communications. It has formed some leading industries, such as in electronics, machinery and plastics.
- **Dalian Hi-Tech Industrial Development Zone** This was approved as a national-level development zone in 1991. It has a total area of 35.6 km². All necessary infrastructure is available within the zone. It focuses on and encourages electronic information, bio-pharmaceuticals and new materials. The zone has 86 scientific research institutes, 39 training centers and over 2,300 enterprises.
- **Dandong Border Economic Corporation Zone** This was approved as a national-level development zone in 1992. It is located on the

banks of the Yalu River and opposite Sinuiju City in North Korea. Its infrastructure is complete. It has formed and encourages such industries as electronic information, machinery manufacturing and bio-pharmaceuticals.

As of 2010 the top five companies were as follows:

1. Angang Steel Co (SHE: 000898, HKG: 0347) is a producer and distributor of hot rolled sheets, cold rolled sheets, galvanized steel sheets, color coating plates, silicon steel, medium and thick plates, wire rods, heavy section and seamless steel pipes. It posted ¥92.43 billion in revenues and ¥2.04 billion in net profits for 2010.
2. GD Power Development Co (SHA: 600795) is an electric and heat power generator and distributor. It posted ¥40.77 billion in revenues and ¥2.4 billion in net profits for 2010.
3. Liaoning Cheng Da Co (SHA: 600739) is a trader of commodities and a biological drug manufacturer. It posted ¥5.25 billion in revenues and ¥1.26 billion in net profits for 2010.
4. Neusoft Corp (SHA: 600718) is a software company that offers digital products, services and solutions. It posted ¥4.94 billion in revenues and ¥484.68 million in net profits for 2010.
5. Bengang Steel Plates Co (SHE: 000761) is engaged in smelting of steel and rolling and processing of steel plates. It posted ¥45.69 billion in revenues and ¥925.37 million in net profits for 2010.

Indicators for the ease of doing business

A. Starting a business

Procedures: 14
Time (days): 41
Cost (% of provincial GRP per capita): 6

B. Registering property

Procedures: 12
Time (days): 51
Cost (% of property value): 3.1

C. Getting credit – creating and registering collateral

Time (days): 20
Cost (% of loan value): 2.8

D. Enforcing contracts

Time (days): 260
Cost (% of claim): 24.8

Further reading

Atherton, Andrew, Alaric Fairbanks (2006). "Stimulating private sector development in China: The emergence of enterprise development centers in Liaoning
and Sichuan provinces," *Asia Pacific Business Review*, vol. 12, issue 3, July,
pp. 333–354.

Bo, Hong, Zhihai Zhang (2002). "The impact of uncertainty on firm investment:
Evidence from machinery industry in Liaoning Province of China," *Economic
Systems*, vol. 26, issue 4, December, pp. 335–352.

Chen, Junjie, Gale Summerfield (2007). "Gender and rural reforms in China:
A case study of population control and land rights policies in northern
liaoning," *Feminist Economics*, vol. 13, issue 3–4, July, pp. 63–92.

Cui, Riming, Bao Yan, Zhang Nan (2010). *Northeast Asia Economic Cooperation and
the Promotion of the Old Industrial Base in Liaoning* (dongbeiya quyu jingji hezuo
yu liaoning laogongye jidi zhenxing hudong yanjiu). Beijing: Economy and
Science Publishing House.

Fang, Bingzhu (2002). *Two Fundamental Changes and the Promotion of the Liaoning
Economy* (liangge genben zhuanbian yu Liaoning jingji zhenxing). Shenyang:
The Northeast University of Economic and Finance Publishing House.

Feng, Dianshu, Benjamin K. Sovacool, Khuong Minh Vu (2010). "The barriers to
energy efficiency in China: Assessing household electricity savings and consumer behavior in Liaoning Province," *Energy Policy*, vol. 38, issue 2, February,
pp. 1202–1209.

Foreign Languages Press (2006, ed.). *Liaoning, Home of the Manchus and Cradle of
Qing Empire* (Panoramic China). Beijing: Foreign Languages Press.

Leppman, Elizabeth J. (2002). "Breakfast in Liaoning Province, China," *Journal of
Cultural Geography*, vol. 20, issue 1, September 2002, pp. 77–90.

Li, Chunfang (2009). *Theory and Practice of Regional Economic Development: The
New Way for Liaoning's Regional Economic Development* (quyu jingji fazhan lilun
yu shijian: liaoning quyu jingji fazhan xinsilu ji dianxing pouxi). Beijing:
China Social and Science Publishing House.

Liang, Qidong (2009). *A Study of the Comprehensive Reform for the Shenyang Economic Zone* (laoshen jingjiqu zonghe peitao gaige yanjiu). Shenyang: Liaoning
University Publishing House.

LiuFeng, Chao, Xu Guanhua (2011). *The Promotion and Strategic Upgrade of
Liaoning Old Industry Bases* (liaoning lao gongye jidi zhenxing yu zhanlue
shengji). Beijing: Science Publishing.

Lu, Tong (2011). *The Strategy of New Technological Improvement in the Rising Old
Industry Bases* (laogongye jidi zhenxing zhongde xinjishu gaizao zhanlue).
Beijing: Science Publishing House.

Schueller, Margot (1997). "Liaoning: Struggling with the burden of the past," in
Goodman, David S.G. (ed.), *China's Provinces in Reform: Class, Community and
Political Culture*. London and New York: Routledge, pp. 93–126.

Smyth, Russell, Zhai Qingguo (2003). "Economic restructuring in China's large
and medium-sized state-owned enterprises: Evidence from Liaoning," *Journal
of Contemporary China*, vol. 12, issue 34, February, pp. 173–205.

Sun, Xinbo, Zhang Lizhi (2009). *Studies of Structural Adjustment of Industrial Enterprises in Liaoning Province* (liaoningsheng gongye qiye zuzhi jiegou tiaozheng
yanjiu). Beijing: Economic and Management Publishing House.

Thomas, Stephen C. (1990). "Catching up: Liaoning Province is courting – and wining – foreign investment," *China Business Review*, November–December, pp. 6–11.

Torbert, Preston M. (1984). "Window on Liaoning Province," *China Business Review*, November–December, pp. 20–3.

Wang, Dachao, Zhao Huie, et al. (2010). *Strategic Studies of the Changing Way of Liaoning Economic Development* (liaoning zhuanbian jingji fazhan fangshi duice yanjiu). Beijing: People Publishing House.

Wu, Jingxue (2008). *Technological Upgrade and Agro-economic Growth: A Case Analysis of Liaoning* (jishu jinbu yu nongye jingji zengzhang: dui liaoning de shizheng fenxi). Beijing: China Agriculture Science and Technology Publishing House.

Xia, Qingjie, Colin Simmons (2004). "The determinants of labor-time allocation between farm and off-farm work in rural China: The case of Liaoning Province," *Journal of Chinese Economic and Business Studies*, vol. 2, issue 2, May, pp. 169–184.

Xu, Ming, Xiao-Ping Jia, Lei Shi, Tian-Zhu Zhang (2008). "Societal metabolism in Northeast China: Case study of Liaoning Province," *Resources, Conservation and Recycling*, vol. 52, issues 8–9, July, pp. 1082–1086.

Ningxia

Source: The author, based on a file from the Wikimedia Commons.

Table A   The administrative divisions of Ningxia

Name	Administrative seat	Population
Guyuan PM	Yuanzhou District	1,228,156
Shizuishan PM	Dawukou District	725,482
Wuzhong PM	Litong District	1,273,792
Yinchuan PM	Xingqing District	1,993,088
Zhongwei PM	Shapotou District	1,080,832

Notes: PM = prefectural level municipality. All data are as of 2010.

Quick facts

Official name: Ningxia Hui Autonomous Region
Abbreviated name: Ning
Land area: 66,000 km^2
Population: 6,301,350
Population density: 89/km^2
GRP per capita of 2010: ¥26,860
HDI of 2008: 0.766
Capital: Yinchuan
Government office address: 217 West Jiefang Street, Yinchuan
Website: www.nx.gov.cn

Ningxia Hui Autonomous Region ("Ning" for short) of the PRC is located in northwest China. As part of the Loess Plateau, it is crossed by the Yellow River. It lies along the western part of the Yellow River and is bordered by Inner Mongolia Autonomous Region to the north and west, Shaanxi Province to the east and Gansu Province to the south. The Great Wall of China runs along its northeastern boundary Home of the Hui people, the region was once a part of the Silk Road that connected China with central Asia and Europe.

Ningxia is one of China's five autonomous regions inhabited by the minority groups. Formerly a province, it was incorporated into Gansu Province in 1954 but was detached and reconstituted as an autonomous region for the Hui people in 1958. This sparsely settled area is a relatively dry, desert-like region. Significant irrigation supports the growing of wolfberries, a commonly consumed fruit throughout the area. Its deserts include the Tengger Desert in Shapotou. Its ecosystem is one of the least studied regions in the world. Some plant genera have been estimated at more than 40,000 years old. Over the years an extensive system of canals has been built. Significant land reclamation and irrigation projects have made increased cultivation possible. The northern section, through which the Yellow River flows, supports the best agricultural land. A railroad linking Lanzhou with Baotou crosses the region and a highway has been built across the Yellow River at Yinchuan, the capital.

The topography of Ningxia slants toward the north with an elevation from 1,100 m to 2,000 m. The highest point is 3,556 m above sea level. The region is 1,200 km from the sea and has a continental climate with average summer temperatures rising to 17–24°C in July and average winter temperatures dropping to between −7 and −10 °C in January. Seasonal extreme temperatures can reach 39 °C in summer and −30 °C in winter. The diurnal temperature variation can reach above 17 °C, especially in spring. The average annual rainfall is 190–700 mm, with more rain falling in the south.

Ningxia boasts 0.71 million ha of wasteland suitable for farming, one of China's eight areas that each have more than 0.63 million ha of wasteland suitable for agriculture. There are 3 million ha of exploitable meadows, making the region one of the ten major pastures in China. The Weining Plain, which features 0.37 million ha of land irrigated with water diverted from the Yellow River, is one of the four principal areas with gravity irrigation in northwest China. For years the annual runoff from the Yellow River there has remained at 32.5 billion m^3 and the water resources allocated to Ningxia by the state for irrigation are 4 billion m^3. Owing to irrigation the region is known as "an oasis in a desert".

The rich land resources, convenient conditions for diverting water from the Yellow River and abundant sunshine offer a solid foundation for the area's the development of agriculture. Its major crops include rice, wheat, maize, beans, sugar beet and Chinese wolfberries. Rice is its most famous produce, giving Ningxia the nickname of "the Pearl of the Northern Frontier" or "the Southern Yangtze of Northern China". Watermelons, apples and grapes from the irrigated area have a 15–20% higher sugar content than those produced in central China. The per-hectare yield of single-cropping paddy reaches 10,500 kg, placing first among the provinces and autonomous regions in western China and making it one of the nation's 12 grain production bases. The mountain area in the south of Ningxia is suitable for both forestry and animal husbandry. The region has broad prospects for the development of the stock rearing and livestock processing industries. Efforts have been made to build Ningxia into a national agricultural demonstration area with high yield, efficiency and quality.

Livestock breeding makes up 29% of local agriculture. Of the 82,000 ha water surfaces, 10,000 ha can be used for aquaculture. Ningxia produces various species of carp, river shrimp and river crabs. In recent years, aquatic production has developed rapidly. It leads other provinces and autonomous regions in the northwest in per capita output of aquatic products.

Ningxia is rich in minerals, with verified deposits of 50 kinds of minerals, including coal, gypsum, oil, natural gas, pottery clay, quartz sandstone and barite. The potential value of these natural resources per capita is 163.5% of the nation's average, putting the region fifth in the country. There are abundant reserves of various kinds of coal and the area undertakes coal production on a considerable scale. It leads the country in terms of gypsum reserves, with verified deposits of more than 4.5 billion tons. Top-grade gypsum makes up half of these. The Huojiakouzi deposit in Tongxin County features a reserve of 20 tons of gypsum in 20 layers with a total thickness of 100 m. The reserves of oil and natural gas are ideal for the large-scale development of oil, natural gas and chemical industries. There are considerable deposits of quartz sandstone, of which 17 million tons have been confirmed. In addition are phosphorus, firestone, copper, iron and Helan stone (a special clay stone).

Ningxia has the third smallest GRP in China, even though its neighbors, Inner Mongolia and Shaanxi, are among the strongest emerging provincial economies in the country. The region's fundamental resources are weak, lacking the rich natural resources of Inner Mongolia or the talent that drives high value-added industries and services in Shaanxi. It also has to invest heavily to maintain its agricultural production in the face of natural disadvantages, such as a dry climate, shortage of water and sand storms.

Table B   Demographic and socioeconomic profile: Ningxia

Indicator	2000	2010
Population (thousands)	5,620	6,330
Illiteracy rate of population aged 15 or over (%)	13.40	6.22
GRP (¥ billions)	26.56	168.97
Composition of GRP (%)		
Primary sector	17.3	9.4
Secondary sector	45.2	49.0
Tertiary sector	37.5	41.6
Fixed asset investment (¥ billions)	15.75	144.42

Table B   (Continued)

Indicator	2000	2010
Status of foreign-funded enterprises		
Number of registered enterprises	408	529
Total investment (US$ millions)	940	3,964
Registered capital (US$ millions)	696	1,785
Foreign trade (US$ millions)		
Export	354	1,552
Import	178	1,015
Sales of consumer goods (¥ billions)	9	40
Per capita annual disposable income of urban residents (¥)	4,912.40	15,344.49
Engle's coefficient (%)	40.88	39.37
Per capita annual net income of rural residents (¥)	1,724.30	4,674.89
Engle's coefficient (%)	29.76	38.42
Number of patent applications granted	224	1,081
Inventions	21	61
Utility models	166	307
Designs	37	713

Note: All monetary values are measured at current prices.
Source: *Ningxia Statistical Yearbook*, 2001 and 2011.

Unlike some poor regions with low labor costs, the average wage in Ningxia is higher than that in two-thirds of other provinces, making it less attractive as a base for manufacturers. At the same time, it does not have the population size to be a consumption hub. Its key industries are chemical manufacturing and metal smelting, both of which consume large amounts of energy. This problem is exacerbated by outdated equipment and technology that make it the least energy-efficient region in China.

The manufacturing sector receives the largest amount of fixed asset investment. Real estate, production and supply of electricity, gas and water, transportation and storage, and mining rank in the top five in terms of total fixed asset investment.

Major consumer markets in this region are located in the capital of Yinchuan, and major department stores and shopping centers include Xinghua Shopping Center, Yingchuan Department Store, Ningxia Hualian Commercial Building and Yinchuan Xincheng Department Store. Clothing, household articles, medicine and medical services, transportation and communication, recreation, cultural activities and education, and residential housing account for other significant expenditures.

Industry in Ningxia is developing very rapidly. Many industrial enterprises, such as those in the coal, electric power, metal, petroleum, machinery, chemical, building materials and textile industries, have been established there. The coal industry is the pillar of the industrial sector. Based in the Shizuishan mining area, a complete system has been set up – from excavating and washing to comprehensive utilization. Much of the coal mined in the area is supplied to the steelworks in Baotou and Jiuquan for steelmaking.

The region offers abundant tourism resources, including desert landscapes and the cultural heritages along the Yellow River. These have attracted both domestic and foreign tourists.

Ningxia has traded with 115 countries. Key trade partners include the US, Japan and Australia. Important export goods include machinery, chemicals, rubber tires, cashmere, anthracite, and farm and sideline products. Import items include rubber, chemicals and light industrial products. Hong Kong is still the largest investor in the region but other major investors include Taiwan, Canada and Japan.

As of 2010, compared with those of other provinces, "production and distribution of electricity, gas and water", "mining" and "management of water conservancy, environment and public facilities" were relatively strong, while "services to households and other services", "hotels and catering services" and "construction" were relatively weak sectors (see Table C).

Table C Ningxia's comparative (dis)advantage index by sector, 2010

Sector	Index
Agriculture, forestry, animal husbandry and fishery	1.54
Mining	2.26
Manufacturing	0.64
Production and distribution of electricity, gas and water	2.61
Construction	0.52
Transport, storage and post	1.00
Information transmission, computer service and software	0.76
Wholesale and retail trades	0.63
Hotels and catering services	0.44
Financial intermediation	1.25
Real estate	0.84
Leasing and business services	0.99
Scientific research, technical services and geological prospecting	0.90
Management of water conservancy, environment and public facilities	1.79
Services to households and other services	0.00
Education	1.10

Table C   (Continued)

Sector	Index
Health, social security and social welfare	1.15
Culture, sports and entertainment	1.28
Public management and social organization	1.28

Notes: All the sectors included in this table are determined according to China's official definitions and for urban areas only. Numerals greater than, equal to and less than 1 indicate that the province's sectors have advantages, no apparent (dis)advantages and disadvantages, respectively.
Sources: Calculated by author based on *China Statistical Yearbook*, 2011. See Appendix for a detailed methodological description.

There are two major economic and technological development zones in Ningxia. These are described below.

- **Yinchuan New- and High-Tech Development Zone** Established in 1992, this is a key development zone in the region and was given the status of a state-level high-tech industrial development zone in 2001. It has an area of 32 km² and enjoys similar preferential policies to other such zones in order to encourage the development of new technology. The pillar industries include electronics and information, bioengineering technology and modern agricultural technology. Currently it has more than 1,400 enterprises, of which 170 industrial high-tech enterprises accounted for 58% of the region's total. The annual industrial value has reached ¥23.7 billion (about US$3.5 billion). Major investors include local enterprises such as Kocel Steel Foundry, FAG Railway Bearing (Ningxia) and Ningxia Little Giant Machine Tools. Major industries include machinery and equipment manufacturing, new materials, fine chemicals and animation.
- **Desheng Industrial Park** Located in Helan County, this is a base for about 400 enterprises. It has industrial chains from Muslim food and commodities to trade and logistics, new materials and bio-pharmaceuticals, which have ¥80 billion in fixed assets. It is the most promising industrial park in the city. It achieved a total output value of 4.85 billion in 2008, up by 40% year on year. Local government plans to cut taxes and other fees to reduce the burden on local enterprises. The industrial output value reached ¥2.68 billion in 2008, an increase of 48% from the previous year. Ningxia wines are a promising area of development. The Chinese authorities have given approval to develop the eastern base of the Helan Mountains as an area suitable for wine production. Several large Chinese wine companies, including Changyu and Dynasty Wine, are developing in the western region of the province. Together they

now own 20,000 acres of land for wine plantations, and Dynasty has ploughed ¥100 million into Ningxia. In addition, major oil company China Petroleum and Chemical Corporation has established a grape plantation near the Helan Mountains. The household appliance company Midea has also begun participating in Ningxia's wine industry.

As of 2010 the top five companies were as follows:

1. Yichuan Xinhua Department Store Co (SHA: 600785) is a retailer and commercial real-estate developer. It posted ¥3.99 billion in revenues and ¥215.22 million in net profits for 2010.
2. Ningxia Orient Tantalum Industry Co (SHE: 000962) is a precious metal smelter. It posted ¥1.64 billion in revenues and ¥82.19 million in net profits for 2010.
3. Ningxia Saima Industry Co (SHA: 600449) is a cement and concrete manufacturer and distributor. It posted ¥2.43 billion in revenues and ¥561.79 million in net profits for 2010.
4. Ningxia Dayuan Chemical Co (SHA: 600146) is a plastics and biochemical manufacturer and distributor. It posted ¥72.11 million in revenues and ¥4.01 million in net profits for 2010.
5. Ningxia Zhongyin Cashmere Co (SHE: 000982) is engaged in the production and sale of cashmere, cashmere tops, cashmere yarns and cashmere sweaters. It posted ¥1.18 billion in revenues and ¥76.77 million in net profits for 2010.

Indicators for the ease of doing business

A. Starting a business
Procedures: 14
Time (days): 55
Cost (% of provincial GRP per capita): 12

B. Registering property
Procedures: 10
Time (days): 59
Cost (% of property value): 4.4

C. Getting credit – creating and registering collateral
Time (days): 25
Cost (% of loan value): 3.6

D. Enforcing contracts
Time (days): 270
Cost (% of claim): 28.7

Further reading

Edmonds, Richard Louis (2005). "Great western development in the Ningxia Hui autonomous region: A cultural remake of a cultural remake?" *Provincial China*, vol. 8, issue 2, October, pp. 144–163.

Liang, Chunyang, Wu Zhilie (2007). *A Study of the Interactions between Imformationization, Industrialization, Urbanization and Agricultural Industrialization in Ningxia*. Yinchuan: Ningxia People Publishing House.

Liu, Changzong (2006). *Ningxia, All and Blessed by the Yellow River* (Panoramic China). Beijing: Foreign Languages Press.

Liu, Ying, Zeng Yuping (2009). *Great Leap: Studies of Ningxia's Economic and Social Development* (kuayue: ningxia jingji shehui fazhan yanjiu). Yinchuan: Ningxia People Publishing House.

Merkle, Rita (2003). "Ningxia's third road to rural development: Resettlement schemes as a last means to poverty reduction?" *Journal of Peasant Studies*, vol. 30, issue 3–4, April, pp. 160–191.

Niu, Guoyuan (2011). *The Strategic Studies of Regional Economic Development in Ningxia* (ningxia quyu jingji fazhan zhanlue yanjiu). Yinchuan: Ningxia People Education Publishing House.

People Government of Ningxia Hui Autonomous Region (2006). *The Eleventh Five-Year-Plan Compendium of National Economic and Social Development in Ningxia Hui Autonomous Region* (ningxia huizu zizhiqu guomin jingji he shehui fazhan di shiyi ge wunianguihua gangyao). Yinchuan: Ningxia People Publishing House.

Ren, Zhenghong (2011). "Utilisation of antenatal care in four counties in Ningxia, China," *Midwifery*, vol. 27, issue 6, December, pp. 260–266.

Wang, Jianmin (2008). *Footprints: A Memoir of Economic Development and Reform Work in Ningxia* (zuji: ningxia jingjia fazhan he gaige gongzuo huiyilu). Yinchuan: Ningxia People Publishing House.

Wu, Haiying, Tao Yuan, Ma Xushu (2007). *Analysis and the Forecast of the Ningxia Economic and Social Situation* (ningxia jingji shehui xingshi fenxi yu yuce). Yinchuan: Ningxia People Publishing House.

Xu, Anlun, Yang Xudong (1988). *Ningxia Economic History* (jingxia jingjishi). Yinchuan: Ningxia People Publishing House.

Yang, Guolin (2007). *In Search of the Great Leap Development in Ningxia* (ningxia kuayueshi fazhan xintansuo). Yinchuan: Ningxia People Publishing House.

Zhang, Jinhai (2011). *Blue Cover Book of Ningxia, 2011* (2011 ningxia jingji lanpishu). Yinchuan: Ningxia People Publishing House, Yellow River Publishing Pte, Ltd.

Zhang, Tianzheng (2011). *Studies in the Construction of Modern Ningxia: Theory and Practice* (jindai ningxia kaifa sixiang ji shijian yanjiu). Beijing: People Publishing House.

Qinghai

Source: The author, based on a file from the Wikimedia Commons.

Table A   The administrative divisions of Qinghai

Name	Administrative seat	Population
Golog Tibetan AP	Maqen County	181,682
Haibei Tibetan AP	Haiyan County	273,304
Haidong P	Ping'an County	1,396,846
Hainan Tibetan AP	Gonghe County	441,689
Haixi Mongol & Tibetan AP	Delhi	489,338
Huangnan Tibetan AP	Tongren County	256,716
Xining PM	Chengzhong District	2,208,708
Yushu Tibetan AP	Yushu County	378,439

Notes: AP = autonomous prefecture; P = prefecture; PM = prefectural level municipality.
All data are as of 2010.

Quick facts

Official name: Qinghai Province
Abbreviated name: Qing
Land area: 721,000 km^2
Population: 5,626,722
Population density: 7/km^2
GRP per capita of 2010: ¥24,115
HDI of 2008: 0.720
Capital: Xining
Government office telephone: 0971-848 3618
Website: www.qh.gov.cn

Qinghai is a province of the PRC, named after Lake Qinghai. It borders Gansu Province to the northeast, Xinjiang Autonomous Region to the northwest, Sichuan Province to the southeast and Tibet Autonomous Region to the southwest. It is located in northwestern China on the Qinghai–Tibet Plateau. The Yellow River originates in the middle of the province, while the Yangtze and Mekong have their headwaters in the south. More than 42% of the population is Tibetan, Hui, Tu, Salar, Mongol or of another ethnicity.

The province is rich in cultural history. It is the source of the Chinese Kunlun legend that was spread throughout the country before finally blending into mainstream Chinese culture. The area is attractive not only for its beautiful scenery but also for its colorful local customs.

Qinghai is located on the northeastern part of the Tibetan Plateau. The Yellow River originates in the south while the Yangtze and Mekong have their sources in the southwest. The average elevation is more than

3,000 m above sea level, varying from 1,650 m to 6,860 m, while 54% of the area is between 4,000 m and 5,000 m. The province is divided into the Qilian Mountains, the Qaidam Basin and the Qingnan Plateau. It has a plateau continental climate thanks to its elevation, topography, latitude and atmospheric circulation. The region has a long, warm winter and a short, cool summer. The temperature varies with an annual average of −5. 6 to 8.7 °C. The precipitation also varies noticeably, with the southeast receiving 450–600 mm of rainfall annually and the rest of the region being rather dry. It is also prone to heavy winds as well as sand storms from February to April.

Qinghai is the fourth largest provincial administration in China after Xinjiang, Inner Mongolia and Tibet. It has the largest saltwater lake in China and the second largest in the world. Qaidam basin lies in the northwest. About a third of this resource-rich basin is desert. It is at an altitude of 3,000 m to 3,500 m. The Sanjiangyuan National Nature Reserve (also referred to as the Sanjiangyuan Nature Reserve or the Three Rivers Nature Reserve) contains the headwaters of the Yellow River, the Yangtze River and the Mekong River. It was established to protect the headwaters of these three rivers. It consists of 18 subareas, each containing three zones which are managed with differing degrees of strictness.

There are deposits of 107 minerals in the province. Of these, 50 are among the top ten in the country and 11, including potassium chloride and magnesium salts, have the largest deposits of their kinds in China. Of the 45 urgently needed minerals in China, 21 have been found in the province, their deposits all ranking among the top ten in the country. In addition, Qinghai has more than 30 salt lakes with proven reserves of 70 billion tons. It is also rich in non-ferrous metals and non-metallic minerals. Its reserve of asbestos leads other provinces and regions in China. The famed Qaidam Basin is abundant in natural gas and oil. The total oil reserve is 1.244 billion tons, of which 200 million tons has been explored. The explored gas reserve is 47.2 billion m^3. At present there are 16 oilfields and 6 natural gas fields in the region.

The province has 178 hydropower stations with a total installed generation capacity of 21.66 million kw. The province plans to build seven more medium-sized hydropower stations which, with a total installed generation capacity of 11 million kw, will produce 36.8 billion kw h each year. The construction cost of each power station in Qinghai is 20–40% lower than the national average. The province is also rich in solar, wind and geothermal energy.

It is one of the five major pasture lands in China, boasting 31.6 million ha of grazing land which accounts for 15% of the country's total.

Among the 940 species of grass growing in its grasslands, 190 are of high nutrition with crude protein, crude fat and low coarse fiber. The livestock kept there include sheep, yak, horse, camel and goat, all of which are cold-resistant. Qinghai has the most domestic yaks in the country, accounting for one-third of the world's total.

Of the wild plants discovered in Qinghai, some 1,000 have economic value, including over 100 medicinal herbs. Its Chinese caterpillar fungus, in particular, is. There are 290 kinds of birds and 109 species of mammals, of which 21 are under first-class state protection, 53 are under second-class state protection, 36 are under provincial protection and 22 have been listed in the International Trade Convention on Endangered Wild Animals and Plants, appendixes I and II. By the end of 2005 there were 11 nature reserves in the province covering a total area of 21.76 million ha and accounting for 30.12% of the province's region.

As the origin of the Yangtze, Yellow and Mekong rivers, Qinghai has an area of 720,000 km², including 31.6 million ha of grassland, 589,900 ha of cultivated land and 250,000 ha of forests. The remaining land is mountains, lakes, deserts and glaciers.

The population of is approximately 5.2 million, among which the Han account for 54.5%. Other groups include the Tibetans (20.87%), Hui (16%), Tu (4%), Salar and Mongols.

Qinghai's economy is among the smallest in China. Its nominal GRP for 2010 was just ¥135.04 billion (about US$20 billion) and it

Table B Demographic and socioeconomic profile: Qinghai

Indicator	2000	2010
Population (thousands)	5,180	5,630
Illiteracy rate of population aged 15 or over (%)	18.03	10.23
GRP (¥ billions)	26,36	135.04
Composition of GRP (%)		
Primary sector	14.6	10.0
Secondary sector	43.3	55.1
Tertiary sector	42.1	34.9
Fixed asset investment (¥ billions)	15.11	101.69
Status of foreign-funded enterprises		
Number of registered enterprises	113	499
Total investment (US$ millions)	577	2,349
Registered capital (US$ millions)	332	1,389
Foreign trade (US$ millions)		
Export	134	318
Import	93	500
Sales of consumer goods (¥ billions)	8	35

Per capita annual disposable income of urban residents (¥)	5,169.96	13,854.99
Engle's coefficient (%)	35.82	37.06
Per capita annual net income of rural residents (¥)	1,490.49	3,862.68
Engle's coefficient (%)	34.31	38.23
Number of patent applications granted	117	264
Inventions	16	41
Utility models	67	134
Designs	34	89

Note: All monetary values are measured at current prices.
Source: *Qinghai Statistical Yearbook*, 2001 and 2011.

contributes to about 0.3% of the country's economy. The per capita GRP was ¥19,407 (about US$2,841), the second lowest in China.

The region's economy is based on minerals, hydropower and agro-husbandry. The province also plays an important ecological role as the source of major rivers. Oil and natural gas production at the Chaidamu Basin also contributes to the economy. Outside Xining, most of the province remains underdeveloped. Qinghai ranks second lowest in China in terms of highway length and only with significant infrastructure will the province be able to fully capitalize on its natural resources. Looking forward, Qinghai plans to focus on solar, wind and low-carbon energy projects. The area's heavy industry includes iron and steel production, located near its capital.

The industrial sector leads the economy with a contribution of more than a half of GRP, while the service sector follows relatively close behind with 37.60%. Agriculture brings up the rear with 10.80%. The industries with the highest amount of fixed asset investments are in the areas of production and supply of electricity, gas and water, manufacturing, transportation and storage, mining and real estate.

The area's livestock include sheep, yaks and horses. Qinghai produces large quantities of meat, sheep's wool, leather and sausage casings for other parts of the country. It is also an important producer of medicinal materials, such as caterpillar fungus, antlers, musk and rhubarb. The province grows spring wheat, highland barley, broad beans, potatoes and rapeseed.

Qinghai is rich in resources, such as hydropower, lead, zinc, minerals, saline and petroleum and gas. The natural resources have had a great influence in shaping the province's industry structure so the pillar industries depend largely on these resources to develop. The four pillar industries include petroleum and natural gas, hydropower, non-ferrous metals and saline chemicals.

Many tourist attractions center on Xining, the provincial seat of Qinghai. During the hot summer months, many tourists from the hot southern and eastern parts of China travel to the city as the climate there in July and August is quite mild and comfortable, making it an ideal summer retreat.

Lake Qinghai is another tourist attraction, albeit further from Xining than Kumbum. It is located on the "Roof of the World", the Tibetan Plateau. The lake lies at an elevation of 3,600 m. The surrounding area is made up of rolling grasslands and is populated by ethnic Tibetans. Most pre-arranged tours stop at Birds Island. An international bicycle race takes place annually from Xining to Lake Qinghai.

The province features ethnic custom tours unique to the plateau. It has more than ten scenic spots, including the Birds Islet, the Mengda Natural Reserves, Ta'er Monastery, snow-capped A'Nyemaqen Mountain, Sun-and-Moon Hill, Gold and Silver Meadow, Longyang Gorge Reservoir (the largest artificial reservoir in China) and the Dulan International Game Land. Together these account for the growing tourist industry in the area.

The Qinghai–Tibet Railway is the world's highest railway line and it weaves between Xining and Lhasa. It has a favorable impact on the local logistics industry and on sightseeing. The operation of the railway in 2007 helped boost goods exchanges between the secluded Qinghai–Tibet Plateau and other parts of China.

Major export items included aluminum and rolled aluminum, silicon, yarn, woolen fiber and carpets. Major export markets included Japan, Hong Kong and the US. Key import products are aluminum oxide, semiconductors, parts for auto data-processing equipment, motor vehicles and chassis. Major sources of imports are Australia, India and Bosnia.

Foreign investments in Qinghai are mainly channeled into the manufacturing industries. Hong Kong is an important source of FDI, accounting for 28.4% of the province's contracted FDI in 2006.

As of 2010, compared with those of other provinces, "scientific research, technical services and geological prospecting", "public management and social organization" and "culture, sports and entertainment" were relatively strong, while "hotels and catering services", "leasing and business services" and "manufacturing" were relatively weak sectors (see Table C).

Table C   Qinghai's comparative (dis)advantage index by sector, 2010

Sector	Index
Agriculture, forestry, animal husbandry and fishery	1.15
Mining	0.88
Manufacturing	0.67
Production and distribution of electricity, gas and water	0.99
Construction	0.79
Transport, storage and post	1.29
Information transmission, computer service and software	1.05
Wholesale and retail trades	0.81
Hotels and catering services	0.56
Financial intermediation	1.04
Real estate	0.74
Leasing and business services	0.66
Scientific research, technical services and geological prospecting	1.96
Management of water conservancy, environment and public facilities	1.28
Services to households and other services	1.26
Education	1.18
Health, social security and social welfare	1.25
Culture, sports and entertainment	1.38
Public management and social organization	1.55

Notes: All the sectors included in this table are determined according to China's official definitions and for urban areas only. Numerals greater than, equal to and less than 1 indicate that the province's sectors have advantages, no apparent (dis)advantages and disadvantages, respectively.
Sources: Calculated by author based on *China Statistical Yearbook*, 2011. See Appendix for a detailed methodological description.

- **Xining Economic and Technological Development Zone (XETDZ)** This was approved as a state-level development zone in July 2000. Lying in the east of Xining, it has an area of 12.79 km^2. It is 4 km from the railway station, 5 km from the downtown area and 15 km from Xi'ning Airport, a grade 4D airport with 14 airlines to other cities, such as Beijing, Guangzhou, Shanghai, Chengdu and Xi'an. The zone enjoys a convenient transportation system, connected by the Xining–Lanzhou expressway and crossed by the two broadest roads of the city. Xining is Qinghai province's passage to the outside world – a transportation center with more than ten highways, over 100 roads and two railways: Lanzhou–Qinghai and Qinghai–Tibet railways in and out of the city.
- XETDZ is the first of its kind at the national level on the Qinghai–Tibet Plateau. It was established to fulfill the strategy of developing the west of the country. It gives priority to export-oriented industrial

projects and those utilizing foreign capital. It focuses on development industries based on local resources, including chemicals based on salt-lake materials, non-ferrous metals, petroleum and natural gas processing, special medicine, foods, bio-chemicals using local plateau animals and plants, new products involving ecological and environmental protection, high technology, new materials, IT, and services such as logistics, banking, real estate, tourism, hotels, catering, agency and international trade. In 2007 there were 100 investment enterprises with a total fixed asset investment of ¥3 billion. Industrial output value in that year reached ¥4.5 billion.

As of 2010 the top five companies were as follows:

1. Qinghai Salt Lake Industry Group Co (SHE: 000578) is a leading producer and distributor of potassium fertilizers. It posted ¥5.9 billion in revenues and ¥1.5 billion in net profits for 2010.
2. Qinghai Salt Lake Potash Co (SHE: 000792) is a leading producer and distributor of chemical fertilizers. It posted ¥4.95 billion in revenues and ¥1.11 billion in net profits for 2010.
3. West Mining Co (SHA: 601168) is a miner, smelter and trader in zinc, lead, copper and aluminum. It posted ¥18.51 billion in revenues and ¥989.43 million in net profits for 2010.
4. Xining Special Steel Co (SHA: 600117) is a producer of steel bars and reinforced bars and machinery. It posted ¥7.05 billion in revenues and ¥233.12 million in net profits for 2010.
5. Qinghai Jinrui Mineral Development Co (SHA: 600714) is a coal and strontium carbonate producer and distributor. It posted ¥377.93 million in revenues and ¥34.81 million in net profits for 2010.

Indicators for the ease of doing business

A. Starting a business

Procedures: 14
Time (days): 51
Cost (% of provincial GRP per capita): 12

B. Registering property

Procedures: 8
Time (days): 60
Cost (% of property value): 5.3

C. Getting credit – creating and registering collateral
Time (days): 20
Cost (% of loan value): 3.8

D. Enforcing contracts
Time (days): 458
Cost (% of claim): 24.8

Further reading

Cheng, Joseph Y.S (2003). "Qinghai's economic development strategy," *Issues and Studies*, vol. 39, issue 2, June, pp. 189–218.
Cooke, Susette (2008). "Surviving state and society in Northwest China: The Hui Experience in Qinghai Province under the PRC," *Journal of Muslim Minority Affairs*, vol. 28, issue 3, December, pp. 401–420.
Fan, Guangming (2007). *Qinghai, Source land of Three Great Rivers* (Panoramic China). Beijing: Foreign Languages Press.
Gao, Xincai, Jiang Anyin (2008). *The Blue Cover Book: Qinghai* (xibei quyu jingji fazhan lanpishu: qinghaijuan). Beijing: People Publishing House.
Goodman, David S.G (2004). "Qinghai and the emergence of the West: Nationalities, communal interaction and national integration," *The China Quarterly*, vol. 178, July, pp. 379–399.
Ma, Hongbo (2011). *Implementing the Strategies of Founding the Province Based on Ecology: A Study of Qinghai Province* (qinghai shishi shengtai lisheng zhanlue yanjiu). Beijing: China Economics Publishing House.
Nie, Hualin, Gao kaishan, Bai Qirui (2006). *Regional Economic Integration: Studies of Economic Issues in the Small Northwest Areas* (xiaoxibei jingji wenti yanjiu: diqu jingji yitihua chanye jiqun sannong wenti). Beijing: China Social Sicence Publishing House.
Su, Duoming (2012). *The Research of Technological Innovation Ability in Qinghai Province* (qinghai keji chuangxin nengli yanjiu). Beijing: China Economics Publishig House.
Su, Ming Ming, Geoffrey Wall (2009). "The Qinghai–Tibet Railway and Tibetan Tourism: Travelers' Perspectives," *Tourism Management*, vol. 30, issue 5, October, pp. 650–657.
Wang, Jianjun, Qu Bo (2009). *Studies of Resource Enterprise and Regional Economic Sustainable Development: A Case in Qinghai Province* (ziyuanxing qiye yu quyu jingji kechixu fazhan yanjiu: yi qinghai weili). Beijing: Ethnological Publishing House.
Xu, Xianli, Keli Zhang, Yaping Kong, Jiding Chen, Bofu Yu (2006). "Effectiveness of erosion control measures along the Qinghai–Tibet highway, Tibetan Plateau, China," *Transportation Research Part D: Transport and Environment*, vol. 11, issue 4, July, pp. 302–309.
Zhang, Hongyan (2010). *Research of Regional Economic and Social Coordinated Development in the Tibetan Ethnic Area, Qinghai Province* (qinghaisheng zangzu diqu jingji yu shehui xietiao fazhan yanjiu). Beijing: Central Ethnic University Publishing House.

Shaanxi

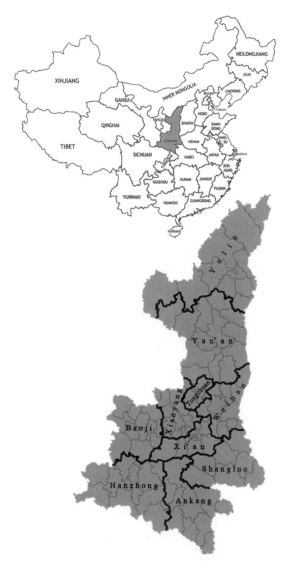

Source: The author, based on a file from the Wikimedia Commons.

Table A The administrative divisions of Shaanxi

Name	Administrative seat	Population
Ankang PM	Hanbin District	2,629,906
Baoji PM	Weibin District	3,716,731
Hanzhong PM	Hantai District	3,416,196
Shangluo PM	Shangzhou District	2,341,742
Tongchuan PM	Yaozhou District	834,437
Weinan PM	Linwei District	5,286,077
Xi'an SPM	Weiyang District	8,467,837
Xianyang PM	Qindu District	4,894,834
Yan'an PM	Baota District	2,187,009
Yulin PM	Yuyang District	3,351,437

Notes: PM = prefectural level municipality; SPM = sub-provincial level municipality. All data are as of 2010.

Quick facts

Official name: Shaanxi Province
Abbreviated name: Shaan
Land area: 205,800 km²
Population: 37,327,378
Population density: 180/km²
GRP per capita of 2010: ¥27,133
HDI of 2008: 0.773
Capital: Xi'an
Government office address: Xincheng Square, Xi'an
Postcode: 710004
Website: www.shaanxi.gov.cn

Shaanxi is a province of the PRC. It includes a portion of the Loess Plateau on the middle reaches of the Yellow River in addition to the Qinling Mountains across the southern part of the region. It borders Ningxia Hui Autonomous Region and Inner Mongolia Autonomous Region to the north, Shanxi Province to the northeast, Henan Province to the east, Hubei Province to the southeast, Sichuan Province and Chongqing Municipality to the south and Gansu Province to the west.

Shaanxi is the official spelling of this province. It is the only name of a Chinese province that is not written according to the Chinese pinyin system. By standard Pinyin rules, both Shaanxi and its neighboring province of Shanxi should be spelled "Shanxi". The difference is in the tone: *Shǎnxī* for Shaanxi and *Shānxī* for Shanxi. The abbreviated name for the region is Shaan (*Shǎn* in Chinese).

The area is composed of several distinct areas. In the north is desert along the border with Inner Mongolia Autonomous Region. The Loess Plateau further south has an elevation of 800–1,300 m and accounts for 45% of the total area of the province. The Central Shaanxi Plain in the middle averages an elevation of 520 m. The Qinling Mountains (elevation 1,000–3,000 m), Daba Mountains (1,500–2,000 m) and Hanjiang River Valley account for 36% of the region. Taibaishan is the highest peak in the Qinling Range. Finally the sub-tropical area is south of the Qinling Mountains.

An inland province along the middle reaches of the Yellow River and a gateway to northwest China, it links the west to the east and the north to the south. The Eurasia Continental Bridge, an international economic link starting from Lianyungang in the east and ending in Rotterdam in the Netherlands, traverses the region.

The northern part of Shaanxi is cold in winter and very hot in summer, with dry winter and spring seasons. Its southern portion generally receives more rain. The average annual temperature is 8–16 °C, with January temperatures ranging from −11 to 3.5 °C and July of 21–28 °C.

The province produces a large quantity of nature's treasures and is endowed with rich natural resources. With substantial development of the west, Shaanxi will become the nation's important area for the transportation of energy sources, such as gasses, electricity and coal from west to east.

Reserves of 91 kinds of minerals have been identified in Shaanxi, of which 58 rank among the top ten in the country, 18 (including coal, natural gas, molybdenum, mercury and gadolinite) take second or third place and 12 (including strontium, rhenium and cement rock) rank first. The reserves and output of gold rank fifth and fourth in China, respectively. The output of molybdenum amounts to half of the country's total. Proven deposits of coal, the most abundant mineral in the province, amount to 161.8 billion tons. The Shenmu-Fugu Coalfield in northern Shaanxi has reserves of 134 billion tons. It is one of the best fields in the world because of its thick coal layer and its easy access and exploitation. In addition, northern Shaanxi has a gas field with proven reserves of 350 billion m³. The region has an area of 50,000 km² that contains coal, the recoverable deposits of which are 161.8 billion tons. Few other coalfields for quality power like this one exist in the world. Northern Shaanxi Natural-Gas Field has proven reserves of

350 billion m^3 and is a word-class continental self-contained natural gas field.

The northern part of the Qinling Mountains is characterized by the Yellow River system, including the Weihe, the Jinghe, the Luohe and the Wuding rivers. South of the mountains is the Yangtze River system consisting of the Hanjiang, Danjiang and Jialing rivers. The Hanjiang, the largest river in the province, provides more than half of the province's total water runoff. Shaanxi has 583 rivers with an annual runoff of 42.6 billion m^3, representing 14,000,000 kw of waterpower storage. Through development over the years, 80,000 irrigation projects of various types have been constructed and 1,410,000 ha of land are irrigated, accounting for 42% of the cultivated land.

The region has more than 750 species of wild vertebrates, which include 79 rare species. It is also home to 12 species of animal – such as giant pandas, golden-haired monkeys and clouded leopards – which are national treasures under the state's priority protection, and rare ibis. Qinchuan cattle, which are bred in the province, are well known all over the world. The number of improved breeds of milking goats is the highest number in the country and the breeding of boar goats is on a significant scale.

The province has 5.93 million ha of forest in the Qinling, Daba, Guanshan, Huanglong and Qiaoshan mountain areas with 28.8% forest coverage. It has 3,300-plus species of wild plants, 37 of which are rare. Some 800 species of medicinal plants are of great economic value, including sea buckthorn and *Gynostemma pentaphylla*. The region leads the country in the output and quality of raw lacquer. The traditional exports of the province are dates, walnut meat and tung oil. By 2005 the number of nature reserves in the province had reached 45, covering a total area of 995,000 ha.

Shaanxi Province is an important place concerning the origin of ancient Chinese civilization. The Banpo Neolithic village is located near Xi'an. Dispersed across the region are 72 imperial mausoleums, witness to the ancient economy and culture of the area. It is best known for ten scenic spots, including the Mausoleum of Huangdi, the Qin Terra-cotta Warriors and Horses, the Xi'an Forest of Stone Tablets, the Shaanxi Museum of History and the city gate and wall of Xi'an. The Qin Terra-cotta Warriors and Horses, known as the "eighth wonder of the world", has been included by UNESCO on the list of World Cultural Heritage Sites. In addition, Yan'an was the destination of the Long March of and the center of the Chinese Communist Revolution from 1935 to 1948.

Shaanxi's nominal GRP for 2010 was ¥1,012.35 billion (about US$150 billion) and its GRP per capita was ¥27,133 (about US$3,500), ranking 14th in the PRC.

Table B   Demographic and socioeconomic profile: Shaanxi

Indicator	2000	2010
Population (thousands)	36,050	37,352
Illiteracy rate of population aged 15 or over (%)	7.29	3.74
GRP (¥ billions)	166.09	1,012.35
Composition of GRP (%)		
Primary sector	16.8	9.8
Secondary sector	44.1	53.8
Tertiary sector	39.1	36.4
Fixed asset investment (¥ billions)	65.37	796.37
Status of foreign-funded enterprises		
Number of registered enterprises	2,761	5,378
Total investment (US$ millions)	8,322	18,044
Registered capital (US$ millions)	5,071	11,012
Foreign trade (US$ millions)		
Export	1,327	5,635
Import	1,061	6,069
Sales of consumer goods (¥ billions)	61	320
Per capita annual disposable income of urban residents (¥)	5,124.24	15,695.21
Engle's coefficient (%)	34.73	32.06
Per capita annual net income of rural residents (¥)	1,443.86	4,104.98
Engle's coefficient (%)	32.53	34.25
Number of patent applications granted	1,462	10,034
Inventions	188	1,887
Utility models	1,022	6,093
Designs	252	2,054

Note: All monetary values are measured at current prices.
Source: *Shaanxi Statistical Yearbook*, 2001 and 2011.

The fossil fuel and high technology sectors compose the two largest industries in Shaanxi. It is a major producer of fossil fuels. In 2009 it produced 296 million tons of coal, 27 million tons of crude oil and 18,950 million m^3 of natural gas, all ranked among the top three in China. The reserves of these resources are large and have yet to be fully explored. The capital, Xi'an City, has a high-tech industrial zone that is supported by several of the best universities and research institutions in western China. The focus is on software development, aerospace technology, new materials and aircraft technology, all of which are among China's new priority industries. Transforming Shaanxi's high-tech advantages into actual production will be the main challenge for the future. Some areas, such as space technology, where the province leads the country, may take longer to commercialize.

As of 2010, compared with those of other provinces, "mining", "scientific research, technical services and geological prospecting" and "information transmission, computer service and software" were relatively strong, while "leasing and business services", "agriculture, forestry, animal husbandry and fishery" and "construction" were relatively weak sectors (see Table C).

Table C   Shaanxi's comparative (dis)advantage index by sector, 2010

Sector	Index
Agriculture, forestry, animal husbandry and fishery	0.42
Mining	1.57
Manufacturing	0.80
Production and distribution of electricity, gas and water	1.27
Construction	0.71
Transport, storage and post	1.08
Information transmission, computer service and software	1.36
Wholesale and retail trades	0.83
Hotels and catering services	1.08
Financial intermediation	1.08
Real estate	0.87
Leasing and business services	0.40
Scientific research, technical services and geological prospecting	1.57
Management of water conservancy, environment and public facilities	1.29
Services to households and other services	1.02
Education	1.25
Health, social security and social welfare	1.09
Culture, sports and entertainment	1.26
Public management and social organization	1.24

Notes: All the sectors included in this table are determined according to China's official definitions and for urban areas only. Numerals greater than, equal to and less than 1 indicate that the province's sectors have advantages, no apparent (dis)advantages and disadvantages, respectively.
Sources: Calculated by author based on *China Statistical Yearbook*, 2011. See Appendix for a detailed methodological description.

In Shaanxi Province there are various economic and technological development zones. These are described below.

- **Baoji Hi-Tech Industrial Development Zone** Established in 1992, this was approved as a national hi-tech zone by the State Council.

It has a long-term planned area of 40 km^2. The transportation system around the zone includes Xi'an Xianyang International Airport and national highway 310. Its encouraged industries are auto parts, electronics, IT, pharmaceuticals and bioengineering, and new materials. At present there are more than 500 enterprises, of which over 100 are new- and high-tech corporations. Leading industries are electronics, IT, electromechanical integration and new materials. A Sino-German joint venture for new chemical materials with a total investment of US$200 million is now underway.

- **Xi'an Export Processing Zone (XEPZ)** This was approved in 2002 by the State Council and was put into operation in 2004. As the first state-level export processing zone in northwest China, it has become one of the seven pioneer export processing zones with the function of bonded logistics in China. It occupies an area of 2.8 km^2. Enterprises there can enjoy the preferential policy of zero customs duty, zero export tariff and zero consumption tax. "One-time declaration, one-time document examination and one-time inspection" is adopted from port to export processing zone. With enterprises from home and abroad, it has become a new growth point of the processing trade in Shaanxi Province. The zone is under the leadership of the Administrative Committee of the Xi'an Economic and Technological Development Zone, which is designated by Xi'an municipal government to exercise economic and administrative power within the zone. XEPZ is a special economic zone. By now there are more than 40 enterprises settled there, and the pillar industries of aviation, machinery, electronics and new energy have taken shape.

- **Xi'an Economic and Technological Development Zone** Established in 1993, this was approved at state level in 2000. It is only 20 minutes from the Xi'an Xianyang International Airport and has several national highway links. It has formed four pillar industries, namely automotive, electronics, food and new materials. So far it has attracted more than 1,700 enterprises. Covering an area of 23.5 km, the zone is a base for machine-building and electronics, light industry, food, medicine and new materials, among others. Some world-class enterprises, such as Coca-Cola, HP, Siemens, Mitsubishi and Volvo, and famous enterprises from Hong Kong and Taiwan, have established their offices and plants there.

- **Xi'an High-Tech Industrial Development Zone** Established in August 1991, this covers an area of 34 km. Ten science and technology parks and industrial bases for software, photoelectronics, new materials and medicine have been built up there. To date more than

4,000 enterprises have been established, of which 703 are new- and high-tech corporations and 488 are foreign-invested ventures. There are 83 risk-investment enterprises there. The zone was established as a "pivotal location" for investment by high-tech industry companies in central and northwest China. It is linked to several national highways and is within 30 minutes of Xi'an Xianyang International Airport. Furthermore, it is ranked in the top three high-tech zones in China.

- **Xi'an Software Park** Established in December 1998, this is the professional park for Xi'an to develop software and service outsourcing industries. It has been appraised as a software industry base under the National Torch Program, a national software industry base, a national software export base and a city demonstrational area of national service outsourcing base. The park houses 90% of enterprises engaging in software and service outsourcing in Xi'an. By the end of 2008 there were nearly 780 companies, of which 170 were foreign-funded, offering more than 71,000 jobs.
- **Yangling Demonstration Zone for Agricultural High-Tech Industries** As the only state-level high-tech agricultural demonstration zone, this covers an area of 94 km with a population of 140,000. It was approved as a national-level hi-tech development zone by the State Council in 1997. It is only 82 km from Xi'an to the east and 70 km from Xi'an Xianyang International Airport. There are 110 laboratories with 5,000 R&D and educational staff in more than 70 subjects. Research into wheat breeding, dry farming, plant protection, poultry procreation and embryo engineering take the lead in China. Technologies relating to animal cloning, stem cell research and cross-breeding wheat rank first worldwide. Since the zone's establishment six years ago, more than 1,600 improved varieties of animals and plants have been produced and over 1,000 agricultural technologies transferred.

As of 2010 the top five companies were as follows:

1. Jinduicheng Molybdenum Co (SHA: 601958) is a molybdenum miner, smelter and distributor. It posted ¥7.06 billion in revenues and ¥835.63 million in net profits for 2010.
2. China Xd Electric Co (SHA: 601179) is engaged in design, research, development, manufacture and distribution of power transmission, distribution and control equipment. It posted ¥12.93 billion in revenues and ¥639.45 million in net profits for 2010.

3. Xian Aircraft International Corp (SHE: 000768) is engaged in the aviation, road transportation and construction material industries. It posted ¥10.53 billion in revenues and ¥345.56 million in net profits for 2010.
4. Xian Shaangu Power Co (SHA: 601369) is a turbine machines manufacturer and distributor. It posted ¥4.35 billion in revenues and ¥664.67 million in net profits for 2010.
5. Shaanxi Provincial Natural Gas Co (SHE: 002267) is a long-distance natural gas pipeline constructor and operator. It posted ¥2.48 billion in revenues and ¥403.94 million in net profits for 2010.

Indicators for the ease of doing business

A. Starting a business

Procedures: 14
Time (days): 43
Cost (% of provincial GRP per capita): 15.2

B. Registering property

Procedures: 8
Time (days): 50
Cost (% of property value): 5.1

C. Getting credit – creating and registering collateral

Time (days): 21
Cost (% of loan value): 4

D. Enforcing contracts

Time (days): 235
Cost (% of claim): 21.7

Further reading

Cao, Aihong, Qi Antian (2010). *Economic Development and Financial Support in the Less-Developed Area: A Case in Ankang, Shaanxi Province* (qian fada diqu de jingji fazhan he jinrong zhichi: yi shanxi sheng ankang wei li). Beijing: Economic Management Publishing House.
Cao, Shixiong, Chenguang Xu, Li Chen, Xiuqing Wang (2009). "Attitudes of farmers in China's northern Shaanxi Province towards the land-use changes required under the grain for green project, and implications for the project's Success," *Land Use Policy*, vol. 26, issue 4, October, pp. 1182–1194.
Cao, Shixiong, Li Chen, Qi Feng, Zhande Liu (2007). "Soft-riser bench terrace design for the hilly loess region of Shaanxi Province, China," *Landscape and Urban Planning*, vol. 80, issues 1–2, 28 March, pp. 184–191.

Feng, Wang, Ann Reisner (2011). "Factors influencing private and public environmental protection behaviors: Results from a survey of residents in Shaanxi, China," *Journal of Environmental Management*, vol. 92, issue 3, March, pp. 429–436.

Foreign Languages Press (2006, ed.). *Shaanxi* (Panoramic China). Beijing: Foreign Languages Press.

Gao, Xincai, Cao Zijian (2008). *Blue Cover Book: Shaanxi* (xibei quyu jingji fazhan lanpishu: shanxijuan). Beijing: People Publishing House.

Huang, Baosheng (1998, ed.). *Survey of Southern Shaanxi Culture* (shannan wenhua diaocha). Xi'an: Taibai Cultural and Arts Press.

Keating, Pauline (1997). *Two Revolutions: Village Reconstruction and the Cooperative Movement in Northern Shaanxi, 1934–1945*. Stanford, CA: Stanford University Press.

Lee, Pak K. (1997). "The political economy of state enterprise relations in China's Shaanxi Province," *Journal of Contemporary Asia*, vol. 27, issue 3, January, pp. 287–314.

Liu, Shijin (2011, ed.). *The New Growth Pole in China's Western Area: The Case of the Yulin-Yuheng New Zone, Shaanxi Province* (zhongguo xibu xinzengzhangji: shanxi yulin yuheng xinqu fazhan zhanlue baogao yanjiu). Beijing: China Development Publishng House.

Shi, Ying (2003, ed.). *Shaanxi Economy and Society in 2002* (2002 nian de shanxi jinji yu shehui). Xi'an: Shaanxi People's Publishing House.

Tian, Peidong (2007). *A History of Shaanxi's Social Economy* (shanxi shehui jingji shi). Xi'an: San Qing Publishing House.

Wadson, Adrew (1999). "Shaanxi, the search for comparative advantage," in Hendrischke, Hans (ed.), *The Political Economy of China's Provinces: Competitive and Comparative Advantage*. London and New York: Routledge, pp. 73–112.

Yang, Shangqin, Shi Ying, Fei Chengrong (2012). *Economic Development Report in Shaanxi, 2012* (2012 ban shanxi jingji fazhan baogao). Beijing: Social Science Reference Publishing House.

Zhou, Hongjian, Anton Van Rompaey, Jing'ai Wang (2009). "Detecting the impact of the 'Grain for Green' Program on the Mean Annual Vegetation Cover in the Shaanxi Province, China using SPOT-VGT NDVI data," *Land Use Policy*, vol. 26, issue 4, October, pp. 954–960.

Shandong

Source: The author, based on a file from the Wikimedia Commons.

Table A The administrative divisions of Shandong

Name	Administrative seat	Population
Binzhou PM	Bincheng District	3,748,500
Dezhou PM	Decheng District	5,568,200
Dongying PM	Dongying District	2,035,300
Heze PM	Mudan District	8,287,800
Ji'nan SPM	Shizhong District	6,814,000
Jining PM	Shizhong District	8,081,900
Laiwu PM	Laicheng District	1,298,500
Liaocheng PM	Dongchangfu District	5,789,900
Linyi PM	Lanshan District	10,039,400
Qingdao SPM	Shinan District	8,715,100
Rizhao PM	Donggang District	2,801,100
Tai'an PM	Taishan District	5,494,200
Weifang PM	Kuiwen District	9,086,200
Weihai PM	Huancui District	2,804,800
Yantai PM	Laishan District	6,968,200
Zaozhuang PM	Shizhong District	3,729,300
Zibo PM	Zhangdian District	4,530,600

Notes: PM = prefectural level municipality; SPM = sub-provincial level municipality. All data are as of 2010.

Quick facts

Official name: Shandong Province
Abbreviated name: Lu
Land area: 156,700 km^2
Population: 95,793,065
Population density: 600/km^2
GRP per capita of 2010: ¥41,106
HDI of 2008: 0.828
Capital: Jinan
Government office address: 1 Shengfu Qianjie, Jinan City
Tel: 531–8606–2094
Postcode: 250011
Website: www.sd.gov.cn

Shandong is a province of the PRC and is part of the east China region. Situated in the lower reaches of the Yellow River, its territory consists of the Shandong Peninsular and adjacent inland. It borders the Bohai Sea to the north, Hebei Province to the northwest, Henan Province to the west, Jiangsu Province to the south and the Yellow Sea to the southeast. It also shares a very short border with Anhui Province. The region stretches 420 km from south to north and 700 km from east to west. Its coastline is 3,000 km long.

In Chinese "Shandong" means "mountain" (*shan*) and "east" (*dong*). The name can thus be translated literally as "east of the mountain" and it refers to the province's location to the east of Mount Taihang. A common nickname for the province is Qilu, after the states of Qi and Lu that existed in the area during the Eastern Zhou Dynasty (771–221 BC). Whereas the state of Qi was a major power of its era, that of Lu became renowned for being the home of Confucius. The cultural dominance of Lu is reflected in the official abbreviation for Shandong, which is "Lu."

The Yellow River passes through Shandong's western areas, entering the sea along the northern coast. The Grand Canal of China enters the province from the northwest and leaves on the southwest. Lake Weishan is the largest lake of the region. Shandong Peninsula has a rocky coastline with cliffs, bays and islands. The large Laizhou Bay, the southernmost of the three bays of the Bohai Sea, is found to the north between Dongying and Penglai; Jiaozhou Bay, which is much smaller, is found to the south, next to Qingdao. The Miaodao Islands extend northwards from the northern coast of the peninsula. The 17 administrative divisions of Shandong Province are subdivided into 140 county-level divisions (49 districts, 31 county-level cities and 60 counties). These are in turn divided into 1,941 township-level divisions (1,223 towns, 293 townships, 2 ethnic townships and 423 sub-districts).

The area's topography is complicated and interwoven with nine types of landform, including plains, basins, hills, terraces, deltas and mountains. Mountain area and plains account for 15.5% and 55% of the province's territory, respectively, while hilly areas take up 13.2%, and rivers and lakes 1.1%. The center of the province is mountainous, with the summit of Mount Taishan, 1,545 m above sea level, being the highest point. Most hills distributed in the eastern part are at the altitude of 500 m and lower. Plains lying to the west and north are mostly below 50 m in elevation. The lowest area of the province is the Yellow River Delta, which is generally 2–10 m above sea level.

Shandong has a warm temperate monsoon climate with most rainfall concentrated in the hot summer. It has a short spring and autumn but a long winter and summer. The average temperature is 11–14 °C. The annual average rainfall is between 550 mm and 950 mm. Mainly relying on rainfall, the province's water resources are scarce, with only 520 m^3 available per resident, accounting for 18.8% of the national average of 2,770 m^3 per head. Currently the water supply is 19.224

billion m³, including 7.844 billion m³ of surface water, 5.88 billion m³ of underground water and 5.5 billion m³ diverted from the Yellow River.

Some 128 minerals, 78% of which are found elsewhere in China, have been discovered in the province, of which 33 have their surveyed deposits listed among the top ten of the nation: gold, natural sulfur and gypsum rank first; petroleum, diamond, magnetite, cobalt, hafnium and granite rank second; and kali salt, graphite, talc, bentonite and limestone rank third. The reserves of many other minerals, such as natural gas, iron, aluminum, barite, diatomite, zircon, bauxite and refractory clay, are also plentiful. Shandong produces approximately 26% of China's gold, and the country is the world's fourth largest producer. A famous gold producer in Shandong is the Shandong Gold Mining Co. Ltd. It is the second largest China listed gold producer behind Zhongjin Gold.

The province is one of China's important energy bases: the crude oil produced in Shandong makes up one-third of the nation's total. The province has 50,000 km² of coalfields and is one of China's ten major coal-production bases. Coal mines are mainly found in the cities of Zibo, Zaozhuang, Yanzhou and Linyi. Intensive petroleum exploration is carried out along the Yellow River Delta. Its Shengli Oilfield is the second largest oil-production base in China, accounting for a large portion of the national total. The Shengli Oilfield extends over an area of 61,000 km² in northern Shandong, producing more than 200 million barrels of crude oil annually. The region is also a rich source of electricity. The Shandong power network is one of the country's six major power networks that are operated separately on a provincial basis.

The region has abundant agricultural and marine resources. With provincial rivers like the Yellow River, the Haihe River and the Huaihe River passing through, Shandong comprises mainly low-lying land with some mountainous terrain. There are more than 3,100 varieties of plant there. Among the 450 species of wild vertebrates (accounting for 21% of the nation's total), 55 are mammals, 362 are birds, 8 are amphibians and 25 are reptiles. In addition, there are many species of land invertebrates, insects in particular, making the province rank first in the country.

One of China's major agricultural production bases, Shandong is known as "a warehouse of grains, cotton and oil, and the land of fruits and aquatic products". It's also an important producer of wheat, peanuts, tobacco, hemp, silkworms and traditional Chinese medicinal herbs and materials. The apples produced in Yantai, pears from Laiyang, peaches from Feicheng and Leling's golden-threaded jujubes are all famous specialties.

The province is rich in marine resources too. Its offshore area makes up 37% of the total surface area of the Bohai and the Yellow seas, with a shoal area accounting for 15% of the nation's total. There are about 260 species of fish and prawn in its seas, including more than 40 major cash species of fish and 100 species of shellfish. Shandong leads the country in the production of prawns, shellfish, abalones, sea slugs and urchins. Meanwhile, with many large and medium-sized salt works, it is also one of China's four major salt producers. In its 266,000 ha of freshwater, there are more than 40 species of freshwater plants and more than 70 species of fish.

The region has played a major role in Chinese history from the beginning of Chinese civilization along the lower reaches of the Yellow River, and it served as a pivotal cultural and religious site for Taoism, Chinese Buddhism and Confucianism. Mount Tai is the most revered mountain of Taoism and the site with the longest history of continuous religious worship worldwide. The Buddhist temples in the mountains to the south of the provincial capital of Jinan were once among the foremost Buddhist sites in China. The city of Qufu is the birthplace of Confucius and was later established as the center of Confucianism.

With beautiful natural landscapes and numerous historical and cultural relics, Shandong has rich tourist resources. It offers a string of attractions, such as two World Heritage Sites – Mount Taishan and the Temple, and the Mansion and Cemetery of Confucius; Lingzi, capital of the ancient Qi State; Penglai, the well-known "fairyland on earth"; Mount Laoshan, a sacred land of Taoism; Weifang, the "world capital of kites"; Qingdao, a charming coastal city famous for its annual International Beer Fair; Yantai, known worldwide as a wine producer; Rongcheng, a place considered as "the edge of the world" by the ancient Chinese; Jinan, the provincial capital honored as "the city of springs"; and a site for watching the wonderful scene of the Yellow River running into the sea.

The province is the second largest economy and consumer market in China next to Guangdong. In 2010 its nominal GRP was ¥3.92 trillion (about US$603 billion), ranking third in the country (behind Guangdong and Jiangsu provinces). Its GRP per capita was ¥42,014 (about US$6,365), ranking eighth. It is one of the rich regions in China and its economic development focuses on large enterprises with well-known brand names. Shandong is the biggest industrial producer and one of the top manufacturing provinces in the country. The richest part is the Shandong Peninsula. Its growing purchasing power has led to the widespread development of major commercial centers, mainly situated in the cities of Ji'nan, Qingdao, Weifang and Yantai.

Table B   Demographic and socioeconomic profile: Shandong

Indicator	2000	2010
Population (thousands)	90,790	95,879
Illiteracy rate of population aged 15 or over (%)	8.46	4.97
GRP (¥ billions)	854.24	3,916.99
Composition of GRP (%)		
Primary sector	14.9	9.2
Secondary sector	49.7	54.2
Tertiary sector	35.5	36.6
Fixed asset investment (¥ billions)	253.11	2,328.05
Status of foreign-funded enterprises		
Number of registered enterprises	12,389	29,486
Total investment (US$ millions)	38,950	124,523
Registered capital (US$ millions)	23,097	72,865
Foreign trade (US$ millions)		
Export	16,093	110,301
Import	12,157	114,860
Sales of consumer goods (¥ billions)	255	1,462
Per capita annual disposable income of urban residents (¥)	6,489.97	19,945.83
Engle's coefficient (%)	44.15	33.52
Per capita annual net income of rural residents (¥)	2,659.20	6,990.28
Engle's coefficient (%)	34.18	37.54
Number of patent applications granted	6,962	51,490
Inventions	363	4,106
Utility models	4,627	36,391
Designs	1,972	10,993

Note: All monetary values are measured at current prices.
Source: *Shandong Statistical Yearbook*, 2001 and 2011.

Shandong ranks first among the provinces in the production of a variety of products, including cotton and wheat, as well as precious metals (such as gold) and diamonds. It also has one of the biggest sapphire deposits in the world. Other important crops include sorghum and maize. It has extensive petroleum deposits too, especially in the Dongying area in the Yellow River Delta, the location of Shengli Oilfield, one of the country's major oilfields. It also produces bromine from underground wells and salt from seawater.

The region boasts a strong food manufacturing and processing industry, focusing on vegetables and seafood. It also has a strong excavating and energy industry related to coal and oil. Its high-tech industry has been growing quickly and local government will continue to champion this sector, particularly the development of computers and software related to network communications. The province also benefits from a large consumer market, notable South Korean investment and tourism directed at Shandong Peninsula. Among the various sectors, manufacturing accounts for the largest fixed asset investment.

Other noteworthy industries within the province include the electronics industry, the automobile industry in Ji'nan City, the locomotive industry in Qingdao City and the cotton textile industry in Qingdao and Ji'nan. A renowned company in Shandong's electronics industry is Haier Electronics, which controls about 30% and 20% of China's refrigerator and air-conditioner market, respectively. Shandong has 93 products that have been awarded "Chinese Famous Brand Names", marginally behind Zhejiang and Guangdong provinces. These include Haier Electronics, Tsingdao Beer, Hisense Electronics and China Qingqi Motorcycles.

Foreign trade in the province continues to display excellent growth. The major import source is South Korea, followed by the US and Japan. The main imports include machinery, steel, equipment and technology. Trailing behind Japan, Korea and the US, the fourth largest trading partner is Hong Kong. The area's manufacturing sector receives the largest amount of utilized FDI, followed by real estate.

As of 2010, compared with those of other provinces, "mining" and "manufacturing" were relatively strong, while "agriculture, forestry, animal husbandry and fishery", "information transmission, computer service and software" and "scientific research, technical services and geological prospecting" were relatively weak sectors (see Table C).

Table C   Shandong's comparative (dis)advantage index by sector, 2010

Sector	Index
Agriculture, forestry, animal husbandry and fishery	0.18
Mining	1.62
Manufacturing	1.30
Production and distribution of electricity, gas and water	0.89
Construction	0.86
Transport, storage and post	0.75
Information transmission, computer service and software	0.48
Wholesale and retail trades	0.98
Hotels and catering services	0.72
Financial intermediation	0.97
Real estate	0.73
Leasing and business services	0.52
Scientific research, technical services and geological prospecting	0.51

Management of water conservancy, environment and public facilities	0.72
Services to households and other services	0.80
Education	0.94
Health, social security and social welfare	0.94
Culture, sports and entertainment	0.69
Public management and social organization	1.00

Notes: All the sectors included in this table are determined according to China's official definitions and for urban areas only. Numerals greater than, equal to and less than 1 indicate that the province's sectors have advantages, no apparent (dis)advantages and disadvantages, respectively.

Sources: Calculated by author based on *China Statistical Yearbook,* 2011. See Appendix for a detailed methodological description.

There are various development zones of different kinds in Shandong Province. Some examples are described below.

- **Jinan High-Tech Industrial Development Zone (JHTIDZ)** Founded in 1991, this was one of the first of its kind approved by the State Council. It is located to the east of the city and covers a planning area of 83 km², divided into a central area covering 33 km², an export processing district of 10 km² and an eastern extension area of 40 km². Since its foundation, the zone has attracted enterprises such as LG, Panasonic, Volvo and Sanyo. In 2000 it joined the world science and technology association and set up a China-Ukraine High-Tech Cooperation Park. The Qilu Software Park of the zone became the sister park of Bangalore Park of India.

- **Jinan Export Processing Zone** This is located in the eastern suburbs of Jinan, to the east of JHTIDZ and to the north of Jiwang Highway. The distance from the highway and Jinan Airport are 9 km and 18 km, respectively.

- **Qingdao Economic and Technological Development Area** This was among the first state-level development zones to be approved and established by the Country Council in 1984. Situated on the western coast of the Jiaozhou Bay, its development area spans about 220 km². Major industries there include high-tech household appliances, shipping, petrochemicals, building materials, pharmaceuticals and mechanical products. Companies listed among the Global Fortune 500 have invested in 48 projects, with Haier, Hisense, Aucma, Sinopec, CSIC, CNOOC, CIMC and others being located in the zone.

- **Qingdao Free Trade Zone** This was established by the State Council in 1992. It is 60 km from Qingdao Liuting Airport and is also close to

Qingdao Qianwan Harbor. More than 40 foreign-invested enterprises have moved in and 2,000 projects have been approved. It is one of the special economic zones enjoying the most favorable investment policies on customs, foreign exchange, foreign trade and taxation in China.

- **Qingdao High-Tech Industrial Zone** This was approved by the State Council in 1992. It is close to Qingdao Liuting Airport and Qingdao Harbor. The area spans approximately $58\,km^2$ and it is 17 km from Qingdao International Airport. There are three subsidiary zones within the high-tech park: the "electronic information zone", the "bioengineering zone" and the "new materials zone". Major industries there include consumer electronics, information and communication technology, bioengineering, new materials and other advanced technologies.

- **Weifang Binhai Economic and Technological Development Area** Established in August 1995, this is a national economic and technological development area approved by the State Council. Covering an area of $677\,km^2$, it possesses $400\,km^2$ of state-owned industrial land. This can guarantee the demand of any project construction and provide broad development space for the enterprises in the area. The zone has been accredited as a National Demonstration Zone invigorating the Sea by Science and Technology, National Innovation Base for Rejuvenating Trade through Science and Technology and National Demonstration Eco-Industry Park.

- **Weihai Economic and Technological Development Zone** This is a state-level development zone approved by the State Council in 1992. The administrative area occupies $194\,km^2$, including the programmed area of $36\,km^2$ and an initial area of $11.88\,km^2$. Nearby are Weihai Port and Wuhai Airport.

- **Weihai Torch Hi-Tech Science Park** This is a state-level development zone approved by the State Council on March 1991. Located in Weihai's northwest zone of culture, education and science, it has an area of $111.9\,km^2$, a coastal line of 30.5 km and 150,000 residents. It is 3 km from the city center, 4 km from Weihai Port, 10 km from Weihai Railway Station, 30 km from Weihai Airport and 80 km from Yantai Airport.

- **Yantai Economic and Technological Development Area** This is one of the first few national development zones approved by government. Located in Yantai, along the Shandong Peninsula, it has an area of about $16\,km^2$ and is strategically centered between the important cities of Beijing, Shanghai and Seoul. Major industries there include machinery, automobile and auto parts, electronics and pharmaceuticals. It has attracted many foreign companies, such as General Motors, Hyundai and Asahi Kasei.

- **Yantai Export Processing Zone** This is one of the first 15 export processing zones approved by the State Council. Its construction area is 4.17 km² and the initial zone covers 3 km². After several years' development its construction is complete, and standard workshops of 120,000 m² and bonded warehouses of 40,000 m² have been built. Up to now, offering an ideal investment environment, the zone has attracted investors from Japan, Korea, Singapore, Hong Kong, Taiwan, Sweden, the US, Canada and others, and from the domestic regions.

As of 2010 the top five companies were as follows:

1. Yanzhou Coal Mining Co (NYSE: YZC, SHA: 600188, HKG: 1171) is a leading coal miner and transporter. It posted ¥34.84 billion in revenues and ¥9.01 billion in net profits for 2010.
2. Weichai Power Co (SHE: 000338) is an automotive and engine researcher, developer and manufacturer. It posted ¥63.28 billion in revenues and ¥6.78 billion in net profits for 2010.
3. Shandong Gold Mining Co (SHA: 600547) is a leading gold mining and smelting giant. It posted ¥31.51 billion in revenues and ¥1.22 billion in net profits for 2010.
4. Yantai Changyu Pioneer Wine Co (SHE: 000869) is a leading wine and other alcoholic beverage maker and distributor. It posted ¥4.98 billion in revenues and ¥1.43 billion in net profits for 2010.
5. Tsingtao Brewery Co (SHA: 600600) is China's most famous brand of beer. It posted ¥19.9 billion in revenues and ¥1.52 billion in net profits for 2010.

Indicators for the ease of doing business

A. Starting a business

Procedures: 13
Time (days): 33
Cost (% of provincial GRP per capita): 6

B. Registering property

Procedures: 8

Time (days): 39
Cost (% of property value): 4.1

C. Getting credit – creating and registering collateral

Time (days): 10
Cost (% of loan value): 2.9

D. Enforcing contracts

Time (days): 210
Cost (% of claim): 22

Further reading

Chen, Kai, Colin Brown (2001). "Addressing shortcomings in the household responsibility system: Empirical analysis of the two-farmland system in Shandong Province," *China Economic Review*, vol. 12, issue 4, pp. 280–292.

Chung, Jae Ho (1997). "Shandong: The political economy of development and inequality," in Goodman, David S.G. (ed.), *China's Provinces in Reform: Class, Community and Political Culture*. London and New York: Routledge, pp. 127–162.

Di, Jiaping, Yujiang Li (2008). "Rural labor transfer mode and regional nonequilibrium degree comparative study in Shandong and Henan provinces," *China Population, Resources and Environment*, vol. 18, issue 5, October, pp. 189–193.

Dong, Xiao-Yuan, Fiona MacPhail, Paul Bowles, Samuel P.S. Ho (2004). "Gender segmentation at work in China's privatized rural industry: Some evidence from Shandong and Jiangsu," *World Development*, vol. 32, issue 6, June, pp. 979–998.

Gnansounou, Edgard, Jun Dong (2004). "Opportunity for inter-regional integration of electricity markets: The case of Shandong and Shanghai in East China," *Energy Policy*, vol. 32, issue 15, October, pp. 1737–1751.

Ho, Samuel P.S., Paul Bowles, Xiaoyuan Dong (2003). "Letting go of the small: An analysis of the privatization of rural enterprises in Jiangsu and Shandong," *Journal of Development Studies*, vol. 39, issue 4, April, pp. 1–26.

Kaneko, Shinji, Asaka Yonamine, Tae Yong Jung (2006). "Technology choice and CDM projects in China: Case study of a small steel company in Shandong Province," *Energy Policy*, vol. 34, issue 10, July, pp. 1139–1151.

Liang, X., L. Goel (1997). "The achievements and trend of tariff reform in China – The experience in Shandong Province," *Utilities Policy*, vol. 6, issue 4, December, pp. 341–348.

Liu, Ling (2008). "Local government and big business in the people's Republic of China – Case study evidence from Shandong Province," *Asia Pacific Business Review*, vol. 14, issue 4, October, pp. 473–489.

MacPhail, Fiona, Xiao-yuan Dong (2007). "Women's market work and household status in rural China: Evidence from Jiangsu and Shandong in the late 1990s," *Feminist Economics*, vol. 13, issue 3–4, July, pp. 93–124.

Park, Bohm, Keun Lee (2003). "Comparative analysis of foreign direct investment in China firms from South Korea, Hong Kong, and the United States in Shandong Province," *Journal of the Asia Pacific Economy*, vol. 8, issue 1, January, pp. 57–84.

Underhill, Anne P., Gary M. Feinman, Linda M. Nicholas, Hui Fang, Fengshi Luan, Haiguang Yu, Fengshu Cai (2008). "Changes in regional settlement patterns and the development of complex societies in southeastern Shandong, China," *Journal of Anthropological Archaeology*, vol. 27, issue 1, March, pp. 1–29.

Wang, Luxiang (2006). *Shandong* (Panoramic China). Beijing: Foreign Languages Press.

Wang, Shujun, Jian Liu, Lijun Ren, Kai Zhang, Renqing Wang (2009). "The development and practices of Strategic Environmental Assessment in Shandong Province, China," *Environmental Impact Assessment Review*, vol. 29, issue 6, November, pp. 408–420.

Wang, Zhenbo, Chuangeng Zhu, Fenghua Sun (2007). "Employment spatial models and mechanism of Shandong Province," *China Population, Resources and Environment*, vol. 17, issue 2, March, pp. 131–135.

Zheng, Bofu, Qinghai Guo, Yuansong Wei, Hongbing Deng, Keming Ma, Junxin Liu, Jingzhu Zhao, Xingshan Zhang, Yu Zhao (2008). "Water source protection and industrial development in the Shandong Peninsula, China from 1995 to 2004: A case study," *Resources, Conservation and Recycling*, vol. 52, issues 8–9, July, pp. 1065–1076.

Shanghai

1 = Yangpu
2 = Jingan
3 = Huangpu
4 = Putuo
5 = Changning
6 = Xuhui
7 = Luwan
7 = Hongkou
8 = Zhabei

Source: The author.

Table A　The administrative divisions of Shanghai

Name	Administrative seat	Population
Baoshan PD	Youyi Rd	1,904,886
Changning PD	yuyuan Rd	690,571
Chongming C	Renmin Rd	703,722
Fengxian PD	Jiefang Middle Rd	1,083,463
Hongkou PD	Feihong Rd	852,476
Huangpu PD	Yanan East Rd	678,670
Jiading PD	Bole South Rd	1,471,231
Jing'an PD	Yanan Middle Rd	246,788
Jinshan PD	Jinshan Avenue	732,410
Minhang PD	Humin Rd	2,429,372
Pudong ND	Eshan Rd	5,044,430
Putuo PD	Daduhe Rd	1,288,881
Qingpu PD	Gongyuan Rd	1,081,022
Songjiang PD	Jiasong South Rd	1,582,398
Xuhui PD	Caoxi North Rd	1,085,130
Yangpu PD	Huaide Rd	1,313,222
Zhabei PD	Datong Rd	830,476

Notes: C = county, which is at the prefectural level; ND = new district, which is a sub-provincial level district; PD = prefectural level district. All data are as of 2010 or 2011.

Quick facts

Official name: Shanghai Municipality
Abbreviated name: Hu
Land area: 6,340.5 km^2
Population: 23,026,600
Population density: 3,966/km^2
GRP per capita of 2010: ¥76,074
HDI of 2008: 0.908
Government office address: 19 Gao'an Road, Shanghai
Tel: 021–6321–2810
Website: www.shanghai.gov.cn

Shanghai is a province-level municipality of the PRC. It is also the largest city proper by population in the world. Located in the Yangtze River Delta in eastern China, it sits at the mouth of the river in the middle portion of the Chinese coast. The municipality consists of a peninsula between the Yangtze and the Hangzhou Bay, Chongming (mainland China's second-largest island) and a number of smaller islands. It is bordered to the north and west by Jiangsu Province, to the south by Zhejiang Province and to the east by the East China Sea.

The Chinese characters of Shanghai's name mean "upon the sea". The earliest occurrence of this name dates from the 11th-century Song Dynasty, when there was already a river confluence and a town with this name in the area. Shanghai is officially abbreviated to *Hu* in Chinese. An older name for it is "Shen", from "Chun Shen Jun", a nobleman and locally revered hero of the 3rd-century BC state of Chu. From this it is also called the "City of Shen".

The city is bisected by the Huangpu River, a tributary of the Yangtze. The traditional center, the Puxi area, is on the western side of the Huangpu, while the newly developed Pudong, containing the central financial district Lujiazui, developed on the eastern bank. Shanghai is administratively equal to a province and is divided into 17 county-level divisions (16 districts and 1 county). As of 2009, these county-level divisions were further divided into 210 township-level divisions (109 towns, 2 townships and 99 sub-districts). These were in turn divided into the village-level divisions (3,661 neighborhood committees and 1,704 village committees).

The average elevation is about 4 m above sea level. Except for a few hills lying in the southwest corner, most parts of the region are flat and belong to the alluvial plain of the Yangtze River Delta. Shanghai is known for its rich water resources, with the water area accounting for 11% of its total territory. The region includes 122 km^2 of water. It extends 120 km from south to north and 100 km from east to west. The city's location on the flat alluvial plain has meant that new skyscrapers must be built with deep concrete piles to prevent them from sinking into the soft ground. The highest point is at the peak of Dajinshan Island at 103 m. As part of the Taihu drainage area, the city has many rivers, canals, streams and lakes and is known for its rich water resources.

With a pleasant northern sub-tropical maritime monsoon climate, Shanghai enjoys four distinct seasons, with generous sunshine and abundant rainfall. Its spring and autumn are relatively short compared with the summer and winter. The average annual temperature is about 17.6 °C (averaging 4.2 °C in January and 27.9 °C in July). Winters are chilly and damp, and cold northwesterly winds can cause night-time temperatures to drop below freezing. Summers are hot and humid, with an average of 8.7 days exceeding 35 °C annually. The city has a frost-free period of some 300 days and it receives an annual rainfall of around 1,300 mm. However, nearly 50% of the precipitation comes during the May–September flooding season, which is divided into three rainy periods: the spring rains, the plum rains and the autumn rains. The most pleasant seasons are spring, although it is changeable and often rainy, and autumn, which is generally sunny and dry. Shanghai experiences on average 1,878 hours of sunshine per year, with the hottest temperature ever recorded at 40.2 °C, and the lowest at −12.1 °C.

The wide river mouth of the Yangtze is home to 108 species of fish, including 20 that are economically important. Shanghai also boasts a number of natural lakes with abundant bottom living things, such as conch, a fresh-water variety of bivalve and clams. Originating from Taihu Lake, the 113 km Huangpu River winds through the downtown area of the city. It is varies between 300 m and 770 m wide with an average width of 360 m. The ice-free river is the main waterway in the Shanghai area. The total water reserve in Shanghai stands at 2.7 billion m³.

Shanghai is a popular tourist destination renowned for its historical landmarks, such as The Bund, City God Temple and Yuyuan Garden, as well as the extensive and growing Pudong skyline. It has been described as the "showpiece" of the booming economy of mainland China. Because of the city's status as the cultural and economic center of East Asia for the first half of the 20th century, it is popularly seen as the birthplace of everything considered modern in China. It was there, for example, that the first motor car was driven, and (technically) the first train tracks and modern sewers were laid. As a city of long history, it has 13 historical sites under state protection, including characteristic gardens built during the Tang, Song, Yuan, Ming and Qing dynasties. A group of buildings constructed since the 1990s have added something new to the scenic attractions of the city.

Well-known parks in Shanghai include People's Square Park, Gongqing Forest Park, Fuxing Park, Zhongshan Park, Lu Xun Park, Century Park and Jing'an Park. The Shanghai Disney Resort Project, approved by government in 2009, should be operational by 2016. The city boasts several museums of regional and national importance. The Shanghai Museum of Art and History has one of the best collections of Chinese historical artifacts in the world, including important archaeological finds since 1949. The Shanghai Art Museum, located in the former Shanghai Race Club building in People's Square, is a major art museum holding both permanent and temporary exhibitions. The Shanghai Natural History Museum also houses a large collection of exhibits. In addition, there are a variety of smaller, specialist museums, some housed in important historical sites such as that of the Provisional Government of the Republic of Korea and the site of the First National Congress of the Chinese Communist Party (CCP).

In the last two decades, Shanghai has been one of the fastest-developing cities in the world. Since 1992 it has recorded a double-digit GRP growth rate almost every year. In 2010 its total GRP grew to ¥1.72 trillion (about US$297 billion), with GRP per capita of ¥82,560 (about US$12,784). The three largest service industries are financial services, retail and real estate. The manufacturing and agricultural sectors account for 42.1% and 0.7% of GRP, respectively (see Table B).

Table B   Demographic and socioeconomic profile: Shanghai

Indicator	2000	2010
Population (thousands)	16,740	23,027
Illiteracy rate of population aged 15 or over (%)	5.40	2.74
GRP (¥ billions)	455.12	1,716.60
Composition of GRP (%)		
Primary sector	1.8	0.7
Secondary sector	47.5	42.1
Tertiary sector	50.6	57.3
Fixed asset investment (¥ billions)	186.94	510.89
Status of foreign-funded enterprises		
Number of registered enterprises	15,930	55,666
Total investment (US$ millions)	98,540	339,385
Registered capital (US$ millions)	53,345	200,919
Foreign trade (US$ millions)		
Export	24,640	173,255
Import	30,064	192,189
Sales of consumer goods (¥ billions)	172	607
Per capita annual disposable income of urban residents (¥)	11,718.01	31,838.08
Engle's coefficient (%)	34.91	31.17
Per capita annual net income of rural residents (¥)	5,596.37	13,977.96
Engle's coefficient (%)	38.56	37.28
Number of patent applications granted	4,050	48,215
Inventions	304	6,867
Utility models	2,083	21,821
Designs	1,663	19,527

Note: All monetary values are measured at current prices.
Source: Shanghai Statistical Yearbook, 2001 and 2011.

Once a fishing and textiles town, Shanghai, thanks to its favorable port location, grew in importance in the 19th century. It was one of the cities opened to foreign trade by the 1842 Treaty of Nanking, which allowed the establishment of the Shanghai International Settlement. The city then flourished as a center of commerce and became the undisputed financial hub of Asia Pacific in the 1930s. With the Chinese Communist Party takeover of the mainland in 1949, the city's international influence declined. Since the 1980s, China's economic reform and opening-up policies have resulted in intense re-development, aiding the return of finance and foreign investment to the city.

Shanghai is one of four province-level municipalities of the PRC, with a total population of over 23 million as of 2010. It is a global city, having an influence in commerce, culture, finance, media, fashion, technology and transport. It is a major financial center and the busiest container port in the world. In 2009 the Shanghai Stock Exchange (SHA) ranked third among worldwide stock exchanges in terms of trading volume, and sixth in terms of the total capitalization of listed companies, and the trading volume of six key commodities, including rubber, copper and zinc, on the Shanghai Futures Exchange all ranked first in the world.

The municipality is one of the main industrial centers in China, playing a key role in the country's heavy industry. A large number of industrial zones, including Hongqiao Economic and Technological Development Zone, Jinqiao Export Economic Processing Zone, Minhang Economic and Technological Development Zone and Caohejing High-Tech Development Zone, form the backbone of Shanghai's secondary industry. Heavy industry accounted for 78% of the gross industrial output in 2009. China's largest steelmaker, Baosteel Group, and Jiangnan Shipyard, one of China's oldest shipbuilders, are both located there. Auto manufacture is another important industry. Shanghai Automotive Industry (Group) Corporation is one of the top three automotive companies in China. It has a strategic partnership with Volkswagen and General Motors.

Shanghai is the commercial and financial center of mainland China, as exemplified by Pudong district, a pilot area for integrated economic reforms. Major capital markets in the city include the Shanghai Stock Exchange, the Shanghai Futures Exchange and the Shanghai Gold Exchange. It is a clear leader in terms of the quality of its growth – 60.7% of GRP comes from the service sector, while the remaining 39.3% comes from relatively high-end manufacturing of automobiles, electronics, petrochemicals, iron and steel, and equipment. It has the highest average wage and disposable income, and the lowest urban to rural income gap in China. Its GRP was ¥1.68 trillion ($256 billion) in 2010. It still lags far behind global financial centers, such as London, New York and Tokyo, in terms of the "soft" environment, such as financial innovation and products, the rules of law, free capital flows and human capital. The cost of living in Shanghai has increased, catching up with its global peers. The city still faces numerous challenges, such as traffic congestion, affordable housing, pollution control and population.

As of 2010, compared with those of other provinces, "Scientific research, technical services and geological prospecting", "leasing and business services" and "transport, storage and post" were relatively strong, while "mining", "agriculture, forestry, animal husbandry and fishery" and "construction" were relatively weak sectors (see Table C).

Table C   Shanghai's comparative (dis)advantage index by sector, 2010

Sector	Index
Agriculture, forestry, animal husbandry and fishery	0.14
Mining	0.01
Manufacturing	1.29
Production and distribution of electricity, gas and water	0.58
Construction	0.30
Transport, storage and post	1.91
Information transmission, computer service and software	1.20
Wholesale and retail trades	1.64
Hotels and catering services	1.85
Financial intermediation	1.67
Real estate	1.75
Leasing and business services	2.00
Scientific research, technical services and geological prospecting	2.64
Management of water conservancy, environment and public facilities	0.89
Services to households and other services	1.82
Education	0.55
Health, social security and social welfare	0.88
Culture, sports and entertainment	1.19
Public management and social organization	0.43

Notes: All the sectors included in this table are determined according to China's official definitions and for urban areas only. Numerals greater than, equal to and less than 1 indicate that the province's sectors have advantages, no apparent (dis)advantages and disadvantages, respectively.
Sources: Calculated by author based on *China Statistical Yearbook*, 2011. See Appendix for a detailed methodological description.

There are dozens of economic and technological development zones in Shanghai. Some examples are described below.

- **Caohejing Export Processing Zone** This was set up in Pujiang Hi-Tech Park with a first-stage developed area of 0.9 km². It is situated close to Xupu Bridge and the Outer Ring Road. It focuses on developing new electronic and IT manufacturing, specializing in computers, new electronic parts, communications and network equipment.

- **Caohejing Hi-Tech Park** Located in the southwest of Shanghai, this is only 11 km from the city center and 7 km from Hongqiao International Airport. Its planned area is 14.3 km². It specializes in the development of computers and computer software, large-scale integrated circuits and microelectronics technology, numerical controlled communication, precision instruments, bioengineering, space technology and advanced-electronic technology. By the end of 2001, 280 foreign-invested enterprises had settled in the park. The amount of foreign investment has reached $1.8 billion.

- **Caohejing Pujiang Hi-Tech Park** This was established in 2004 as an expansion of Caohejing Hi-Tech Park with the approval of the State Council. It is composed of three parts: an export processing zone, a hi-tech industrial area and a business-supporting area, covering an area of 10.7 km². It focuses on hi-tech industry development, such as electronics, computers and software, aeronautics and astronautics, new energy, new materials, modern media and so on, and it will introduce the relevant supporting industries to facilitate this hi-tech development. As a state-level economic and technological development zone, it has also been listed by Shanghai Municipal Government as one of the five key industrial parks in the municipality.

- **Hongqiao Economic and Technological Development Zone** This is located in the west of the urban area of Shanghai. It covers an area of 65.2 ha with a construction area of 31.09 ha, a greenery area of 19.54 ha and a road area of 14.39 ha. It plans to construct 300,000 m² of exhibition and display space, office buildings, a hotel and restaurant, housing, and complementary facilities. A foreign consular area has been established there. The zone is characterized as a foreign trade center, and it is the sole commercial and trade development zone in China that integrates the businesses of exhibitions, office service, housing, catering and shopping.

- **Jiading Hi-Tech Park** This was approved in 1991 by the State Council. The planned area is 2 km² and 1.6 km² has already been developed. Industries encouraged there include advanced manufacturing industries such as mechatronics, photoelectronics and IT, regional and functional industry (automotive industry), and modern service industries.

- **Jiading Export Processing Zone** Established in 2005 with the approval of the State Council, this completed construction and began operating in 2008. It is located in the northwest of Jiading Industrial Zone. With a designed area of 5.96 km², it is divided into an export-processing area, a developing spare area and a supporting area. The designed area in phase 1 is 0.989 km².

- **Jinqiao Export Processing Zone** This is a key state-level development zone approved by the Chinese government. It is mainly for the development of modern industry, modern housing, modern commerce and trade. It is a high-level, multifunctional development zone that integrates manufacturing, trade, commercial services and community administration. It is administered in accordance with international practices. With a planned area of 20 km², the zone is divided into two parts by the north–south Jinqiao Road. The eastern part, of about 16 km², is for a modern industrial park, modern commerce and a trade park, and the western part, of about 4 km², is for a modern residential park, administration and a service center.

- **Minhang Economic and Technological Development Zone** This was established in 1983. It now has a developed area of 3.5 km². It is only 30 km from the city center and 27 km from Hongqiao International Airport. Direct access to Pudong International Airport is also available via the outer ring road. The zone emphasizes the development of mechanical and electrical equipment industry, modern biological and pharmaceutical industry, and the food and beverage industry. The establishment of R&D units and high-tech enterprises are also encouraged.

- **Qingpu Export Processing Zone** Established in 2003 with the approval of the State Council, this is a special zone under the regulation of Shanghai Customs enjoying a planned area of 3 km². It is located in the planned territory of Qingpu Industrial Zone, a municipal industrial park in the west of Shanghai. Closed management is adopted in Qingpu Export Processing Zone, where organizations and facilities for customs, commodities inspection, taxation, industrial and commercial administration, banking, foreign trade, transportation and customs clearance are available.

- **Shanghai Chemical Industry Park** This was established in the late 1990s with major expansion in the early 2000s, with MNCs (such as BASF, Huntsman and Bayer) building plants to make MDI, chlorine, acrylics and other polymers. It is located some 20 km southwest of the city near the village of Caojing.

- **Songjiang Export Processing Zone** Established in 2000, this is one of the first state-level export processing zones. The enterprises there enjoy preferential policies like those in state-level industrial zones and their export products are exempt from value added tax. Its programmed phase 1 area is 1.98 km², the development of which is complete. Some 35 companies have settled there. The aim is to attract an investment of US$1.6 billion in the zone with the current level at US$400 million. The companies in the zone all engage in electronics and IT manufacturing, especially laptop manufacture. The zone's programmed phase 2 area is 2 km², which is undergoing expansion.
- **Waigaoqiao Free Trade Zone** Covering an area of 10 km², this is one of the first and largest free trade zones in China. Owing to its outstanding business environment and preferential policies, it is been well recognized as a bridge of international trade and the hottest investment zone for foreign companies in China. To date it has attracted over 9,300 companies, among which more than 80% are trading companies. The number of foreign enterprises set up there has accounted for one-third of the total in Shanghai. Among these are 135 from the Top Fortune 500 companies. In terms of GRP, import and export value, and investment, the zone accounts for over 60% of all 15 free trade zones in China.

As of 2010 the top five companies were as follows:

1. SAIC Motor Corp Ltd (SHA: 600104) is principally engaged in automobile manufacture and distribution. It posted ¥313.38 billion in revenues and ¥13.73 billion in net profits for 2010.
2. Baoshan Iron & Steel Co (SHA: 600019) is principally engaged in the manufacture and trading of steel products. It posted ¥202.41 billion in revenues and ¥12.89 billion in net profits for 2010.
3. Shanghai Bailian Group Co (SHA: 600631) is principally engaged in the operation of department stores and supermarkets, office building leasing, and the provision of tourism and restaurant services. It posted ¥12.84 billion in revenues and ¥614.85 million in net profits for 2010.
4. Shanghai Electric Group Co (SHA: 601727, HKG:2727) is principally engaged in the design, manufacture and distribution of electric power and industrial equipment. It posted ¥63.18 billion in revenues and ¥2.82 billion in net profits for 2010.
5. Bright Dairy & Food Co (SHA: 600597) is principally engaged in the processing, production and distribution of dairy products. It posted ¥9.57 billion in revenues and ¥194.38 million in net profits for 2010.

Indicators for the ease of doing business

A. Starting a business

Procedures: 14
Time (days): 35
Cost (% of provincial GRP per capita): 3.1

B. Registering property

Procedures: 4
Time (days): 29
Cost (% of property value): 3.6

C. Getting credit – creating and registering collateral

Time (days): 8
Cost (% of loan value): 2.9

D. Enforcing contracts

Time (days): 292
Cost (% of claim): 9

Further reading

Bathelt, Harald, Gang Zeng (2012). "Strong growth in weakly-developed networks: Producer–user interaction and knowledge brokers in the greater Shanghai Chemical Industry," *Applied Geography*, vol. 32, issue 1, January, pp. 158–170.

Chen, X., Y. Zong (1999). "Major impacts of sea-level rise on agriculture in the Yangtze delta area around Shanghai," *Applied Geography*, vol. 19, issue 1, January, pp. 69–84.

Chow, Clement Kong Wing, Michael Ka Yiu Fung (1998). "Ownership structure, lending bias, and liquidity constraints: Evidence from Shanghai's manufacturing sector," *Journal of Comparative Economics*, vol. 26, issue 2, June, pp. 301–316.

Copeland, Laurence, Woon K. Wong, Yong Zeng (2009). "Information-based trade in the Shanghai stock market," *Global Finance Journal*, vol. 20, issue 2, pp. 180–190.

Danielson, Eric N. (2004). *Shanghai and the Yangzi Delta*. Singapore: Marshall Cavendish/Times Editions.

Danielson, Eric N. (2010). *Discover Shanghai*. Singapore: Marshall Cavendish.

Gielen, Dolf, Chen Changhong (2001). "The CO2 emission reduction benefits of Chinese energy policies and environmental policies: A case study for Shanghai, period 1995–2020," *Ecological Economics*, vol. 39, issue 2, November, pp. 257–270.

Han, Ji, Yoshitsugu Hayashi, Xin Cao, Hidefumi Imura (2009). "Application of an integrated system dynamics and cellular automata model for urban growth assessment: A case study of Shanghai, China," *Landscape and Urban Planning*, vol. 91, issue 3, 30 June, pp. 133–141.

Han, Xuehui (2010). "Housing demand in Shanghai: A discrete choice approach," *China Economic Review*, vol. 21, issue 2, June, pp. 355–376.

Heilmann, Sebastian (2005). "Policy-making and political supervision in Shanghai's financial industry," *Journal of Contemporary China*, vol. 14, issue 45, January, pp. 643–668.

Horesh, Niv (2009). *Shanghai's Bund and Beyond*. New Haven, CT: Yale University Press.

Huang, Fu-Xiang (1991). "Planning in Shanghai," *Habitat International*, vol. 15, issue 3, pp. 87–98.

Jacobs, J. Bruce (1994). "Shanghai and the lower Yangtze valley," in Goodman, David S.G., Gerald Segal (eds), *China Deconstructs: Politics, Trade and Regionalism* (Routledge in Asia). London and New York: Routledge, pp. 224–252.

Jacobs, J. Bruce (1997). "Shanghai: An alternative center?" in Goodman, David S.G. (ed.), *China's Provinces in Reform: Class, Community and Political Culture*. London and New York: Routledge, pp. 163–198.

Johnson, Linda Cooke (1995). *Shanghai: From Market Town to Treaty Port*. Stanford, CA: Stanford University Press.

Law, W.-W. (2007). "Globalisation, city development and citizenship education in China's Shanghai," *International Journal of Educational Development*, vol. 27, issue 1, January, pp. 18–38.

Li, L.H. (2011). "The dynamics of the Shanghai land market – An intra city analysis," *Cities*, vol. 28, issue 5, October, pp. 372–380.

Li, Li, Changhong Chen, Shichen Xie, Cheng Huang, Zhen Cheng, Hongli Wang, Yangjun Wang, Haiying Huang, Jun Lu, Shobhakar Dhakal (2010). "Energy demand and carbon emissions under different development scenarios for Shanghai, China," *Energy Policy*, vol. 38, issue 9, September, pp. 4797–4807.

Li, Limei, Si-ming Li, Yingfang Chen (2010). "Better city, better life, but for whom?: The Hukou and resident card system and the consequential citizenship stratification in Shanghai," *City, Culture and Society*, vol. 1, issue 3, September, pp. 145–154.

Li, Linda Chelan (1998a). "Investment in Shanghai: Central policy and provincial implementation," in Li, Linda Chelan (ed.), *Center and Provinces: China 1978–1993: Power as Non-Zero-Sum* (Studies on Contemporary China). Oxford: Oxford University Press, pp. 114–149.

Li, Linda Chelan (1998b). "Discretion and strategies in Shanghai," in Li, Linda Chelan (ed.), *Center and Provinces: China 1978–1993: Power as Non-Zero-Sum* (Studies on Contemporary China). Oxford: Oxford University Press, pp. 218–46.

Li, Zhigang, Fulong Wu (2006). "Socioeconomic transformations in Shanghai (1990–2000): Policy impacts in global–national–local contexts," *Cities*, vol. 23, issue 4, August, pp. 250–268.

Liefner, Ingo, Christian Brömer, Gang Zeng (2012). "Knowledge absorption of optical technology companies in Shanghai, Pudong: Successes, barriers and structural impediments," *Applied Geography*, vol. 32, issue 1, January, pp. 171–184.

Liu, Chunrong (2006). "Social changes and neighbourhood policy in Shanghai," *Policy and Society*, vol. 25, issue 1, pp. 133–155.

Liu, Gang (2007). "A behavioral model of work-trip mode choice in Shanghai," *China Economic Review*, vol. 18, issue 4, pp. 456–476.

Liu, Jung-Chao, Lilai Xu (1997). "Household savings and investment: The case of Shanghai," *Journal of Asian Economics*, vol. 8, issue 1, Spring, pp. 77–91.

Ma, Xufei, Andrew Delios (2007). "A new tale of two cities: Japanese FDIs in Shanghai and Beijing, 1979–2003," *International Business Review*, vol. 16, issue 2, April, pp. 207–228.

Manuhutu, Chassty, Anthony D. Owen (2010). "Gas-on-gas competition in Shanghai," *Energy Policy*, vol. 38, issue 5, May, pp. 2101–2106.

Olds, Kris (1997). "Globalizing Shanghai: The 'global intelligence corps' and the building of Pudong," *Cities*, vol. 14, issue 2, April, pp. 109–123.

Roberts, Kenneth D. (2001). "The determinants of job choice by rural labor migrants in Shanghai," *China Economic Review*, vol. 12, issue 1, Spring, pp. 15–39.

Shi, C., S.M. Hutchinson, S. Xu (2004). "Evaluation of coastal zone sustainability: An integrated approach applied in Shanghai municipality and Chong Ming Island," *Journal of Environmental Management*, vol. 71, issue 4, July, pp. 335–344.

Shao, Shuai, Lili Yang, Mingbo Yu, Mingliang Yu (2011). "Estimation, characteristics, and determinants of energy-related industrial CO_2 emissions in Shanghai (China), 1994–2009," *Energy Policy*, vol. 39, issue 10, October, pp. 6476–6494.

Shen, Junyi, Tatsuyoshi Saijo (2008). "Reexamining the relations between socio-demographic characteristics and individual environmental concern: Evidence from Shanghai data," *Journal of Environmental Psychology*, vol. 28, issue 1, March, pp. 42–50.

Walcott, Susan M., Clifton W. Pannell (2006). "Metropolitan spatial dynamics: Shanghai," *Habitat International*, vol. 30, issue 2, June, pp. 199–211.

Wei, Yehua Dennis, Chi Kin Leung, Jun Luo (2006). "Globalizing Shanghai: Foreign investment and urban restructuring," *Habitat International*, vol. 30, issue 2, June, pp. 231–244.

Wolde-Rufael, Yemane (2004). "Disaggregated industrial energy consumption and GRP: The case of Shanghai, 1952–1999," *Energy Economics*, vol. 26, issue 1, January, pp. 69–75.

Wong, Woon K., Bo Liu, Yong Zeng (2009). "Can price limits help when the price is falling? Evidence from transactions data on the Shanghai stock exchange," *China Economic Review*, vol. 20, issue 1, March, pp. 91–102.

Wu, Fulong (2000). "Place Promotion in Shanghai, PRC," *Cities*, vol. 17, issue 5, October, pp. 349–361.

Wu, Jiaping, Ian Radbone (2005). "Global integration and the intra-urban determinants of foreign direct investment in Shanghai," *Cities*, vol. 22, issue 4, August, pp. 275–286.

Wu, Jiaping, Tony Barnes (2008). "Local planning and global implementation: Foreign investment and urban development of Pudong, Shanghai," *Habitat International*, vol. 32, issue 3, September, pp. 364–374.

Wu, Weiping (1999). "City profile: Shanghai," *Cities*, vol. 16, issue 3, June, pp. 207–216.

Wu, Weiping (2007). "Cultivating research universities and industrial linkages in China: The Case of Shanghai," *World Development*, vol. 35, issue 6, June, pp. 1075–1093.

Wu, Zhou (2006). *Shanghai* (Panoramic China) (Chinese Edition). Beijing: Foreign Languages Press.

Yuan, W., P. James (2002). "Evolution of the Shanghai city region 1978–1998: An analysis of indicators," *Journal of Environmental Management*, vol. 64, issue 3, March, pp. 299–309.

Zhu, Jieming, Loo-Lee Sim, Xing-Quan Zhang (2006). "Global real estate investments and local cultural capital in the making of Shanghai's new office locations," *Habitat International*, vol. 30, issue 3, September, pp. 462–481.

Zhu, Pingfang, Weimin Xu, Nannan Lundin (2006). "The impact of government's fundings and tax incentives on industrial R&D investments – Empirical evidences from industrial sectors in Shanghai," *China Economic Review*, vol. 17, issue 1, pp. 51–69.

Shanxi

Source: The author, based on a file from the Wikimedia Commons.

Table A The administrative divisions of Shanxi

Name	Administrative seat	Population
Changzhi PM	Chengqu District	3,334,564
Datong PM	Chengqu District	3,318,057
Jincheng PM	Chengqu District	2,279,151
Jinzhong PM	Yuci District	3,249,425
Linfen PM	Yaodu District	4,316,612
Lvliang PM	Lishi District	3,727,057
Shuozhou PM	Shuocheng District	1,714,857
Taiyuan PM	Xinghualing District	4,201,591
Xinzhou PM	Xinfu District	3,067,501
Yangquan PM	Chengqu District	1,368,502
Yuncheng PM	Yanhu District	5,134,794

Notes: PM = prefectural level municipality. All data are as of 2010.

Quick facts

Official name: Shanxi Province
Abbreviated name: Jin
Land area: 156,800 km^2
Population: 35,712,100
Population density: 217/km^2
GRP per capita of 2010: ¥26,283
HDI of 2008: 0.800
Capital: Taiyuan
Government office address: 101 Shifu Dongjie, Taiyuan City
Tel: 0351–304–4451
Postcode: 030072
Website: www.shanxi.gov.cn

Shanxi is a province of the PRC. The name literally means "mountain's west", which refers to its location west of the Taihang Mountains. Situated in the middle of the Yellow River Valley, it borders Hebei Province to the east, Henan Province to the south, Shaanxi Province to the west and Inner Mongolia Autonomous Region to the north. Its abbreviation is "Jin" in Chinese, after the state of Jin that existed here during the Eastern Zhou Dynasty (771–221 BC).

Shanxi is located on a plateau made up of higher ground to the east (Taihang Mountains) and the west (Lvliang Mountains) and a series of valleys in the center through which the Fen River runs. The highest peak is Mount Wutai in the northeast, which has an altitude of 3,058 m. The Great Wall of China forms most of the northern border with Inner Mongolia Autonomous Region. The Zhongtiao Mountains run along part of the southern border and separate Shanxi from the east–west part of the Yellow River. This river forms the western border of Shanxi with Shaanxi. The Fen and the Qin rivers, tributaries of the Yellow River, run north-to-south through the province and drain much of the area. The north of the province is drained by tributaries of the Hai River, such as Sanggan and Hutuo rivers. The largest natural lake is Xiechi Lake, a salt lake near Yuncheng in southwestern Shanxi.

Originating from eastern and western mountain areas, all rivers in the province have their outlets in other regions. The rivers running west and south belong to the Yellow River system, while those flowing east belong to the Haihe River system. The Yellow River drainage area totals 97,503 km^2, accounting for 62.2% of Shanxi's land area. The Haihe River drainage area covers 59,320 km^2, constituting 37.8%. The 11 prefecture-level divisions of Shanxi are subdivided into 119 county-level divisions (23 districts, 11 county-level cities and 85 counties). These are in turn divided into 1,388 township-level divisions (561 towns, 634 townships and 193 sub-districts).

The area has a continental monsoon climate and is rather arid. Average January temperatures are below 0 °C, while average July temperatures are around 21–26 °C. Winter is long, dry and cold, while summer is warm and humid. Spring is extremely dry and prone to dust storms. Shanxi is one of the sunniest parts of China and early summer heatwaves are common. The average annual precipitation is around 350–700 mm, with 60% of it concentrated between June and August.

The province abounds in mineral resources. Of more than 120 kinds of underground minerals so far discovered, 53 have proven reserves. Of these, reserves of coal, bauxite, pearlite, gallium and zeolite rank first in the nation. It is especially noted as the "kingdom of coal", with proven reserves amounting to 261.2 billion tons, accounting for one-third of the nation's total. As a result, Shanxi is a leading producer of coal in China and has more coal companies than any other area, with its annual production exceeding 300 million tons. The Datong, Ningwu, Xishan, Hedong, Qinshui and Huoxi coalfields are the most important there. It also has about 500 million tons of bauxite deposits, about one-third of the country's total Chinese.

Shanxi has 1,214.6 billion m^3 of underground water resources but only 45% of them are recoverable. These are mainly distributed on the fringe of basins and in provincial border areas. There is a lack of surface water, but the available resources are evenly distributed. There are eight rivers, each over 150 km. The total volume of river water runoff stands at 11.4 billion m³, a figure slightly more than that in Ningxia Hui Autonomous Region and so ranking last but one nationally.

The province has about 1,700 species of known seed plants in 134 families, including more than 480 kinds of woody plants. The southern and southeastern parts of the province are richest in diversity of vegetation types and plant species. These include broadleaved deciduous forests, estival (summer) broadleaved forests composed chiefly of secondary deciduous shrubs, and mixed coniferous and broadleaved forests. The central part has vast expanses of forests, mainly composed of coniferous forests, mesophytic deciduous scrub forests and estival broadleaved forests. The north and northwest are rich in temperate bush and semi-arid grassland, but have fewer forests. Dominant plants there include Chinese silver grass, xeric wormwood, *Caragana microphylla* and sea buckthorn. In general, Shanxi lacks forest resources, being one of China's most deficient provinces. Of the more than 1,000 species of wild plants so far discovered, there are over 90 species of wild medicinal plants widely distributed in the hilly areas. Famous ones include *Codonopsis pilosola, Astragalus membranaceus*, liquorice and weeping golden bell. Major wild fiber plants include nilghiri nettle, splendid achnatherum, Chinese small iris, kudzu vines, chaste trees and Chinese alpine rush.

There are more than 400 species of terrestrial wild animals in the region, including some 70 species of rare animals under state protection. The 14 species under first-class protection include white stork, black stork, golden eagle, sea eagle, vulture, brown pheasant, red-crowned crane, great bustard, leopard, tiger and sika deer. The 56 species under second-class protection comprise 40 kinds of birds, two kinds of amphibians and 14 kinds of mammals. In addition, there are more than 20 species of fur-bearing animals, including otter, Marten foina, raccoon-dog, leopard cat, yellow weasel, badger and fox. Table animals include hare, wild boar, ring-necked pheasant, rock partridge and partridge. There are also more than 70 species of medicine-supplying animals.

Shanxi abounds in tourism resources. It now has 31,401 unmovable cultural relics of different kinds. They comprise 2,639 ruins of ancient monuments, 1,666 ancient graves, 18,118 old buildings and memorial structures of historic interest, 300 grottoes and temples, 360 sites bearing ancient vertebrate fossils, 6,852 sites with stone inscriptions and 1,466 memorial buildings. There are 12,345 painted sculptures in these old buildings and memorial structures of historic interest and 26,751 m^2 of murals in old temples. The province therefore has the opportunity to develop tourism based on its rich cultural relics and to make it a pillar sector of the economy. The Ancient City of Pingyao is a World Heritage Site near Taiyuan. Once a great financial center of China, it is noted for its preservation of many features of northern Han Chinese culture, architecture and the way of life during the Ming and Qing dynasties. The Yungang Grottoes (literal translation "The Cloud Ridge Caves") are shallow caves near Datong. There are over 50,000 carved images and statues of Buddhas and Bodhisatvas within these grottoes, ranging from 4 cm to 7 m tall.

In addition, Mount Wutai (Wutai Shan) is known as the residence of the bodhisattva Manjusri, and as a result is also a major Buddhist pilgrimage destination, with many temples and natural sights. Points of interest include the Tang Dynasty (AD 618–907) era timber halls located at Nanchan Temple and Foguang Temple, as well as a giant white stupa at Tayuan Temple built during the Ming Dynasty (AD 1368–1644). Mount Hengshan in Hunyuan County is one of the "Five Great Peaks" of China and is also a major Taoist site. Not far away is the Hanging Temple, located on the side of a cliff, which has survived for 1,400 years despite earthquakes in the area. The Pagoda of Fogong Temple in Ying County was built in AD 1056 during the Liao Dynasty. It is octagonal with nine levels (five are visible from outside), and at 67 m high it is the tallest wooden pagoda in the world. It is also the oldest in China, although many existing stone and brick pagodas predate it by centuries.

The region's nominal GRP in 2010 was ¥920.09 billion (about US$150 billion), ranking 18th in China. The GRP per capita is below the national average. Compared with the provinces in East China, it is less developed for many reasons. Its geographic location limits its participation in international trade, which involves mostly eastern coastal provinces. The local climate and dwindling water resources limits agriculture in Shanxi, but important crops there include wheat, maize, millet, legumes and potatoes.

Situated in the north of China, Shanxi is an important energy source base with abundant reserves of coal, magnesium, bauxite and fireclay. As a result its economy depends heavily on the mining industry, in particular coal extraction, and it is home to the largest group of coal companies in the country. Huge reserves of coal have drawn investment into railways, power plants, and coal- and chemical-related research and products.

Table B Demographic and socioeconomic profile: Shanxi

Indicator	2000	2010
Population (thousands)	32,970	35,741
Illiteracy rate of population aged 15 or over (%)	4.18	2.13
GRP (¥ billions)	164.38	920.09
Composition of GRP (%)		
Primary sector	10.9	6.0
Secondary sector	50.4	56.9
Tertiary sector	38.7	37.1
Fixed asset investment (¥ billions)	54.82	606.32
Status of foreign-funded enterprises		
Number of registered enterprises	959	3,665
Total investment (US$ millions)	4,827	22,929
Registered capital (US$ millions)	2,560	11,128
Foreign trade (US$ millions)		
Export	2,091	6,741
Import	701	7,119
Sales of consumer goods (¥ billions)	63	332
Per capita annual disposable income of urban residents (¥)	4,724.11	15,647.66
Engle's coefficient (%)	41.48	39.48
Per capita annual net income of rural residents (¥)	1,905.61	4,736.25
Engle's coefficient (%)	34.78	37.46
Number of patent applications granted	968	4,752
Inventions	173	739
Utility models	627	3,096
Designs	168	917

Note: All monetary values are measured at current prices.
Source: *Shanxi Statistical Yearbook*, 2001 and 2011.

Industry is centered on heavy industries, such as coal and chemical production, power generation and metal refining. There are many military-related industries in the province due to its geographic location and history (it is used to be the base of the People's Liberation Army). Taiyuan Satellite Launch Center, one of three in China, is located in the middle of the province with the country's largest stockpile of nuclear missiles.

Many private corporations have invested in Shanxi's mining industry. Hong Kong billionaire Li Ka-shing made one of his largest investments ever in China in exploiting coal gas there. Foreign investors include mining companies from Canada, the US, Japan, the UK, Germany and Italy. Mining-related companies include Daqin Railway Co. Ltd, which runs one of the busiest and most technologically advanced railways in China, connecting Datong and Qinhuangdao and exclusively used for coal shipping.

The area's industrial share in total GRP is the highest among all the provinces. The pillar industries in the province are coal mining, metallurgy, chemicals and machinery. The deposit volume and output of coal account for one-third and one-quarter of the country's total, respectively. Major coalfields are located near Taiyuan and Datong, and the Datong Coal Group Corp is one of the most renowned coal enterprises in the nation.

Benefiting from the abundant mineral resources as well as the electricity generated from coal, a large and comprehensive metallurgy system has been set up with ferrous and non-ferrous metallurgy industries. Taiyuan Iron and Steel Group Corp is a large iron and steel company in China and is also a key stainless steel producer. Shanxi Aluminum Plant is one of the nation's biggest aluminum production bases. The chemical industry's current strategy is to utilize coal resources. Besides this resource advantage, Shanxi also has a good industrial base and a high concentration of industrial groups for developing the coal chemical industry. The Shanxi Fertilizer Plant has become the largest compound fertilizer production base that uses coal as raw material in Asia. The development of coal-related industries, however, brings with it heavy pollution and serious mining accidents. Many cities in Shanxi are rated as the most polluted cities in China.

As one of the steel and aluminum production bases in China, Shanxi has cheap raw material as well as convenient transportation for machinery manufacturing. Types of machines produced include trucks, coal machines, railway equipment, textile machinery, and auto engines and parts. Taiyuan Heavy and Mining Machinery Works and Taiyuan First Machine Tool Works are among the more well-known companies in this field.

Major export products include minerals, base metals, machinery, chemicals, gypsum and cement, while major import products are minerals, machinery, base metals, chemicals and optical products. The main import sources are Australia, Germany, India, Japan and Cuba, while key export destinations are the US, South Korea, Japan, Belgium and Italy.

During recent years, Shanxi has encouraged foreign investors to participate in the technological improvement of traditionally advantageous industries, such as the coal and coke, metallurgy and electric power industries. As a result, most of the FDI received is channeled into manufacturing and mining. Real estate, energy supply and logistics also receive some FDI. Most of this investment comes from the Virgin Islands, the Bahamas, Hong Kong, the UK and the US.

As of 2010, compared with those of other provinces, "mining", "public management and social organization" and "culture, sports and entertainment" were relatively strong, while "agriculture, forestry, animal husbandry and fishery", "services to households and other services" and "real estate" were relatively weak sectors (see Table C).

Table C   Shanxi's comparative (dis)advantage index by sector, 2010

Sector	Index
Agriculture, forestry, animal husbandry and fishery	0.28
Mining	4.69
Manufacturing	0.65
Production and distribution of electricity, gas and water	1.06
Construction	0.59
Transport, storage and post	1.07
Information transmission, computer service and software	0.73
Wholesale and retail trades	1.09
Hotels and catering services	0.67
Financial intermediation	0.97
Real estate	0.40
Leasing and business services	0.68
Scientific research, technical services and geological prospecting	0.68
Management of water conservancy, environment and public facilities	0.96
Services to households and other services	0.40
Education	1.02
Health, social security and social welfare	0.84
Culture, sports and entertainment	1.17
Public management and social organization	1.30

Notes: All the sectors included in this table are determined according to China's official definitions and for urban areas only. Numerals greater than, equal to and less than 1 indicate that the province's sectors have advantages, no apparent (dis)advantages and disadvantages, respectively.
Sources: Calculated by author based on *China Statistical Yearbook*, 2011. See Appendix for a detailed methodological description.

There are three major development zones in Shanxi. These are described below.

- **Taiyuan Economic and Technology Development Zone** This is a state-level development zone approved by the State Council in 2001 with a planned area of 9.6 km². It is only 2 km from Taiyuan Airport and 3 km from a railway station, national highways 208 and 307 pass through the zone. So far it has formed a "four industrial base, professional industry park" development pattern.
- **Taiyuan Hi-Tech Industrial Development Zone** Established in 1991, this is the only state-level hi-tech development zone in the province, with an area of 24 km². It is close to Taiyuan Wusu Airport and Highway G208. The nearest port is Tianjin Port.
- **Datong Economic and Technological Development Zone** This was established in 1992. It has an area of 37.2 km² with a population of 8,800. The three villages of Fanzhuang, Yuzhoutong and Qili are under its jurisdiction. It has also developed five key industries: food processing, new materials, coal deep processing, automobile sales and mechanical manufacturing. These industries have given a powerful boost to the economic development of the zone. The "Medical Industrial Park" within this zone was established with the approval of provincial government in 2003 and 14 medical manufacturing enterprises have settled there.

As of 2010 the top five companies were as follows:

1. Daqin Railway Co (SHA: 601006) is a provider of coal transport services from Shanxi and Inner Mongolia to eastern China. It posted ¥42.01 billion in revenues and ¥10.41 billion in net profits for 2010.
2. Shanxi Xishan Coal and Electricity Power (SHE: 000983) is a coal miner and supplier of electricity. It posted ¥16.94 billion in revenues and ¥2.64 billion in net profits for 2010.
3. Shanxi Luan Environmental Energy Development Co (SHA: 601699) is engaged in the mining, washing, processing and distribution of coal. It posted ¥21.43 billion in revenues and ¥3.44 billion in net profits for 2010.
4. Shanxi Guo Yang New Energy Co (SHA: 600348) is engaged in the mining, washing, processing and distribution of coal as well as generation and distribution of electricity and heat. It posted ¥27.94 billion in revenues and ¥2.41 billion in net profits for 2010.

5. Shanxi Taigang Stainless Steel Co (SHE: 000825) is an iron and steel smelter. It posted ¥87.2 billion in revenues and ¥1.37 billion in net profits for 2010.

Indicators for the ease of doing business

A. Starting a business
Procedures: 14
Time (days): 55
Cost (% of provincial GRP per capita): 9.3

B. Registering property
Procedures: 10
Time (days): 62
Cost (% of property value): 5.4

C. Getting credit – creating and registering collateral
Time (days): 16
Cost (% of loan value): 2.9

D. Enforcing contracts
Time (days): 300
Cost (% of claim): 26.4

Further reading

Aunan, Kristin, Jinghua Fang, Haakon Vennemo, Kenneth Oye, Hans M. Seip (2004). "Co-benefits of climate policy – Lessons learned from a study in Shanxi, China," *Energy Policy*, vol. 32, issue 4, March, pp. 567–581.

Chen, Xinfeng (2010). *The Studies of Shanxi's Sustainable Development during the Economic Transition Era* (jingjizhuanxingqi shanxisheng kechixu fazhan yanjiu). Taiyuan: Shanxi People Publishing House and Shanxi Publication Group.

Goodman, David S.G. (1998). "In search of China's new middle classes: The creation of wealth and diversity in Shanxi during the 1990s," *Asian Studies Review*, vol. 22, issue 1, March, pp. 39–62.

Goodman, David S.G. (1999). "King Coal and Secretary Hu: Shanxi's third modernization," in Hendrischke, Hans (ed.), *The Political Economy of China's Provinces: Competitive and Comparative Advantage*. London and New York: Routledge, pp. 211–248.

Goodman, David S.G. (2000). "Structuring local identity: Nation, province, and county in Shanxi during the 1990," *China Quarterly*, vol. 172, issue 1, pp. 840–863.

Goodman, David S.G. (2000). "The localism of local leadership cadres in reform Shanxi," *Journal of Contemporary China*, vol. 9, issue 24, July, pp. 159–183.

Huang, Dongsheng (2003). *An Introduction to the Shanxi Economy and Culture* (shanxi jingji yu wenhua gailun). Beijing: China Economics Publishing House.

Li, Weidong, Peng Jianxun (2006). *The Circulation Economy: The Only Way of Sustainable Development in Shanxi* (xunhuanjingji: shanxi chixu fazhan de biyou zhilu). Beijing: China Society Publishing House.

Li, Zhiqiang, Rong Heping (2012). *The Development Report of Resource-Based Economic Transform of Shanxi* (shanxi ziyuanxing jingji zhuanxing fazhan baogao). Beijing: Social Science Reference Publishing House.

Liu, Chunyang (2009). *Shanxi's Energy: Finding a Way Out* (shanxi nengyuan silu yu chulu). Taiyuan: Shanxi People Publishing House.

Miao, Z., R. Marrs (2000). "Ecological Restoration and Land Reclamation in Open-Cast Mines in Shanxi Province, China," *Journal of Environmental Management*, vol. 59, issue 3, July, pp. 205–215.

Niu, Renliang, Ling Zhengce (2010). *The Studies of Major Economic and Social Issues in Shanxi Province* (shanxi zhongda jingji shehui wenti yanjiu). Beijing: China Society Publishing House.

Sands, Barbara N. (1989). "Agricultural decision-making under uncertainty: The case of the Shanxi Farmers, 1931–1936," *Explorations in Economic History*, vol. 26, issue 3, July, pp. 339–359.

Sun, Jianzhong, Zhou Xinsheng, et al. (2006). *The Studies of Implementing the Grant Open Strategies for Shanxi Province* (shanxisheng shishi dakaifang zhanlue yanjiu). Beijing: Economics and Science Publishing House.

Veeck, Gregory, Li Zhou, Gao Ling (1995). "Terrace Construction and Productivity on Loessal Soils in Zhongyang County, Shanxi Province, PRC," *Annals of the Association of American Geographers*, vol. 85, issue 3, September, pp. 450–467.

Wang, Xiaojun, Zhenrong Yu, Steve Cinderby, John Forrester (2008). "Enhancing Participation: Experiences of Participatory Geographic Information Systems in Shanxi Province, China," *Applied Geography*, vol. 28, issue 2, April, pp. 96–109.

Zhang, Daisheng, Kristin Aunan, Hans Martin Seip, Haakon Vennemo (2011). "The energy intensity target in China's 11th Five-Year Plan period – Local implementation and achievements in Shanxi Province," *Energy Policy*, vol. 39, issue 7, July, pp. 4115–4124.

Zhang, Daisheng, Kristin Aunan, Hans Martin Seip, Steinar Larssen, Jianhui Liu, Dingsheng Zhang (2010). "The assessment of health damage caused by air pollution and its implication for policy making in Taiyuan, Shanxi, China," *Energy Policy*, vol. 38, issue 1, January, pp. 491–502.

Zhang, Jianjun, Meichen Fu, Yuhuan Geng, Jin Tao (2011). "Energy saving and emission reduction: A project of coal-resource integration in Shanxi Province, China," *Energy Policy*, vol. 39, issue 6, June, pp. 3029–3032.

Zhao, Rongda (2005). *Shanxi* (Panoramic China) (Chinese Edition). Beijing: Foreign Languages Press.

Zheng, Jianguo, Shen Changping (2007). *The Environment and the Social Economic Development of Shanxi* (huanjing yu shanxi shehui jingji fazhan). Beijing: Economics and Science Publishing House.

Sichuan

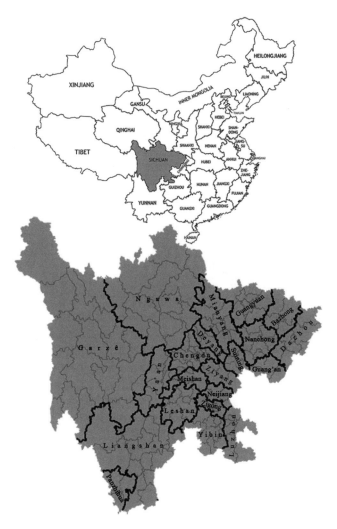

Source: The author, based on a file from the Wikimedia Commons.

Table A   The administrative divisions of Sichuan

Name	Administrative seat	Population
Aba Tibetan & Qiang AP	Barkam County	898,713
Bazhong PM	Bazhou District	3,283,771
Chengdu SPM	Qingyang District	14,047,625
Dazhou PM	Tongchuan District	5,468,092
Deyang PM	Jingyang District	3,615,759
Ganzi Tibetan AP	Kangding County	1,091,872
Guang'an PM	Guang'an District	3,205,476
Guangyuan PM	Lizhou District	2,484,125
Leshan PM	Shizhong District	3,235,756
Liangshan Yi AP	Xichang	4,532,809
Luzhou PM	Jiangyang District	4,218,426
Meishan PM	Dongpo District	2,950,548
Mianyang PM	Fucheng District	4,613,862
Nanchong PM	Shunqing District	6,278,622
Neijiang PM	Shizhong District	3,702,847
Panzhihua PM	Dongqu District	1,214,121
Suining PM	Chuanshan District	3,252,551
Ya'an PM	Yucheng District	1,507,264
Yibin PM	Cuiping District	4,472,001
Zigong PM	Ziliujing District	2,678,898
Ziyang PM	Yanjiang District	3,665,064

Notes: AP = autonomous prefecture; PM = prefectural level municipality; SPM = sub-provincial level municipality. All data are as of 2010.

Quick facts

Official name: Sichuan Province
Abbreviated name: Chuan
Land area: 485,000 km^2
Population: 80,418,200
Population density: 180/km^2
GRP per capita of 2010: ¥21,182
HDI of 2008: 0.763
Capital: Chengdu
Government office address: 30 Duyuan Street, Chengdu
Tel: 028-8666-3798
Website: www.sc.gov.cn

Sichuan is a province of the PRC. It is located along the upper Yangtze River in the southwest of China and borders Qinghai Province to the northwest, Gansu Province to the north, Shaanxi Province to the northeast, Chongqing Municipality to the east, Guizhou Province to the southeast, Yunnan Province to the south and Tibet Autonomous Region to the west. Its name is abbreviated to "Chuan" in Chinese.

The Yangtze River and its tributaries flow through the mountains of western Sichuan and the Sichuan Basin, thus the province is upstream of the great cities that stand along the Yangtze River in central and eastern China, such as Chongqing, Wuhan, Nanjing and Shanghai. One of the major tributaries of the Yangtze within the province is the Minjiang River of central Sichuan, which joins the Yangtze at Yibin.

The region is high in the west and low in the east in terms of its topography. The western part includes plateaus and mountainous regions, with some 4,000 m above sea level; while the eastern part is the basin and hilly land, with an elevation of between 1,000 m and 3,000 m. Western Sichuan consists of the numerous mountain ranges forming the easternmost part of the Tibetan Plateau, which are known generically as Hengduan Mountains. One of these ranges, Daxue Shan, contains the highest point of the province, Gongga Shan, at 7,556 m. Lesser mountain ranges surround the basin on the north, east and south. Among them are the Daba Mountains in the province's northeast. The Longmen Shan fault runs under the north-easterly mountain location of the 2008 earthquake.

Sichuan Province covers most of the Sichuan Basin. The Sichuan Basin, covering an area of 165,000 km², is one of the four largest in China. The elevation within the basin is between 200 m and 750 m, sloping down from north to south. Surrounded by mountains, it has a mild climate. This provides a favorable environment for plants and animals. The forests cover 7.46 million ha. Sichuan is home to one-fifth of the country's dawn redwoods and *Cathaya argyrophylla*, two species so old that they are regarded as living fossils. The region is also rich in animal resources. There are over 1,000 kinds of vertebrates, accounting for 40% of those in the whole country. Among them are 55 rare species. The well-known giant panda lives mainly in 36 of the counties and in the natural reserves of four mountain ranges within Sichuan's territory.

Due to the great differences in the terrain, the climate is very variable. The Sichuan Basin (including Chengdu) in the eastern half of the province experiences a sub-tropical monsoon climate with long, warm to hot, humid summers and short, mild to cool, dry and cloudy winters, with China's lowest sunshine totals. The western areas have a mountainous climate characterized by very cold winters and mild summers with plentiful sunshine. The south, including Panzhihua, has a sunny, sub-tropical climate with very mild winters and hot summers.

Sichuan is rich in minerals. It has more than 132 kinds of proven underground resources, of which reserves of 11 kinds, including vanadium, mirabilite, fluorite, sulfur iron, titanium and lithium, are the largest in China. The Panxi region alone possesses 13.3% of the country's reserves of iron, 93% of titanium, 69% of vanadium and 83% of the cobalt. It also possesses China's largest proven natural gas reserves, and large amounts of Sichuan's natural gas production is transported to eastern, more developed provinces.

The reserves of hydropower resources in the area amount to 150 million kw, second only to Tibet, and the exploitable potential is over 100 million kw, more than any other area in China. It is also the hometown of the world-famous giant panda.

Sichuan has historically been known as the "Province of Abundance". The crops produced there are those that survive in sub-tropical and cool temperate zones. The region is a leading producer of rice and also a major producer of other crops, such as corn, sweet potatoes, wheat, rapeseed, sorghum, barley, soybeans and millet. It has a long history of silk production and it is famous for hemp and other fiber crops, which normally rank second in China. Sichuan is the only region in which both the oxen of north China and the water buffaloes of south China are found living side by side. It also has the largest output of pork among all the provinces and the second largest output of silkworm cocoons in the country.

The province has one of the most diverse ranges of ethnic groups in China. The majority of the population are Han, who are found scattered throughout the region with the exception of the far west. Thus significant numbers of other minorities, such as the Tibetans, the Yi, the Qiang and the Naxi, reside in the west, forming a traditional transition zone between Central Asian and East Asian cultures. Most of the minority ethnic groups have maintained their traditional lifestyles and practices – often a mixture of agriculture, animal husbandry and hunting.

Sichuan's beautiful landscapes and rich historical relics have made the province a major center for tourism. The UNESCO World Heritage Sites list includes five world heritages – three natural heritages, one cultural heritage and one mixed heritage. These are the Huanglong Scenic, Jiuzhaigou Valley, Emei Mountain, Qingcheng Mountain and Dujiangyan Irrigation System, and the Sichuan Giant Panda Sanctuaries. In addition there are 9 state-class scenic areas, 11 national forest parks, 40 nature reserves and 44 provincial-class scenic areas. Almost every variety of landscape of interest to tourists is available here: plateaus, mountains, ravines, basins, hills, plains, rivers, lakes, hot springs, waterfalls, limestone caves and even danxia formation.

Sichuan's nominal GRP for 2010 was ¥1.72 trillion (about US$250 billion), equivalent to a per capita level of ¥17,380 (about US$2,545).

Table B   Demographic and socioeconomic profile: Sichuan

Indicator	2000	2010
Population (thousands)	83,290	80,449
Illiteracy rate of population aged 15 or over (%)	7.64	5.44
GRP (¥ billions)	401.03	1,718.55
Composition of GRP (%)		
Primary sector	23.6	14.4
Secondary sector	42.4	50.5
Tertiary sector	34.0	35.1
Fixed asset investment (¥ billions)	141.80	1,311.67
Status of foreign-funded enterprises		
Number of registered enterprises	3,539	12,050
Total investment (US$ millions)	10,107	54,383
Registered capital (US$ millions)	7,028	33,457
Foreign trade (US$ millions)		
Export	1,434	12,403
Import	1,344	13,893
Sales of consumer goods (¥ billions)	152	681
Per capita annual disposable income of urban residents (¥)	5,894.27	15,461.16
Engle's coefficient (%)	40.10	35.87
Per capita annual net income of rural residents (¥)	1,903.60	5,086.89
Engle's coefficient (%)	36.83	48.27
Number of patent applications granted	3,218	32,212
Inventions	248	2,204
Utility models	1,699	12,724
Designs	1,271	17,284

Note: All monetary values are measured at current prices.
Source: *Sichuan Statistical Yearbook*, 2001 and 2011.

The province is one of the most industrialized areas in western China and thrives in such light industries as building materials, wood processing, food processing and silk processing. There are also several world-famous wine breweries in the province, such as Wu Liangye

Group, Jian Nanchun Group and Luzhou Laojiao, accounting for about one-fifth of the country's total production. The region's high-tech industry has been developing fast and has attracted a number of internationally renowned IT companies, such as Microsoft, Cisco, Intel, IBM and Motorola, to set up manufacturing centers there.

In addition to heavy industries, such as coal, energy, iron and steel production, the auto industry is a key sector of the machinery industry in Sichuan. Most of the auto manufacturing companies are located in Chengdu, Mianyang, Nanchong and Luzhou. Other important industries there include aerospace and defense (military). A number of China's rockets (Long March rockets) and satellites have been launched from the Xichang Satellite Launch Center, located in the city of Xichang.

Great strides have been made in developing Sichuan into a modern hi-tech industrial base by encouraging both domestic and foreign investments in electronics and IT (such as software), machinery and metallurgy (including automobiles), hydropower, pharmaceuticals and the food and beverage industries.

As the economy grows the province must focus on growth outside the capital, where cities face inadequate transport infrastructure and an expressway system that does not link many cities to each other. Local government plans to improve transportation linkages between cities in the northeast and south. Sichuan is the biggest consumer market in Western China. In recent years the expansion of foreign retail enterprises there has sped up since China fully liberalized the retail and wholesale distribution sectors. Major foreign retail enterprises include Carrefour and Auchan from France, Metro from Germany, Wal-Mart from the US, Ito-yokado from Japan and Parkson from Malaysia.

Thanks to significant improvement in the local business environment, there have been major achievements in foreign trade. Key export markets include the US, Hong Kong, India and Japan. The main exports are machinery and electrical equipment, video and audio appliances, textiles, and base metals and related products. The US and Japan are also key import sources, in addition to Germany and South Korea. Major imports include machinery and electric equipments video and audio appliances, transport equipments and minerals.

Sichuan has attracted the most FDI among all the western provinces. The actual utilized FDI comes from the British Virgin Islands, Hong Kong, Taiwan, Singapore, the US, Samoa, Cayman Islands and Malaysia. Most of it is channeled into real estate and manufacturing.

As of 2010, compared with those of other provinces, "construction" and "public management and social organization" were relatively

Table C   Sichuan's comparative (dis)advantage index by sector, 2010

Sector	Index
Agriculture, forestry, animal husbandry and fishery	0.31
Mining	0.83
Manufacturing	0.78
Production and distribution of electricity, gas and water	1.12
Construction	1.80
Transport, storage and post	0.84
Information transmission, computer service and software	0.78
Wholesale and retail trades	0.73
Hotels and catering services	0.60
Financial intermediation	1.04
Real estate	0.58
Leasing and business services	0.44
Scientific research, technical services and geological prospecting	1.07
Management of water conservancy, environment and public facilities	1.02
Services to households and other services	0.36
Education	1.19
Health, social security and social welfare	1.19
Culture, sports and entertainment	0.77
Public management and social organization	1.24

Notes: All the sectors included in this table are determined according to China's official definitions and for urban areas only. Numerals greater than, equal to and less than 1 indicate that the province's sectors have advantages, no apparent (dis)advantages and disadvantages, respectively.
Sources: Calculated by author based on *China Statistical Yearbook*, 2011. See Appendix for a detailed methodological description.

strong, while "agriculture, forestry, animal husbandry and fishery", "services to households and other services" and "leasing and business services" were relatively weak sectors (see Table C).

Sichuan Province has various economic and technological development zones. Some examples are described below.

- **Chengdu Economic and Technological Development Zone** This was approved as a state-level development zone in 2000. It now has a developed area of 10.25 km² and a planned area of 26 km². It lies 13.6 km east of Chengdu, the capital city of the province and the hub of transportation and communication in southwest China. The zone has attracted investors and developers from more than 20 countries to carry out their projects there. Industries encouraged there include mechanical, electronic, new building materials, medicine and food processing.

- **Chengdu Export Processing Zone** This was ratified by the State Council as one of the first 15 export processing zones in the country in 2000. In 2002 the state approved the establishment of the Sichuan Chengdu Export Processing West Zone with a planned area of 1.5 km^2, located inside the west region of the Chengdu Hi-Tech Industrial Development Zone.
- **Chengdu Hi-Tech Industrial Development Zone** Established in 1988, this was approved as one of the first national hi-tech development zones in 1991. In 2000 it was opened to the Asia Pacific Economic Cooperation and it has been recognized as a national advanced hi-tech development zone in successive assessment activities held by China's Ministry of Science and Technology. It ranks fifth among the 53 national hi-tech development zones in China in terms of comprehensive strength. It covers an area of 82.5 km^2, consisting of the South Park and the West Park. By relying on the city sub-center, which is under construction, the South Park is focusing on creating a modernized industrial park with scientific and technological innovation, incubation R&D and modern service industry playing leading roles. Priority has been given to the development of the software industry. Located on both sides of the "Chengdu–Dujiangyan–Jiuzhaigou" golden tourism channel, the West Park aims to build a comprehensive industrial park targeting industrial clustering with complete supportive functions. The West Park gives priority to three major industries: electronic information, biomedicine and precision machinery. The pillar industries of the zone include IT, pharmaceuticals and precision machinery. There are over 11,800 companies registered in the zone, of which 674 are foreign-invested enterprises with 33 being Fortune 500 companies.
- **Mianyang New and Hi-Tech Industrial Development Zone** This was established in 1992 with a planned area of 43 km^2. It is situated 96 km from Chengdu and is 8 km from Mianyang Airport. There are more than 136 high-tech enterprises in the zone and they account for more than 90% of total industrial output. The zone is a leader in the electronic information industry, biological medicine, new materials and the production of motor vehicles and parts.

As of 2010 the top five companies were as follows:

1. Wuliangye Yibin Co (SHE: 000858) is a leading traditional Chinese white liquor distiller. It posted ¥15.54 billion in revenues and ¥4.4 billion in net profits for 2010.

2. Panzhihua New Steel Vanadium and Titanium Co (SHE: 000629) is a manufacturer of hot rolled and cold rolled plates, steel tubes, special steel, vanadium and titanium products. It posted ¥43.27 billion in revenues and ¥1.06 billion in net profits for 2010.
3. Dongfang Electric Corp (SHA: 600875) is an electric power generating equipment manufacturer and distributor. It posted ¥38.08 billion in revenues and ¥2.58 billion in net profits for 2010.
4. Luzhou Lao Jiao Co (SHE: 000568) is a leading traditional Chinese white liquor distiller. It posted ¥5.37 billion in revenues and ¥2.21 billion in net profits for 2010.
5. Kelun Pharmaceutical (SHE: 002422) is an IV solutions and injectable powder manufacturer. It posted ¥4.03 billion in revenues and ¥661.23 million in net profits for 2010.

Indicators for the ease of doing business

A. Starting a business

Procedures: 13
Time (days): 35
Cost (% of provincial GRP per capita): 19.1

B. Registering property

Procedures: 11
Time (days): 39
Cost (% of property value): 3.9

C. Getting credit – creating and registering collateral

Time (days): 12
Cost (% of loan value): 3.2

D. Enforcing contracts

Time (days): 295
Cost (% of claim): 35.5

Further reading

Bramall, Chris (2009). "Origins of the agricultural 'miracle': Some evidence from Sichuan," *The China Quarterly*, vol. 143, February, pp. 731–755.
Chen, Ni (2009). "Institutionalizing public relations: A case study of Chinese government crisis communication on the 2008 Sichuan earthquake," *Public Relations Review*, vol. 35, issue 3, September, pp. 187–198.
Choi, Susanne Y.P., Yuet Wah Cheung, Kanglin Chen (2006). "Gender and HIV risk behavior among intravenous drug users in Sichuan Province, China," *Social Science and Medicine*, vol. 62, issue 7, April, pp. 1672–1684.

Christopher, A. McNally (2004). "Sichuan: Driving capitalist development westward," *The China Quarterly*, vol. 178, pp. 426–447.

Eyferth, Jacob (2003). "How not to industrialize: Observations from a village in Sichuan," *Journal of Peasant Studies*, vol. 30, issue 3–4, April, pp. 75–92.

Foreign Languages Press (2006, ed.). *Sichuan, Land of Natural Abundance* (Panoramic China). Beijing: Foreign Languages Press.

Goodman, David S.G. (1998). *Center and Province in the People's Republic of China: Sichuan and Guizhou, 1955–1965* (Contemporary China Institute Publications). Cambridge: Cambridge University Press.

Hong, Lijian (1997). "Sichuan: Disadvantage and mismanagement in the heavenly kingdom," in Goodman, David S.G. (ed.), *China's Provinces in Reform: Class, Community and Political Culture*. London and New York: Routledge, pp. 199–236.

Hu, Junmei, Min Yang, Xiaoqi Huang, Xiehe Liu, Jeremy Coid (2010). "Forensic psychiatry assessments in Sichuan Province, People's Republic of China, 1997–2006," *Journal of Forensic Psychiatry and Psychology*, vol. 21, issue 4, August, pp. 604–619.

Ku, Hok Bun, David Ip, Yue-gen Xiong (2009). "Social work in disaster intervention: Accounts from the grounds of Sichuan," *China Journal of Social Work*, vol. 2, issue 3, November, pp. 145–149.

Liu, Chun (2012). "The myth of informatization in rural areas: The case of China's Sichuan Province," *Government Information Quarterly*, vol. 29, issue 1, January, pp. 85–97.

McCulloch, Neil, Michele Calandrino (2003). "Vulnerability and chronic poverty in rural Sichuan," *World Development*, vol. 31, issue 3, March, pp. 611–628.

Mobrand, Erik (2009). "Endorsing the exodus: How local leaders backed peasant migrations in 1980s Sichuan," *Journal of Contemporary China*, vol. 18, issue 58, January, pp. 137–156.

Tsui, Kai-yuen (1998). "Trends and inequalities of rural welfare in China: Evidence from rural households in Guangdong and Sichuan," *Journal of Comparative Economics*, vol. 26, issue 4, December, pp. 783–804.

Umeno, Yuki (2008). "From immigrants to stayers: Micro-demography of a historical lineage in Sichuan, China," *The History of the Family*, vol. 13, issue 3, January, pp. 268–282.

Wang, Jieying (2010). "Beyond information: The sociocultural role of the internet in the 2008 Sichuan earthquake," *The Journal of Comparative Asian Development*, vol. 9, issue 2, December, pp. 243–292.

Wang, Xiaoyan, Sheung-tak Cheng (2009). "A comparative analysis of the rural and urban older victims of the 5.12 Sichuan earthquake," *The Journal of Comparative Asian Development*, vol. 8, issue 1, March, pp. 43–66.

Tianjin

XINJIANG

GANSU

INNER MONGOLIA

HEILONGJIANG

JILIN

LIAONING

BEIJING

TIANJIN

HEBEI

NINGXIA

SHANXI

SHAN-
DONG

QINGHAI

TIBET

SHAANXI

HENAN

JIANG-
SU

SICHUAN

HUBEI

ANHUI

SHANGHAI

ZHE-
JIANG

GUIZHOU

HUNAN

JIANGXI

FUJIAN

YUNNAN

GUANGXI

GUANGDONG

HAINAN

Jixian

Baodi

Wuqing

Ninghe

Beichen

Lidong

Xiqing

Jinnan

Binhai New District

Jinghai

1 = Hongqiao
2 = Heping
3 = Nankai
4 = Hebei
5 = Hedong
6 = Hexi

Source: The author.

Table A   The administrative divisions of Tianjin

Name	Administrative seat	Population
Baodi PD	Jianshe Rd	799,057
Beichen PD	Beichen Ave	669,031
Binhai NA	Xingang No. 2 Rd	2,482,065
Dongli PD	Yuejin Rd	569,955
Hebei PD	Shizilin Ave	788,368
Hedong PD	Taixing South Rd	860,852
Heping PD	Qufu Ave	273,466
Hexi PD	Fujian Rd	870,632
Hongqiao PD	Qinjian Ave	531,526
Ji C	Ji Town	784,789
Jinghai C	Jinhai	646,978
Jinnan PD	Keji Ave	593,063
Nankai PD	Huanghe Ave	1,018,196
Ninghe C	Ninghe Town	416,143
Wuqing PD	Yongyang West Ave	949,413
Xiqing PD	Liukou Rd	684,690

Notes: C = county; NA = new area, which is a prefectural level district; PD = prefectural level district. All data are as of 2010.

Quick facts

Official name: Tianjin Municipality
Abbreviated name: Jin
Land area: 11,760 km^2
Population: 12,938,224
Population density: 1,173/km^2
GRP per capita of 2010: ¥72,994
HDI of 2008: 0.875
Government office address: 167 Dagu Road, Heping District
Tel: 022–2330–5555
Website: www.tj.gov.cn

Tianjin is a province-level municipality of the PRC. It is under the direct administration of Chinese central government. It is located on the northeast side of the North China Plain, facing the Bohai Sea in the east, with a coast stretching about 133 km. It adjoins Beijing Municipality to the north and borders Hebei Province to the east, west and south. Tianjin is officially abbreviated as "Jin" in Chinese.

The municipality is located on both sides of the lower reaches of the Haihe River. Several other rivers run into the sea in the area, such as the New Ziya River, the Duliujian River, the New Yongding River, the New

Chaobai River and the Canal Ji. The distance from the city proper to the seacoast is 50 km and that to Beijing is 120 km. It is an important passage by sea to Beijing, having served as fort and gateway to Beijing since ancient times. It is also a communication hub linking north, northeast and northwest China. The city boasts the largest man-made harbor in the north. Tianjin Port is an important passage linking a dozen provinces and cities in the north with the sea. Tianjin's geographical position and strategic importance is unmatchable. With more than 30 navigation routes leading to more than 300 international ports, it serves as a major channel linking the continents of Asia and Europe by sea.

Tianjin's name first appeared in the early years of the Yongle reign of the Ming Dynasty (AD 1368–1644) and it refers to the ferry port used by the emperor. In AD 1404 it became a military position of strategic importance, and construction of city walls and garrison installations began. It was eventually called the Tianjin Fort. It is divided into the old city and the Binhai New Area. The latter is a focus for expansion and has maintained an annual growth rate of nearly 30% of GRP since its establishment in 2009. As of the end of 2010, 285 Fortune Global 500 companies had established branch offices there. It is a base for advanced industry, financial reform and innovation.

The municipality is generally flat, and swampy near the coast, but hilly in the far north, where the Yan Mountains intrude into northern Tianjin. The highest point is Jiushanding Peak on the northern border with Hebei, at an altitude of 1,078 m. The city is located across the River Haihe, the largest river in north China, which has at its upper reaches more than 300 tributaries of more than 10 km long. These converge into North Canal, Yongdin River, Daqing River, Ziya River and South Canal, which then join in the Haihe River at Sanchakou near the Jin'gang Bridge of Tianjin. The Haihe River, which flows into the Bohai Sea at Dagukou, is 72 km long with an average width of 100 m and a depth of 3–5 m. It used to carry 3,000-ton ships. Since the project of diverting water from the Luanhe River to Tianjin was finished in the 1980s, 1 billion m^3 of water has been sent to the city every year. Tianjin also has a rich deposit of underground water. In the mountain area, quality mineral water with low mineral content oozes from the cracks of rocks at a rate of 7.2–14.6 tons per hour, and the flow can reach 720–800 tons per hour during the rainy season. There are three large reservoirs there with a total capacity of 340 million m^3.

The municipality features a four-season, monsoon-influenced climate, typical of East Asia. In winter the wind often blows from the north because of the cold high pressure from Mongolia. In summer, affected by the sub-tropical high pressure from the western Pacific, the city sees much southerly wind. The region has a semi-moist warm temperate continental monsoon climate with an apparent feature of transit from continental climate to marine climate. The seasons are distinct but the duration of each is different. Precipitation is not substantial with uneven distribution over the year. The monsoon wind is significant and sunshine is adequate. The annual average temperature is 12.3 °C. The hottest month is July, during which the average temperature can reach 26 °C. January is the coldest month with an average temperature of −4 °C. The yearly average rainfall is 550–680 mm, 80% of which is concentrated in the summer.

More than 20 varieties of minerals worthy of excavation have been discovered in the area. These include manganese, manganese-boron stone, gold, tungsten, molybdenum, copper, aluminum, zinc, limestone, marble, medical stone, barite and natural oilstone. There are petroleum and natural gas reserves underground in the plain and in the continental framework of the Bohai Sea. Tianjin also has about 1 billion tons of petroleum deposits, with Dagang District (in the Binhai New Area) containing important oilfields. Salt is also important, with Changlu Yanqu being one of China's most important salt-production areas. Geothermal energy is another resource.

Farmland takes up about 40% of the municipality's total area. Wheat, rice and maize are the key crops. Fishing is important along the coast. Tianjin is also significant industrial base. Major industries include petrochemicals, textiles, car manufacturing, mechanical industries and metalworking.

In the coastal area there are a lot of salt- and alkali-resistant plants. In the wetlands there are reeds, calamus, and cultivated water chestnut and lotus root. In the northern mountain area there are Chinese pine, Chinese walnut, walnut, haw and persimmon. The wild animals are mostly herbivores, such as wild goat, river deer, hedgehog, squirrel and birds. There are about 30 varieties of freshwater fish in ponds and reservoirs, including common carp, snail carp, grass carp, silver carp and mullet. Tianjin cuisine focuses heavily on seafood. It also has several famous snack items.

The majority of Tianjin residents are Han Chinese. There are also 51 of the 55 minor Chinese ethnic groups living there. Major minorities include Hui, Koreans, Manchus and Mongols. Despite its proximity to Beijing, the local dialect sounds quite different but provides the basis for Putonghua, the official spoken language of the PRC.

The main attractions of the region include Luzutang (Boxer Rebellion Museum), Guwenhua Jie, Ancient culture street, Tianjin Wen Miao (an important temple of Confucius), Yuhuangge Taoist Temple, Temple of Great Compassion Zen Buddhist Temple, Tianhou Palace, a temple dedicated to the goddess Mazu and the biggest in the North China region, Tianjin Water Park, the largest urban park and recreation area in the region, Tianjin Zoo, home to approximately 3,000 animals and 200 species, Italian Town and a polar marine animals theme park in Tianjin. The city is the respected home base of Beijing opera, one of the most prestigious forms of Chinese opera.

The nominal GRP of Tianjin was approximately ¥922 billion (about US$145 billion) with a per capita GRP of ¥72,994 in 2010. The manufacturing sector is the largest and the fastest-growing sector of Tianjin's economy (see Table B).

Table B Demographic and socioeconomic profile: Tianjin

Indicator	2000	2010
Population (thousands)	10,010	12,993
Illiteracy rate of population aged 15 or over (%)	4.93	2.10
GRP (¥ billions)	163.94	922.45
Composition of GRP (%)		
Primary sector	4.5	1.6
Secondary sector	50.0	52.5
Tertiary sector	45.5	46.0
Fixed asset investment (¥ billions)	61.09	627.81
Status of foreign-funded enterprises		
Number of registered enterprises	9,942	12,918
Total investment (US$ millions)	33,086	109,624
Registered capital (US$ millions)	18,510	62,044
Foreign trade (US$ millions)		
Export	7,674	37,771
Import	9,482	53,841
Sales of consumer goods (¥ billions)	74	290
Per capita annual disposable income of urban residents (¥)	8,140.50	24,292.60
Engle's coefficient (%)	46.27	50.05
Per capita annual net income of rural residents (¥)	3,622.39	10,074.86
Engle's coefficient (%)	35.47	41.74
Number of patent applications granted	1,611	11,006
Inventions	163	1,930
Utility models	994	6,718
Designs	454	2,358

Note: All monetary values are measured at current prices.
Source: *Tianjin Statistical Yearbook*, 2001 and 2011.

Although the output value of primary industry has continued to grow in recent years, its share of GRP has gradually decreased. The agriculture sector is currently undergoing strategic restructuring. Fish breeding, poultry raising and high-quality planting have become the main agriculture industries of the area.

The municipality is an important industrial center in northern China. Its pillar industries include electronics, automobiles, metallurgy and petrochemicals, of which the electronics and telecommunications are the most important and have developed rapidly.

In recent years, more than ten large business establishments, including Gulou Trade Street, have been reconstructed. Currently there are more than 50 shopping centers with an area of more than 10,000 m². Modern sales channels and new trade forms have developed quickly. Some internationally famous supermarket companies have established chain stores in Tianjin, including Metro, Makro, Walmart, Osun and Trust-mart. Shanghai Lianhua, Jiangsu Suning, Beijing Gome and other well-known domestic enterprises have also set up supermarkets in Tianjin. Its indigenous retailer, Family World, is also competitive.

The region's industrial development owes much to the rapid growth of hi-tech industries – electronics and IT in particular. Meanwhile, a lot of hi-tech enterprises, such as GMCC, Jinyao Group, Nankai Guard Group and Tasly Group, have become competitive. EADS Airbus is an important manufacturer and has opened an assembly plant in the municipality for its Airbus A320 series airliners, operational since 2009.

In the short term, infrastructure spending will buoy the economy. There are substantial projects underway to extend the metro system (which currently has only one line) and to improve road and rail links with Beijing.

Foreign investments are mainly in manufacturing (including textiles and garments, chemical products, machinery and equipment, electronics and telecommunication), trade, catering, and real estate. Some 95 of the world's top 500 enterprises have invested in Tianjin, such as Motorola, Samsung, BridgeStone, LG, GE, TOYOTA, Honda, Sanyo, 3M and Kyocera. Foreign-invested enterprises are playing an important role in the economy. Hong Kong is traditionally the biggest investor in Tianjin but US and Japanese investment has increased rapidly in recent years. Other major sources of foreign investment are Korea, Germany and Taiwan.

Tianjin has a highly externally oriented economy. Manufactured goods account for the majority of its exports, of which machinery and electronic products (such as mobile phones, displays and compact disc players) are the most important. The export of hi-tech products has seen rapid growth in recent years. Other export items include textiles and related products, mineral products and metallurgy products. Foreign-, Hong Kong-, Macau- and Taiwan-funded enterprises continue to be the largest players in the city's foreign trade. The major export markets are Japan, the US, South Korea, Hong Kong, the Netherlands and Germany. The key import sources are Japan, the US, South Korea, Hong Kong and Germany. Over the past five years, imports from these countries have grown rapidly – in particular, imports from Korea, Taiwan, Germany and France.

As of 2010, compared with those of other provinces, "services to households and other services", "wholesale and retail trades" and "hotels and catering services" were relatively strong, while "agriculture, forestry, animal husbandry and fishery", "construction" and "public management and social organization" were relatively weak sectors (see Table C).

Table C   Tianjin's comparative (dis)advantage index by sector, 2010

Sector	Index
Agriculture, forestry, animal husbandry and fishery	0.12
Mining	1.01
Manufacturing	1.31
Production and distribution of electricity, gas and water	0.67
Construction	0.51
Transport, storage and post	1.26
Information transmission, computer service and software	0.77
Wholesale and retail trades	1.47
Hotels and catering services	1.47
Financial intermediation	0.94
Real estate	1.08
Leasing and business services	1.42
Scientific research, technical services and geological prospecting	1.40
Management of water conservancy, environment and public facilities	1.03
Services to households and other services	7.24
Education	0.66
Health, social security and social welfare	0.90
Culture, sports and entertainment	0.85
Public management and social organization	0.61

Notes: All the sectors included in this table are determined according to China's official definitions and for urban areas only. Numerals greater than, equal to and less than 1 indicate that the province's sectors have advantages, no apparent (dis)advantages and disadvantages, respectively.
Sources: Calculated by author based on *China Statistical Yearbook*, 2011. See Appendix for a detailed methodological description.

Tianjin Municipality has established more than ten economic and technological development zones. Some examples are described below.

- **Tianjin Airport International Logistics Zone** This is jointly invested in by Tianjin Port Free Trade Zone and Tianjin Binhai International Airport. It is located inside the airfreight area of Tianjin Binhai International Airport. It has excellent domestic and foreign airfreight logistics enterprises engaged in sorting, warehousing, distribution, processing and exhibitions. It is in the process of constructing the largest airfreight base in northern China.
- **Tianjin Export Processing Zone** Located in the northeast of Tianjin Economy Development Area, this has a planned area of 2.54 km^2, and the development area in Phase I is 1 km^2. The zone enjoys a convenient transport network and is located 40 km from Tianjin, 145 km from Beijing and 5 km from Tianjin Port.
- **Tianjin Port Free Trade Zone** This is the largest free trade zone in northern China as well as the only one in northern China and northwestern China. It was approved in 1991 by the State Council. It is 30 km from Tianjin City, less than 1 km from the wharf and only 38 km from Tianjin Binhai International Airport.
- **Tianjin Tanggu National Marine High-Tech Development Area** This was established in 1992 and was upgraded to a national-level high-tech development area by the State Council in 1995, the only one specializing in developing the marine hi-tech industry. By the end of 2008 it had 2,068 corporations and 5 industries, including new materials, oil manufacturing, modern machinery manufacturing and electronic information.
- **National Supercomputing Center** The current second fastest supercomputer in the world, Tianhe-1A, is located in this center.

As of 2010 the top five companies were as follows:

1. Tianjin Tasly Pharmaceutical Co (SHA: 600535) is engaged in the manufacture and distribution of pharmaceutical products. It posted ¥4.65 billion in revenues and ¥450.3 million in net profits for 2010.
2. Tianjin Zhonghuan Semiconductor Co (SHE: 002129) is engaged in the semiconductor industry. It posted ¥1.31 billion in revenues and ¥97.53 million in net profits for 2010.
3. Tianjin Port Holdings Co (SHA: 600717) is engaged in cargo loading and unloading, as well as the provision of port services. It posted

¥11.48 billion in revenues and ¥803.28 million in net profits for 2010.

4. Tianjin FAW Xiali Automobile Co (SHE: 000927) is engaged in the manufacture and sale of automobiles and spare parts. It posted ¥9.89 billion in revenues and ¥299.68 million in net profits for 2010.

5. Tianjin Teda Co (SHE: 000652) is engaged in the wholesale of chemical products. It posted ¥6.95 billion in revenues and ¥286.43 million in net profits for 2010.

Indicators for the ease of doing business

A. Starting a business

Procedures: 14
Time (days): 41
Cost (% of provincial GRP per capita): 3.7

B. Registering property

Procedures: 5
Time (days): 42
Cost (% of property value): 4.4

C. Getting credit – creating and registering collateral

Time (days): 14
Cost (% of loan value): 2.7

D. Enforcing contracts

Time (days): 300
Cost (% of claim): 11.3

Further reading

Chaichian, Mohammad A. (1991). "Urban public housing in China: The case of Tianjin," *Habitat International*, vol. 15, issues 1–2, pp. 127–140.

Edgington, David W. (1986). "Tianjin," *Cities*, vol. 3, issue 2, May, pp. 117–124.

Foreign Languages Press (2005, ed.). *Tianjin* (Panoramic China) (Chinese Edition). Beijing: Foreign Languages Press.

Hendrischke, Hans (1999). "Tianjin – Quiet achiever?" in Hendrischke, Hans (ed.), *The Political Economy of China's Provinces: Competitive and Comparative Advantage*. London and New York: Routledge, pp. 183–210.

Hook, Brian (1998). *Beijing and Tianjin: Towards a Millennial Megalopolis* (Regional Development in China). Oxford: Oxford University Press.

Jia, Hongwei, Chen Zhiping (2010). *The Regional Society and Port Trade: A Case in Tianjin, 1867–1931* (quyu sheshui yu kouan maoyi: yi tianjin wei zhongxin, 1867–1931). Tianjin: Tianjin Ancient Book Publishing House.

Leitmann, Josef (1994). "Tianjin," *Cities*, vol. 11, issue 5, October, pp. 297–302.

Li, Jingyuan (2011). *Connecting Beijing and Tianjin and the Urban Economic Integration: the Economic Belt around the Capital and the Rise of Jing-jin Corridor* (duijie jingjin yu dushiqu jingji yitihua: goujian huanshoudu jingji quan yu jingjin zoulang de jueqi). Beijing: China Economic Publishing House.

Li, Jinkun (2006). *The Analysis and Forcast of Economic and Social Situation in Tianjin* (tianjinshi jingji shehui xingshi fenxi yu yuce). Tianjin: Tianjin Academy of Social Science Publishing House.

Li, Jun, Michel Colombier, Pierre-Noël Giraud (2009). "Decision on optimal building energy efficiency standard in China – The case for Tianjin," *Energy Policy*, vol. 37, issue 7, July, pp. 2546–2559.

Li, Shitai, Liang Chuansong (2009). *The Theory and Practice of Regional Industrial Cooperation: Connecting Yantai and the Binhai New Zone in Tianjin* (quyu chanye hezuo de lilun yu shijian: yantaishi duijie Tianjin binhai xinqu). Beijing: Economics and Science Publishing House.

Lu, Zhigang, Shunfeng Song (2006). "Rural–urban migration and wage determination: The case of Tianjin, China," *China Economic Review*, vol. 17, issue 3, pp. 337–345.

Song, Lianxin (2009). *To Witness the Rise of the Third Growth Pole: The Extraordinary Development Record of the Binhai New Zone in Tianjin* (jianzheng disanzengzhangji de jueqi: tianjin binhai xinqu bupingfan de fazhan lichen shiji). Beijing: Economics and Science Publishing House.

Sun, Tao, Hongwei Zhang, Yuan Wang, Xiangming Meng, Chenwan Wang (2010). "The application of environmental Gini coefficient (EGC) in allocating wastewater discharge permit: The case study of watershed total mass control in Tianjin, China," *Resources, Conservation and Recycling*, vol. 54, issue 9, July, pp. 601–608.

Tan, Minghong, Xiubin Li, Hui Xie, Changhe Lu (2005). "Urban land expansion and arable land loss in China – A case study of Beijing–Tianjin–Hebei region," *Land Use Policy*, vol. 22, issue 3, July, pp. 187–196.

The Archive of Tianjin (2009). *The Development Record of the Binhai New Zone in Tianjin* (tianjin binhai xinqu jingji fazhan shilu). Tianjin: Tianjin People Publishing House.

Todd, Daniel (1994). "Changing technology, economic growth and port development: The transformation of Tianjin," *Geoforum*, vol. 25, issue 3, August, pp. 285–303.

Wang, Jiating (2009). *The Theory and Case Studies of Experimental Zone's Comprehensive Reform: A Case in the Binhai New Zone, Tianjin* (guojia zonghe peitao gaige shiyanqu de lilun yu shizheng yanjiu: yi tianjin binhai xinqu weili). Nanking: Nanking University Publishing House.

Wang, Shuzu (2001). *WTO and the Development of Tianjin* (WTO yu Tianjin jingji fazhan). Tianjin: Tianjin People Publishing House.

Warner, Malcolm (1990). "Developing key human resources in China: An assessment of University Management Schools in Beijing, Shanghai and Tianjin in the decade 1979–88," *The International Journal of Human Resource Management*, vol. 1, issue 1, June, pp. 87–106.

Wei, Yehua Dennis, Yanjie Jia (2003). "The geographical foundations of local state initiatives: Globalizing Tianjin, China," *Cities*, vol. 20, issue 2, April, pp. 101–114.

Wu, Jinghua (2009). *The Rise of Tianjin: The Strategy of Tianjin Development* (tianjinjueqi: huanyu tianjin fazhan zhanlue de baogao). Tianjin: Tianjin People Publishing House.

Xing, Chunsheng (2010). *Economic Growth Pole with Chinese Characteristics and the Binhai New Zone in Tianjin* (zhongguo tese jingji zengzhangji yu tianjin binhai xinqu). Tianjin: Tianjin People Publishing House.

Zhai, Guofang, Takeshi Suzuki (2008). "Public willingness to pay for environmental management, risk reduction and economic development: Evidence from Tianjin, China," *China Economic Review*, vol. 19, issue 4, December, pp. 551–566.

Zhang, Ruigang (2008). *The Economic and Technological Development Zone of Tianjin: Managing Performance Pattern* (Tianjin jingji jishu kaifaqu: guifanhua neikong guanlixing jixiao yusuan moshi). Beijing: China Economic and Finance Publishing House.

Tibet

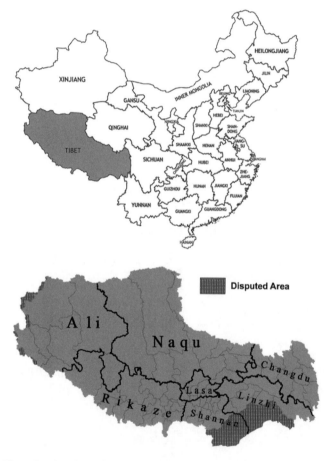

Source: The author, based on a file from the Wikimedia Commons.

Table A   The administrative divisions of Tibet

Name	Administrative seat	Population
Ali P	Gar Town	95,465
Changdu P	Changdu Town	657,505
Lhasa PM	Chengguan District	559,423
Linzhi P	Linzhi Town	195,109
Naqu P	Naqu Town	462,382
Rikaze P	Rikaze Town	703,292
Shannan P	Naidong Town	328,990
Zangnan D	Itanagar	NA

Notes: D = district; P = prefecture; PM = prefectural level municipality. Zangnan (called Arunachal Pradesh in India), which is claimed by the PRC as a district of Tibet Autonomous Region, is currently under Indian administration. All data are as of 2010.

Quick facts

Official name: Tibet Autonomous Region
Abbreviated name: Zang
Land area: 1,228,400 km²
Population: 3,002,166
Population density: 2/km²
GRP per capita of 2010: ¥17,319
HDI of 2008: 0.630
Capital: Lhasa
Government office address: Central Gyinzhu Road, Lhasa
Website: www.xizhang.gov.cn

Tibet Autonomous Region is in the PRC. It is a plateau on the northeast side of the Himalayas. It adjoins Xinjiang Uygur Autonomous Region and Qinghai Province to the north, Sichuan Province to the east and Yunnan Province to the southeast, and it shares international borders with Myanmar, India, Bhutan and Nepal to the south and west. It is the traditional homeland of the Tibetan people as well as of other ethnic groups, such as the Monpas, the Qiang and the Lhobas. Tibet is now also inhabited by considerable numbers of the Han and the Hui people.

The modern Chinese pinyin for "Tibet" is "Xizang", which derives from two Chinese characters, "xi" (west) and "zang". Zang refers to Tibetan people, language and culture, regardless of where they are from. The term "Xizang" was coined during the Qing Dynasty during the reign of Emperor Jiaqing (AD 1796–1820). Following the collapse of the Qing

Dynasty in 1911, Tibet declared its independence. The region maintained its autonomy until 1951, when it was incorporated into the PRC. The previous Tibetan government was abolished in 1959. Today the PRC divides the western and central parts of Tibet to be Tibet Autonomous Region, while the northeastern, eastern and southeast areas are under the administrations of Qinghai, Sichuan and Yunnan provinces, respectively. In addition, Arunachal Pradesh (called Zangnan or Shannan in Chinese), which is currently under Indian administration, is claimed by the PRC as a district of Tibet Autonomous Region.

The region, averaging more than 4,000 m above sea level, forms the main part of the Qinghai–Tibet Plateau and is well known as the "Roof of the World". Mount Everest (about 8,848 m above sea level), located on the border with Nepal, is the highest mountain on earth. Several major rivers have their source on the Tibetan Plateau (mostly in Qinghai Province). These include the Yangtze, the Yellow, the Indus, the Mekong, the Ganges, the Salween and the Yarlung Tsangpo (Brahmaputra) rivers. The Yarlung Tsangpo Grand Canyon is among the deepest and longest in the world. The Indus and Brahmaputra originate from western Tibet.

The atmosphere is severely dry for nine months each year, and the average annual snowfall is only 460 mm. The Indian monsoon exerts some influence on eastern Tibet. Northern Tibet is subject to high temperatures in summer and intense cold in winter. Western passes receive a small amount of fresh snow each year but remain traversable all year round. Low temperatures are prevalent throughout these western regions, where bleak desolation is unrelieved by any vegetation bigger than a low bush, and where wind sweeps unchecked across vast expanses of arid plain.

There are more than 90 known mineral types in the area, of which 26 have proven reserves and 11 rank among the top five in China. The minerals include chromite, lithium, copper, gypsum, boron, magnesite, barite, arsenic, mica, peat, kaolin, salt, natural soda, mirabilite, sulfur, phosphorus, potassium, diatomaceous earth, iceland spar, corundum, rock quartz and agate. In 2007 Chinese central government issued a report outlining the discovery of a large mineral deposit in Tibet. This may double China's previous reserves of zinc, copper and lead. Government sees this as a way to alleviate the nation's dependence on foreign mineral imports for its growing economy. However, the exploitation of these vast resources could harm Tibet's fragile ecosystem and also undermine its culture.

Tibet is rich in hydro, geothermal, solar and wind energy. It produces approximately 200 million kw of natural hydroenergy annually, about 30% of the nation's total. It has 354.8 billion m³ of surface water resources, about 13.5% of the nation's total, and 330 billion m³ of glacial water resources. The region has 56.59 million kw exploitable hydroenergy resources, about 15% of the nation's total. It also leads China in geothermal energy. The Yangbajain geothermal field in Damxung County, Lhasa, is the country's largest high-temperature steam geothermal field and also one of the largest in the world.

Tibet is like a giant plant kingdom with more than 5,000 species of high-grade plants. It is also one of China's largest forest areas and includes intact primeval forests. Most plant species from the tropical to the frigid zones of the northern hemisphere are found there. Forestry reserves exceed 2.08 billion m³ and the forest coverage rate is 9.84%. Common species include Himalayan pine, alpine larch, *Pinus yunnanensis*, *Pinus armandis*, Himalayan spruce, Himalayan fir, hard-stemmed long bract fir, hemlock, Monterey *Larix potaniniis*, Tibetan larch, Tibetan cypress and Chinese juniper. There are about 926,000 ha of pine forest in Tibet. Two species, Tibetan longleaf pine and Tibetan lacebark pine, are among those species under state protection. There are more than 1,000 wild plants used for medicine, 400 of which are common medicinal herbs. Particularly well known medicinal plants include Chinese caterpillar fungus, *Fritillaria thunbergii*, *Rhizoma picrorhizae*, rhubarb, *Rhizoma gastrodiae*, pseudo-ginseng, *Codonopsis pilosula*, *Radix gentiane*, Macrophyllae, *Radix salviae miltiorrhizae*, glossy ganoderma and *Caulis spatholobi*. There are over 200 known species of fungi, including famous edible fungi, such as songrong, hedgehog hydnum, zhangzi fungus, mushrooms, black fungi, tremellas and yellow fungi. Fungi for medical use include tuckahoes, songganlan and stone-like omphalias.

There are 142 species of mammals, 473 species of birds, 49 species of reptiles, 44 species of amphibians, 64 species of fish and more than 2,300 species of insects. Wild animals include old world monkeys, Assamese macaque, rhesus monkey, muntjak, head-haired deer, wild cattle, red-spotted antelope, serows, leopards, clouded leopards, black bears, wild cats, weasels, little pandas, red deer, river deer, whitelipped deer, wild yaks, Tibetan antelopes, wild donkeys, argalis, Mongolian gazelles, foxes, wolves, Iynxes, brown bears, jackals, blue sheep and snow leopards. The Tibetan antelope, wild yak, wild donkey and argali are all rare species particular to the Qinghai–Tibet Plateau and they are under state protection. The white-lipped deer, found only in China, is particularly rare. The black-necked crane and the Tibetan pheasant are under first-grade state protection.

Historically, the population of the region consisted of primarily ethnic Tibetans and some other ethnic groups. The original ancestors of the Tibetan people, as represented by the six red bands in the old Tibetan flag, are Se, Mu, Dong, Tong, Dru and Ra. Other traditional ethnic groups with a significant population or with the majority of the ethnic group residing in Tibet (excluding the area disputed with India) include the Bai, Blang, Bonan, Dongxiang, Han, Hui people, Lhoba, Lisu people, Miao, Mongols, Monguor (Tu people), Menba (Monpa), Mosuo, Nakhi, Qiang, Nu people, Pumi, Salar and Yi.

The area's cultural influences extend to the neighboring states of Bhutan and Nepal, as well as regions of India (such as Sikkim, Ladakh, Lahaul and Spiti), in addition to the Tibetan autonomous areas that are under the administration of adjacent Chinese provinces (such as Qinghai, Sichuan and Yunnan). Lhasa is the traditional center of Tibetan culture and the capital of Tibet Autonomous Region. It contains two World Heritage Sites – the Potala Palace and Norbulingka, which were the residences of the Dalai Lama. Lhasa contains a number of significant temples and monasteries, including Jokhang and Ramoche Temple.

Tibet is the so-called rooftop of the world. It draws visitors because of its great religious significance. Many tourists and pilgrims from Nepal and India enter through the Burang port of entry to visit the area's sacred mountains and lakes. The southwest Tibet tourist district is a place for mountaineers, many of whom are Nepalese, who come to Tibet through the Zhamu entry/exit port to enjoy the mountain scenery or do some climbing. In southern Tibet, centered on Nyingchi, one can pass through the four seasons of the year in a single day. There are snow-capped mountains, dense primeval forests, surging rivers and azalea-covered mountainsides. This beautiful scenery is easy to enjoy given the pleasantly humid and mild climate.

The region has continually developed and exploited its unique tourism resources, both human and natural. It currently has four tourist areas of Lhasa, the west, the southwest and the south. The Lhasa tourist area includes Lhasa, Yangbajain, Damxung, Gyangze, Zetang, Xigaze and Yamzhoyum Co Lake. Lhasa is not only Tibet's political, economic, cultural and transportation hub but also the center of Tibetan Buddhism. Major tourist sites include the Jokhang Temple, Ramoche Temple, Potala Palace, Barkhor Bazaar, Norbulingka Palace and three great monasteries of Ganden, Drepung and Sera. The Jokhang Temple, the Potala and Norbulingka palaces and Ganden, Drepung and Sera monasteries are key cultural relics under state-level protection.

New tourist routes and specialty tours have been added in recent years. They are Lhasa–Nyingschi–Shannan–Lhasa (eastern circle line) and Lhasa–Xigaze–Ngari–Xigaze (western circle line). Tours include exploration by automobile, trekking and scientific investigation tours. Other special events include the Shoton Theatrical Festival in Lhasa, the Qangtam Horseracing Festival on the North Tibet Plateau and the Yarlung Culture and Arts Festival in Shannan.

At the westernmost end of China, Tibet is the least urbanized area, with an economy that depends on agriculture, finance from central government and a thriving tourism industry. Economic development in the area is stunted by low population density, high transportation costs and high exploration costs. While it could be a large producer of natural resources and raw materials, there have been few advances in these areas. The focus is on expanding secondary industries, in particular energy, mining and new building materials.

Table B Demographic and socioeconomic profile: Tibet

Indicator	2000	2010
Population (thousands)	2,620	3,007
Illiteracy rate of population aged 15 or over (%)	32.50	24.42
GRP (¥ billions)	11.75	50.75
Composition of GRP (%)		
Primary sector	30.9	13.5
Secondary sector	23.2	32.3
Tertiary sector	45.9	54.2
Fixed asset investment (¥ billions)	6.41	46.27
Status of foreign-funded enterprises		
Number of registered enterprises	78	264
Total investment (US$ millions)	335	534
Registered capital (US$ millions)	188	296
Foreign trade (US$ millions)		
Export	109	538
Import	40	52
Sales of consumer goods (¥ billions)	4	19
Per capita annual disposable income of urban residents (¥)	7,426.32	14,980.47
Engle's coefficient (%)	36.38	36.23
Per capita annual net income of rural residents (¥)	1,330.81	4,138.71
Engle's coefficient (%)	53.83	49.71
Number of patent applications granted	17	124
Inventions	4	16
Utility models	4	49
Designs	9	59

Note: All monetary values are measured at current prices.
Source: *Tibet Statistical Yearbook*, 2001 and 2011.

At present, central government exempts Tibet from all taxation and provides most of its government expenditures. Due to limited arable land, the primary occupation on the Tibetan Plateau is raising livestock, such as sheep, cattle, goats, camels, yaks, dzo and horses. The main crops grown are barley, wheat, buckwheat, rye, potatoes, and assorted fruits and vegetables. The development of agriculture and animal husbandry has been given top priority in the Tibetan economy. The major agricultural products, such as broad beans, barley, wheat, rapeseed, garlic and mushrooms, have great competitive advantage in terms of quality due to several unique natural conditions.

In recent years, due to increased interest in Tibetan Buddhism, tourism has become an increasingly important sector and is actively promoted by the authorities. This brings in most income from the sale of handicrafts. These include Tibetan hats, jewelry (silver and gold), wooden items, clothing, quilts, fabrics, rugs and carpets.

Industry still plays an important role in the economy although its service sectors have developed rapidly over the last few decades. Industrial products such as minerals, medicine, Qingke barley wine, carpets and building materials are renowned globally. Traditional Tibetan medicine, in particular, boasts a history of more than 2,000 years.

In 2006 the construction of the 1,956 km Qinghai–Tibet Railway was completed. This stretches from Xining, capital of Qinghai Province, to Lhasa, and across the Kunlun Mountains and Tanggulashan. For 960 km it is constructed 4,000 m above sea level and is thus the world's highest railway. Its completion makes Tibet more accessible. It is also responsible for 75% of cargo, which greatly reduces transportation costs.

The economy of the region is dominated by subsistence agriculture, though tourism has been growing in recent decades. Major consumer markets are located in Lhasa and Shigatse. Traditional shopping districts are located around Jokhang Square, Beijing Road and Barkhor Street. In Lhasa, Barkhor Street is a famous market for buying small commodities, such as carpets, ethnic costumes and jewelry. Tibet has consistently developed and exploited its unique tourism resources, both human and natural. The region is home to unique folk customs and stunningly beautiful natural scenery, such as Namtso Lake, the Great Gorges of Yarlung, Tsangpu River, Potala Palace and Jokhang.

Major exports include light industry products, livestock products, traditional Chinese medicine and carpets. The main imports are motor vehicles and machinery products. Tibet's cross-border trade plays an important role in its economy as a result of its special geographic location.

Priority for foreign investments are given in the following areas: infrastructure (such as transportation and communications), education, agriculture (plateau agriculture, water-conservative agriculture and food processing) and Tibetan medicine. Foreign investments come mainly from Nepal, Japan, the US, the UK, South Korea, Denmark, Canada and Australia.

As of 2010, compared with those of other provinces, "public management and social organization" and "culture, sports and entertainment" were relatively strong, while "services to households and other services", "real estate", "manufacturing" and "mining" were relatively weak sectors (see Table C).

Table C   Tibet's comparative (dis)advantage index by sector, 2010

Sector	Index
Agriculture, forestry, animal husbandry and fishery	1.38
Mining	0.23
Manufacturing	0.13
Production and distribution of electricity, gas and water	1.45
Construction	0.36
Transport, storage and post	0.64
Information transmission, computer service and software	1.16
Wholesale and retail trades	0.65
Hotels and catering services	0.96
Financial intermediation	1.03
Real estate	0.00
Leasing and business services	0.27
Scientific research, technical services and geological prospecting	1.36
Management of water conservancy, environment and public facilities	0.45
Services to households and other services	0.00
Education	1.47
Health, social security and social welfare	1.41
Culture, sports and entertainment	2.78
Public management and social organization	3.63

Notes: All the sectors included in this table are determined according to China's official definitions and for urban areas only. Numerals greater than, equal to and less than 1 indicate that the province's sectors have advantages, no apparent (dis)advantages and disadvantages, respectively.
Sources: Calculated by author based on *China Statistical Yearbook*, 2011. See Appendix for a detailed methodological description.

- **Lhasa Economic and Technological Development Zone** This is the only development zone in Tibet. It was approved by the State Council as a state-level economic and technological development zone in 2001. It is located in the western suburbs of Lhasa, the capital of

Tibet Autonomous Region. It is 50 km from Gonggar Airport, 2 km from Lhasa Railway Station and 2 km from the 318 national highway. Its area spans 5.46 km^2 and it consists of "A" and "B" zones. The zone encourages overseas investments in high-tech, export-oriented industrial projects. Sectors and projects concentrate on the development and processing of agricultural and pastoral products, Tibetan medicine, foodstuffs and tourism products.

As of 2010 the top five companies were as follows:

1. Cheezheng TTM (SHE: 002287) is a traditional Tibetan medicine maker. It posted ¥523.64 million in revenues and ¥170.46 million in net profits for 2010.
2. Tibet Mineral Development Co (SHE: 000762) is a ferrochrome, copper, lithium and boron explorer. It posted ¥468.85 million in revenues and ¥32.6 million in net profits for 2010.
3. Tibet Tianlu Co (SHA: 600326) is a road and bridge construction company. It posted ¥1.13 billion in revenues and ¥74.62 million in net profits for 2010.
4. Along Tibet Co (SHA: 600773) is a property developer. It posted ¥864.65 million in revenues and ¥115.23 million in net profits for 2010.
5. Tibet Galaxy Science and Technology Development Co (SHE: 000752) is a mineral water and alcohol maker under the brand name of Lhasa. It posted ¥415.51 million in revenues and ¥15.1 million in net profits for 2010.

Further reading

Allen, Charles (2004). *Duel in the Snows: The True Story of the Younghusb and Mission to Lhasa*. London: John Murray.

Bell, Charles (1924). *Tibet: Past and Present*. Oxford: Clarendon Press.

Dowman, Keith (1988). *The Power-Places of Central Tibet: The Pilgrim's Guide*. London and New York: Routledge and Kegan Paul.

Feigon, Lee (1998). *Demystifying Tibet: Unlocking the Secrets of the Land of the Snows*. Chicago: Ivan R. Dee.

Foreign Languages Press (2006, ed.). *Tibet, Roof of the World* (Panoramic China). Beijing: Foreign Languages Press.

Gyatso, Palden (1997). *The Autobiography of a Tibetan Monk*. New York: Grove Press.

Johnson, Bonnie (2000). "The politics, policies, and practices in linguistic minority education in the people's Republic of China: The case of Tibet," *International Journal of Educational Research*, vol. 33, issue 6, pp. 593–600.

Le Sueur, Alec (2001). *The Hotel on the Roof of the World – Five Years in Tibet*. Chichester: Summersdale. Oakland: RDR Books.

Mackerras, Colin (2011). "Managing ethnic minority crises: The Tibetan areas and Xinjiang," in Chung, Jae Ho (ed.), *China's Crisis Management* (China Policy Series). London and New York: Routledge, pp. 65–86.

McKay, Alex (1997). *Tibet and the British Raj: The Frontier Cadre 1904–1947*. London: Curzon.

Mercille, Julien (2005). "Media effects on image: The case of Tibet," *Annals of Tourism Research*, vol. 32, issue 4, October, pp. 1039–1055.

Norbu, Thubten Jigme, Colin Turnbull (1968; 1987). *Tibet: Its History, Religion and People*. London: Penguin Books.

Pachen, Ani, Adelaide Donnely (2000). *Sorrow Mountain: The Journey of a Tibetan Warrior Nun*. Kodansha America, Inc.

Petech, Luciano (1997). *China and Tibet in the Early XVIIIth Century: History of the Establishment of Chinese Protectorate in Tibet*. T'oung Pao Monographies, Boston, MA: Brill Academic Publishers.

Rabgey, Tashi, Tseten Wangchuk Sharlho (2004) (PDF). *Sino-Tibetan Dialogue in the Post-Mao Era: Lessons and Prospects*. Washington, DC: East-West Center.

Ramachandran, K.N. (1980). "Tibet in focus," *Strategic Analysis*, vol. 4, issue 3, June, pp. 101–106.

Samuel, Geoffrey (1993). *Civilized Shamans: Buddhism in Tibetan Societies*. Washington, DC: Smithsonian Institution.

Smith, Warren W. (1996). *History of Tibet: Nationalism and Self-Determination*. Boulder, CO: Westview Press.

Smith, Warren W. (2004). *China's Policy on Tibetan Autonomy*. EWC Working Papers series No. 2. Washington, DC: East-West Center. Available at http://www.eastwestcenter.org/fileadmin/stored/pdfs/EWCWwp002.pdf. Accessed on March 26, 2012.

Smith, Warren W. (2008). *China's Tibet?: Autonomy or Assimilation*. Lanham, MD: Rowman and Littlefield Publishers.

Sperling, Elliot (2004). *The Tibet-China Conflict: History and Polemics*. Washington, DC: East-West Center.

Su, Ming Ming, Geoffrey Wall (2009). "The Qinghai–Tibet railway and Tibetan tourism: Travelers' perspectives," *Tourism Management*, vol. 30, issue 5, October, pp. 650–657.

Taylor, Annie E. (1894). "My experiences in Tibet," *Scottish Geographical Magazine*, vol. 10, issue 1, January, pp. 1–8.

Van Walt van Praag, Michael C. (1987). *The Status of Tibet: History, Rights, and Prospects in International Law*. Boulder, CO: Westview Press.

Wylie, Turrell V. (1977). "The first Mongol conquest of Tibet reinterpreted," *Harvard Journal of Asiatic Studies*, vol. 37, Number 1, June.

Yan, Z., N. Wu, D. Yeshi, J. Ru (2005). "A review of rangeland privatization and implications in the Tibetan Plateau, China," *Nomadic Peoples*, vol. 9, issue 1, pp. 31–52.

Zhou, Jinxing, Yang Jun, Peng Gong (2008). "Constructing a green railway on the Tibet Plateau: Evaluating the effectiveness of mitigation measures," *Transportation Research Part D: Transport and Environment*, vol. 13, issue 6, August, pp. 369–376.

Xinjiang

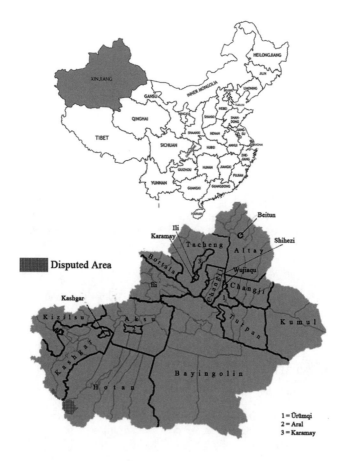

Table A The administrative divisions of Xinjiang

Name	Administrative seat	Population
Aksu P	Aksu	2,370,887
Altay P	Altay	526,980
Aral SPM	Aral	166,205
Bayingolin Mongol AP	Korla	1,278,492
Beitun SPM	Beitun	76,300
Bortala Mongol AP	Bole	443,680
Changji Hui AP	Changji	1,428,592
Hotan P	Hotan	2,014,365
Ili Kazakh AP	Yining	2,482,627
Karamay PM	Karamay District	391,008
Kashgar P	Kashgar	3,979,362
Kizilsu Kirgiz AP	Artux	525,599
Kumul P	Kumul	572,400
Shihezi SPM	Shihezi	635,582
Tacheng P	Tacheng	1,219,212
Tumxuk SPM	Tumxuk	147,465
Turpan P	Turpan	622,679
Urumqi PM	Tianshan District	3,110,280
Wujiaqu SPM	Wujiaqu	72,613

Notes: AP = autonomous prefecture; P = prefecture; PM = prefectural level municipality; SPM = sub-prefectural-level municipality (administered by the Xinjiang Production and Construction Corps). All data are as of 2010.

Quick facts

Official name: Xinjiang Uyghur Autonomous Region
Abbreviated name: Jiang
Land area: 1,660,000 km^2
Population: 21,813,334
Population density: 12/km^2
GRP per capita of 2010: ¥25,034
HDI of 2008: 0.774
Capital: Urumqi
Government office address: 2 Zhongshan Road, Urumqi
Tel: 0991–280–3114
Postcode: 830041
Website: www.xinjiang.gov.cn

Xinjiang Uyghur Autonomous Region is in the PRC. It is a large, sparsely populated area (comparable in size to Iran) which takes up about one-sixth of the country's territory. It borders Tibet Autonomous Region and India's Leh District to the south, and Qinghai and Gansu provinces to the southeast. The region shares a 5,000 km land border with eight countries (including Mongolia to the northeast, Russia to the north and Kazakhstan, Kyrgyzstan, Tajikistan, Afghanistan, Pakistan and India to the west). The name "Xinjiang", which was first given to it during the Qing Dynasty (AD 1644–1911), literally means "new frontier/territory". It has the abbreviated name "Jiang".

In ancient times, Xinjiang was known in China as the Western Territory. It is split by the Tian Shan mountain range. This east–west chain of mountains separate Dzungaria in the north from the Tarim Basin in the south. Dzungaria is dry steppe. The Tarim Basin is desert surrounded by oases. On the east side is the Turpan Depression, while the Tian Shan split in the west forms the Ili River Valley. Much of the Tarim Basin is dominated by the Taklamakan Desert. The lowest point in Xinjiang, and in the entire PRC, is the Turpan Depression, 155 m below sea level. Its highest point is the mountain K2, about 8,611 m above sea level, on the border with Pakistan. Other mountain ranges include the Pamir Mountains to the southeast, the Karakoram to the south and the Altai Mountains to the north.

Xinjiang is the largest political subdivision of China. It is divided into two prefecture-level cities, seven prefectures and five autonomous prefectures for Mongol, Kirgiz, Kazakh and Hui minorities. These are then divided into 11 districts, 20 county-level cities, 62 counties and 6 autonomous counties, then 5 sub-prefectural-level cities (Aral, Beitun, Shihezi, Tumxuk and Wujiaq), which do not belong to any prefecture, are administered by the Xinjiang Production and Construction Corps – a de facto sub-provincial unit directly under Chinese central government. The Tian Shan mountain range marks the Xinjiang–Kyrgyzstan border at the Torugart Pass. The Karakorum Highway links Islamabad in Pakistan with Kashgar over the Khunjerab Pass.

About 68 million ha or 41.2% of Xinjiang's total area are considered suitable for agriculture, forestry and animal husbandry. Of this there are some 48 million ha of natural grassland for grazing, 9 million ha available for reclamation, over 4 million ha under cultivation and 666,700 ha of man-made pastures. The region is one of the country's five major grazing areas. In addition there are some 4.8 million ha of land available for forestry, including 1.5 million ha in production with reserves of some 250 million m^3 of timber.

Fruits such as the Yili apple, Korla pear, seedless white grape and Hami melon are famous both locally and abroad. The region is famed for its unique natural environment and resources that nurture the growth of specific fruits which cannot be easily farmed elsewhere. Xinjiang is also China's largest and fastest-growing base for cotton, hops and lavender. Additionally, with the second largest pastureland in the country, the region is one of China's major sheep-farming areas and fine-wool production bases.

Among the 122 minerals that have been discovered in Xinjiang, several are the largest reserves nationwide. These include beryllium, muscovite, natron saltpeter, pottery clay and serpentine. Known reserves of iron ore are put at 730 million tons, while those for salt are 318 million tons, mirabilite 170 million tons and natron saltpeter over 2 million tons. With its deposits of more than 70 non-metallic minerals, the region is well known for its muscovite, gemstones, asbestos and Khotan (Hetian) jade. In addition, estimates put its coal reserves at more than one-third of the national total. Petroleum and natural gas reserves are estimated at 30 billion tons and account for more than 25% of the national total. Xinjiang is noted for producing salt, soda, borax, gold, jade and coal. It is also known for its fruits and produce, including grapes, melons, pears, cotton, wheat, silk, walnuts and sheep.

Xinjiang has an annual runoff of some 88 billion m^3 of surface water together with 25 billion m^3 of exploitable groundwater. Glaciers covering 24,000 km^2 lock away over 2,580 billion m^3 of water.

Xinjiang is home to 699 species of wild fauna, including 85 species of fish, 7 species of amphibians, 45 species of reptiles and 137 species of mammals. More than 4,000 species of wild flora have been identified, of which over 1,000 varieties, such as bluish dogbane and Russian dandelion, are of significant economic value.

The region is home to a number of different ethnic groups, including the Uyghur, the Han, the Kazakh, the Hui, the Kyrgyz and the Mongol. These follow various religious traditions, with the majority of the population adhering to Islam. Afaq Khoja Mausoleum and Id Kah Mosque in Kashgar are among the most important Islamic sites in Xinjiang. Emin Minaret is another key Islamic site, in Turfan. Bezeklik Thousand Buddha Caves is a major Buddhist site. According to one source, more than 2% of the population are Christians. Action against Christian activity tends to be stricter than in other parts of China. Home to 47 ethnic groups, a diverse range of religions co-exist there. Lamaism (Tibetan Buddhism), Islam, Buddhism, Taoism, Christianity, Catholicism, Eastern Orthodoxy and Shamanism all thrive side by side in the country's foremost multicultural melting pot.

Xinjiang has an abundance of valuable tourism resources and the region is notably famous for the ancient Silk Road. It is also home to 256 ancient cultural sites, tombs, ruins, Buddhist caves, stone sculptures and numerous contemporary monuments. Approximately 154 of the sites are under state protection. Popular scenic and historical attractions include Heavenly Lake, Bosteng Lake, Gaochang Ancient City and the ruins of Loulan.

The region's nominal GRP was ¥543.75 billion (about US$85 billion) in 2010. Southern Xinjiang, with its 95% non-Han population, has an average per capita income half that of the area as a whole.

Table B   Demographic and socioeconomic profile: Xinjiang

Indicator	2000	2010
Population (thousands)	19,250	21,851
Illiteracy rate of population aged 15 or over (%)	5.56	2.36
GRP (¥ billions)	136.44	543.75
Composition of GRP (%)		
Primary sector	21.1	19.8
Secondary sector	43.0	47.7
Tertiary sector	35.9	32.5
Fixed asset investment (¥ billions)	61.04	342.32
Status of foreign-funded enterprises		
Number of registered enterprises	371	1,751
Total investment (US$ millions)	1,143	5,229
Registered capital (US$ millions)	749	3,330
Foreign trade (US$ millions)		
Export	1,147	12,555
Import	1,439	8,809
Sales of consumer goods (¥ billion)	37	138
Per capita annual disposable income of urban residents (¥)	5,644.86	13,643.77
Engle's coefficient (%)	40.34	41.48
Per capita annual net income of rural residents (¥)	1,618.08	4,642.67
Engle's coefficient (%)	31.05	40.32
Number of patent applications granted	717	2,562
Inventions	66	189
Utility models	475	2,012
Designs	176	361

Note: All monetary values are measured at current prices.
Source: *Xinjiang Statistical Yearbook*, 2001 and 2011.

Thanks to its abundant reserves of coal, crude oil and natural gas on the one hand, and China's Western Development Policy introduced by the State Council on the other, Xinjiang has achieved rapid economic development during the past decade. Its GRP doubled between 2004 and 2010. The oil and gas extraction industry in Aksu and Karamay is booming, with the West–East Gas Pipeline connecting to Shanghai. The oil and petrochemical sector accounts for 60% of the local economy.

The region has recently become one of the most important energy producers in China. While the discovery of natural resources has certainly been a boost for the province, these remain scattered about an uninhabited and undeveloped landscape. Development in the areas of production and transportation will be necessary to maximize the region's economic growth. In 2009 Xinjiang produced more natural gas than any other province, the fourth most crude oil in China and large amount of coal. It also has a thriving agriculture sector.

Ever since the initiation of China's opening-up and reform drive in 1979, the area's economy has been changed dramatically. Industry leads with a contribution of 47.7% to the GRP. The service sector also makes a substantial contribution at 32.5%; while agriculture contributes the remaining 19.8%.

Urumqi, the capital city of Xinjiang, is the region's largest consumer center. Major department stores and shopping centers include Urumqi Tianshan Department Store, Urumqi Pacific Department Store and Urumqi Youhao Department Store. The French international hypermarket chain Carrefour has also established outlets and its northwest headquarters in the city.

Thanks to its wealth of natural resources, Xinjiang's well-developed industrial infrastructure focuses on a variety of industries, such as raw and refined oil, iron and steel, metallurgy, machinery, chemicals and power generation. The region's natural resources include coal, oil, iron, manganese, chromium, lead, molybdenum, zinc, beryllium, lithium, niobium, tantalum, cesium, white mica, asbestos and crystal. Oil and petrochemicals, food and beverages, textiles, metallurgy, building materials and electric power are the region's pillar industries of Xinjiang.

Most of the imports and exports are directed to and from Kazakhstan through the Ala Pass. China's first border free trade zone (Horgos Free Trade Zone) is located in the Xinjiang–Kazakhstan border city of Horgos. This is the largest "land port" in China's western region and it has easy access to the Central Asian market. Xinjiang also opened its second border trade market to Kazakhstan in 2006, the Jeminay Border Trade Zone.

Major imports in the region include rolled steel, medical equipment, crude oil, oil products and fertilizers. Due to the area's sparse population and underdeveloped transport network, FDI remains relatively low.

However, in recent years, growth in FDI has increased dramatically. The top three sectors that utilize the most foreign capital are manufacturing, mining and quarrying, and the production and distribution of electricity, gas and water. Denmark has injected the most FDI into the region. Other key sources are Australia, Hong Kong and Singapore.

As of 2010, compared with those of other provinces, "agriculture, forestry, animal husbandry and fishery", "mining" and "public management and social organization" were relatively strong, while "manufacturing", "services to households and other services" and "information transmission, computer service and software" were relatively weak sectors (see Table C).

Table C   Xinjiang's comparative (dis)advantage index by sector, 2010

Sector	Index
Agriculture, forestry, animal husbandry and fishery	7.95
Mining	1.60
Manufacturing	0.37
Production and distribution of electricity, gas and water	1.00
Construction	0.61
Transport, storage and post	0.90
Information transmission, computer service and software	0.51
Wholesale and retail trades	0.61
Hotels and catering services	0.56
Financial intermediation	0.78
Real estate	0.56
Leasing and business services	0.80
Scientific research, technical services and geological prospecting	0.84
Management of water conservancy, environment and public facilities	1.19
Services to households and other services	0.49
Education	1.10
Health, social security and social welfare	1.12
Culture, sports and entertainment	1.04
Public management and social organization	1.27

Notes: All the sectors included in this table are determined according to China's official definitions and for urban areas only. Numerals greater than, equal to and less than 1 indicate that the province's sectors have advantages, no apparent (dis)advantages and disadvantages, respectively.
Sources: Calculated by author based on *China Statistical Yearbook*, 2011. See Appendix for a detailed methodological description.

Xinjiang has seven economic and technological development zones: Bole Border Economic Cooperation Area, Shihezi Border Economic

Cooperation Area, Tacheng Border Economic Cooperation Area, Urumqi Economic and Technological Development Zone, Urumqi Export Processing Zone, Urumqi New and Hi-Tech Industrial Development Zone and Yining Border Economic Cooperation Area. Some examples are described below.

- **Urumqi Economic and Technological Development Zone** This is located northwest of Urumqi. It was approved in 1994 by the State Council as a national-level economic and technological development zone. It is located 1.5 km from Urumqi International Airport, 2 km from North Railway Station and 10 km from the city center. The Wu-Chang Expressway and 312 national highway pass through it. As a leading economic zone, it brings together the resources of Xinjiang's industrial development, capital, technology, information, personnel and other factors of production. With an area spanning 36.3 km^2, the development zone focuses on machinery manufacturing, new building materials, molds, furniture, food and beverages, pharmaceuticals, modern logistics and export processing. In 2006 the total industrial output reached ¥6.9 billion – an increase of 37.3% on the previous year.
- **Shihezi Economic and Technological Development Zone** This is located in the central area of the northern slope of Mount Tianshan and is the state-level development zone in the west of China. It was approved as a state-level development zone in 2000. With a land area of 5.3 km^2, it is oriented toward the countries along the Eurasian Continental Bridge. Many pillar industries have taken shape there: food processing, beverage production, plastics and chemicals, textiles, water-saving devices, foodstuffs, specialized fertilizers and building materials. It gives priority to the development of new technologies, new processes and new materials related to agricultural and husbandry production, and high-tech, high-value-added and high-return techniques and processes for processing farm products and byproducts. The infrastructure, fundamental industries and services of those industries concerned will also be developed.
- **Urumqi Export Processing Zone** This is located in Urumqi Economic and Technology Development Zone. It was established in 2007 as a state-level export processing zone.
- **Urumqi New and Hi-Tech Industrial Development Zone** This was established in 1992 and is the only high-tech development zone in the region. There are more than 3,470 enterprises there, of which 23

are Fortune 500 companies. It has a planned area of 9.8 km² and is divided into four zones. There are plans for expansion.

As of 2010 the top five companies were as follows:

1. Xinjiang Goldwind Science and Technology Co (SHE: 002202, HKG: 2208) is a wind turbine generator manufacturer and distributor. It posted ¥17.6 billion in revenues and ¥2.29 billion in net profits for 2010.
2. Xinjiang Guanghui Industry Co (SHA: 600256) is engaged in property development, distribution of liquefied natural gas, commodities wholesaling and retailing, and mining. It posted ¥3.79 billion in revenues and ¥688.38 million in net profits for 2010.
3. TBEA Co (SHA: 600089) is a power transmission and transformation equipment manufacturer and distributor. It posted ¥17.77 billion in revenues and ¥1.61 billion in net profits for 2010.
4. Hong Yuan Securities Co (SHE: 000562) offers services in brokerage, investment banking, securities investment and asset management. It posted ¥3.3 billion in revenues and ¥1.31 billion in net profits for 2010.
5. Xinjiang Zhongtai Chemical Co (SHE: 002092) is a chemical raw materials manufacturer and distributor. It posted ¥4.08 billion in revenues and ¥291.27 million in net profits for 2010.

Indicators for the ease of doing business

A. Starting a business

Procedures: 13
Time (days): 44
Cost (% of provincial GRP per capita): 9

B. Registering property

Procedures: 11
Time (days): 45
Cost (% of property value): 4.2

C. Getting credit – creating and registering collateral

Time (days): 24
Cost (% of loan value): 3.4

D. Enforcing contracts

Time (days): 392
Cost (% of claim): 20.5

Further reading

Becquelin, Nicolas (2004). "Staged development in Xinjiang," *The China Quarterly*, vol. 178, July, pp. 358–378.

Blank, Stephen (2003). "Xinjiang and China's security," *Global Economic Review*, vol. 32, issue 4, January, pp. 121–148.

Chen, Yu-Wen (2012). "'Xinjiang 13' revisited," *Asian Ethnicity*, vol. 13, issue 1, January, pp. 111–113.

Dillon, Michael (2011). *Xinjiang and the Expansion of Chinese Communist Power: Kashghar in the Twentieth Century*. London and New York: Routledge.

Ferdinand, Peter (1994). "Xinjiang: Relations with China and abroad," in Goodman, David S.G., Gerald Segal (eds), *China Deconstructs: Politics, Trade and Regionalism* (Routledge in Asia). London and New York: Routledge, pp. 271–285.

Hou, P., R.J.S. Beeton, R.W. Carter, X.G. Dong, X. Li (2007a). "Response to environmental flows in the lower Tarim River, Xinjiang, China: Ground water," *Journal of Environmental Management*, vol. 83, issue 4, June, pp. 371–382.

Hou, P., R.J.S. Beeton, R.W. Carter, X.G. Dong, X. Li (2007b). "Response to environmental flows in the lower Tarim River, Xinjiang, China: An ecological interpretation of water-table dynamics," *Journal of Environmental Management*, vol. 83, issue 4, June, pp. 383–391.

Luo, G.P., C.H. Zhou, X. Chen, Y. Li (2008). "A methodology of characterizing status and trend of land changes in oases: A case study of Sangong River Watershed, Xinjiang, China," *Journal of Environmental Management*, vol. 88, issue 4, September, pp. 775–783.

Mackerras, Colin (2011). "Managing ethnic minority crises: The Tibetan areas and Xinjiang," in Chung, Jae Ho (ed.), *China's Crisis Management* (China Policy Series). London and New York: Routledge, pp. 65–86.

Millward, James A. (2007). *Eurasian Crossroads: A History of Xinjiang*. London: Hurst and Company.

Morrison, Peter (1985). "Islam in Xinjiang," *Religion in Communist Lands*, vol. 13, issue 3, December, pp. 244–249.

Naby, Eden (1986). "Uighur elites in Xinjiang," *Central Asian Survey*, vol. 5, issue 3–4, January, pp. 241–254.

Shen, Yuling (2009). "The social and environmental costs associated with water management practices in state environmental protection projects in Xinjiang, China," *Environmental Science and Policy*, vol. 12, issue 7, November, pp. 970–980.

Steele, Liza, Raymond Kuo (2007). "Terrorism in Xinjiang?" *Ethnopolitics*, vol. 6, issue 1, March, pp. 1–19.

Toops, Stanley (1992a). "Tourism in Xinjiang, China," *Journal of Cultural Geography*, vol. 12, issue 2, March, pp. 19–34.

Toops, Stanley (1992b). "Recent Uygur leaders in Xinjiang," *Central Asian Survey*, vol. 11, issue 2, June, pp. 77–99.

Toops, Stanley (1993). "Xinjiang's handicraft industry," *Annals of Tourism Research*, vol. 20, issue 1, pp. 88–106.

Wang, David (1996). "Soviet citizenship in Xinjiang," *Asian Studies Review*, vol. 19, issue 3, April, pp. 87–97.

Wang, Hui, Zhaoping Yang, Li Chen, Jingjing Yang, Rui Li (2010). "Minority community participation in tourism: A case of Kanas Tuva villages in Xinjiang, China," *Tourism Management*, vol. 31, issue 6, December, pp. 759–764.

Wang, Yuan-Kang (2001). "Toward a synthesis of the theories of peripheral nationalism: A comparative study of China's Xinjiang and Guangdong," *Asian Ethnicity*, vol. 2, issue 2, September, pp. 177–195.

Zhao, Yueyao (2001). "Pivot or periphery? Xinjiang's regional development," *Asian Ethnicity*, vol. 2, issue 2, September, pp. 197–224.

Yunnan

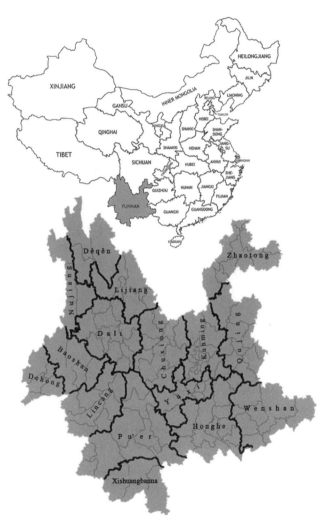

Source: The author, based on a file from the Wikimedia Commons.

Table A   The administrative divisions of Yunnan

Name	Administrative seat	Population
Baoshan PM	Longyang District	2,506,000
Chuxiong Yi AP	Chuxiong	2,684,000
Dali Bai AP	Dali	3,456,000
Dehong Dai & Jingpo AP	Luxi	1,211,000
Diqing Tibetan AP	Xamgyi'nyilha County	400,000
Honghe Hani & Yi AP	Mengzi County	4,501,000
Kunming PM	Panlong District	6,432,000
Lijiang PM	Gucheng District	1,245,000
Lincang PM	Linxiang District	2,430,000
Nujiang Lisu AP	Lushui County	534,000
Pu'er PM	Simao District	2,543,000
Qujing PM	Qilin District	5,855,000
Wenshan Zhuang & Miao AP	Wenshan County	3,518,000
Xishuangbanna Dai AP	Jinghong	1,134,000
Yuxi PM	Hongta District	2,304,000
Zhaotong PM	Zhaoyang District	5,213,000

Notes: AP = autonomous prefecture; PM = prefectural level municipality. All data are as of 2010.

Quick facts

Official name: Yunnan Province
Abbreviated names: Dian; Yun
Land area: 394,100 km^2
Population: 45,966,000
Population density: 112/km^2
GRP per capita of 2010: ¥15,752
HDI of 2008: 0.710
Yunnan Province
Capital: Kunming
Government office address: Wuhuashan, Kunming
Tel: 0871–362–1773
Website: www.yn.gov.cn

Yunnan is a province of the PRC, located in the far southwest of the country, with the Tropic of Cancer running through its southern part. The north of the province forms part of the Yunnan–Guizhou Plateau. The province borders Guangxi Zhuang Autonomous Region and Guizhou Province to the east, Sichuan Province to the north and Tibet Autonomous Region to the northwest. It shares 4,060 km of land borders with Vietnam, Laos and Myanmar, and it is connected to Thailand and Cambodia via waterways. Yunnan has two abbreviated names: "Dian" and "Yun".

The region is situated in a mountainous area with high elevations in the northwest and low elevations in the southeast. Most of the population lives in the east. In the west, the relative height from mountain peaks to river valleys can be as much as 3,000 m. There are a relatively large number of ethnic groups living in the province: 25 are found in Yunnan, which include Yi, Bai, Hani, Zhuang, the Dai, Miao, Lisu, Hui, Lahu, Va, Naxi, Yao, Tibetan, Jingpo and Blang. In its 16 prefecture-level divisions, it has 129 county-level divisions and 1,455 township-level divisions

The area has a generally mild climate with pleasant weather because its location on south-facing mountain slopes, receiving the influence of both the Pacific and Indian oceans. The January average temperature is 8–17 °C and July is 21–27 °C. Average annual rainfall is 600–2,300 mm, with over half falling between June and August. The plateau region has moderate temperatures. The western canyon region is hot and humid at the valley bottoms but freezing winds are common on the mountaintops.

More than 150 kinds of minerals have been discovered in 2,700 places in the province. The most valuable proven deposits are of fuel and non-metallic minerals. Some 13% of the proven deposits of minerals are the largest of their kind in China, and two-thirds are among the largest of their kind in the Yangtze River valley and in south China. Yunnan ranks first in the country with respect to deposits of zinc, lead, tin, cadmium, indium, thallium and crocidolite, and it has large deposits of iron, coal, lead, copper, gold, mercury, silver, antimony and sulfur. Gejiu city is well known as "the Kingdom of Zinc" with its reserves ranked first in the country. In addition, reserves of germanium, zirconium, platinum, rock salt, nickel, phosphate, arsenic and blue asbestos are also substantial.

The area is rich in natural resources and has the largest diversity of plant life in China. It has over 600 rivers and lakes, providing about 200 billion m^3 of water supply per year, three times that of the Yellow River. The rivers flowing into the province from outside add 160 billion m^3. The rich water resources offer abundant hydroenergy.

Yunnan is known as the kingdom of plants and animals. At the end of 2005 there were 198 nature reserves, covering a total area of 3.55 million ha. The province is China's most diverse, biologically as well as culturally. It contains snow-capped mountains and true tropical environments, thus supporting an unusually full spectrum of species and vegetation types. During the summer the Great Plateau of Tibet acts as a barrier to monsoon winds, trapping moisture in the province. This gives the alpine flora in particular what one source has called a "lushness found nowhere else".

This topographic range combined with tropical moisture sustains extremely high biodiversity and high degrees of endemism, probably the richest botanically in the world's temperate regions. The province not only has more plant species of tropical, sub-tropical, temperate and frozen zones than any other province in the country but also has many ancient, derivative plants, as well as species introduced from foreign countries. Among the 30,000 species of plants in China, 18,000 can be found in Yunnan. Some 144 species of plants are now under Class I and Class II protection.

Yunnan offers rich tourism resources, including beautiful landscape, colorful ethnic customs and a pleasant climate. Its most popular tourist spots include Kunming, Dali, Lijiang, Xishuangbanna and Shangri-la. Most visitors are Chinese tourists, although trips to Yunnan are organized by an increasing number of foreign travel agencies. Also a new trend is developing: small-scale ecotourism. UNESCO World Heritage Sites include the Old Town of Lijiang (accepted in 1997 as a cultural site), the Three Parallel Rivers of Yunnan Protected Areas (accepted in 2003 as a natural site) and the South China Karst (accepted in 2007 as a natural site).

Yunnan is one of China's relatively undeveloped areas with more poverty-stricken counties than other provinces. Its nominal GRP in 2010 was ¥722.42 billion (about US$110 billion). Its per capita GRP was ¥13,494 (about US$1,975). The shares of GRP of Yunnan's primary, secondary and tertiary industries are 15.3%, 44.6% and 40.0%, respectively (see Table B).

Table B Demographic and socioeconomic profile: Yunnan

Indicator	2000	2010
Population (thousands)	42,880	46,016
Illiteracy rate of population aged 15 or over (%)	11.39	6.03
GRP (¥ billions)	195.51	722.42
Composition of GRP (%)		
Primary sector	22.3	15.3
Secondary sector	43.1	44.6
Tertiary sector	34.6	40.0
Fixed asset investment (¥ billions)	68.40	552.87

Status of foreign-funded enterprises		
Number of registered enterprises	1,634	3,833
Total investment (US$ millions)	4,819	17,949
Registered capital (US$ millions)	3,101	10,450
Foreign trade (US$ millions)		
Export	1,093	5,108
Import	791	5,225
Sales of consumer goods (¥ billions)	58	250
Per capita annual disposable income of urban residents (¥)	6,324.64	16,064.54
Engle's coefficient (%)	39.20	34.26
Per capita annual net income of rural residents (¥)	1,478.60	3,952.03
Engle's coefficient (%)	37.83	47.21
Number of patent applications granted	1,217	3,823
Inventions	140	652
Utility models	606	2,026
Designs	471	1,145

Note: All monetary values are measured at current prices.
Source: *Yunnan Statistical Yearbook*, 2001 and 2011.

A poverty-alleviation plan includes five large projects aimed at improving infrastructure facilities. These include attempts at soil improvement, water conservation, electric power, roads and "green belt" building. The province hopes that this will alleviate the shortages of grain, water, electric power and roads.

Yunnan lags behind the east coast in relation to socioeconomic development. However, because of its geographic location it has comparative advantages in regional and border trade with countries in southeast Asia. The Lancang River (upper reaches of the Mekong River) is the waterway to Southeast Asia. In recent years, land transportation has been improved to strengthen economic and trade co-operation among countries in the Greater Mekong Subregion. Yunnan's abundance of resources means that its pillar industries are agriculture, tobacco, mining, hydroelectric power and tourism.

The main manufacturing industries are iron and steel production and copper smelting, commercial vehicles, chemicals, fertilizers, textiles and optical instruments. Tobacco is the biggest industry in Yunnan. Hongta Group is one of the most important tobacco-production bases and the nation's largest cigarette manufacturer. With the imposition of tougher smoking regulations, this industry is stalling, as is its GRP growth. As a result there is a need to find a new economic driver.

The electricity industry is another important economic pillar of Yunnan and this plays a key role in the West-East Electricity

Transmission Project. The electricity produced in the region is mainly transported to Guangdong Province. Production and supply of electricity, gas and water have the highest amount of fixed asset investment. The other four industries with substantial investments in fixed assets are transport, storage and post, real estate, manufacturing, and water, environment and public facilities management.

The largest consumer center is in Kunming and a number of foreign retail enterprises have invested there. These include Wal-Mart from the US, Carrefour from France and Price-Mart and Trust-Mart from Taiwan.

Yunnan is one of China's largest forest zones. Its forest area accounts for 24.2% of the country's total. The province also yields a large number of plant and animal species, and these provide the foundation for its Chinese medicine and food industries. The flowers, tea leaves, fruits and vegetables of the province are well known.

Tobacco is the main export product and makes up a large part of the provincial GRP. Yunnan also has strong competitive potential in the fruit and vegetable industries, especially in low value-added commodities, such as fresh and dried vegetables and fresh apples.

The region is currently China's most important producer of Arabica coffee. Besides the export of roasted coffee, coffee-related products such as extracts, essences and substitutes may be promising products. Yunnan is the birthplace of tea and ancient tea trees can still be found there. Tea is becoming an important export product and in the US and Japan the demand is growing.

As a result of the country's growing consumption of dairy products (a trend heavily supported by national government), the province's dairy industry is developing rapidly and receiving large subsidies to develop a competitive edge in southwest China. Exports to its ASEAN neighbors are also planned.

A growing sector heavily supported by local government is horticulture. The flower industry in Yunnan started to develop toward the end of the 1980s. Currently it is the most important province nationwide in terms of flower growing. It accounts for 50% of China's total cut-flower production. The size of the planting area for cut flowers in the province amounts to 4,000 ha. Apart from sales on the domestic market, it also exports to a number of foreign countries and regions, such as Japan, Korea, Hong Kong, Thailand and Singapore. Rapid developments in this sector soon attracted the attention of Dutch horticultural companies, and Dutch investments in flower-related projects and businesses are steadily growing.

The transport sector has maintained steady development. The area has more than 1,700 km of railways (the Guiyang–Kunming,

Chengdu–Kunming, Kunming–Hekou and Mengzi–Baoxiu railways) and a highway network of 44,000 km. The Jinsha, Nanpan, Yuanjiang and Lancang rivers are also navigable by boat. Telecommunications and postal services developed rapidly there.

The province has trade contacts with more than 70 countries and regions in the world. It established the Muse border trade zone (located in Ruili) along its border with Burma. It mainly exports tobacco, machinery and electrical equipment, chemical and agricultural products and non-ferrous metals. ASEAN is the region's largest trading partner. Imports are mainly minerals, machinery and electrical appliances, electronics and telecommunications equipment. Major import sources include Hong Kong, the EU and Myanmar.

The largest investment is in manufacturing. Other areas include production and supply of electricity, gas and water, business services and mining and quarrying. Hong Kong is the largest source of foreign investment in Yunnan. Hong Kong companies, such as New World, invested in the development of Chinese medicine there. Other major investors are Singapore, the US, the Virgin Islands and Taiwan.

As of 2010, compared with those of other provinces, "agriculture, forestry, animal husbandry and fishery", "education" and "public management and social organization" were relatively strong, while "services to households and other services", "manufacturing" and "information transmission, computer service and software" were relatively weak sectors (see Table C).

Table C   Yunnan's comparative (dis)advantage index by sector, 2010

Sector	Index
Agriculture, forestry, animal husbandry and fishery	1.56
Mining	1.09
Manufacturing	0.65
Production and distribution of electricity, gas and water	1.11
Construction	1.20
Transport, storage and post	0.86
Information transmission, computer service and software	0.76
Wholesale and retail trades	1.18
Hotels and catering services	1.12
Financial intermediation	0.78
Real estate	0.79
Leasing and business services	0.94
Scientific research, technical services and geological prospecting	0.86
Management of water conservancy, environment and public facilities	0.98
Services to households and other services	0.52

Table C   (Continued)

Sector	Index
Education	1.32
Health, social security and social welfare	1.01
Culture, sports and entertainment	1.09
Public management and social organization	1.31

Notes: All the sectors included in this table are determined according to China's official definitions and for urban areas only. Numerals greater than, equal to and less than 1 indicate that the province's sectors have advantages, no apparent (dis)advantages and disadvantages, respectively.

Sources: Calculated by author based on *China Statistical Yearbook*, 2011. See Appendix for a detailed methodological description.

Yunnan Province has more than a dozen economic and technological development zones. Some examples are described below.

- **Kunming Economic and Technological Development Zone** This was established in 1992 as a national-level zone approved by the State Council. It has a preferential location in east-central Yunnan. It has an area of 55.7 km². After several years of development, the zone has formed its pillar industries, which include tobacco processing, machinery manufacturing, electronic information and biotechnology.
- **Kunming New and Hi-Tech Industrial Development Zone** This is a state-level high-tech industrial zone established in 1992 in northwest Kunming. It is administratively under Kunming Prefecture. Covering an area of 9 km², it is located in the northwest part of Kunming City, 4 m from Kunming Railway Station and 5 km from Kunming International Airport.
- **Ruili Border Trade Economic Cooperation Zone** This is a State Council-approved industrial park based in Ruili City. It was founded in 1992 to promote trade between China and Burma. The area's import and export trade include the processing industry and local agriculture, and biological resources are very promising. Sino-Burmese business is growing fast and Burma is now one of the region's biggest foreign trade partners. In 1999, Sino-Burmese trade accounted for 77.4% of Yunnan's foreign trade. In the same year, exports of electromechanical equipment reached US$55.28 million. The main exports include fiber cloth, cotton yarn, ceresin wax, mechanical equipment, fruits, rice seeds, fiber yarn and tobacco.

- **Wanding Border Economic Cooperation Zone** This is a State Council-approved industrial park based in Wanding Town. Founded in 1992, it was established to promote trade between China and Burma. The zone spans 6 km² and focuses on developing trading, processing, agriculture resources and tourism.
- **Qujing Economic and Technological Development Zone** This is a provincial development zone approved by provincial government in 1992. It is located in the east of urban Qujing, the second largest city in Yunnan in terms of economic strength. As an agency under Qujing Municipal Party committee and municipal government, its administrative commission functions as an economy supervising body at the prefecture level and an administration body at the county level. It has 106 km² under its jurisdiction. It shoulders the task of building a new 40 km² city area and providing services for a population of 400,000 in the next ten years.
- **Chuxiong Economic and Technological Development Zone** This is an important zone in Yunnan. It has attracted a number of investment projects and is key to the development of a new type of industry platform. The zone covers an area of 12 km² and comprises four parks.
- **Hekou Border Economic Cooperation Zone** First established in 1992, this is a border zone approved by the State Council to promote trade between China and Vietnam. It has a planned area of 4.02 km². The zone has implemented several policies to serve its clients in China from various industries and sectors, including investment, trade, finance, taxation and immigration.

As of 2010 the top five companies were as follows:

1. Yunnan Baiyao Group Co (SHE: 000538) is China's largest TCM drug maker.
2. Yunnan Copper Co (SHE: 000878) is a producer and distributor of copper concentrates, precious metals and chemical products.
3. Yunnan Chihong Zinc and Germanium Co (SHA: 600497) is a non-ferrous metal miner and smelter.
4. The Pacific Securities Co (SHA: 601099) offers services in securities brokering, investment banking and securities underwriting.
5. Yunnan Tin Co (SHE: 000960) is a miner and processor of tin and other non-ferrous metals.

For complete access to our database of all Yunnan Province Companies earnings, revenues, margins and other corporate

Indicators for the ease of doing business

A. Starting a business

Procedures: 14
Time (days): 42
Cost (% of provincial GRP per capita): 13.9

B. Registering property

Procedures: 9
Time (days): 66
Cost (% of property value): 5.4

C. Getting credit – creating and registering collateral

Time (days): 18
Cost (% of loan value): 4

D. Enforcing contracts

Time (days): 365
Cost (% of claim): 36.4

Further reading

Booz, Patrick R. (1998). *Yunnan.* Odyssey Passport: McGraw-Hill Contemporary.
Bryce, E.J. (1935). "Yunnan," *Australian Geographer*, vol. 2, issue 7, September, pp. 23–26.
d'Hooghe, Ingrid (1994). "Regional economic integration in Yunnan," in Goodman, David S.G., Gerald Segal (eds), *China Deconstructs: Politics, Trade and Regionalism* (Routledge in Asia). London and New York: Routledge, pp. 286–176.
Ding, Shijun, Laura Meriluoto, W. Robert Reed, Dayun Tao, Haitao Wu (2011). "The impact of agricultural technology adoption on income inequality in rural China: Evidence from southern Yunnan Province," *China Economic Review*, vol. 22, issue 3, September, pp. 344–356.
Foggin, Peter, Nagib Armijo-Hussein, Céline Marigaux, Hui Zhu, Zeyuan Liu (2001). "Risk Factors and child mortality among the Miao in Yunnan, Southwest China," *Social Science and Medicine*, vol. 53, issue 12, December, pp. 1683–1696.
Goodman, Jim (2006). *The Exploration of Yunnan.* Kunming: Yunnan People's Publishing House.
Guo, Huijun, Christine Padoch (1995). "Patterns and management of agroforestry systems in Yunnan: An approach to upland rural development," *Global Environmental Change*, vol. 5, issue 4, September, pp. 273–279.
Guo, Huijun, Christine Padoch, Kevin Coffey, Chen Aiguo, Fu Yongneng (2002). "Economic development, land use and biodiversity change in the tropical mountains of Xishuangbanna, Yunnan, Southwest China," *Environmental Science and Policy*, vol. 5, issue 6, December, pp. 471–479.

Lu, Qi, Yang Chunyue (2008). "Characteristics of rural labor emigration in minority areas of Honghe, Yunnan and its impact on new socialist countryside construction in the 21st century," *China Population, Resources and Environment*, vol. 18, issue 4, August, pp. 85–86.

Mansfield, Stephen (2007). *China: Yunnan Province*. Buckinghamshire: Bradt Travel Guide.

McCarthy, Susan K. (2009). *Communist Multiculturalism: Ethnic Revival in Southwest China*. Seattle, WA: University of Washington Press.

Nyaupane, Gyan P., Duarte B. Morais, Lorraine Dowler (2006). "The role of community involvement and number/type of visitors on tourism impacts: A controlled comparison of Annapurna, Nepal and northwest Yunnan, China," *Tourism Management*, vol. 27, issue 6, December, pp. 1373–1385.

Ou, Zhide (2006). *Yunnan, Shangrila over the Horizon* (Panoramic China). Beijing: Foreign Languages Press.

Poncet, Sandra (2006). "Economic integration of Yunnan with the greater Mekong subregion," *Asian Economic Journal*, vol. 20, issue 3, pp. 303–317.

Solinger, Dorothy J. (2009). "Politics in Yunnan Province in the decade of disorder: Elite factional strategies and central-local relations, 1967–1980," *The China Quarterly*, vol. 92, February, pp. 628–662.

Summers, Tim (2012). "(Re)positioning Yunnan: Region and nation in contemporary provincial narratives," *Journal of Contemporary China*, vol. 21, issue 75, pp. 445–459.

Swain, Margaret (2002). "Looking South: Local identities and transnational linkages in Yunnan," in Fitzgerald, John (ed.), *Rethinking China's Provinces*. London and New York: Routledge, pp. 179–220.

Tapp, Nicholas (2010). "Yunnan: Ethnicity and economies–markets and mobility," *The Asia Pacific Journal of Anthropology*, vol. 11, issue 2, June, pp. 97–110.

Turner, Carol (2005). "Yunnan, China: Minority peoples observed," *Asian Affairs*, vol. 36, issue 1, March, pp. 12–34.

Unger, Anne Helen, Walter Unger (2002). *Yunnan: China's Most Beautiful Province*. München: Hirmer Verlag.

Unger, Anne Helen, Walter Unger (2007). *Yunnan: China's Most Beautiful Province*. Bangkok: Orchid Press.

Wang, Jianping (1992). "Islam in Yunnan," *Journal of Institute of Muslim Minority Affairs*, vol. 13, issue 2, July, pp. 364–374.

Ward, Captain F. Kingdon (1937). "Yunnan and the Tai peoples," *Journal of The Royal Central Asian Society*, vol. 24, issue 4, October, pp. 624–636.

White, Sydney D. (2010). "The political economy of ethnicity in Yunnan's Lijiang Basin," *The Asia Pacific Journal of Anthropology*, vol. 11, issue 2, June, pp. 142–158.

Yang, Li, Geoffrey Wall (2008). "Ethnic tourism and entrepreneurship: Xishuangbanna, Yunnan, China," *Tourism Geographies*, vol. 10, issue 4, October, pp. 522–544.

Yuan, Jingxue Jessica, Chikang Kenny Wu, Jianren Zhang, Ben K. Goh, Betty L. Stout (2008). "Chinese tourist satisfaction with Yunnan Province, China," *Journal of Hospitality and Leisure Marketing*, vol. 16, issue 1–2, April, pp. 181–202.

Zhejiang

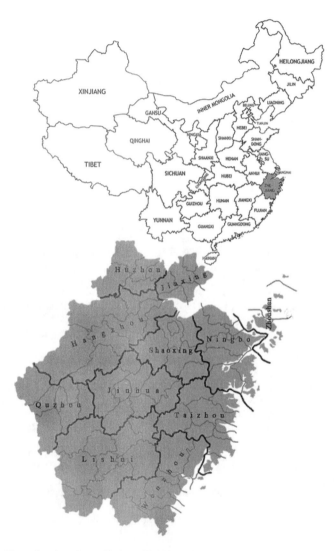

Table A   The administrative divisions of Zhejiang

Name	Administrative seat	Population
Hangzhou SPM	Gongshu District	8,700,400
Huzhou PM	Wuxing District	2,893,500
Jiaxing PM	Nanhu District	4,501,700
Jinhua PM	Wucheng District	5,361,600
Lishui PM	Liandu District	2,117,000
Ningbo SPM	Haishu District	7,605,700
Quzhou PM	Kecheng District	2,122,700
Shaoxing PM	Yuecheng District	4,912,200
Taizhou PM	Jiaojiang District	5,968,800
Wenzhou PM	Lucheng District	9,122,100
Zhoushan PM	Dinghai District	1,121,300

Notes: PM = prefectural municipality; and SPM = sub-provincial level municipality. All data are as of 2010.

Quick facts

Official name: Zhejiang Province
Abbreviated name: Zhe
Land area: 101,800 km^2
Population: 54,426,900
Population density: 464/km^2
GRP per capita of 2010: ¥51,711
HDI of 2008: 0.841
Capital: Hangzhou
Government office address: Building I, 8 Shengfu Road, Hangzhou
Tel: 0571–8705–2467
Postcode: 310025
Website: www.zj.gov.cn

Zhejiang is a province of the PRC, situated on China's southeastern coast, on the southern part of the Yangtze River Delta. It borders Jiangsu Province and Shanghai Municipality to the north, Anhui Province to the northwest, Jiangxi Province to the west and Fujian Province to the south. To the east is the East China Sea. The name Zhejiang ("crooked river") derives from the old name of the Qiantang River, which passes through Hangzhou, the provincial capital. The name is often abbreviated to "Zhe".

The territory slopes down from the southwest to the northeast. The former is mountainous with an average height of 800 m above sea level.

Most of the province's mountains with a height of over 1,500 m are found in this area. Huangmaojian in Longquan County, 1,929 m above sea level, is the highest peak. The middle region is hilly and scattered with many large and small basins. The northeast is a low, flat alluvial plain covered with a thick layer of fertile soil and crisscrossed with waterways. The mountain ranges stretch toward the East China Sea forming many peninsulas and islands.

Of its total land area, the mountainous and hilly regions account for 70.4% and the plains and basins make up 23.2%. The coastline stretches for 6,486 km. Zhejiang has 3,061 islands, the largest number in China. Its 11 administrative divisions are subdivided into 90 county-level divisions (32 districts, 22 county-level cities, 35 counties and 1 autonomous county). These are in turn divided into 1,570 township-level divisions (761 towns, 505 townships, 14 ethnic townships and 290 sub-districts).

The region has a sub-tropical monsoon climate with four distinct seasons and abundant sunshine. Spring starts in March and is rainy with changeable weather. Summer, from June to September, is long, hot, rainy and humid. Autumn is generally dry, warm and sunny. Winter is short and cold, except in the far south. The average annual temperature is around 15–19 °C, with January temperatures around 2–8 °C and July temperatures around 27–30 °C. The annual precipitation is about 1,000–1,900 mm. There is plenty of rainfall in early summer, and by late summer the area is directly threatened by typhoons forming in the Pacific.

More than 100 minerals have been found in Zhejiang, including 12 non-metallic ones, ranking among the top three in China in terms of the size of reserves. Five new mineral reserves were proven in 2004. Its reserves of stone coal, alunite, pyrophyllite, limestone for cement-making and limestone for construction rank first in the country. Fluorite occupies second place in China and diatomite third. The reserves of silica, pearlite, granite, zeolite, silver, zinc, vanadium and cadmium rank among the country's top ten.

The province has a coastline (including island lines) of 6,486 km with a domestic sea area of 30,900 km². It has the country's largest in-shore fishery, with 400 km² of shallow sea and 2,886 m² of low beach for aquaculture. In addition the continental shelf of the East China Sea is rich in petroleum and natural gas.

Zhejiang is famed as "a treasure house of plants in southeastern China" with substantial forest coverage. It has as many as 3,800 species of plants. Among these, gingko and more than 50 others are listed as rare plants under state protection. There are more than 1,900 species of wild animals in the province, 120 of which are listed as the first or second grade of wild animals under state protection, making up on-third of China's total protected rare animals.

Zhejiang is a favored tourist destination. It has 11 state-level scenic areas, including West Lake, Fuchun River, Xin'an River, Thousand-islet Lake, Mount Yantang, Nanxi River, Mount Putuo, the Shengsi Islands, Mount Tiantai, Mount Mogan, Mount Xuedou, Twin-Dragon Cave and Mount Xiandu, in addition to 35 province-level scenic spots. The Hangzhou River is a national holiday resort, and ten other resorts, including Lake Xianghu in Xiaoshan, Oujiang River in Wenzhou and Mount Huiji in Shaoxing, are of provincial level. The Surging Qiantang Tides, a unique natural site, attracts numerous visitors from both home and abroad.

Longjing tea (also called "dragon well tea"), originating in Hangzhou, is one of the most famous Chinese teas. Hangzhou is also renowned for its silk umbrellas and hand fans. Zhejiang cuisine (subdivided into many traditions, including Hangzhou cuisine) is one of the eight great traditions of Chinese cuisine.

Zhejiang's nominal GRP for 2010 was ¥2.78 trillion (about US$402 billion) with a per capita GRP of ¥44,335 (about US$6,490). After more than 20 years of development since the reforms and opening-up of China, the province now has a strong economy, with industry as its leading sector. It has become one of the most commercial and richest provinces in China. Compared with many other regions, the development of different areas in Zhejiang is more balanced.

Table B   Demographic and socioeconomic profile: Zhejiang

Indicator	2000	2010
Population (thousands)	46,770	54,465
Illiteracy rate of population aged 15 or over (%)	7.06	5.62
GRP (¥ billions)	603.63	2,772.23
Composition of GRP (%)		
Primary sector	11.0	4.9
Secondary sector	52.7	51.6
Tertiary sector	36.3	43.5
Fixed asset investment (¥ billions)	235.00	1,237.60
Status of foreign-funded enterprises		
Number of registered enterprises	10,002	28,769
Total investment (US$ millions)	29,313	183,233
Registered capital (US$ millions)	17,122	106,942

Table B   (Continued)

Indicator	2000	2010
Foreign trade (US$ millions)		
Export	20,482	200,944
Import	11,040	86,306
Sales of consumer goods (¥ billions)	230	1,025
Per capita annual disposable income of urban residents (¥)	9,279.16	27,359.02
Engle's coefficient (%)	34.46	30.09
Per capita annual net income of rural residents (¥)	4,253.67	11,302.55
Engle's coefficient (%)	37.72	34.22
Number of patent applications granted	7,495	114,643
Inventions	184	6,410
Utility models	3,439	47,617
Designs	3,872	60,616

Note: All monetary values are measured at current prices.
Source: *Zhejiang Statistical Yearbook*, 2001 and 2011.

The fourth largest economy and the third largest exporter in China, the region leads all provinces in rankings of GRP per capita in both urban and rural areas. As a result of local government's business-friendly policies, this region witnessed the success of thousands of small and medium-sized enterprises. Compared with the rest of the country, people in Zhejiang are the most entrepreneurial, which has also helped the province to achieve a small urban-to-rural income gap.

An important maker of electronics and other equipment, its manufacturers have a significant competitive advantage: a combination of low prices, cheap labor, low resource costs and high volumes. However, as other provinces become cheaper, Zhejiang's growth is shrinking and structural reform is needed. Additionally, high incomes and limited investment choices have resulted in high property costs.

Rice is the area's main crop, followed by wheat. North Zhejiang is also a center of aquaculture, and the Zhoushan fishery is the largest in the country. The main cash crops include jute and cotton, and the region also leads the provinces of China in tea production. (The renowned Longjing tea is a product of Hangzhou.) The region's towns are known for the hand production of goods such as silk, for which it is ranked second among the provinces. Its many market towns connect the cities with the countryside.

Southern Zhejiang was traditionally poor and underdeveloped due to its mountainous geography. Economic reforms of the late 1970s brought huge changes to the region. However, the private sector has seen rapid growth, especially in the cities of Wenzhou, Ningbo and Shaoxing. The region, together with the more developed north Zhejiang, has helped the province to leapfrog over other regions and become one of the richest in China.

The main manufacturing sectors are electromechanical industries, textiles, food and construction materials. In recent years the province has followed its own development model, dubbed the "Zhejiang model", which is based on prioritizing and encouraging entrepreneurship, an emphasis on small businesses responsive to the whims of the market, large public investments in infrastructure, and the production of low-cost goods in bulk for both domestic consumption and export. As a result it has made itself one of the richest provinces, and the "Zhejiang spirit" has become something of a legend within the country. It encourages and gives autonomy to township enterprises. Although being the majority shareholder of many township enterprises, local government normally refrains from intervening in their investment and operation decisions. Completely independent, they are essentially the same as private enterprises.

In the past, light industry played a major role in the economy. However, fuelled by the development of the economy and foreign investment, the industrial structure has changed since 2003. In 2006, heavy industry contributed 56.4% of the total value-added industrial output in Zhejiang. The four pillar industries are textiles, electrical equipment and machinery, power, and general-purpose equipment manufacturing. The province has always been the leading textile and garment production base in China. It is the second largest producer in the country with about 20% market share, while its rival, Guangdong Province, took 26% in 2006. In addition, it is a major export market for textiles and garments.

Compared with Guangdong, Zhejiang has an advantage in terms of labor costs as it is equipped to draw on low-cost labor from neighboring provinces, such as Anhui and Jiangxi. It has a more convenient and cheaper transportation system than Guangdong. The province also has five ports in Ningbo, Zhoushan, Zhapu, Haimen and Wenzhou. Famous garment producers include Younger, Meters Bonwe, Shan Shan, Langsha and Peacebird. Most of the textile and garment enterprises are located in Ningbo, Wenzhou, Shaoxing and Hangzhou.

The electronics industry is a fast-growing sector in the region. Zhejiang has set up a relatively strong industrial base in this. Hangzhou,

Ningbo, Jiaxing and Shaoxing are major production bases of electronic products. Geely Group is a major contributor to the auto industry there. It is a private enterprise, located in Hangzhou, with four manufacturing bases in Linhai, Ningbo, Taizhou and Shanghai, specializing in the production of auto parts. The company was among the first batch of automakers that launched self-developed brands. It is one of the fastest-growing automakers in China. While it started out as a refrigerator manufacturer in 1986, the company moved to motorcycle manufacturing in 1994 and commenced auto production in 1998.

Zhejiang has more than 1,000 software enterprises with over 50,000 employees. Famous software enterprises include Insigma Technology, Alibaba.com Corporation, Huansun Technology and SUPCON Group. In 2007 the Hangzhou-based e-business provider Alibaba was listed on the Stock Exchange of Hong Kong Limited (SEHK), raising a sum of US$1.7 billion. This is a record high for an internet company from mainland China. Other industries dealing with software, IT service outsourcing and on-line games provided by Zhejiang enterprises have also expanded quickly.

The province has four major ports. Among them, the Ningbo-Zhoushan Port is the largest iron ore and oil transshipment base in China. Together with Shanghai Port, Zhejiang is the gateway to the world for China. Ningbo, Wenzhou, Taizhou and Zhoushan are important commercial ports. The Hangzhou Bay Bridge between Haiyan County and Cixi is the longest bridge over a continuous body of seawater in the world.

Zhejiang is also a major player in China's foreign trade. Exports include machinery and electronic products. Private companies and foreign-invested enterprises are the major exporters and the key export destinations include the EU, the US and Japan, while the main import sources are Japan, Korea and Taiwan.

At the same time, a lot of foreign investment has rushed into the area. Most of the investments have been injected into the developed regions of the province, such as Hangzhou, Ningbo, Shaoxing, Jiaxing, Huzhou and Zhoushan. Among the various sectors, manufacturing (specifically textiles, chemicals, mechanical and electronics industries) has attracted the most foreign investment.

As of 2010, compared with those of other provinces, "construction", "manufacturing" and "leasing and business services" were relatively strong, while "mining", "agriculture, forestry, animal husbandry and fishery" and "services to households and other services" were relatively weak sectors (see Table C).

Table C   Zhejiang's comparative (dis)advantage index by sector, 2010

Sector	Index
Agriculture, forestry, animal husbandry and fishery	0.06
Mining	0.05
Manufacturing	1.43
Production and distribution of electricity, gas and water	0.60
Construction	2.10
Transport, storage and post	0.59
Information transmission, computer service and software	0.89
Wholesale and retail trades	0.86
Hotels and catering services	1.10
Financial intermediation	0.92
Real estate	0.95
Leasing and business services	1.24
Scientific research, technical services and geological prospecting	0.71
Management of water conservancy, environment and public facilities	0.74
Services to households and other services	0.40
Education	0.57
Health, social security and social welfare	0.76
Culture, sports and entertainment	0.70
Public management and social organization	0.60

Notes: All the sectors included in this table are determined according to China's official definitions and for urban areas only. Numerals greater than, equal to and less than 1 indicate that the province's sectors have advantages, no apparent (dis)advantages and disadvantages, respectively.
Sources: Calculated by author based on *China Statistical Yearbook*, 2011. See Appendix for a detailed methodological description.

By the end of 2006, Zhejiang had 13 state-level and 57 provincial-level development zones. In 2006 the total GRP of the zones accounted for 11% of the province's total GRP. Among them, high-tech industries contributed about 40% of the total. In 2006 these development zones attracted utilized FDI of US$4.5 billion, accounting for 50% of the province's total. Major developments zones are clustered in the cities of Hangzhou, Ningbo and Shaoxing. Two examples are described below.

- **Hangzhou Economic and Technological Development Zone (HETDZ)** Located in the east of Hangzhou, this zone is 20 km from the downtown area. It was established in 1993 with the aim of encouraging research and manufacturing in fields such as IT and electronics, machinery, pharmaceuticals and textiles. To further boost the export-oriented manufacturing industry, Hangzhou Export Processing Zone was established in 2000 with a planned area of 2.92 km². This is the first state-level export processing zone in Zhejiang. By the end of 2006, HZEDTZ had attracted 404 foreign enterprises from 32 countries to set up business in the zone. Some 31 Fortune 500 enterprises invested in 50 projects there. In 2006 the total industrial output of the zone reached ¥111.3 billion (high-tech industries such as electronics and IT contributed 61% of the total). In addition, its exports amounted to US$7.1 billion. In terms of overall competitiveness, it ranked 12th among all state-level development zones in 2006. Major investors include Motorola, Toshiba, Siemens, Terumo and LG.

- **Hangzhou Hi-tech Park** This was established in 1990 and was approved as a state-level high-tech park in 1991. Ever since it has attracted more than 5,000 high-tech enterprises to set up business there, accounting for more than 70% of the city's total (or 25% of the province's total). By the end of 2006, 475 foreign enterprises from 32 counties had invested in the park with a total investment of US$3.5 billion. The US, the UK, Japan and Korea are the major investment sources. In 2006 the GRP of the park amounted to 17.1 billion and exports reached US$3 billion, up 13.2% and 44%, respectively. Among all 53 state-level high-tech parks, Hangzhou High-Tech Park was ranked 11th in the same year. Major investors include Bosch, Nokia, Huawei and Utstarcom.

As of 2010 the top five companies were as follows:

1. Hik Vision (SHE: 002415) is a leading surveillance and monitoring devices solutions supplier. It posted ¥3.61 billion in revenues and ¥1.05 billion in net profits for 2010.
2. Zhejiang China Commodities City Group Co (SHA: 600415) is China's largest operator of small articles trading platform. It posted ¥3.17 billion in revenues and ¥808.9 million in net profits for 2010.
3. Bank of Ningbo Co (SHE: 002142) is a city-level lender based in Ningbo, an economic powerhouse in Zhejiang. It posted ¥5.91 billion in revenues and ¥2.32 billion in net profits for 2010.
4. Xinhu Zhongbao Co (SHA: 600208) is a property developer that also runs education, hospitality and finance subsidiaries. It posted ¥8.14 billion in revenues and ¥1.56 billion in net profits for 2010.
5. Youngor Group Co (SHA: 600177) is one of China's leading garment producers and also develops real estate. It posted ¥14.51 billion in revenues and ¥2.67 billion in net profits for 2010.

Indicators for the ease of doing business

A. Starting a business

Procedures: 12
Time (days): 30
Cost (% of provincial GRP per capita): 5.7

B. Registering property

Procedures: 8
Time (days): 50
Cost (% of property value): 3.7

C. Getting credit – creating and registering collateral

Time (days): 11
Cost (% of loan value): 3

D. Enforcing contracts

Time (days): 285
Cost (% of claim): 11.2

Further reading

Foreign Languages Press (2006, ed.). *Zhejiang, Riding the Tides of History* (Panoramic China). Beijing: Foreign Languages Press.

Forster, Keith (1997). "Zhejiang: Paradoxes of restoration, reinvigoration and renewal," in Goodman, David S.G. (ed.), *China's Provinces in Reform: Class, Community and Political Culture*. London and New York: Routledge, pp. 237–271.

Forster, Keith (1998). *Zhejiang in Reform*. Sydney, NSW: Wild Peony.

Glauben, Thomas, Thomas Herzfeld, Xiaobing Wang (2008). "Labor market participation of Chinese agricultural households: Empirical evidence from Zhejiang Province," *Food Policy*, vol. 33, issue 4, August, pp. 329–340.

He, Baogang (2005). "Village citizenship in China: A case study of Zhejiang," *Citizenship Studies*, vol. 9, issue 2, May, pp. 205–219.

Hendrischke, Hans (2003). "How local are local enterprises? Privatization and translocality of small firms in Zhejiang and Jiangsu," *Provincial China*, vol. 8, issue 1, April, pp. 27–39.

Li, Mingshi, Zhiliang Zhu, James E. Vogelmann, Da Xu, Weisong Wen, Anxing Liu (2011). "Characterizing fragmentation of the collective forests in southern China from multitemporal landsat imagery: A case study from Kecheng District of Zhejiang Province," *Applied Geography*, vol. 31, issue 3, July, pp. 1026–1035.

Liu, Renyi, Liu Nan (2002). "Flood area and damage estimation in Zhejiang, China," *Journal of Environmental Management*, vol. 66, issue 1, September, pp. 1–8.

Pérez, Manuel Ruiz, Zhong Maogong, Brian Belcher, Xie Chen, Fu Maoyi, Xie Jinzhong (1999). "The role of bamboo plantations in rural development: The case of Anji County, Zhejiang, China," *World Development*, vol. 27, issue 1, January, pp. 101–114.

Shi, Zulin, Bi Liangliang (2007). "Trans-jurisdictional River Basin Water Pollution Management and Cooperation in China: Case study of Jiangsu/Zhejiang Province in comparative global context," *China Population, Resources and Environment*, vol. 17, issue 3, May, pp. 3–9.

Skinner, Mark W., Richard G. Kuhn, Alun E. Joseph (2001). "Agricultural land protection in China: A case study of local governance in Zhejiang Province," *Land Use Policy*, vol. 18, issue 4, October, pp. 329–340.

Tong, Shaosu (2010). *Folk Culture in China's Zhejiang Province*. Paramus, NJ: Homa and Sekey Books.

Wang, Hui, Ran Tao, Lanlan Wang, Fubing Su (2010). "Farmland preservation and land development rights trading in Zhejiang, China," *Habitat International*, vol. 34, issue 4, October, pp. 454–463.

Xu, Wei, K.C Tan (2001). "Reform and the process of economic restructuring in rural China: A case study of Yuhang, Zhejiang," *Journal of Rural Studies*, vol. 17, issue 2, April, pp. 165–181.

Xu, Wei, K.C. Tan (2002). "Impact of reform and economic restructuring on rural systems in China: A case study of Yuhang, Zhejiang," *Journal of Rural Studies*, vol. 18, issue 1, January, pp. 65–81.

Zhao, Xingshu, Axel Michaelowa (2006). "CDM potential for rural transition in China case study: Options in Yinzhou District, Zhejiang Province," *Energy Policy*, vol. 34, issue 14, September, pp. 1867–1882.

Zhou, Jiehong, Jensen H. Helen, Jing Liang (2011). "Implementation of food safety and quality standards: A case study of vegetable processing industry in Zhejiang, China," *The Social Science Journal*, vol. 48, issue 3, September, pp. 543–552.

Part II
Ranking the Provinces

Per capita gross regional product

Province	1952 rank	1980 rank	1990 rank	2000 rank	2010 rank
Anhui	22	27	24	24	25
Beijing	3	2	2	2	2
Chongqing	NP	NP	NP	19	18
Fujian	14	20	12	7	9
Gansu	16	16	27	30	30
Guangdong	18	18	5	5	6
Guangxi	27	28	29	29	26
Guizhou	29	29	30	31	31
Hainan	NP	NP	15	15	22
Hebei	9	7	17	11	12
Heilongjiang	4	5	8	10	14
Henan	23	21	28	18	15
Hubei	20	17	13	13	13
Hunan	21	22	20	17	20
Inner Mongolia	7	14	18	16	7
Jiangsu	13	10	7	6	5
Jiangxi	11	24	23	25	27
Jilin	8	6	10	14	11
Liaoning	5	4[a]	4	8	9
Ningxia	10	19	19	22	19
Qinghai	15	9	14	20	23
Shaanxi	24	12	21	27	17
Shandong	19	13	11	9	8
Shanghai	1	1	1	1	1
Shanxi	17	15	16	21	16
Sichuan	28	26	26	23	24
Tianjin	2	3	3	3	3
Tibet	25	23	22	26	28
Xinjiang	6	11	9	12	21
Yunnan	26	25	25	28	29
Zhejiang	12	8	6	4	4

Note: NP = not a province for the year.
Sources: Rongxing Guo, *How the Chinese Economy Works* – 3E, Basingstoke, Hampshire: Palgrave Macmillan, 2009, p. 169; and Rongxing Guo, *Understanding the Chinese Economies*. Santiago, CA: Academic Press/Elsevier, 2012, p. 150.

354

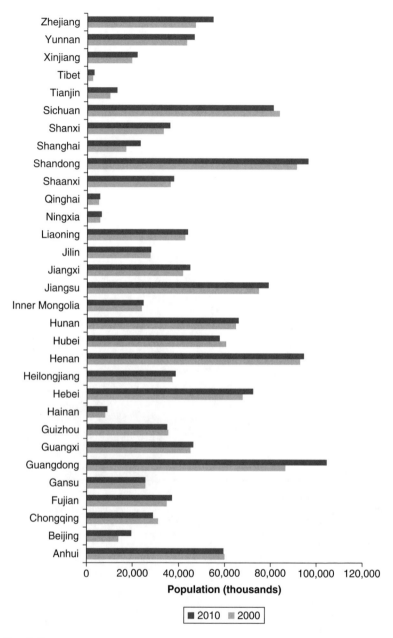

Population (thousands)

■ 2010 ■ 2000

Population

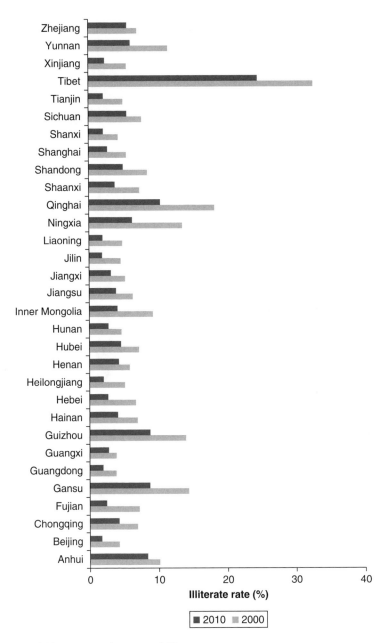

Ratio of illiterate population aged 15 or over

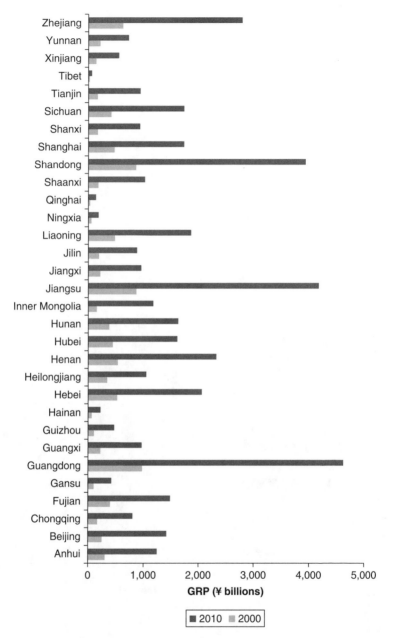

GRP (¥ billions)

■ 2010 ■ 2000

Gross regional product

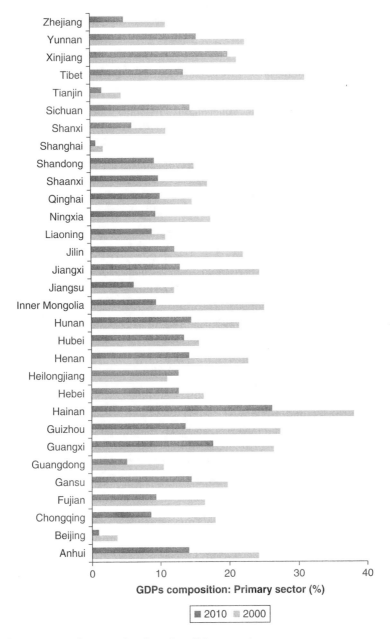

Composition of gross regional product: Primary sector

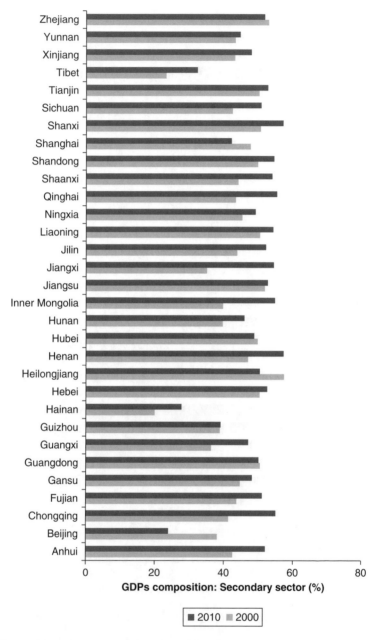

GDPs composition: Secondary sector (%)

■ 2010 ■ 2000

Composition of gross regional product: Secondary sector

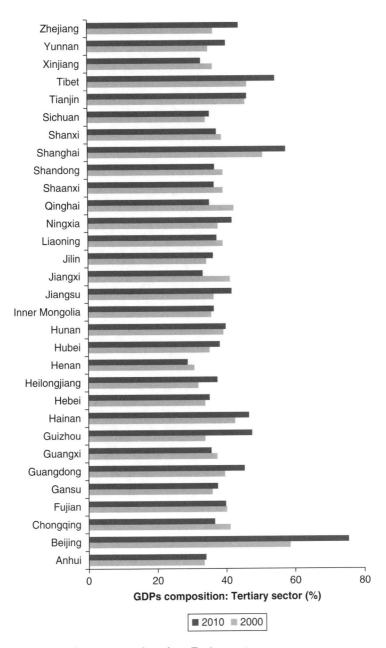

Composition of gross regional product: Tertiary sector

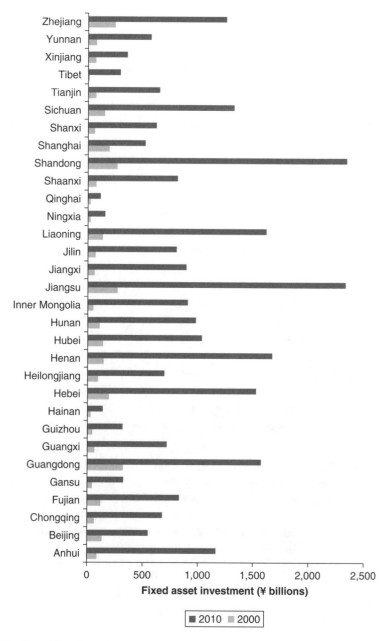

Fixed asset investment (¥ billions)

2010 ■ 2000 ■

Fixed asset investment

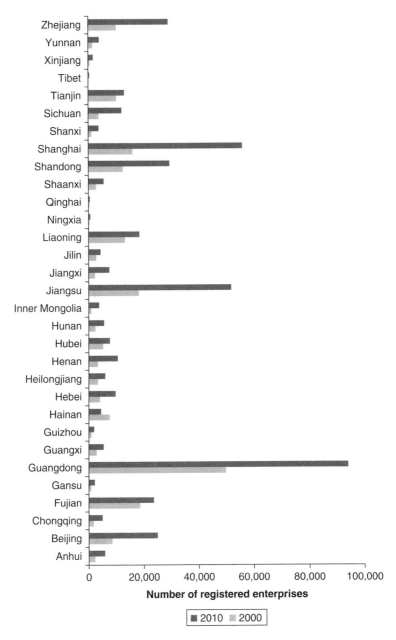

Number of registered enterprises

■ 2010 ■ 2000

Status of foreign-funded enterprises: Number of registered enterprises

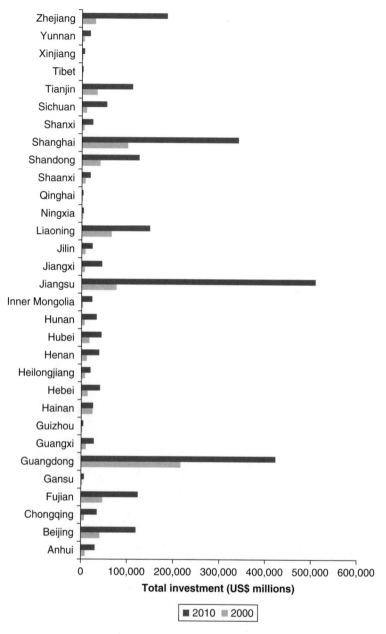

Total investment (US$ millions)

■ 2010 ■ 2000

Status of foreign-funded enterprises: Total investment

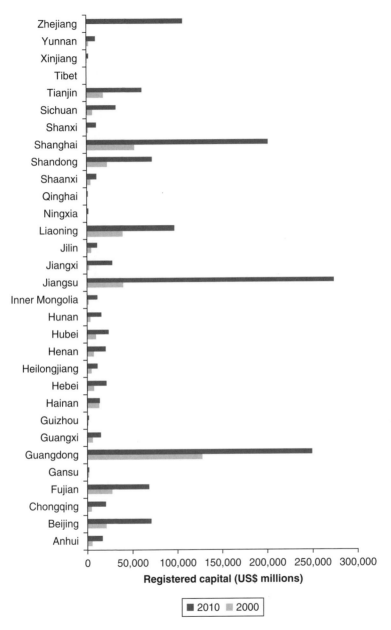

Status of foreign-funded enterprises: Registered capital

364

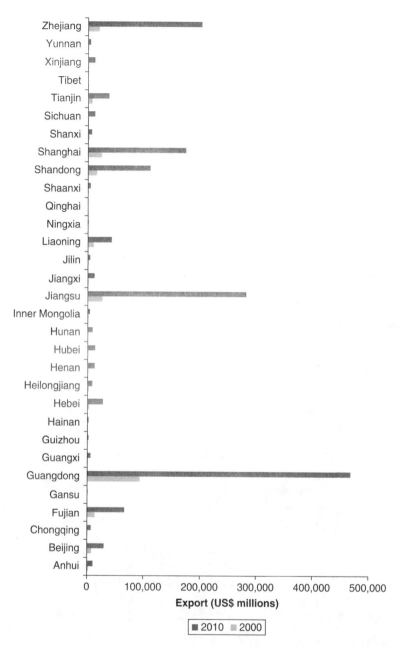

Foreign trade: Export

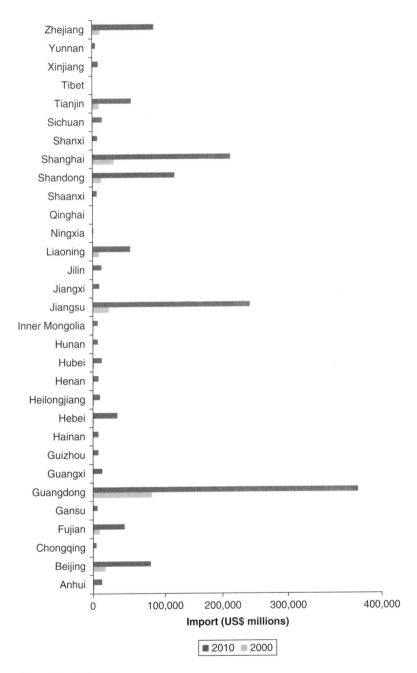

Import (US$ millions)

■ 2010 ■ 2000

Foreign trade: Import

366

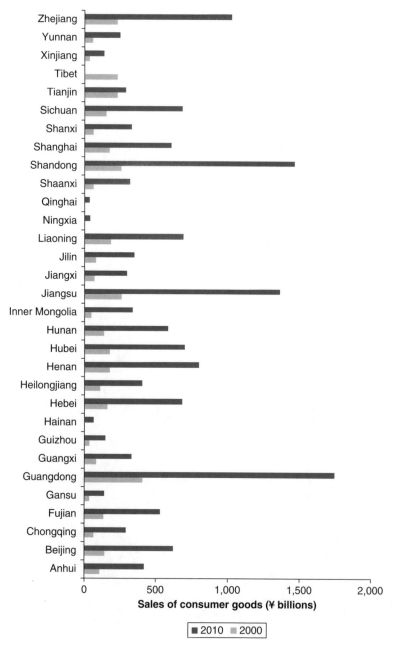

Sales of consumer goods

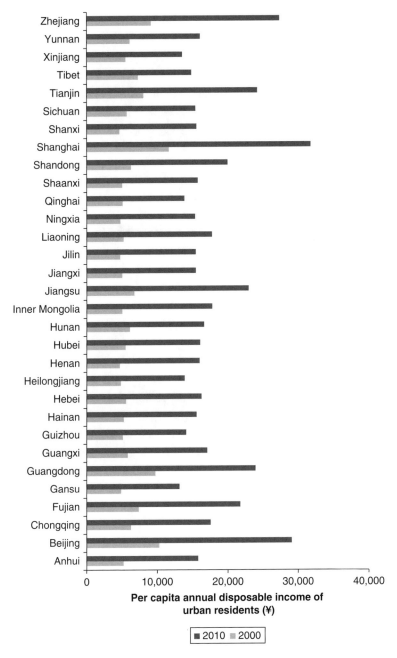

Per capita annual disposable income of urban residents (¥)

■ 2010 ■ 2000

Per capita annual disposable income of urban residents

368

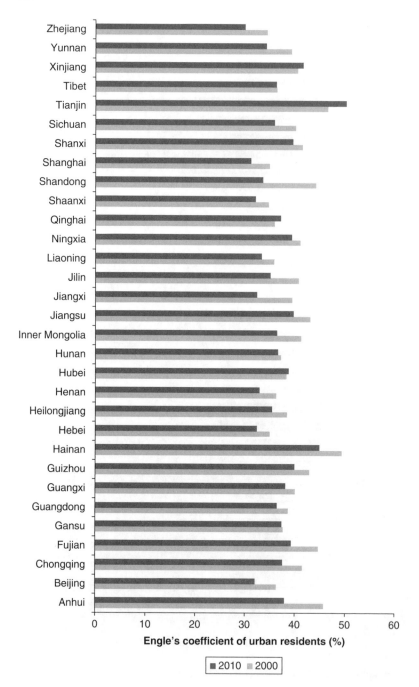

Engle's coefficient of urban residents

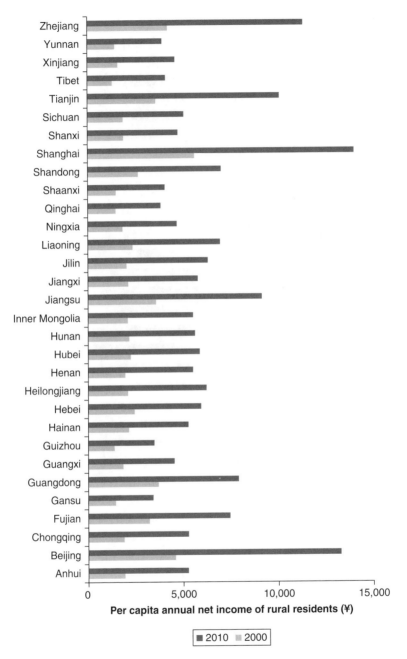

Per capita annual net income of rural residents

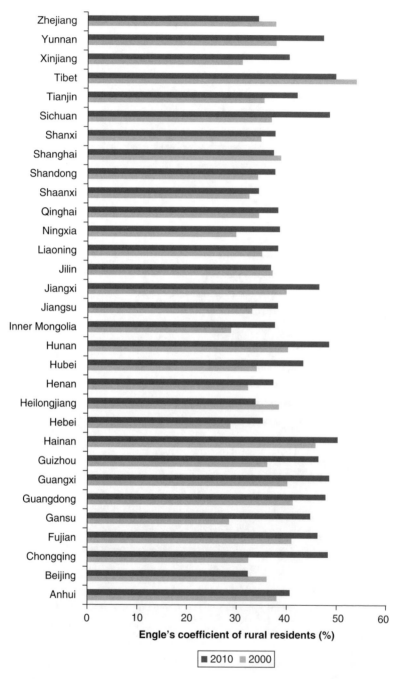

Engle's coefficient of rural residents

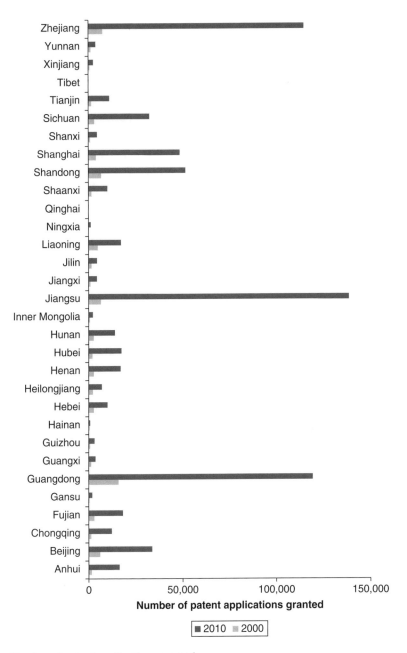

Number of patent applications granted

■ 2010 ▨ 2000

Number of patent applications granted

372

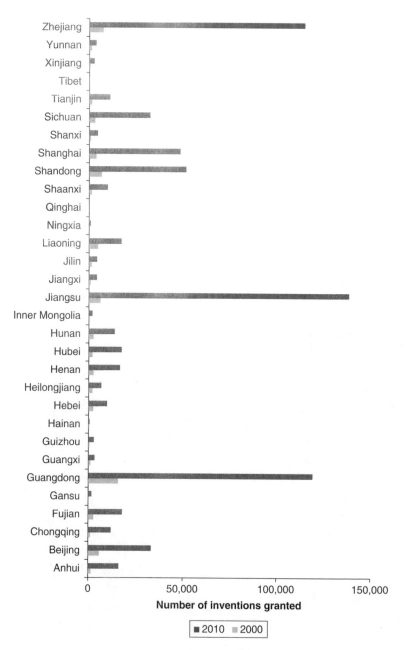

Number of inventions granted

■ 2010 ■ 2000

Number of patent applications granted: Inventions

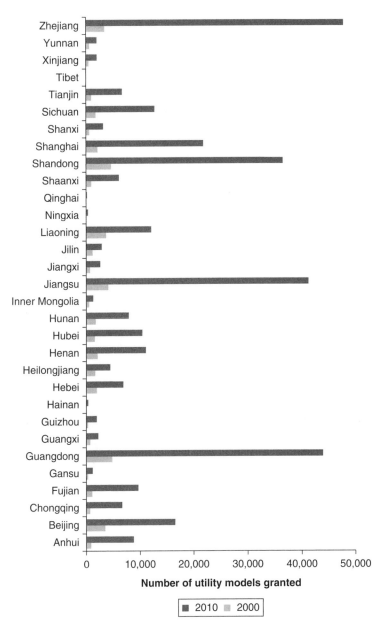

Number of utility models granted

■ 2010 ▨ 2000

Number of patent applications granted: Utility models

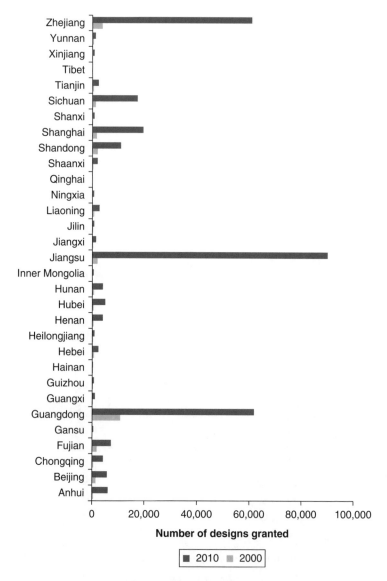

Number of designs granted

2010 ■ 2000 ■

Number of patent applications granted: Designs

Ease of doing business: Starting a business

Province	Procedures	Time (days)	Cost (% of provincial GRP per capita)	Rank
Zhejiang	12	30	5.7	1
Jiangsu	12	31	5.8	2
Guangdong	13	28	6.3	3
Shandong	13	33	6.0	4
Shanghai	14	35	3.1	5
Fujian	12	40	6.7	7
Jilin	14	37	9.5	8
Tianjin	14	41	3.7	8
Liaoning	14	41	6.0	9
Beijing	14	37	3.2	10
Hunan	14	42	14.6	10
Inner Mongolia	14	45	7.9	11
Sichuan	13	35	19.1	11
Henan	13	41	11.6	12
Hainan	13	38	12.1	13
Xinjiang	13	44	9.0	14
Hubei	13	36	13.6	15
Heibei	14	42	9.8	16
Chongqing	14	39	9.5	17
Heilongjiang	14	42	11.9	18
Shanxi	14	55	9.3	20
Jiangxi	14	46	14.6	21
Qinghai	14	51	12.0	23
Yunnan	14	42	13.9	23
Shaanxi	14	43	15.2	25
Ningxia	14	55	12.0	26
Anhui	14	42	19.4	27
Guangxi	14	46	16.5	28
Gansu	14	47	14.1	29
Guizhou	14	50	26.6	30

Notes: (1) This table records all procedures that are officially required for an entrepreneur to start up and formally operate an industrial or commercial business. These include obtaining all necessary licenses and permits, and completing any required notifications, verifications or inscriptions for the company and employees with relevant authorities. The ranking of the ease of starting a business is the simple average of the percentile rankings of its component indicators. (2) Each province is represented by its capital city.

Source: World Bank (2008) *Doing Business in China 2008*. Washington, DC: The World Bank Group and Beijing: Social Science Academic Press (China).

Ease of doing business: Registering property

Province	Procedures	Time (days)	Cost (% of property value)	Rank
Shanghai	4	29	3.6	1
Guangdong	8	35	3.7	2
Fujian	7	37	4.1	3
Shandong	8	39	4.1	4
Jiangsu	7	31	4.6	5
Tianjin	5	42	4.4	6
Zhejiang	8	50	3.7	7
Jilin	8	55	4.2	8
Chongqing	7	28	7.0	9
Shaanxi	8	50	5.1	10
Sichuan	11	39	3.9	11
Beijing	10	59	3.1	12
Xinjiang	11	45	4.2	13
Heilongjiang	8	55	6.1	14
Liaoning	12	51	3.1	14
Ningxia	10	59	4.4	16
Anhui	10	46	5.6	17
Inner Mongolia	11	47	4.6	18
Qinghai	8	60	5.3	19
Jiangxi	10	50	6.1	20
Heibei	10	58	3.2	21
Yunnan	9	66	5.4	22
Hainan	16	76	4.8	23
Hunan	10	53	6.9	24
Hubei	9	60	6.2	25
Shanxi	10	62	5.4	26
Henan	11	60	5.1	27
Guizhou	9	77	12.6	28
Gansu	10	78	7.8	29
Guangxi	12	68	6.8	30

Notes: (1) This table records the full sequence of procedures necessary for a business (buyer) to purchase a property from another business (seller) and to transfer the property title to the buyer's name so that the buyer can use the property for expanding its business, use the property as collateral in taking new loans or, if necessary, sell the property to another business. (2) Each province is represented by its capital city.

Source: World Bank (2008) *Doing Business in China 2008*. Washington, DC: The World Bank Group and Beijing: Social Science Academic Press (China).

Ease of doing business: Getting credit – creating and registering collateral

Province	Time (days)	Cost (% of loan value)	Rank
Fujian	7	2.3	1
Jiangsu	10	2.1	2
Guangdong	11	2.4	3
Shandong	10	2.9	4
Shanghai	8	2.9	4
Tianjin	14	2.7	6
Beijing	15	2.7	7
Zhejiang	11	3.0	8
Heibei	15	2.8	9
Heilongjiang	13	3.1	10
Sichuan	12	3.2	11
Hubei	13	3.3	12
Shanxi	16	2.9	12
Anhui	20	2.8	14
Liaoning	20	2.8	15
Inner Mongolia	15	3.3	16
Henan	16	3.3	17
Hainan	14	5.1	18
Chongqing	15	5.0	19
Hunan	20	3.7	20
Jilin	22	3.3	21
Qinghai	20	3.8	22
Yunnan	18	4.0	23
Jiangxi	17	5.9	24
Guizhou	17	6.9	25
Xinjiang	24	3.4	26
Ningxia	25	3.6	27
Shaanxi	21	4.0	28
Gansu	20	8.0	29
Guangxi	47	3.9	30

Notes: (1) This table measures the legal rights of borrowers and lenders with respect to secured transactions through one set of indicators and the sharing of credit information through another. The first set of indicators describes how well collateral and bankruptcy laws facilitate lending. The second set measures the coverage, scope and accessibility of credit information available through public credit registries and private credit bureaus. The ranking of the ease of getting credit is the simple average of the percentile rankings of its component indicators. (2) Each province is represented by its capital city.
Source: World Bank (2008) *Doing Business in China 2008*. Washington, DC: The World Bank Group and Beijing: Social Science Academic Press (China).

Ease of doing business: Enforcing contracts

Province	Time (days)	Cost (% of claim)	Rank
Guangdong	120	9.7	1
Jiangsu	112	13.6	2
Zhejiang	285	11.2	3
Shanghai	292	9.0	4
Shaanxi	235	21.7	5
Shandong	210	22.0	5
Tianjin	300	11.3	5
Chongqing	286	14.8	8
Beijing	340	9.6	9
Liaoning	260	24.8	10
Hainan	310	14.5	11
Fujian	342	13.7	12
Ningxia	270	28.7	13
Heibei	397	12.2	14
Jiangxi	365	16.5	15
Henan	285	31.5	16
Hubei	277	33.1	17
Shanxi	300	26.4	18
Guangxi	397	17.1	20
Heilongjiang	290	31.5	20
Xinjiang	392	20.5	22
Sichuan	295	35.5	23
Guizhou	397	23.0	24
Jilin	540	18.4	25
Anhui	300	41.8	26
Hunan	382	26.6	27
Qinghai	458	24.8	28
Yunnan	365	36.4	29
Gansu	440	29.9	30
Inner Mongolia	330	23.7	30

Notes: (1) This table measures the efficiency of the judicial system in resolving a commercial dispute. The data are built by following the step-by-step evolution of a commercial sale dispute before local courts. The data are collected through study of the codes of civil procedure and other court regulations as well as surveys completed by local litigation lawyers and by judges. The ranking of the ease of enforcing contracts is the simple average of the percentile rankings of its component indicators. (2) Each province is represented by its capital city.
Source: World Bank (2008) *Doing Business in China 2008*. Washington, DC: The World Bank Group and Beijing: Social Science Academic Press (China).

Appendix

There exist many multiregional differences in terms of natural and social resources, industrial structure and economic development in China. In order to gain a better understanding of the comparative (dis)advantages of China's provinces, let us calculate the location quotient of China's provinces.

The Location Quotient Technique is the most commonly utilized spatial economic analysis method. It was developed in part to add a slightly more complex model to the variety of analytical tools available to economic base analysts.[1] It compares the local economy to a reference economy, in the process attempting to identify specializations in the local economy. The location quotient compares the regional share of economic activity in a particular industry with the national share of economic activity in the same industry. The result reveals the degree of regional specialization in each industry.

If the location quotient for a particular industry is less than one, the region is less specialized than the nation, while location quotients greater than one reveal greater specialization of the industry in the local economy than in the national economy. Also, observing location quotients over time shows if an industry is becoming more or less specialized in the region.

To calculate any location quotient, the following formula is applied. Note that here we are comparing the regional economy (often a province) with the national economy. The location quotient (LQ) of region j in industry i can be calculated as:

$$LQ(i,j) = \frac{\text{Provincial employment in industry } i / \text{Total provincial employment}}{\text{National employment in industry } i / \text{Total national employment}}$$

Mathematically, if x_{ij} is the employment of the ith industry ($i = 1, 2, \ldots$) in the jth province ($j = 1, 2, \ldots$), the value of LQ can be calculated as follows:

$$LQ(i,j) = \frac{x_{ij} \left/ \sum_i x_{ij} \right.}{\sum_j x_{ij} \left/ \sum_i \sum_i x_{ij} \right.}.$$

Interpreting the location quotient (LQ_{ij}) is very simple and only three general outcomes are possible – that is, $LQ_{ij} < 1$, $LQ_{ij} = 1$ and $LQ_{ij} > 1$. Their implications are as follows:

If LQ_{ij} is less than one, it suggests that province j is less than expected for industry i. Therefore industry j is not even meeting local demand for a given good or service; in other words, it has comparative advantages.

If LQ_{ij} is equal to one, it suggests that province j is exactly sufficient to meet the local demand for a given industry i. Therefore industry j is meeting local demand for a given good or service; in other words, it has no comparative (dis)advantages.

If LQ_{ij} is greater than one, it suggests that province j is greater than expected. It is therefore assumed that there is an "extra" part of goods and services for industry i. This extra economy then must export its goods and services to other areas; in other words, industry i has comparative disadvantages.

Note

1. See, for example, A.M. Isserman (1977) "The location quotient approach for estimating regional economic impacts," *Journal of the American Institute of Planners*, vol. 43, pp. 33–41.

Index

Notes: (1) Only the administrative divisions that are directly under provinces, autonomous regions and central municipalities are included in this index. (2) The types of the administrative divisions are shown within parentheses.

Abbreviations: AC=autonomous county; AP=autonomous prefecture; C=county; CM=county level municipality; D=district; FD=forestry district; NA=new prefectural-level area; P=prefecture; PD=prefectural level district; PL=prefectural level league; PM= prefectural level municipality; SPC= sub-prefectural level country; and SPM=sub-provincial level municipality.

Printed and bound in the United States of America